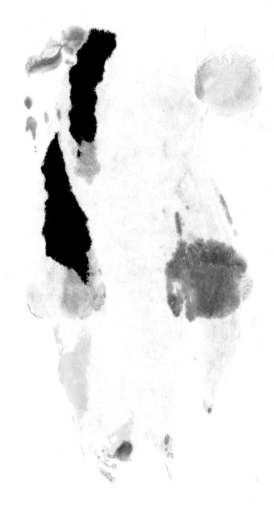

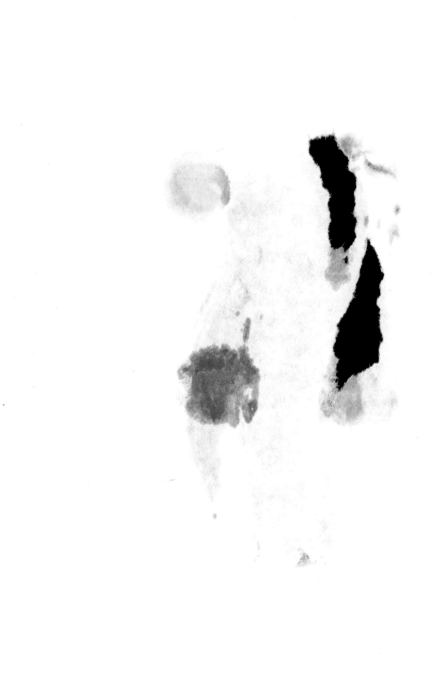

Granville Barker

A Secret Life

Drawing by John Singer Sargent of Harley Granville Barker, in 1900 (the drawing was owned by Bernard Shaw, who bequethed it to the National Gallery, by whose permission it is here reproduced).

Granville Barker
A Secret Life

Eric Salmon

HEINEMANN EDUCATIONAL BOOKS
LONDON

Heinemann Educational Books Ltd
22 Bedford Square, London WC1B 3HH
LONDON   EDINBURGH   MELBOURNE   AUCKLAND
HONG KONG   SINGAPORE   KUALA LUMPUR   NEW DELHI
IBADAN   NAIROBI   JOHANNESBURG
EXETER (NH)   KINGSTON   PORT OF SPAIN

British Library Cataloguing in Publication Data

Salmon, Eric
Granville Barker: a secret life.
1. Barker, Granville—Biography
2. Dramatists, English—20th century—
Biography
I. Title
822'.912   PR6003.B/

ISBN 0-435-18790-2

Typeset by Inforum Ltd, Portsmouth
Printed and bound in Great Britain by
Biddles Ltd, Guildford and King's Lynn

for
JANET
with love always

Contents

Illustrations

*A*cknowledgements

I am deeply indebted to a very large number of people for their ready and generous co-operation in the work of assembling the materials for this book. In listing them here, I tender to each of them my most sincere thanks and if, in assembling their names, I have inadvertently missed anyone out, I hope that he or she will believe that the omission is due to inefficiency rather than ingratitude and will accept my thanks just the same.

For permission to quote from Granville Barker's works I am indebted to Messrs. Sidgwick & Jackson Ltd., Messrs. Chatto & Windus Ltd., and Cambridge University Press; for permission to quote from his letters and unpublished manuscripts, and also the letters of Helen Huntington Granville-Barker, my thanks are due to Mr. J.C. Medley and the Society of Authors; to Mrs. Elinor Finley I tender my sincere thanks for permission to quote the letters of William Archer as also to Mr. Alexander Murray for quotations from the letters of Gilbert Murray; to the Trustees of the Estate of the late Mrs. J.H.T. Cassel for quotations from the letters of T.E. Lawrence; to the Trustees of the Estate of the late Sir Max Beerbohm for permission to quote two of his poems.

For access to original letters and papers (and in many cases the most generous loan of them for copying purposes) I gratefully thank the following: Mr. Charles Aukin, Mrs. Rose Banks, Mr. M.V. Carey of Kennedy, Ponsonby & Prideaux (London), Mr. Robert Eddison, Sir John Gielgud, Miss Athene Seyler, Mr. Robin Whitworth. As well as individual owners of letters and documents, the research librarians, keepers of manuscripts and general staffs of the following institutions have assisted by placing documents at my disposal and by sending photo-copies of relevant papers to me: the Berg Collection of the New York Public Library (Dr. Lola Szladits), the Bodleian Library (Miss Helen Langley), the British Library (many people), the Theatre Museum, Victoria & Albert Museum (Mr. Alexander Schouvaloff and staff), the Huntington Library (Mrs. Valerie Franco), the George Arents Research Library, University of Syracuse (Ms. Carolyn A. Davis), the University of London Library (Miss H.M. Young) and the Humanities Research Center, University of Texas (Mrs. Ellen Dunlap, to whom I owe very special thanks, and her entire staff).

A vast number of people have helped me to sort out various puzzles and elucidate various mysteries connected with Granville Barker. Many of these people have allowed me to interview them in person, receiving me graciously and giving generously of their time. Others have been equally co-operative and helpful in replying to importunate enquiries which I addressed to them through the mail or by telephone. Inevitably I shall miss somebody out in a list like this and can only hope to be forgiven for such omissions. The catalogue of my creditors herein, compiled as carefully as possible, is as follows: Mr. Jesse Banks, Mrs. Rose Banks, Mr. Anthony Beaumont, Lady Beckett, Sir Isaiah Berlin, Mr. Peter de Brant, Miss Frances Briggs, Mr. Anthony Curtis, Mrs. H.F. Dimond, Sir John Gielgud, Mr. Robert Gittings, Miss Eileen Gosney, Mr. Piers Haggard, Mr. M.B. Harris (of Stone & Co., Exeter), Professor James Hepburn, Mr. Michael Holroyd, Mr. John Huntington, Mr. Montgomery Hyde, Mr. Stanley Kauffmann, Professor Dennis Kennedy, Professor G. Wilson Knight, Professor Dan H. Laurence, Mr. Michael MacOwan, Mr. David Mc.Fall, Mr. Norman Marshall, Miss Margery M. Morgan, Mr. S.W. Mounting, Mr. Stephen Murray, Miss Cathleen Nesbitt, Mr. John J. O'Grady (of Cadwalader, Wickersham & Taft, New York), Mrs. Alfreda Rushmore, Miss Athene Seyler, Mr. Norman Sims, Mr. John Sterling, Mr. and Mrs. Bob Summers, Miss Jessica Tandy, Professor Hugh Trevor-Roper, Lieutenant-Commander Barry Tuke, Mr. Robin Whitworth.

For the supplying of photographs used as illustrations for this book, and for their gracious permission to publish them, I am indebted to Mr. Peter de Brant, Sir John Gielgud, the Hoblitzelle Theatre Arts Collection, University of Texas and the National Portrait Gallery, London.

In addition to these individuals, I must also acknowledge the generous help with enquiries of various sorts of four institutions and their officers, namely the British Theatre Association, Colyton Grammar School (especially its Headmaster, Mr. Ernest Fox and its Librarian, Mrs. Muriel Clayton), the Hispanic Society of America, in New York and the Garrick Club, in London.

I have received much support and encouragement, as well as practical help of various kinds, from my own university – the University of Guelph – more particularly from the Dean of Research and the Librarian, Mrs. Margaret Beckman, and her staff: the value of the contribution made by the Library can scarcely, indeed, be overestimated. To the Social Sciences and Humanities Research Council of Canada I am indebted for generous financial support for the costs of various research journeys over the past three years and the cost of preparing a final typescript. The actual work of typing has fallen to Mrs. Sharon Ballantyne, who – through the many typings and re-typings occasioned by my eccentricities – managed to keep as cheerful as she is efficient and to produce at the end of it a typescript with which it has been a pleasure to work.

For his friendly advice and encouragement, as well as his professional skill and expertise, I am deeply obliged and very grateful to my editor, Edward Thompson – who, in a very real sense, is this book's 'onlie begetter'. I am also extremely grateful to John Russell Brown, who kindly and carefully read my manuscript and made some very valuable comments and suggestions.

I must lastly say a word of special gratitude to my old friend John Trewin. His enthusiasm and encouragement have always been an inspiration to me; but in the case of this particular book he has also given me a great deal of solid practical help by way both of advice and of factual knowledge of the period, drawn from his own vast store of information. He has a better memory than any other man I ever met and is always recklessly ready to place it at the disposal and service of other people: for my own share in this largesse I rest his eternal debtor.

E.S.
University of Guelph

Preface

Harley Granville Barker was, in his day, the most famous and most respected director in the British theatre and his reputation as an actor stood only just short of his reputation as a director. His day was, in rough general terms, the first decade of the present century. In 1915, when he was only thirty-eight, his career as a director – though nobody (including himself) realized it at the time – was virtually over. Throughout the 1920s and 1930s he was enormously respected and enormously influential in the theatre, though he practised as a director only intermittently and as an actor not at all. His case, and the apparent discrepancy between the amount of practical work and degree of influence, is even more curious than that of Edward Gordon Craig. The whole of Barker's career, in fact, is filled with puzzling questions which still remain largely unanswered.

The present book is an attempt to answer some of these questions, to review with a fresh eye both his written work and his practical work in the theatre itself, and to fill in some of the factual gaps which have been left by previous commentators. There is already a biography of Barker which narrates the facts of his life, or most of them, chronologically. It is, with only minor exceptions, accurate and though it is not as thoroughly documented as, in my view, a first biography should be, it does nevertheless contain quotations from and references to a number of the basic documents, particularly the private correspondence between Barker and Gilbert Murray and between Barker and J.M. Barrie. It seems to me to have three weaknesses: it depends too much for its point of view on the conventional, received wisdom of its time (especially its time in the theatre); it is somewhat too awe-stricken, not to say stage-struck, in tone (especially as regards Barker's first wife, under whose direct influence it was written); and it regards Barker's written work – more especially his plays – rather as mere milestones on the road to 'success' and reputation than as actual, living work. Despite these drawbacks it performs its biographical function, at least in the straightforward factual sense, quite well and it would obviously be superfluous to provide another purely chronology-oriented record of Barker's life. What I have tried to do, rather, is to take the various elements and aspects of Barker's life and examine each one separately, giving a chapter to each. For convenience I have arranged the chapters in the order in which the particular aspect in question first began to develop or show itself (so I have not abjured chronology completely) but it should be borne in mind that the events and ideas of one chapter will on this system inevitably overlap with those of several other chapters. I have treated his writing – both creative and critical – as one (a very important one) of these 'elements' of his life and career and have tried to estimate the proper balance between it and the other aspects of him. I do not believe (as Barker himself perhaps *did* believe) that he was a born writer and nothing else; nor do I believe (as, for example, C.B. Purdom and W. Bridges Adams tended to believe) that his writing was simply a secondary, rather self-indulgent activity, merely incidental to his more important work as an actor-manager-director. His writing and his practical theatre work were – and still are – both of great importance and there was an intricate and intrinsic relationship between them which I shall try to illustrate and examine. Barker was, in his chosen field of theatre, that doubly-fascinating thing, a man of action who was also a thinker, a combination of practical executant, critic and creative artist (and, at the personal level, a strange combination of extrovert and introvert). It has been my objective – I cannot tell how successfully carried out – to explore the balance of these disparate parts.

In spite of my reservations, mentioned above, about C.B. Purdom's *Harley Granville Barker* (London: Rockliff, 1955), I am – as will be obvious from the text of my own work – indebted to it for many things and I gratefully acknowledge that indebtedness. Similarly, I must record my debt to Margery Morgan's *A Drama of Political Man* (London: Sidgwick & Jackson, 1961): I disagree with its main thesis but find much of the detail of its analysis of the plays most perceptive and valuable. I have also drawn upon the work of a large number of other biographers, commentators, critics and theatre historians: acknowledgement is made to each work at the appropriate place in the text, but I take this opportunity to record my thanks to the authors generally and collectively.

E.S.
University of Guelph

Chronology

1877   Harley Granville Barker born in London on November 25.

1891   First recorded appearance in a play (Anstey's *Vice Versa* at the Spa Rooms, Harrogate).

1891   Enrolled as a trainee in Sarah Thorne's theatrical school at the Theatre Royal, Margate.

1892   First stage appearance in London, in Charles Brookfield's *The Poet and The Puppets* at the Comedy Theatre.

1894   Engaged as general understudy in Florence Farr's company at the Avenue Theatre, London.

1895   Member of Ben Greet's touring company, in which he played Paris to the Juliet of Lillah McCarthy.

1895   Collaborated with Berte Thomas in writing *A Comedy of Fools*, a play in four acts. Not produced and not published.

1895–96 Collaborated with Berte Thomas in the writing of *The Family of the Oldroyds*, a play in four acts. Not produced and not published.

1896   Played in Charles Hawtrey's company in *Under the Red Robe* at the Haymarket Theatre, London.

1897   With Berte Thomas wrote *The Weather-Hen; or Invertebrata*, a comedy in prologue, two acts and an epilogue. Unpublished.

1898–99 With Berte Thomas wrote *Our Visitor to 'Work-a-Day'*, a play in five acts. Not produced and not published.

1899   Member of Mrs. Patrick Campbell's Company, in London and on tour. Played parts of Gordon Jayne in *The Second Mrs. Tanqueray* and Antonio Poppi in *The Notorious Mrs. Ebbsmith*.

1899   In London, played Selim in *Carlyon Sahib* by Gilbert Murray.

1899   *The Weather-Hen; or Invertebrata* produced at Terry's Theatre, London, with Madge McIntosh in the leading part.

1899   Played the title rôle in Shakespeare's *Richard II*, directed by William Poel.

1899   Wrote *The Marrying of Ann Leete* (probably the first play written by Barker without a collaborator).

1900   Played Bratsberg in first production of Archer's translation of Ibsen's *The League of Youth* for the Stage Society (a single performance).

1900   Wrote a one-act verse play, called *A Miracle*. Unpublished.

1900   Directed *The Death of Tintagiles* (Maeterlinck) for the Stage Society, with two other one-act plays.

1900   Played Lieutenant Wendowski in Sudermann's *Magda* for Mrs. Patrick Campbell's company at the Royalty Theatre, London.

1900   Played Marchbanks in first London production of Shaw's *Candida* for the Stage Society (one performance only).

1900   Played the Earl of Rochester in *English Nell* at the Prince of Wales Theatre, with Marie Tempest as Nell Gwynn.

1900   Played Captain Kearney in first production of Shaw's *Captain Brassbound's Conversion* for two performances at the Stage Society.

1900–01   Wrote *Agnes Colander*, a play in three acts. Not published and not produced.

1901   Directed and played the part of Napoleon in Shaw's *The Man of Destiny* for a single matinée at the Comedy Theatre, London (under J.T. Grein's management).

1901   Played in *The Case of Rebellious Susan* at Wyndham's Theatre and in *Becky Sharp* at the Prince of Wales Theatre.

1901   Joined the Fabian Society.

1902   Directed first production of his own play *The Marrying of Ann Leete* at the Royalty Theatre.

1902   Played Frank in first production of *Mrs. Warren's Profession* (Shaw) at the New Lyric Club.

1902   Played Osric in Johnston Forbes-Robertson's production of *Hamlet* at the Lyric Theatre.

1903   Played Basil Kent in the first production of Somerset Maugham's first play, *A Man of Honour*, at the Imperial Theatre.

1903	Played the title rôle in William Poel's production of Marlowe's *Edward II*.
1903	Directed, at the Imperial Theatre, *The Waters of Bitterness* (S. M. Fox) and *The Admirable Bashville* (Shaw).
1903–05	Wrote *The Voysey Inheritance*.
1904	With William Archer, wrote *A National Theatre* (published in 1907).
1904–07	With J. E. Vedrenne ran the famous 'repertory' seasons at the Court Theatre, Sloane Square, directing and appearing in many plays.[1]
1906	Married Lillah McCarthy.
1906–07	Wrote *Waste*.
1908	First visit to the United States.
1909	Wrote *The Madras House*.
1910	Began writing *The Village Carpenter*; the play was never finished.
1909–10	Directed a repertory season at the Duke of York's theatre, London, with Charles Frohman as producer.
1911	Directed first production of Masefield's *The Witch*, with Lillah McCarthy as Anna Pedersdotter, at the Court Theatre.
1911	Directed and appeared in his own version of Schnitzler's *Anatol* at the Palace Theatre.
1911–12	Wrote *Rococo*, a one-act play.
1912	Directed Eden Phillpotts' censored play *The Secret Woman* for two private performances at the Kingsway Theatre.
1912	Directed *The Winter's Tale* at the Savoy Theatre.
1912	Directed *Twelfth Night* at the Savoy Theatre.
1913	Directed first production of *Androcles and the Lion* at the St. James's Theatre.
1913	Produced and directed a season of repertory at the St. James's Theatre.
1914	Directed *A Midsummer Night's Dream* at the Savoy Theatre.
1914	Wrote *Vote by Ballot*, a one-act play.
1914	Visited Stanislavsky in Moscow.
1914	Revised and continued *The Village Carpenter* under new title of *The Wicked Man*; still did not complete it.

[1] The Court Theatre venture is here treated as a single activity or unit. Since a separate chapter is devoted to the details of that activity in this present volume and since it is excellently documented in Desmond MacCarthy's *The Court Theatre, 1904–1907* which is still the standard work on the subject, it would be confusing rather than illuminating to include in this chronology the titles of all the productions presented. It is more accurate to treat Barker's work at the Court Theatre as a single entity and to show it as a single stage in his career.

1914	Directed Hardy's *The Dynasts* at the Kingsway Theatre, in a stage version which he himself prepared.
1915	Produced and directed a season of repertory at Wallack's Theatre, New York City.
1915	At the request of the Red Cross wrote a book about the Red Cross work with the British army in France.
1915	In the autumn returned to New York to lecture on British theatre.
1916	From New York wrote to Lillah breaking off their marriage.
1916	Wrote *Farewell to the Theatre*.
1917	Accepted commission in British Intelligence.
1918	Divorced Lillah McCarthy and married Helen Huntington.
1919	Bought Netherton Hall in Farway, Devon.
1919	Became Chairman of the newly-founded British Drama League.
1920	Translated Sacha Guitry's *Deburau* from the French for production in New York.
1921	Directed Maeterlinck's *The Betrothal* at the Gaiety Theatre, London.
1922	Published *The Exemplary Theatre*.
1919–22	Wrote and published *The Secret Life*.
1923	Began the writing of *His Majesty*.
1923	Publication of the first volume of *The Players' Shakespeare*, with introduction by Barker.
1927	Published first volume of *Prefaces to Shakespeare* (written from 1922 onward).
1928	Published *His Majesty*.
1929	President of the Royal Society of Literature.
1931	Went to live in Paris.
1937	Became Director of the British Institute in Paris.
1940	In April, spent two weeks in London advising on the Gielgud/Casson production of *King Lear*.
1940	Arrived in Lisbon, from Paris, in June.
1940	Arrived in New York on September 6 and took up residence there.
1942	Lectured at the University of Toronto.
1944	Lectured at Princeton University.
1945	Lectured at Harvard University.
1945	In May, returned to England.
1946	In March, returned to live in Paris.
1946	Died in Paris, August 31.

−1−

The Early Years

There was supposed to be a Mysterious Envelope containing secret and shocking information about Harley Granville Barker, written by Lewis Casson and deposited for safe keeping with the Society for Theatre Research. Sir Lewis's instructions were that the envelope was not to be opened for *x* years, the story says. The Society for Theatre Research says that when it eventually went to open it in 1977 – that being the centenary of Barker's birth – the Mysterious Envelope had mysteriously disappeared. Ann Casson and John Casson, daughter and son of Sir Lewis, tend to believe that the envelope and its revelatory contents never actually existed but were conjured up out of Sir Lewis's innate sense of the theatrical and his awareness of Barker's near-legendary status. The Secretary of the Society for Theatre Research, on the other hand, says he clearly remembers being at the meeting of the Society at which The Envelope was solemnly accepted into trust, but when I asked to see the minutes of that meeting, they were not forthcoming. Quite obviously, nobody is lying: what all are doing is responding to the already-present and constantly-growing sense of Harley Granville Barker as a mythical figure. The Envelope story is not the only one. There are others, all of which tell of a blazingly-public life and hint at the mysterious and carefully-concealed private life behind it. Several of these stories seek to account for the fact that in the early nineteen-twenties Barker, after twenty years of furious and fruitful activity in the theatre, suddenly withdrew totally, or almost totally, from practical theatre work and thenceforward never acted again, directed only occasionally and then only for very specific reasons on a few very special occasions. The usual explanation for this, within the legend, is that his second wife, Helen Huntington, whom he married in 1918, insisted that he leave the theatre and break off his connections with theatre people (most notably, with Shaw). The legend has perhaps some truth in it, but it is surely too simplistic to account for the whole of the matter. Helen may well have 'insisted': but why did Harley yield to that insistence? 'She was very rich and he loved luxury' the legend says: 'She bought him'. But there is a good deal of evidence that calls such a judgment in question. John Casson, in his book *Lewis and Sybil*[1] says 'Lewis [Sir Lewis Casson] oscillated between two theories about the cause of his retreat. One was that he had been eaten alive by his second wife and the other that he had become an agent in the British Secret Service, which later became Lewis's standard explanation when people he knew began behaving with any degree of eccentricity.'

On those rare occasions when he emerged from his self-imposed exile and returned to London as the fabled director, most of the actors who worked with him responded, according to their own accounts, with an almost superstitious awe; but not quite all. A few of them, and especially the younger ones, found him ponderous, overbearing and not particularly helpful. Stephen Murray, who as a young actor played Kent in the 1936 production of *Waste*, thought Barker 'an insensitive and overweening bully'. (Small wonder: Murray had the unfortunate experience of having Barker chant all the lines of his part with him at rehearsal after rehearsal: even at the dress rehearsal Barker sat in the auditorium, booming away; and the play finished with a heart-felt rendering from the stalls of the famous last line: 'Oh, the waste of him . . . oh, the waste . . . the waste!' Murray must have begun to wonder whether this would continue at performances as well.)

Of course, we all belie our appearances. No motives are entirely plain and none is entirely unmixed. But in Barker's case the difference between public face and private soul seems to have been more than the usual and seems also to have been one of which he himself was terribly aware. It became, especially in the latter part of his life, obsessional with him, a matter for conscious concealment. He came to regard the maintaining of that concealment as a vital exercise in the preserving of the integrity of the self.

In 1919, less than two years after his marriage to Helen Huntington, and shortly after they had gone to live at Netherton Hall, in Colyton, Devon – far from London and the life of the theatre – Barker began to write a play to which he gave a particularly significant title. It was called *The Secret Life*. He had written plays before, of course; famous and striking ones. But this one was written away from the theatre, with no immediate production in mind. It has, in fact, never had a professional production and very few of any other kind. In a letter, dated May 13, 1921, to William Archer, Barker said: 'The Madras House is the best play I've written yet – dialogue almost equal to Dekker. I've begun though (P.G.)[2] a better one. And finished (T.G.)[2] my book on the theatre.[3] Helen has just finished a long satirical poem – jolly good!'

So while Helen Huntington wrote long satirical poems and began another novel (*Ada*, published by Chatto & Windus in 1923), Harley Granville Barker settled down at Netherton (Nether Town – the very word is like a bell!) to write a play about private life and public life. The play itself, a remarkable one, will be examined in a later chapter, along with Barker's other plays. It is mentioned here only as evidence of its author's instinct towards withdrawal and his belief in the necessity for and the efficacy of secrecy. Whether this trait was a result of his origins and early life or of inherent psychological factors must remain a matter for conjecture. Certain it is that those origins were obscure, both in the sense of being undistinguished and in the sense of being difficult to establish in any detail.

Shaw, in an obituary article which he wrote when Barker died in 1946[4] said: 'He had a strong strain of Italian blood in him, and looked as if he had stepped out of a picture by Benozzo Gozzoli.' Certainly his mother's name was half-Italian.

He was born in the sub-district of Kensington Town in the County of Middlesex on November 25, 1877. So much, out of a mass of guesses, suppositions and legends, we know for a fact because the General Register Office at Somerset House has a birth certificate giving this information. The actual place of birth is given as 3a, Sheffield Terrace, Campden Hill; the father's name is given as Albert James Barker, whose occupation is described as 'Gentleman'; the mother is given as Mary Elizabeth Barker, formerly Bozzi-Granville. The birth was registered on December 14, 1877 and in the column headed 'Name entered after registration' the names Harley Granville appear, there being no entry in the earlier column 'Name, if any'. C.B. Purdom, in his *Harley Granville Barker* (London: Rockliff, 1955), gives a quite full history of the antecedents on both sides of the family but since he quotes no authority and gives no indication of the source of his information, much of it must be regarded with some scepticism, especially as the General Register Office has no records to support most of his statements.

St. John Ervine, in his book *Bernard Shaw; His Life, Work and Friends* (London: Constable, 1956) says:

> Inevitably, no doubt, a legend ran round London that Granville-Barker was G.B.S.'s son, though no mother was ever mentioned. When I first heard it, I suggested to my informant that the strongest refutal of it was G.B.S.'s failure to boast about it, as he certainly would have done, had it been true.

Well, perhaps; though we need not feel under obligation to accept St. John Ervine's *bravura* reading of the situation, which is part of another theatrical legend – that of Shaw, which Shaw himself industriously promoted. Shaw, if he did not actually boast about it, knew the rumour and mentions it in a letter to Pinero on March 21, 1910[5]:

> Some of them swear by Barker: others hint that he is my natural son: but most of them reject this hypothesis on the ground that I am physically incapable of parentage.

The rumour was repeated to me as recently as 1978 by Norman Marshall, the producer and director who had started his career as an actor in a rôle secured for him by Barker's recommendation. He was twenty-four years Barker's junior but knew Barker fairly well and seemed certain that the rumour was widely current and probably believed, whether it was true or not.

When Barker died in 1946, Shaw – in addition to the article in *Drama* – wrote a letter to the *Times Literary Supplement*. It has been quoted fairly often before but since it is rather strikingly *à propos* in the present context I shall take the liberty of quoting it again:

> The enclosed photograph of Harley Granville-Barker, taken by me forty years ago at the Old House, Harmer Green, when our collaboration, now historic, was at its inception, may interest readers.
>
> We clicked so well together that I regarded him as my contemporary until one day at rehearsal, when someone remarked that I was fifty, he said, 'You are the same age as my father.' After that it seemed impossible that he should die before me. The shock the news gave me made me realize how I had cherished a hope that our old intimate relation might revive. But
>
> > Marriage and death and division
> > Make barren our lives
>
> and the elderly professor could have little use for a nonagenarian ex-playwright.

In two respects at least Shaw treated Barker as if he were his son. One of those ways is hinted at in the 1946 letter – in their work together at the Court Theatre between 1904 and 1907 the artistic relationship was not only remarkably close but was in some ways of a filial-paternal kind. It was Shaw who created the opportunity for Barker by giving him the part of Marchbanks in *Candida* in 1900, when Barker was twenty-two and Shaw was nearly forty-four. In the Barker-Vedrenne seasons (1904–07) at the Court, while Barker himself directed all the other plays, Shaw directed his own plays and Barker was almost invariably one of the cast. Shaw lent Barker money – quite large sums – for various theatrical ventures, including the Court seasons and unhesitatingly cancelled the debts on those occasions upon which the financial burden on Barker became too great. But in addition to the artistic relationship there was a personal relation of a very close kind also. Both Shaw and his wife were obviously extremely fond of Barker and he was a constant visitor in their various homes. During the 1914–18 war, while he was in the process of obtaining a divorce from Lillah McCarthy, Barker treated the Shaws' house at Ayot St. Lawrence as his own home, keeping a spare suit of civilian clothes there and slipping away from London whenever he could to spend a day or two there, whether Shaw and Charlotte were in residence at the time or not. Earlier than that, during and immediately after the famous years at the Court Theatre, Barker and Shaw fairly frequently took holidays together, sometimes with their wives, sometimes alone. As Stanley Weintraub points out, both in *Shaw: An Autobiography* (New York: Weybright and Talley, 1969) and in *Journey to Heartbreak* (New York: Weybright and Talley, 1971), Shaw looked upon Barker as a 'surrogate son'.

Bernard Shaw, aged almost twenty, arrived in London in April, 1876: Granville Barker was born in November, 1877. Shaw lived with his mother and sister at 13, Victoria Grove, S.W. 10 (the street is now called Netherton Grove); Barker was born at 3a, Sheffield Terrace, W8. The two addresses are within fifteen minutes' walk of each other. Mrs. Barker was an entertainer, appearing (under the name of Miss Granville) at concerts both as a reciter of verse and as a bird-mimic. Shaw, in his first years in London[6], fairly often appeared at local concerts as a pianist, sometimes accompanying his sister's singing, sometimes as a soloist. He also, under his mother's tuition, developed a passable baritone voice himself and could thus perform as a singer as well as a pianist. He describes the kind of concert and the kind of programme in the opening chapter of his second novel, *The Irrational Knot*, written in 1880. The group of performers in this concert, which the novel says is given at Wandsworth Town Hall, includes a young man of Irish descent, recently arrived in London, who can both sing and play the piano but is rather looked down on socially by the rest of the company. It also includes a lady who gives poetry recitations. The young man, Edward Conolly, lodges in London with his sister, who is a professional singer.

All of this *proves* nothing, of course. But it indicates a possibility. Shaw performed at local concerts shortly after arriving in London. He met other performers. One of them could easily have been a lady who lived just across Kensington from him and who earned a little by giving poetry recitals and imitating bird-song. That Shaw was extremely susceptible to feminine charms and tumbled in and out of love with the ease and frequency (and, on occasion, the splash) of a friendly spaniel tumbling into water, is by now well known. Given the shadowy character of Granville Barker's alleged father, the theory seems at least tenable. Purdom (p. 3) says: 'Albert James Barker seems to have made no success of his life, though proud of his family connections; he was of medium height, dark-haired, bald, with a black-pointed beard, thin-faced, active, nervous, excitable, an interminable talker, and consumptive. He died of that disease in France in 1909, aged fifty-three, when his son was already famous.' This and Purdom's other brief comments tell us just enough to make us wonder whether that is all there is to know and where these snatches of disconnected information came from.

As to a possible relationship between Shaw and Granville Barker, there are some other details worth noting. When Shaw moved to a flat in the Adelphi in 1898, Barker took a room close by, at 8, York Buildings and Mary Elizabeth Barker and her husband moved into rooms just across the street: Barker, his mother and Shaw would be within two minutes' walk of each other. Archibald Henderson, Shaw's first biographer, remarks in his *George Bernard Shaw: Man of the Century* (New York: De Capo Press, 1972) 'Among Shaw's younger friends, with whom I was thrown a great deal on my first visit to England, were Harley Granville-Barker, Robert Loraine, Alvin Langdon Coburn, A.R. Orage, and Holbrook Jackson. The others were treated like nephews by the genial and friendly Shaw; but Barker received from him all the tender interest and straight-from-the-shoulder handling of a son.' (p. 795) This was in 1907, the year of Henderson's first visit to England. Barker was then almost thirty. And one last point: both men had red hair – though of different shades of red, apparently. Purdom – who makes no mention of the rumour about Shaw's possible paternity – includes in his book

Bernard Shaw and Granville Barker at about the time of the start of the Court Theatre experiment.

(opposite page 18) a photograph of Shaw and Barker sitting together, both looking serious and intense. About the set of the eyes, mouth and nose there is a distinct resemblance and if one covers the hair line on this picture of Barker, the unsmiling, clean-shaven face bears some likeness to photographs of Shaw in his late teens and early twenties. One is tempted also to cite the famous photograph of Barker with Lillah McCarthy in *Man and Superman* in 1905, but perhaps this is cheating, since when he played Tanner he deliberately made up to look like Shaw. However, the astonishing success with which he could do so – judging from the two photographs reproduced side by side on page 9 – may perhaps be regarded as having some significance. Still, none of this is proof, but it does suggest a reasonable possibility to which later events tend to give an additional degree of credibility.

We do not know where Barker went to school or, indeed, whether he had any formal education at all. We do know that in 1891, when he was fourteen, he was sent to a theatre school in Margate, to train as an actor. The school was run by Sarah Thorne (1837–99), a well-known actress and teacher of acting who also ran a stock company at the Theatre Royal, Margate. Her pupils, when sufficiently skilled, played the smaller parts in the Theatre Royal productions. Barker remained at Margate for six months. One of his fellow-students was a young man called Berte Thomas. Thomas, who later became Barker's collaborator in the writing of several early plays, was Barker's senior by nine years and was, in 1891, himself training to be an actor.

The first direct evidence we have of Barker's employment as an actor is a letter written by him to his mother in 1895. He writes from the Channel Islands Hotel in Guernsey and sends his letter to Poste Restante, Lucerne. He describes briefly the voyage to Guernsey, says that theatrical lodgings on the island are so bad that he and three of the ladies of the company have been forced to seek the shelter of the hotel in spite of its being expensive (five shillings a day). 'A rehearsal this afternoon, then we play the 'Two Roses' tomorrow. Masks then 'Money'. The letter concludes with 'Keep care of yourself, Gracie and Dad. Best love, from Little Dog.'[7]

The touring company of which Barker was a member in 1895 and with which he visited the Channel Islands was that of Ben Greet, who was then thirty-eight and already an inveterate tourer. The leading lady of the company, playing Juliet, Desdemona, Ophelia, Beatrice, Peg Woffington and Lady Teazle, was Lillah McCarthy, aged twenty. This was her first major engagement. Barker played Paris to her Juliet, the

Lillah McCarthy and
Granville Barker as
Ann Whitefield and
Jack Tanner in
Man and Superman.

Bernard Shaw
about 1890.

*Barker in his
early years
as an actor.*

*A silver locket
containing a picture
of his mother before
her marriage. Barker
kept the locket all his life.*

Romeo being H.B. Irving, twenty-five years old, elder son of the newly-knighted Sir Henry.

In the same year, Barker renewed his acquaintance with Berte Thomas and collaborated with him in the writing of a play, called *A Comedy of Fools*. Purdom says: 'but after being offered unsuccessfully to a number of managements the manuscript was torn up', information which he presumably had from Thomas himself, since when he was writing his book about Barker in 1954–55 he talked with Thomas. *A Comedy of Fools* is, nevertheless, significant in that it marks the beginning of Barker as a playwright. During the next year, in spite of being engaged as actors (chiefly in London) for some part of the time, Barker and Thomas managed to complete a second play, called *The Family of the Oldroyds*. The typescript is still extant and is now owned by the British Library, to whom it was given by Berte Thomas in the late 1940s or early 1950s. Even allowing for the fashion of the time, it is a very crude and shallow piece of work but one needs to remember that when it was written Barker was only eighteen and even Thomas, who was presumably the prime mover in the matter, was only twenty-seven. Its typescript is today a fascinating document because it bears very heavy revisions in Barker's hand, all of which – without exception – are attempts to tone down the melodramatic purple of the original dialogue. This does not cure the melodrama or the stereotyping indulged in by the plot, but it does indicate that Barker, even at eighteen, was beginning to be aware of the weakness and the inherent silliness of the over-heated dialogue and the pretentious posturings of the popular drama of the time. The time is important to note: in the five years immediately preceding the writing of *The Family of the Oldroyds* had appeared the following:

1891   *The Dancing Girl* (Jones)
1892   *Lady Windermere's Fan* (Wilde)
1893   *The Second Mrs. Tanqueray* (Pinero)
1893   *A Woman of No Importance* (Wilde)
1894   *The Case of Rebellious Susan* (Jones)
1895   *The Notorious Mrs. Ebbsmith* (Pinero)

These plays have one thing in common: they all centre on that character who held so fixed and firm a fascination for nineteenth-century playwrights and audiences – the 'fallen' woman. It need, therefore, be no surprise to find her, in yet another manifestation, in *The Family of the Oldroyds* in 1895–96. The particular form she assumes in the Barker-Thomas play is interesting, but the lady herself is a stock figure, simply part of that procession which begins with Marguerite Gautier in 1852. The plays in which she appears always register an orthodox official disapproval of her and her falling propensities (always discreetly off-stage) in the sexual field but always (or almost always – Emile Augier provides us, in *Le Mariage d'Olympe* (1855), with a significant but rather lonely exception) reveal a sneaking affection and admiration for her. She is invariably wittier, wiser, kinder and more courageous than her more virtuous sisters – and infinitely more personable and attractive. The twist which Barker and Thomas give to the familiar theme and the stock character in *The Family of the Oldroyds* is to allow us to see their demi-mondaine in embryo, so to speak. Tessa is the adolescent daughter of a woman who has died before the play begins; we hear of the dead mother fragmentarily at first but gradually she is retrospectively revealed in more detail as being the standard theatrical figure of the age. She is equipped with all the usual trappings – physical allure, a passionate nature, contempt for convention, 'Southern blood'[8] and so on. And Tessa, we gradually learn, takes after her. She is a mere slip of a girl when we first see her; but she grows up with astonishing alacrity. The first time she is kissed by a man (on the lips, in Act I, right before our eyes) she leaps to conclusions that a more cautious young lady might consider unwarranted and the curtain line of the act is given to her: 'Naomi – dear, dear Naomi. It has come at last – I am a woman.' Things rapidly go from bad to worse, both in Tessa's character and in the quality of the dialogue, which assumes a deeper and deeper – and more and more embarrassing – shade of purple. In Act II Tessa mocks Naomi, who has inconveniently but much more restrainedly fallen in love with the same man as Tessa. So Tessa begins by doing an imitation of the man's speech (as she imagines it) to Naomi:

TESSA: 'Naomi, I love you.' Loves you! Ah! God curse you both. Loves you? He is mine. He kissed me on the lips, here in this very room. He is mine – mine – mine! Diavoli rossi t'staggiano, you white-lipped English saint. You'll take him from me – you will be his wife – Damn you! Damn you! Damn you!

Then in Act III she talks to her father, Clement, about his dead wife:

It is the truth – it is the truth – you can't deny it. I feel it here, it is written on my heart in letters of fire – I know – I know. If I had been one of your pure-souled English women, the knowledge of it would have killed me long ago, – I wish to God it had. But I'm tainted through and through, from head to foot. The thought of my Mother's life fires me, fascinates me, sucks me into the whirlpool of its glorious passion. I have the Southern sun in my blood – I've none to respect, no God to answer to. I'm the mistress of my own fate – you have taught me that. I live alone, irresponsible, nothing to guide me but my mother's voice: 'Child of shame – child of shame,' it cries; 'who are you to live a pure holy life? You can't remove the taint of blood, for you are weak and I am strong in you. You are damned. You were cursed before you were born, cursed in your life, cursed in your love. Do as your own black heart tells you. Follow your passions, your lusts, your desires – enjoy life while you may, – poor – outcast. Drink your cup of vice to the very dregs, pollute the earth while you must – and die damned everlastingly.' I'll live my life as I must. There is no God to save me – you know it – you have told me so again and again. He is a law – a destiny that judges! Well, let Him judge me if He dare!

Tessa's father is, not unnaturally, extremely worried to hear language of this kind in the mouth of a sixteen-year-old (though he refrains from asking what one would have thought to be the obvious question: 'My dear child, what *have* you been reading?'), but by the end of the play he has decided that the case is a hopeless one and in a fit of passion he cries out: 'Curse her, she has made my life a hell. I would she were dead at my feet, here now before you all. God, if there is a God, strike her dead.' Tessa, who just happens to be hiding behind the long window-curtain, overhears him and reacts with typical exaggeration. The final lines of the play read as follows:

(TESSA *parts the curtains and stands there, the dagger sticking in her breast, her hand clutching it. She walks slowly and firmly to* CLEMENT.)
TESSA: Are you satisfied?
(CLEMENT *gives a gasping cry.* TESSA *falls at his feet.*)
CLEMENT: God's hand, God's law, Oh God, is it just? (*very softly*) Maria! Maria![9]
TESSA: Carissimo. Shall we go together, you and I, out of the world?
CLEMENT (*softly*): My darling.
TESSA: Carissimo.
(TESSA *laughs softly to herself and dies*)

CURTAIN

Barker and Thomas, in 1895, obviously assumed that this is what plays were supposed to be like, with impossibly noble thoughts, high-toned speeches, thrillingly moral posturings of an absurdly unreal kind – all pivoting on adultery or potential adultery or the suspicion of adultery – and all of it as distant from everyday experience and ordinary life as it could possibly be. Their assumption is not very surprising, however, when one considers that list of plays produced in London during the previous five years and when one remembers that these two young men were both actors: they saw the theatre from the inside, knew its ways and its expectations; both had played in the company of that famous charmer, Mrs. Patrick Campbell. It is not surprising that at first they mistook the theatre's florid fantasies for the stuff of real life. What *is* surprising is the rapidity with which one of them, at least, recovered from this myopia and suddenly began to look at real life itself with a fresh sense of vision. Even in his manuscript amendments to the typescript of *The Family of the Oldroyds*, there are indications of the direction in which Barker's thoughts were moving. All the corrections, deletions and additions (and there are many) are in his handwriting and all of them (albeit very, very tentatively at this stage) move toward subtlety and austerity of speech. Already, at the age of eighteen, he is beginning to react against the bombast and the empty rhetoric. The long speech of Tessa's quoted above, was amended to read:

> It is the truth – it is the truth – you can't deny it. I feel it here – I know – I know. If I had been one of your pure-souled English women, the knowledge of it would have killed me long ago, – I wish to God it had. But I'm tainted, through and through, from head to foot. I have the Southern sun in my blood – nothing to guide me but my mother's voice: 'Child of shame – child of shame,' it cries; 'who are you to live a pure holy life? You are doomed. You were cursed before you were born, cursed in your life, cursed in your love. Enjoy life while you may, – poor – outcast.' I'll live my life as I must. There is no God to save me – you know it – you have told me so again and again. He is a law – a destiny that judges! Well, let Him judge me if He dare!

This is still pretty bad, but it is better than the first version. And is it really all that much worse than, say, Agnes in *The Notorious Mrs. Ebbsmith*?

> One supreme hour. Her poor life is like the arch of a crescent; so many years lead up to that hour, so many weary years decline from it. No matter what she may strive for, there is a moment when Circumstance taps her upon the shoulder and says, 'Woman, this hour is the best that Earth has to spare for you.' It may come to her in calm or in tempest, lighted by a steady radiance or by the glitter of evil stars; but however it comes, be it good or evil, *it is her hour* – let her dwell upon every second of it!

Surely no one in real life ever talked like that! But in the plays of the 1880s and 1890s everyone talked that way. And, what is more, took themselves seriously at it and were taken seriously by critics and audience. Nor can this kind of writing be defended on the grounds that it is not intended as a direct representation of ordinary speech but as a poetic distillation of inner senses, the late-Victorian equivalent of Elizabethan blank verse: judged by such a criterion it is even more lamentably wanting – as poetry it is empty, vapid, turgid, over-blown, sentimental and inaccurate. But it did have one quality in common with Elizabethan stage verse – it was the fashion of the time, deeply entrenched, much admired. It took men like Shaw and Barker to recognize its emptiness and to demonstrate against it. William Archer, who was neither foolish nor insensitive, wrote of the first production of *The Second Mrs. Tanqueray*: 'I wonder if Mr. Pinero himself quite realises what an immeasurable advance he has made in *The Second Mrs. Tanqueray* on all his former works? He has written a play which Dumas might sign without a blush. . . . It is not merely the seriousness of the subject that distinguishes this play from its predecessors. . . It is the astonishing advance in philosophical insight and technical skill which places the new play in a new category. . . . Here, without raving, we can praise almost without reservation.' He described the language of *The Second Mrs. Tanqueray* as 'good honest manly prose'. And this was not because he had no other models by which to judge: his own translation of *The Master Builder*, for example, was first produced in London in the same year as *The Second Mrs. Tanqueray* and he had, by that time, translated most of Ibsen's other plays as well. His theatre notices of the time make it clear that he thought of the Pinero of *The Second Mrs. Tanqueray* as being, if not Ibsen's equal, at least in the same league. Yet the situations and the dialogue in *The Second Mrs. Tanqueray* are as inflated and over-heated as those in all the other plays of the period:

AUBREY: Paula, you must have said something – admitted something –
PAULA: I don't think so. It – it's in my face.
AUBREY: What?
PAULA: She tells me so. She's right! I'm tainted through and through; anybody can see it, anybody can find out. You said much the same to me tonight.

And a little later Paula says:

You'll see me then, at last, with other people's eyes; you'll see me just as your daughter does now, as all wholesome folks see women like me. And I shall have no weapon to fight with – not one serviceable little bit of prettiness left me to defend myself with! A worn-out creature – broken up, very likely some time before I ought to be – my hair bright, my eyes dull, my body too thin or too stout, my cheeks raddled and ruddled – a ghost, a wreck, a caricature, a candle that gutters, call such an end what you like!

At the end of the play Paula, like Tessa in *The Family of the Oldroyds* (and like many other heroines of the period), kills herself in order to provide an effective final curtain:

DRUMMLE: She – she has – !

ELLEAN: Killed – herself? (*Nodding*) Yes – yes. So everyone will say. But I know – I helped to kill her. If I had only been merciful! (*She beats her breast. She faints upon the ottoman. He pauses for a moment irresolutely then he goes to the door, opens it, and stands looking off.*)

CURTAIN

Mrs. Erlynne, in *Lady Windermere's Fan*, carries on in much the same vein:

Believe what you choose about me. I am not worth a moment's sorrow. But don't spoil your beautiful young life on my account! You don't know what may be in store for you unless you leave this house at once. You don't know what it is to fall into the pit, to be despised, mocked, abandoned, sneered at – to be an outcast! . . . One pays for one's sin, and then one pays again, and all one's life one pays. . . . As for me, if suffering be an expiation, then at this moment I have expiated all my faults, whatever they have been; for tonight you have made a heart in one who had it not, made it and broken it.

Wilde, in fact, was – in spite of his cynicism and his wit – no better than the rest until he came to write *The Importance of Being Earnest*, which is a horse of a quite different colour. But in the very same year that it was produced (which was also the year in which the young Barker began to write *The Family of the Oldroyds*) Wilde had another play running in which the language of Mrs. Erlynne of two years earlier repeats itself in Mrs. Arbuthnot (in *A Woman of No Importance*):

Before her child was born – for she had a child – she implored him for the child's sake to marry her, that the child might have a name, that her sin might not be visited on the child, who was innocent. He refused. After the child was born she left him, taking the child away, and her life was ruined, and her soul ruined, and all that was sweet and good, and pure in her ruined also. She suffered terribly – she suffers now. She will always suffer. For her there is no joy, no peace, no atonement. She is a woman who drags a chain like a guilty thing. She is a woman who wears a mask, like a thing that is a leper. The fire cannot purify her. The waters cannot quench her anguish. Nothing can heal her! No anodyne can give her sleep, no poppies forgetfulness! She is lost! She is a lost soul!

She is talking about herself, of course. All these ladies are at their best when talking about themselves, especially about what they did in The Past. Here is Drusilla Ives in *The Dancing Girl* of Henry Arthur Jones:

> Strike me then, if you will! You'll be reasonable? – very well! Listen to reason then! You gave me life – you gave me health and strength and beauty ! You brought me up as you thought best – But your mean, narrow life stifled me, crushed me! I couldn't breathe in it! I wanted a larger freer, wider life – I was perishing for want of it! I've kept up a life of deception for five years to spare you pain – for your sake – not for mine! Now it's over! You know me! You see me as I am – I am the topmost rose on the topmost branches and I love the sunshine – I want admiration – applause! I want to live and live in every pulse of me! For every moment of my life – and I will! I will be myself! You cannot change me! Leave me! Let me go!

One scarcely needs to add that this lady, too, is dead by the end of the play. She dies in Shame, after dancing in public on a Sunday evening in New Orleans. Could any circumstance be more conclusive?

These various speeches – the style, the content, the pretentious, high-flown metaphor – are virtually interchangeable from one play to another, regardless of who wrote them. It is little wonder that the eighteen-year-old Barker fell at first into the universal pattern. The wonder is that he realised his error so soon and corrected it so quickly. He had to begin to learn by imitating the thing that he would very quickly reject and scorn. In 1895, while he and Berte Thomas were beginning the writings of *The Family of the Oldroyds*, Shaw was describing *The Notorious Mrs. Ebbsmith*, in one of his *Saturday Review* essays,[10] as 'a piece of claptrap so gross that it absolves me from all obligation to treat Mr. Pinero's art as anything higher than the barest art of theatrical sensation'. But Shaw was already almost forty and already had seen two of his own plays produced in London – *Widowers' Houses* in 1892 and *Arms and the Man* in 1894. Barker would soon catch him up, but in the meantime it is worth noting some of the characteristics of this product of his nonage. The entirely imitative nature of its content, posture and general style is, as has been pointed out already, immediately obvious. If one glances back at those speeches written by Pinero, Wilde and Jones, one can even detect actual phrases which have been borrowed by Barker and Thomas. Note, for example, 'tainted through and through', borrowed from Paula Tanqueray; and Tessa's describing of herself as an 'outcast', just as Mrs. Erlynne does. Not that Barker and Thomas went through the texts of other plays picking out juicy phrases and appropriating them to their own use. There was no need: such language came entirely automatically with the general style and thought (if that is the right word) of the theatre of the period. The cliché phrase was the inevitable concomitant of the stereotyped situation. Cups were, in those days, always 'drained to the very dregs'; people habitually found themselves gazing into symbolic abysses or climbing metaphorical mountains. In spite of Archer's defence, on various occasions, of Pinero's 'realism', you weren't really meant to *believe* the characters on the stage, or to believe that their situations corresponded to ordinary, everyday situations. Bluntschli, in *Arms and the Man*, identifies the normal audience approach when he says to Raina (who gives an operatic-style performance in her ordinary private life): 'I can't help it. When you strike that noble attitude and speak in that thrilling voice, I admire you; but I find it impossible to believe a single word you say.'

As well as echoing the standard melodrama of the time so thoroughly, *The Family of the Oldroyds* is full of other, incidental echoes. Tessa's 'I'm the mistress of my own fate' in Act III is a feminine transcription of Henley's 'I am the master of my fate,/I am the captain of my soul.' Clement's 'I would she were dead at my feet. . . .' in Act IV is a direct memory of Shylock in Act III, Scene I of *The Merchant of Venice*: 'I would my daughter were dead at my foot and the jewels in her ear; I would she were hears'd at my foot and the jewels in her coffin.' Barker would learn in his later plays to use oblique references to other works in ways that served to illuminate his own, but the echoes in *The Family of the Oldroyds* are not of this kind: they are, in themselves, clichés – the grabbing at the most usual and ordinary form of expression that comes to the author's mind. They do not startle the imagination into the recognition of connections hitherto unperceived; they lull the mind into the acceptance of the wholly expected.

The play, however, does have two touches of originality. One is the use of Tessa as symbol both of past and future; a clumsy but brave attempt, whether conscious or unconscious, to show where the stock-character fallen woman came from, how she developed, what motive power drove her. The other is the relationship, clumsily done and undeveloped but nevertheless discernible, between Clement and Tessa, father and daughter. At three moments in the play Clement sees Tessa as if she were his wife, not his daughter; and at the final curtain Tessa herself makes the same kind of assumption. For just a moment there is a real resonance in the play; the imagination stirs and the piece almost comes to life. It is enough, by way of promise, to point us toward what is to come.

Barker's development as a playwright was closely parallel to his development as a performer (and I use the word 'performer', rather than 'actor' because when his career really hit its stride his work as an actor blended so closely with his work as director/producer/manager that it is quite impossible to consider them separately, just as it is impossible to consider the uniqueness of his play-writing, at its maturity, apart from the rest of his work in the theatre). This, indeed, is the special quality of the man. He conceived a new idea of theatre, a theatre capable of a completely new sense of seriousness, and his personal skills in that theatre extended to more facets of it than was the case with any other practitioner of his time and not with many of *any* time.

But in 1896 he was still only eighteen and the skills still had to be nurtured and developed. He was a small-part actor in London and he had collaborated in the writing of two plays, neither of which had been produced and neither of which, it is safe to say, was produceable. He had yet to play a major rôle and had yet to write a play of his own, on his own. The next four years would see him do both.

−2−

Developing Strength

*I*t was in 1899, two weeks before his twenty-second birthday, that he was able to demonstrate fully for the first time that, so far as the field of acting was concerned, the skills were now fully developed and mature. On November 11 of that year he played the title-rôle in Shakespeare's *Richard II* in William Poel's production of the play for the Elizabethan Stage Society. Only one performance of the production was given, in the lecture theatre of the University of London on a Saturday afternoon, but that was sufficient to enable some of the more trusted and perceptive critics to see that Barker was a young actor with talents beyond the ordinary. '. . . the play had hardly started before it was clear that there was one player whose talent would make the performance exceptionally interesting . . .', wrote A.B. Walkley in *The Times* on November 13, 1899, adding that 'Mr. Barker played the later scenes with a decided sense of character and with a pathos that seemed to touch every section of his rather difficult audience.' At the end of his review Walkley mentions that the performance did not finish till 'past seven' and that this was a difficult time at which to discharge an audience upon the town. It must have been difficult for the leading player as well: it left him little enough time, even though the distance is short, to get from Burlington Gardens to the Prince of Wales Theatre in Coventry Street, where he had to be that evening as an understudy in Mrs. Patrick Campbell's production of *The Moonlight Blossom*, by C.B. Fernald. It was the final performance of the Fernald play that night and four days later, on Wednesday, November 15, Mrs. Pat's company at the Prince of Wales opened a new play in which Granville Barker was not merely an understudy but had a small part in the cast. He played Albert Bailey in *The Canary* – described by the *Times* as a 'light comedy' and by Allardyce Nicoll as a 'farce' – by George Fleming.[1] Apart from the Richard II, Barker's London acting had all been of this kind – and not very much of it, either. He had had a very small part in Charles Hawtrey's production of *Under the Red Robe*, at the Haymarket Theatre in 1896; in 1897 and 1898 he had not acted in London at all; in 1899, before *The Canary*, he had played in three other plays with Mrs. Campbell's company: a revival of *The Second Mrs. Tanqueray*, a revival of *The Notorious Mrs. Ebbsmith* and a fortnight's run of a new play by Gilbert Murray, called *Carlyon Sahib*. The gap of 1897–98 he had filled in two ways: he had acted outside London and, again with the collaboration of Berte Thomas, he had written two more plays. In the summers of both of those years he was with A.B. Tapping's company in Hastings. And in July, 1897 he played Hastings in *She Stoops to Conquer* at Kingston-on-Thames, the Marlow being Gordon Craig, who had met Barker several times before and did not much care for him. 'Barker was a sickly youth', says Craig in *Index to the Story of My Days* (London: Hulton Press, 1957), 'and I was a hearty young man some five or six years older than he. But to me he seemed never very young. The first time I met him he was getting out of a bus, and looked rather ill, if not helpless, and I lent him a hand. I remember he sat down on a bench, didn't say thank you, and looked more and more frail.' Elsewhere in the same book Craig says: 'I never knew Barker well, for I was not sufficiently interested in what he seemed to be doing, nor was I attracted by his personality' and, again, 'Barker was to me in nothing *simpatico*'. Strange that the two men who influenced twentieth-century English-speaking theatre more, perhaps, than any others and whose ideas about the seriousness and nobility of the theatre were in many ways the perfect complement each for other should have been at the personal level so antipathetic.

Barker, then, in the years between 1896 and 1900 was a young actor beginning to make his way and not attracting any very marked attention until Poel cast him as Richard II. Just how or why that happened seems not to be known: we must assume that Poel, whose work with Elizabethan plays had begun in 1881, with a production of *Hamlet* in St. George's Hall when he was twenty-nine, had seen Barker act (perhaps in Shakespeare with Ben Greet), had recognized his quality and potential and had also found him sympathetic to the idea of and approach to theatre which he, Poel, was interested in developing. Certain it is that Barker's performance in *Richard II* moved him closer to that pre-eminence as an actor which was soon to be his and also gave him an opportunity to escape for a little while from the frustration of acting in plays which he despised for their shallowness and cheap sensationalism. But for the time being the writing of plays was more interesting and more important to him than acting in them and, though his early training and experience as an actor must have helped to provide him with a sound basis for all his future ideas about and work in the theatre, his early plays – including the two which were written in 1897 and 1898 – are fascinating documents in themselves and crucial evidence for anyone attempting to understand either the stages of Barker's development at this period of his life or the real nature and stature of his mature, later plays.

The two plays which Barker and Thomas wrote at this time were *The Weather-Hen; or Invertebrata* (1897) and *Our Visitor to 'Work-a-day'* (1898–99). Both show a marked advance upon *The Family of the Oldroyds*, of 1895–96, in character-observation and character-drawing, in both the plausibility and the resonance of the plot, and in the suppleness, fluency and 'speakability' of the dialogue. What also stands out is that the women characters, in all three plays, are much more closely and finely observed than the men and that all three plays have women as the main, central character.

The Weather-Hen is much the less ambitious of the two plays: its dialogue stays closer to a straightforward, contemporary, prose-conversational style and its plot and social milieu stay closer to those of the usual, conventional drama of the period. In the former of these traits the play represents something of a modulation from the deep purple of much of *The Family of the Oldroyds*; in the latter trait it represents a simple continuation from *The Family of the Oldroyds*; both plays are peopled by characters who come from that world with which the London theatre of the time was most familiar and most at home – the upper middle classes and the minor aristocracy – though they do acquire, in *The Weather-Hen*, more touches of originality than in *The Family of the Oldroyds* and some of the central figures do succeed in becoming real people in whom one can genuinely believe. The play remains slight, however, and is hobbled, so far as its persuasiveness now is concerned, by its attachment to and dependence upon a sexual and marital code which is no longer acknowledged and scarcely even any longer understood.

The title of the play is provided by a brief passage of dialogue in what was the Prologue of the first version (it became Act I in a revised version, re-written after the sole production of the play in June/July, 1899)[2]:

MACARTNEY:	Men are weather-cocks, my dear lady, once let them get on a steeple to view the country.
EVE:	Useful and ornamental!
MACARTNEY:	But weather-cocks make weather-hens – and weather-hens are neither.
EVE:	They show the way the wind blows.
MACARTNEY:	Not even that – a weather-hen has no glory of tail or feathers. Believe me, she's a disgrace to her sex, my dear.
EVE:	Thank you, doctor.

Eve Prior has married for the sake of comfort and security. She had been a promising actress but found the life too precarious and so married Marvel Prior, a successful but meretricious playwright, deserting James Ferguson to do so. Ferguson, who had been mentor, friend and lover to her bore no resentment but was saddened by the spectacle of her wasting herself. One night, after the opening of a new play of Prior's, he and Eve give a supper-party. When all the guests have gone and Eve is alone, awaiting her husband's return from seeing the leading lady home, Ferguson suddenly drops in on her: suffering from insomnia, he has been strolling in Regent's Park and, passing the house, happens to notice that the front door is open. He comes in, on an impulse, to see Eve. Though he says very little, his visit upsets the careful balance of her artificial existence and, reminding her of the truer and more substantial life which she deserted, sets her longing for some way of escape. When Ferguson has gone, she is restless and discontented and in that mood she lets her husband know that she has for months been aware of his infidelity. Insensitive as he is, he shrugs off the whole incident, not even troubling to deny the accusation. This drives Eve further to desperation and she accepts the advances of Dicky Battye, a very young man who imagines himself in love with her. They plan to elope to a country cottage which Dicky's parents have given him and, on the very day of their planned departure, first Ferguson and then Prior, her husband, accidentally blunder in on the plan. It is at this point that the play acquires one of its touches of originality and variation from the Victorian norm: the husband behaves conventionally enough but the friend, instead of giving moral advice or seizing the lady and running off with her himself, invents a quirky, comic, little plot. Unknown to her or her young swain, he persuades Dicky's parents – without telling them the true state of affairs – that Dicky wishes them to spend a fortnight with him at his cottage because Mrs. Prior is coming to stay with him while her husband is away and he feels that it would be improper for her to be there alone with him.

Though the play does not exploit it thoroughly enough, this has the makings of a high-comedy situation of real quality. As it is, even with the inadequate exploitation of it, it provides in Act II, when the runaway couple arrives at the cottage in a thunderstorm to find Dicky's parents have arrived just ahead of them, several moments of real theatrical worth. The denouement is worked out with real integrity, too: as Ferguson had anticipated, Dicky's courage fails him when faced with his father and mother and, though Eve suggests that they can *still* run away together simply by announcing their intention and leaving the senior Battyes to occupy the cottage alone, he feebly gives in and renounces her; similarly, Eve loses her nerve and asks Ferguson to take her with him to America, where he is just going. He refuses, not because he does not care for her but, rather, because he does: he feels that she must learn how to stop running away, how to stop deceiving herself and others, how to fashion a reality for herself and live by it. The play ends with her acceptance of this: she leaves her trivial husband, returns to her old profession of acting and sets out to make a life of her own.

The main thrust of the play clearly shows the influence of Ibsen: the escape of a young wife from the imprisoning comfort of a loveless marriage, the use of a young woman as a symbol of the 'life principle', the general sense that, as Margery M. Morgan says in her *A Drama of Political Man*,[3] 'The deadly sin is to hold back from full self-commitment'. It is worth remembering that in the six years immediately prior to the writing of *The Weather-Hen*, five of Ibsen's later plays had been given their first London performances – *Rosmersholm* in February, 1891; *Hedda Gabler* in April 1891; *The Master Builder* in February, 1893; *Little Eyolf* in November, 1896; *John Gabriel Borkman* in May, 1897 – and all of them were already published in several languages, including English, before those performances took place. Two of these plays, moreover, contain (or, one could almost say, fail to contain) two of those strange, wild, passionate young women who come 'from the North' and with a purity and ruthlessness of purpose ride like Valkyries through the dead domestic lives of mere town-dwellers. What one might call the general poetic objective of *The Weather-Hen* is very much in tune with Ibsen, even though the work is very slight alongside his and obviously lacks the richness and complexity even of the early Ibsen, let alone of the tremendous final plays which by now were reaching London. The texture of the dialogue, however, is utterly different from Ibsen's and begins to show, faintly yet but nonetheless recognizably, those qualities of allusiveness and obliqueness which gives such resonance to Barker's other plays and which show to the greatest advantage in *The Marrying of Ann Leete* and *The Secret Life*. I agree with Miss Morgan that one can safely talk about 'Barker's dialogue' in *The Weather-Hen*, even though the play was a collaboration. The similarity of tone, of texture and of actual syntactical structure between the dialogue of this play and that of his own solo work done later surely can leave no question that, whatever Berte Thomas contributed to the piece, the talk put into the mouths of the characters was put there by Barker. This curiously evocative dialogue, signs and hints of which we first see in *The Weather-Hen* (it is wholly absent from the earlier *The Family of the Oldroyds*), is very much Barker's own. It owes nothing to any other writer of whom I can think; but it owes a good deal, I would venture, to two other sources, both of them unique to Barker. One of these was, by contraries, his own experience of having to speak high-sounding rhetorical fustian on the stage in his early career as an actor; the other was his own special vision of the world – a curious blend of toughness and timidity, and a longing for passionate commitment which uneasily co-existed in him with a coolly observing and ironic eye. He eventually invented, to express these dichotomies and contradictions, a form of speech that mirrored the hesitations and tentativeness of his own intuitive responses and at the same time nicely caught the stumbling hesitations of conversational expression, thus making the latter a symbol of and a vehicle for the former. It is essentially actors' speech, theatrical and non-literary. This dialogue of Barker's is far less literary than, say, Synge's or Shaw's or – to quote a later example – John Whiting's: certainly far less so than Meredith's. The chief interest and importance of *The Weather-Hen* is that we can see in it not only the beginning of the invention of this highly-charged, highly-convoluted, elliptical form of stage speech, but also we can see, by measuring this play against the earlier Barker-Thomas play and against the normal, standard play of the time, both the structural and the spiritual causes that led to the invention, that made it – for Barker – a necessity.

Since I shall have a good deal more to say further on about this special quality of dialogue, I ought perhaps to clear up one possible misunderstanding, more particularly as the matter has already arisen: I do not intend the word 'literary' as a pejorative when applied to stage dialogue. There are those critics who feel that for stage dialogue to possess literary style or quality or dimension is *ipso facto* a disadvantage. I would dispute this viewpoint and would assert that many of our finest and biggest plays, though they are sound and workable theatrically, nevertheless work in an essentially literary way. All I am insisting on here is that Barker's plays are not among them. While with *The Playboy of the Western World* or *Man and Superman* (both of them very great plays – the two best comedies of the century in English) there is much left, as a poem on paper, even if one does not see the play (either actually or in the mind's eye) in terms of performance, with *The Marrying of Ann Leete* or *The Secret Life* there is almost nothing left unless one sees them in terms of performance. Barker himself said, in a letter[4] to R.A. Scott-James, the editor of the *Mercury*: 'But my main fault [they are discussing his Preface to *Hamlet*] – your review lets me see – is that I have not bridged the gulf between your mainly literary standpoint and my dramatic standpoint, from which plays are only incidentally literature . . . I'm almost tempted to say sometimes that drama is as near to music as it is far from literature.' This view was one which he held consistently throughout his whole career, though it grew stronger and more articulate in the later years. I do not suggest that because this was his view he therefore consciously set out to write 'non-literary' dialogue (this would have been a barren and silly exercise) but, in trying to find adequate means to give expression to reality as he saw it, he gradually hammered out the method which best suited him and that method depended for its imagery and potency on the quick glance, the glancing blow, the half-statement, the suspended thought, of the *spoken* word; but the word spoken privately to another but overheard in public. This dialogue is public speech; but it is theatre-public speech – not declamation or oratory or rhetoric but crafted conversation, knowingly eavesdropped with the connivance of the conversers.

It was a new idea and the force of it and the method of it must have both been only dimly perceptible to the young Granville Barker of 1897, but his instinct was right and his groping towards its expression was not wholly ineffectual. *The Weather-Hen*, though tame, thin and with something of a limp, is a bird of the right feather. Some bits of the technique work well enough already; others will with practice. One of the tests one should keep in mind is the test of 'speakability': and submitted to this test the play scores heavily. Much of the dialogue would ripple marvellously off the tongue of actors and would carry with it in the process an unmistakable sense of tension and of power. The best passages, as one would expect, are those between Eve and James Ferguson. Notice the economy of the following, taken from the Epilogue of the play; notice the tautness and the forward thrust produced by the *non sequiturs* and seeming *non sequiturs*:

JIM:	You were a little fond of the boy.
EVE:	Oh dear no. Still, once or twice, it was a struggle to drift.[5] I'd like you to believe that, Jimmy.
JIM:	You're a better woman than you think.
EVE:	Thank heaven I'm nearly thirty. D'you think I'll live to be old?
JIM:	Who plays Cassandra?
EVE:	Will I be a cat?
JIM:	Shut your eyes tight.
EVE:	Ah – one feels things coming. Just for fun, Jimmy, tell me a remedy.
JIM:	You should never play with edged – rudders.
EVE:	I don't intend to do more than look at it; I'm drifting surely enough. Just show me the physic – I won't make a face.
JIM:	To cure . . .?
EVE:	Being discussed in the library.[6]

A pause

JIM:	Stand alone.
EVE:	How funny.
JIM:	It's the only happiness for the great unmatched.
EVE:	Horrid sour grapes.
JIM:	May be. Disappointment can't afford to be weak. Loneliness is the only test of strength.

EVE *laughs outright.*

EVE:	What a ridiculous fool you are!
JIM:	I'm glad I'm going.
EVE:	So am I – oh, so am I. Don't write to me.
JIM:	I'm burning my boats.
EVE:	Don't forget the rudders, Mr. Impossibilities.

This highly allusive, charged style becomes at once much more pronounced and much more supple in *Our Visitor to 'Work-a-day'*, written about eighteen months later. Like *The Weather-Hen*, its central concern is the necessity for an inner truth and an inner reality, some essential quality of life to which the trivial, chance happenings of the casual work-a-day world can be referred in order to put them in a proper perspective: and as in the earlier play, the vital, purifying force, the fresh gale of invigorating but alarming air from some mysterious northern region, is represented by an impulsive but determined young woman. Her name in this play is Griselda. The mundane, timorous, insensitive world, the 'Work-a-day' of the title, is represented by the industrial town of Cardoxeter, the dreary deadness of which is meant to lie like a visible pall on the play. Barker and Thomas are at some pains to emphasise this: the list of characters at the beginning of the typescript has a note at its head which reads: 'A play in five acts, concerning Cardoxeter, the three men, a young woman and her husband, and another stranger'. The town has been given the status, almost, of a character in the play. The nature of that character is made clear in visual terms during the action: for example, the description of the stage setting at the beginning of the play starts thus: 'The doctor's house in Cardoxeter stands not far from the main street, mid-way between the new railway station and the principal factory; opposite the gasometer. Built not more than thirty years back in a style strictly and solely utilitarian, the house stands, two storeys and a deep basement'; all the action of the play takes place in the doctor's consulting room, 'the chief feature of the room being a twelve-paned window 8 ft. × 6 ft., the half of the lower part covered with a perforated zinc blind on which the passers-by read 'Dr. Greatorex'. There is a window seat. The view consists of a thirty-foot width of street, bounded by the gasometer.' The very first stage direction says: 'The factory bell is ringing, not quite twenty yards off' and this is repeated from time to time, to keep the oppressive presence of the town in our minds. The action of the play starts thus:

At last the bell stops. JOHN *looks at his watch.*

JOHN:	Six o'clock.
VIVIEN:	Have you a timetable?
JOHN:	In the bookcase, by the stethoscope.

Factory hands leaving their work pass the window; old men, young men, some boys, a few women.

VIVIEN:	The faces again.
JOHN:	The last of 'em.
VIVIEN:	Four times a day?
	Repletion, then hunger; then repletion, then hunger –
JOHN:	Then repletion,
	then snores.
VIVIEN:	Are these faces of yours never young?
JOHN:	Now you see, nothing buds to bloom in Cardoxeter.
VIVIEN:	– but withers.
	To work and say nothing and die. They call this the 'black country'[7], don't they?
JOHN:	And, what the devil do you find Birmingham?

The device of having the factory-workers pass the window – visible symbols of that world which the central characters of the play are trying variously to escape or subdue or rejuvenate – is repeated several times during the play so that there is an increasing desperation in the growing sense of a black swamp that threatens to engulf all the sentient and noble parts of life. But the play admirably resists the temptation to wander off into sociological considerations of factory laws and workers' housing. The black factories remain a unified symbol of all human greed and grubbiness and purblind insensitivity: they do not fragment into dramat-ized case histories. The focus of the plays holds surely, though some-times obscurely, on a small group of complex characters – and, for an early play by young dramatists, the complexities are very well drawn.

John Greatorex is the doctor; Vivien is his mistress and is leaving him, not because of any quarrel or jealousy but from a dimly-felt sense of limitation and unease and because she has suddenly conceived a passion for the Catholic Church. She is an immediately interesting character, described by Margery M. Morgan, accurately I think, as 'half-whore, half-nun, a butterfly'. Twice she says: 'I have a very high ideal of marriage, and that I will not fail to keep.' She is patently sincere in this but her ideal and her interpretation of marriage has nothing to do with the conventional view of that institution or with marriage as a mere guarantee of respectability. Her statement, and her formal – almost ritualistic – repetition of it, comes at the very beginning of the play and at a highly significant moment (just as she is leaving John) and, placed so, it constitutes itself a touchstone for the whole play.

Immediately after Vivien's departure, Griselda arrives. She is young, impulsive, attractive and has just married, secretly, a medical student called Evelyn Gurth. She comes to declare her secret and to ask blessings on the new marriage from her dying father and from John, the old family friend. She also has a more practical request to put to the latter: she wants him to take on her new husband as his assistant. He at first refuses and there is a suggestion both of sexual jealousy and of a kind of fatherly disapproval in his refusal: there is also more than an echo of the coming of Hilde to Solness in Act I of *The Master Builder*; before she tells John about her marriage, the following exchange occurs:

JOHN:	Have you been budding to bloom away from Cardoxeter?
GRISELDA:	Doesn't the woman cry out?
JOHN:	I can't say; shadows come first and loom larger.
GRISELDA:	You have no belief in what's to be best in me.

JOHN:	Haven't I?
GRISELDA:	You want me a child.
JOHN:	Do I? I do.
GRISELDA:	Selfish.
JOHN:	Why yes.
GRISELDA:	Not your own way, no way at all, is that it? And you are a man's man, all prose.
JOHN:	And you, green-sick for doggerel.
GRISELDA:	Think of me, poemless, poetless, unsexed at once.
JOHN:	You talk physical nonsense.

She gives her age, when John asks it, as 'twenty-two and two months' – just ten months younger than Hilde. And Evelyn, the young man she has married is, as well as a medical student, a poet. 'I write a little', he says: 'The first lines of an Epic or two. I fail at it.' When John sees them together and sees them happy, he changes his mind, takes Evelyn on as his assistant and invites the young couple to take up residence at his house. But through the dreary months of a Cardoxeter winter the new marriage gradually dries up:

EVELYN:	Here I'm nobody.
JOHN:	Here are others.
EVELYN:	Though look at my luck.
JOHN:	Griselda. Her price.
EVELYN:	That sounds ridiculous.
JOHN:	Wives are always to be bought.
EVELYN:	I emptied my pockets.

There is a pause.

JOHN:	That child is seedy.
EVELYN:	I tell her what to do.
JOHN:	Who blamed you.
EVELYN:	She is still very young.
JOHN:	I haven't that impression. I diagnose: the travailing of change.
EVELYN:	Her fault; not my misfortune! There she goes, on ahead.
JOHN:	Rehabilitation.
EVELYN:	Without me?
JOHN:	Never.
EVELYN:	Hang on behind baggage.
JOHN:	You're a sort of leech.

EVELYN *brings down his book on* JOHN'S *hand, smashing the test-tube he is holding.*

So Evelyn leaves Griselda and goes to London to continue his medical training. Griselda and John move closer together and finally fall in love. Evelyn, in London, meets Vivien and a love-affair develops between them. But at the end of the play Evelyn leaves Vivien and returns to Cardoxeter to fetch Griselda, who goes with him:

JOHN: To love and lose is quite impossible; so I have loved to lose.
GRISELDA: You'll lose. I never wished him dead.
JOHN: He stops the way.
GRISELDA: I want you; but . . .
JOHN: To you he's coming. Why?
GRISELDA: Because I am his wife.
JOHN: And mine.
GRISELDA: How many meanings has the word?

So the play is a play about marriage. It starts with Vivien's rejecting it because it will not live up to her ideals; it ends with Griselda's accepting it because she sees it as structurally and organisationally necessary. But, to Griselda, the ideal lies outside marriage, no matter how necessary marriage is to the structure. She retains her burning sense of a wild reality outside the scope and uses of the everyday, but she declines to let it destroy her: she will live in the everyday but carry the secret in her heart. As a character she is stronger than the Rebecca of *Rosmersholm*, more common-sense than the Hilde of *The Master Builder* (though less well delineated by her author than either). While they are waiting for Evelyn to arrive, John and Griselda talk together:

GRISELDA: John, no woman ever loves a sick man. Will you accept my pity, now and always?
JOHN: No!
GRISELDA: Bravo!
JOHN: To speak true, all this has been my tomorrow lately.
GRISELDA: We must face it without hope.
JOHN: That cruse of oil which fails.
GRISELDA: Pshaw! We work miracles.
JOHN: Think of every day.
GRISELDA: Each without remedy.
JOHN: You call such healthy?
GRISELDA: No: but the truer economy is to live it out.
JOHN: To feed on it.
GRISELDA: To grow fat on it.
JOHN: He blossoms poetry.

GRISELDA:	Our visitor. For a little while; knives, forks, and lighting of the gas, will mean you.
JOHN:	I'm to envy him.
GRISELDA:	Don't be self-conscious; I mean to forget that it's life.
JOHN:	You must recall my ways and be tortured.
GRISELDA:	Thanks, hero.
JOHN:	Curse me this fiction.
GRISELDA:	Be careful what you start believing.
JOHN:	Our . . .
GRISELDA:	love . . .
JOHN:	What do I know? . . . is to be made use of.
GRISELDA:	One may be sure of that.

The final words of this scene, and the end of the play, are these:

GRISELDA:	Pray earnestly.
JOHN:	If you please.
GRISELDA:	John.
JOHN:	I hear.
GRISELDA:	Not his child.
JOHN:	You can't be sure of that; you know I can't be sure of that; he who says we can't be sure . . .[8]

> *The factory bell starts ringing, not quite twenty yards off. Two or three factory hands come quickly from their work for the midday meal.* EVELYN *arrives from the station and is greeted by one of the women workers, outside the window. As he passes, the bell stops. In the silence* JOHN *and* GRISELDA *rise and stand waiting.*

CURTAIN

Something of the curious intensity of the highly condensed, oblique, emotive dialogue of this play can be judged from the excerpts already quoted, but there is a more remarkable passage still, to which brief reference must be made. It is a dialogue between Vivien and Ethelbert Yeo, a priest, at the beginning of Act IV. She has come back to Cardoxeter because she has violently quarrelled with Evelyn. John and Griselda are both out when she arrives but Yeo is there, waiting for them to return. They begin to talk and a little way into the conversation the following appears:

> *She goes to him, baring her neck. He sees bruises.*

| VIVIEN: | Finger prints. |
| YEO: | His? |

VIVIEN:	The Man's way out.
YEO:	From . . .?
VIVIEN:	You always knew me.
YEO:	Bird of prey.[9]
VIVIEN:	You wit.
YEO:	Probably she will bear it well.
VIVIEN:	Griselda.
YEO:	Your coming here is mean.
VIVIEN:	I hate him!
YEO:	Pray.

She kneels to pray. He stands watching her. She begins to cry and looks up.

VIVIEN:	I'm very hungry.
YEO:	No, you are not to eat.

She buries her head. He paces the room. He stops.

YEO:	Are you praying?
VIVIEN:	No.
YEO:	Then get up.

She rises. She pulls off her cap and coat and is dressed in an extravagant evening gown, a poor grey shawl around her shoulders. There is a rent in her gown. She crouches by the fire. YEO *stands watching her.*

VIVIEN:	I'll let the flames lick me.
YEO:	Lust is damnable.
VIVIEN:	Go to school and fie.
YEO:	Away from that.

She moves from the fire and sits at the opposite side of the room. YEO *paces. She shivers.*

VIVIEN:	I'm body o' warmth; please.
YEO:	Pampered and furnished in sexual tricks; little green apple.
VIVIEN:	Always I attract, of course.
YEO:	Are you less than a public nuisance?
VIVIEN:	Not useless.
YEO:	Unideal.
VIVIEN:	Never a fellow-being but I gratified.
YEO:	Lapped in ease.
VIVIEN:	And warmth.

YEO *is close to her and starts away.*

YEO:	And you trepan men from their wives.

VIVIEN:	Evelyn came towards me, striding.
YEO:	Where was your spirit, your spirit discriminate?
VIVIEN:	In my sense of him.
YEO:	Mortification . . .
VIVIEN:	. . . is not beautifully good.
YEO:	. . . would have purged, for our earth-senses are gross.
VIVIEN:	I never yet tried to degrade.
YEO:	But you again and again have felt the subtle stealth of a potent blood-wine, into the head and heart and limbs.
VIVIEN:	And the world is one with me.
YEO:	I'll speak of the cold, grey, morning light; you know.
VIVIEN:	Perhaps.
YEO:	And never strangled self.
VIVIEN:	The blinds were drawn.
YEO:	Calm spirit-light that is, and is for ever; and never strangled strumpet self.

Margery M. Morgan argues (op. cit., pp. 48–50) that this kind of dialogue would never work in the theatre because the audience would have to spend all its time puzzling over obscure literary references, missing five lines while they sorted out the previous five in their heads. The reply to this argument is surely the same as Barker himself gave to critics who, in 1912 and 1913, complained that his actors spoke Shakespeare's verse (in the productions of *The Winter's Tale, Twelfth Night* and *A Midsummer Night's Dream* at the Savoy Theatre) too rapidly for comprehension. He talks, in a letter of September 26, 1912 to the *Daily Mail*, about 'how swift and passionate a thing, how beautiful in its variety, Elizabethan blank verse might be when tongues were trained to speak and ears acute to hear it'. And a little further on in the same letter he advised potential members of his audiences to 'sit there at your ease to listen and watch, and only ask yourself, when the curtain has finally fallen: Was I stirred and amused, has it been enthralling to hear and beautiful to see?' He made the same point many times over and in many different ways during the course of his career: 'meaning' in the theatre comes to the audience subliminally, not as a result of ratiocination and inward intellectual disputation. He expected that to apply not only to Shakespeare but to all plays, including his own. Indeed, he remarks ruefully to William Archer, in a letter written in 1922 about *The Secret Life*, that he does not really *expect* it to be produced since the British theatre at the time had no actors properly trained to speak the lines *and no audience properly trained to listen*. Given such actors and such an audience, I see no overwhelming difficulty in the dialogue of *Our Visitor to 'Work-a-day'*. The method of it seems to me theatrically valid and legitimate and the execution, though a little over-luxuriant, more than competent. The play's main weakness subsists not in its use of a dialogue deliberately designed to provoke a rapid succession of vivid images but in a certain looseness and vagueness of structure. The fault, in other words, is a purely dramaturgical one. The separate elements of the play are not bound together closely and logically enough for the plot to develop what one might call a mythic momentum; the play as a whole fails to become a poem, though it contains fragments of unfinished poems within itself. Of the main characters, on whom this burden would naturally and properly fall, only Griselda is fully realized – and she is admirably drawn. Evelyn, Yeo, Vivien and John all seem uneasily incomplete: they wander out of the play inconsequentially, leaving a gap and a vague sense of frustration. This is particularly true of Vivien and Yeo. Indeed, the whole religion motif, though obviously necessary to the completed pattern of the play, fails to come into focus: either the duologue which has been quoted should have been driven through to a firmer conclusion or Vivien and Yeo should have come back in Act V to develop that part of the complexity to a satisfactory resolution. In a word, there are elements in the plot that seem arbitrary rather than integral; though it quite obviously intends that the level of mere narrative should be transcended it partially fails to live up to this intention, not because the narrative itself is feeble but because the process of transcendence is not always of sufficient power. It does not have about it, at all points, that sense of inevitability which enables a story to function mythically. But its poetic impulse and poetic vision are true and accurate and authentic and are expressed in authentic, workable, theatric terms. Far from regarding the dialogue of *Our Visitor to 'Work-a-day'* as 'theatrically impossible', I would personally cite it as the play's main strength, both theatrically and, so to speak, poetically. It is certainly the sign by which one recognizes the real originality of Barker's touch: its kinship with his later plays – especially *The Marrying of Ann Leete* and *The Secret Life* – is immediately obvious, as is the advance which it represents in comparison with the purely imitative and derivative language of *The Family of the Oldroyds*, written only two and a half years earlier. This matter of the nature of stage dialogue and of the relationship between it and the loose, casual, accidental, unformed nature of ordinary, everyday conversation, is one of some importance. Barker was worried and fascinated by it all his life; and in our own time, when the tendency of most dramatists is to move stage dialogue closer and closer to off-stage speech in both form and content, the question of what is artistically desirable and/or allowable is a central issue.

There is another particular significance in this early play of Barker's and that is the emergence, for the first time, of the 'secret' theme; and it is the tone and texture of the dialogue, rather than the plot or fable, which brings it out. What the play says, in sum, is that one must live as best one can in the everyday world, accepting such compromises as are necessary, but the real life (if there is one) is always separate, apart, lived secretly, owing little or nothing to either the circumstances or the logic of 'work-a-day'. This theme is sounded in various guises and with differing emphases in all his plays from 1899 onward. We find it in *The Marrying of Ann Leete* (the necessity for separating the real and personal contract from the shallow social contract), *Waste* (the destruction wrought by conventional forces against which the only defence is a private code of conduct in which the individual himself passionately believes), *The Voysey Inheritance* (the poisoning of the inner, secret life by false and debased standards and arguments of expediency), *The Madras House* (the stalemate, irresolution and inaction which result when there *is* no secret life), *Farewell to the Theatre* (an asseveration of the necessity for a secret life to make some sense at least of the outward life). Miss Morgan has called her book *A Drama of Political Man* and has asserted that 'His heroes reach, or fail to reach, the fulfillment of their moral being in the public realm; if they seem to move within a domestic circle, still their decisions are made in awareness of their political significance'. To me, the accent in all Barker's work seems the exact reverse of Miss Morgan's statement. His characters, to find their reality, move in neither a public-political nor a private-domestic sphere, but in a secret world of their own which their souls struggle to find and, having found, then defend as best they may, against the tyrannies of both communal and domestic living, against the depredations of both public and private life. And the best defence, Barker's work constantly says, is secrecy, silence. Only two of his plays (*Waste* and *The Secret Life*) are formally about politics in the ordinary, narrow sense of that term; one other (*His Majesty*) is, up to a point, about *government* (which is a different thing) and a further one (*The Marrying of Ann Leete*) has political gossip and scandal as a kind of scaffolding to help support the structure of the piece. But even these, all four of them, are ultimately concerned not with politics and the communal life at all, but with the secret life of the heart, in defiance of and in spite of the cackle of the political world. Their interest in politics is incidental. The central, guiding principle of Barker's vision of things is not politics: it is secrecy. And Barker sees the essential nature of humanity as being, not political, but sexual. His plays, with the exception of *The Voysey Inheritance* (in which the sexual element is much muted), chart the commerce between secrecy and sex and between both of them and the outside world. They are, from first to last, not only full of sexual imagery (in a way in which, for instance, the plays of Shaw and Galsworthy are not) but also full of narrative material dealing with various aspects of the sexual relationship. In other words, as well as having a strong intuitive sense of the importance of sexual ties and sexual responses, he found it necessary in his work to grapple intellectually with sex as a 'problem'. This is not altogether surprising: the Victorian-Edwardian theatre was drenched with sex – actresses like Mrs. Langtry and Mrs. Patrick Campbell (how significant their married status as part of their normal professional titles!) existed on it solely, not only in the subject-matter of the plays in which they appeared but also in their relations with their audiences at the time of performance: their enormous (and it *was* a thing of enormity) popularity was due far more to their physical attractiveness than to their artistic talents and, indeed, these two ladies in particular translated the term 'artistic talent' to mean the presentation of themselves to a devouring audience, the public giving of themselves, a kind of communal orgasm at the final curtain. In a sense, Barker's treatment of sex in his plays is a reaction against this use of the theatre and this use of sex. He is at once more idealistic and more realistic about it. He shuns the hot-house atmosphere and chooses to face the north wind. He seeks to make his plays reflect life rather than reflect the theatre and other plays. The measure of this, again, is the enormous advance which *The Weather-Hen* and *Our Visitor to 'Work-a-day'* show over *The Family of the Oldroyds*: some time in 1896, or thereabouts, he suddenly developed a new sensitivity and a new idea of what, artistically, was needed to express that sensitivity and to oppose the fashionable concept of what the theatre was for. Writing to William Archer on June 11, 1899,[10] he said:

Dear Sir,
    You may remember, some time ago, reading a play of ours 'The Weather-Hen' and saying that you would be glad to see more of our work. 'Weather-Hen' is to be played and we are greatly hoping that in the course of events you will be at the matinee.
    I now send you what we have written since.
    May I only ask you – if you read it – not to approach it from the point of view of what is commonly called an 'actable' play.

This is perhaps a poor apology for what we have tried to do.

I am

very faithfully yours,

H. GRANVILLE BARKER

In other words, Barker and Thomas were perfectly conscious of the challenge they were offering to the theatre of their day; it was a quite deliberate act. Barker, too – we cannot speak for Thomas in this – was also aware of the twin nature of the force at the centre of his vision – sex and alone-ness. In an earlier letter to Archer (April 12, 1898) he describes what to him is the essence of *The Weather-Hen*: 'The crucial point of the play – that Eve who has sacrificed womanhood, real life and Jimmy for position, 'Art' and her husband, should be rescued from this diseased life by Jimmy and placed on the road to healthy humanity by the man whom she has by her wanton misdoing caused to walk that road lonely and so placed him beyond the need of her, she herself acknowledging too late her need of him – at the end of the play – to do penance, alone in his steps.' So, even at the conscious level in the author's mind, the twin themes were already there in that very early play. They are much more thoroughly developed in the next one, *Our Visitor to 'Work-a-day'*.

(Let us, however, be a little careful about this kind of argument. It does not follow that an author's opinions about what the essence of his work is are necessarily the most accurate representation there is of that essence or that because he says the work is 'about' a particular thing, it is really about that thing, or about anything. Conversely, it does not follow that because an author happens not to perceive certain elements in his work, even crucial ones, they are therefore not there: no real work of art is merely a simple vehicle for the author's conscious, intellectual view of what he supposes he should have been writing about. It is, of course, gratifying and reassuring to find that what one now thinks one perceives as the central reality of his plays was also seen as such by Barker himself, but this fact must not be taken as having the force of absolute proof. I note it because it is interesting to do so and because it is not without its significance and importance in our understanding of these early plays and of their relationship to Barker's later work, but I do not seek to argue that because Barker *says* the crucial point of the play is thus and so, we must assume that it necessarily *is* thus and so: he is as likely as the onlooker to be wrong in his sense of what the play's total gesture is – more likely, perhaps.)

In 1899, after the completion of *Our Visitor to 'Work-a-day'* and an attempt to make a stage version of Thackeray's *Henry Esmond* (which was never completed), the play-writing collaboration of Berte Thomas and Granville Barker broke up. Both men went on writing plays, but not together. Thomas's were ordinary, well-crafted, efficient trivialities, several of which were briefly played at various theatres in London and elsewhere in the south of England.[11] Barker's were works of increasing grasp, profundity and importance, some of which are still awaiting their first productions. The first of Barker's solo pieces, written in the busy year of 1899, in between his acting engagements and the directing of *The Weather-Hen*, was *The Marrying of Ann Leete*. It was the first of his plays to receive a major production (in 1902) and the first to be published (in 1909) and for these reasons it is always regarded and referred to as his 'first' play. This is misleading. It seems to me mistaken to discount entirely the merits and the importance of *The Weather-Hen* and *Our Visitor to 'Work-a-day'* and it is not unfair to regard them as mainly Barker's plays. Moreover, the links – both stylistic and thematic – between them and *The Marrying of Ann Leete* are so clear and so strong that any full understanding of the latter play must depend in part upon an appreciation of the two former ones.

We should, on this account alone if no other, be thankful for a piece of innocent deception practised long ago by Charlotte and Bernard Shaw. The typescript of *Our Visitor to 'Work-a-day'* bears a note in Bernard Shaw's hand, which says:

> This play was presented to my wife by Granville Barker with his instruction that it should be destroyed when read. Instead, she had it bound and kept it carefully until her death in 1943, when it came into my possession. On his death in 1946 I lent it to his publishers to copy, and now present it to the British Museum.
>
> G. Bernard Shaw.

That *The Marrying of Ann Leete* is a marked advance on the former works is gratifyingly obvious but that it is a continuation, without any lesion, in both theme and technique from *Our Visitor to 'Work-a-day'* must also be noted. Much of the play's positive gesture is, once again, carried by an honest, sensitive, determined, young woman: Ann Leete is twenty. She is the symbol of life's power to assert and renew itself in the face of corruption, cynicism and decay. This symbol, however, is not arbitrarily appointed and then imposed upon the play; it develops naturally and organically from the life of the piece. Barker sets the piece at the end of the eighteenth century, the time of the French Revolution, and repeatedly invites us by all kinds of glancing references, to regard it as speaking for the end of the nineteenth. A new century is about to begin: the play makes it the symbol of a new life and insists over and over again upon the necessity of rejecting the old life in order to take up the new one. There are multiple reminders in the dialogue of the parallel of the changing of the seasons, the ending of one year and the beginning of a new one. Carnaby Leete is a politician in late middle age; his family is an ancient one, its roots deep in the land it owns, but the family fortunes have fallen on bad times. A prominent member of the Whig government, he has resigned at a time of crisis, ostensibly for reasons of conscience and principle but actually because he was astute enough to foresee his party's forthcoming defeat. Now he is, after a decent interval of lofty and disdainful withdrawal, wooing the Tories. In former days he has, to strengthen his ties with the Whigs, married off his elder daughter Sarah, to Sir Charles Cottesham. He now seeks – but deviously, not in the least openly – to use his younger daughter, Ann, in the same way by marrying her to Lord John Carp, a son of one of the Tory leaders and a man twice her age. Ann herself is not privy to this design and is shown at the beginning of the play as a young woman faced with new sensations and new experiences and just beginning to formulate some coherent sense of life for herself. Leete takes advantage of a foolish bet to further his ends with Carp. At a late-night party Mr. Daniel Tatton, a country gentleman, bets Carp that Ann can walk the length of the garden in the dark, alone, without crying out in fear. The play begins with Ann's scream, heard from a stage in complete darkness; but as the dawn gradually fills the garden with light, we find that Ann screamed not with fear but in protest because Lord John Carp had followed her through the dark garden and had kissed her. 'Miss Leete', asks Tatton, concerned with his bet, 'were you frightened when Lord John kissed you?' Ann does not reply but her attitude to the kiss is revealed to us a little later, in a little private conversation between her and Lord John:

ANN:	I was not frightened.
LORD JOHN:	You kissed me back.
ANN:	Not on purpose. What do two people mean by behaving so . . . in the dark?
LORD JOHN:	I am exceedingly sorry that I hurt your feelings.
ANN:	Thank you, I like to feel.
LORD JOHN:	And you must forgive me.
ANN:	Tell me, why did you do it?
LORD JOHN:	Honestly I don't know. I should do it again.

ANN:	That's not quite true, is it?
LORD JOHN:	I think so.
ANN:	What does it matter at all!
LORD JOHN:	Nothing.

Ann's father, though he treats the whole affair of the bet and the kiss quite lightly and cynically, is nevertheless quick to notice that it gives him a hold over Carp. When they are alone, he deliberately and calculatedly picks a quarrel with Carp, saying that his daughter's honour is compromised (to which Carp replies, 'Nonsense!') and challenges him to a duel. Carp at first refuses to take this seriously but Leete persists and the duel is fought, gentleman-like, and Leete is wounded in the arm. Carp then asks Ann to marry him. 'Thank you very much', she answers him: 'it'll be very convenient for us all.' For a little while she concurs, though the idea is distasteful to her:

LORD JOHN:	Give me your hand.
ANN:	No.
LORD JOHN:	You're beautiful.
ANN:	I don't think so. You don't think so.
LORD JOHN:	I do think so.
ANN:	I should like to say I don't love you.
LORD JOHN:	Last night you kissed me.
ANN:	Last night you were nobody in particular . . . to me.
LORD JOHN:	I love you.
ANN:	Please don't. I can't think clearly.
LORD JOHN:	Look at me.
ANN:	I'm sure I don't love you because you're making me feel very uncomfortable and that wouldn't be so.
LORD JOHN:	Then we'll think.
ANN:	Papa . . . perhaps you'd rather not talk about Papa.
LORD JOHN:	Give yourself to me.
ANN:	(*drawing away from him*) Four words! There ought to be more in such a sentence . . . it's ridiculous. I want a year to think about its meaning. Don't speak.
LORD JOHN:	Papa joins our party.
ANN:	That's what we're after . . . thank you.

She keeps up the charade for a few hours only. Later that same day, in front of the whole family, she suddenly recants and asks the gardener, John Abud, to marry her. She says to Sarah, her sister: 'And I curse you . . . because, we being sisters, I suppose I am much what you were, about to be married; and I think, Sally, you'd have cursed your present self. I could become all that you are and more . . . but I don't choose.' The last act of the play is divided into two scenes: the first is a brilliantly and bitterly satirical treatment of the wedding feast; and the second is a short and simple but powerful coda in the farm cottage belonging to Abud and shows the arrival of Abud and Ann in their new home on their wedding night – having walked nine miles across the fields from Markswayde Hall and the wedding feast. In spite of its shortness this last scene is, as Dennis Kennedy[12] rightly says, 'one of Barker's finest and perhaps one of the best in modern English drama'.

Both Dennis Kennedy and Marjorie Morgan point out quite correctly that the style of the dialogue in *The Marrying of Ann Leete* effectively prevents the plays from bogging down either in the trivia of political intrigue (in spite of the title of Miss Morgan's book) or in the realistic psychological details of individual personal problems. It is as if, from the very start, the way the talk is framed insists that everything be referred to first principles: the play is compelled to function in a mythopoeic way. Yet this is done quite unpretentiously and is done, moreover, in a way that is authentically theatrical and artistically proper: the hesitations of natural conversation are imitated (in the Aristotelian sense) to provide a paradigm, a metaphor for the hesitations of thought, the evasions, the half-hidden meanings which lie behind all utterance. Freed of practical explanation and the exposition of mundane story details, this spare dialogue paradoxically gives access to unexpected richness. John Masefield, in a letter to Barker written on Sepember 10, 1909, praised this allusive quality, the capacity of Barker's poetic prose for raising images. He said: 'I'll tell you what I specially admire in Ann Leete: your power of suggestion of the dawn. You have made your people talk at the beginning like parts of twilight.' But for the mastery exercised by the dialogue, the whole play would be in danger of toppling into a sentimental banality. The plot, after all, is – but for the manner of its handling – dangerously close to the clichés about kind hearts/coronets and love-in-a-cottage. Only Barker's exquisite sureness of touch in the talk he has put into his characters' mouths inhibits such banal clichés and assures us of the complexity and high seriousness of his vision. In one of his early letters to William Archer (April 9, 1900) he said: 'I've always laid it down a rule for myself – never attempt poetry until prose is too poor to express you'. He was referring to the one play he ever wrote in formal verse, a one-act play called *A Miracle*[13], probably written immediately after *The Marrying of Ann Leete*. And though *Ann Leete* is not in verse he found for it a medium as supple and suggestive without going into formal verse, a medium beguilingly like conversation, though not so in any literal sense, yet capable of behaving like poetry, of *becoming* poetry, in fact. At every point the play deliberately avoids surfaces and turns inward to elementals. Take, for example, the announcement at the end of Act II that George, Ann's brother, has just become the father of twins. George has 'married beneath him' (and so invites comparison with Ann in her gesture of marrying the gardener); moreover, he has married a girl who had earlier rejected that gardener, Abud, because she considered herself too good for him. Abud harbours no resentment and is still fond of Dolly: when he hears that she is about to have a baby, his genuine and unaffected concern for her overcomes any reticence which social status might dictate:

ABUD: Mr. George! Mr. George!

GEORGE comes slowly along the terrace, in his hand an open book, which some people might suppose he was reading. He speaks with studied calm.

GEORGE: You are very excited, my good man.

ABUD: She's brought you a child, sir.

ANN: Your child!

GEORGE: Certainly.

ABUD: Thank God, Sir!

GEORGE: I will if I please.

ANN: And she's doing well.

ABUD: There's a messenger come post.

GEORGE: To be sure . . . it might have been bad news.

And slowly he crosses the garden towards the house.

ABUD: *(suddenly beyond all patience)*: Run, damn you!

GEORGE makes one supreme effort to maintain his dignity, but fails utterly. He gasps out . . .

GEORGE: Yes, I will.

and runs off as hard as he can.

ABUD: *(in an ecstasy)*: This is good. Oh, Dolly and God . . . this is good!

ANN: *(round-eyed)*: I wonder that you can be pleased.

ABUD: *(apologizing . . . without apology)*: It's life.

ANN: *(struck)*: Yes, it is.

And she goes towards the house, thinking this over.

The play's central concern is with integrity, the necessity for preserving the true gesture of the self despite the false gestures of organized society, especially 'polite' society, which is at best shallow and at worst vicious. Again, as in the two earlier plays, that integrity depends upon alone-ness, severance, secretness. Ann, who is shown as groping at the beginning of the play towards her first realization of the nature of maturity, is constantly identified with the rose and, as Carnaby Leete points out in the play, the rose is traditionally identified with secrecy – not in any underhand or deceitful sense, but in the sense of preserving within itself the divine mystery, the secret of the inner life. There is more than a suggestion in the play that *all* societal organization is diminishing and deadening, that all communal association will inevitably lead to betrayal: the individual heart is the only true and trustworthy unit. This sense, never articulated in explicit terms, pervades the whole play and is enhanced by the play's being set at the time of both the French and the American Revolutions. But the spirit of this play, in the ultimate analysis, is not revolutionary: it is anarchical – which is not the same thing. The revolutionary times serve only to create in the play a sense of unrest and to emphasize both the need for and the possibility of change; the urge to defy. And, as has already been noted above, the end of one century and social era is clearly intended to stand as a metaphor for the end of another century and another social era. This is underscored in the actual dialogue: George says to Ann, 'You want a new world . . . you new woman.' The use of the strictly and exclusively nineteenth-century term 'new woman', with all its political, sociological and artistic echoes and implications, warns us (and would have even more clearly warned a contemporary audience) not to take that eighteenth-century setting too literally. The play explores and exploits, in fact, the poetic possibilities of the term *fin de siècle*, making the ending of the century a symbol for the ending of a whole system and a signal, therefore, for a new burst of individual resolution and energy. This generalized sense of the movement of night into day, winter into spring, *ennui* into activity, century into century, is much more important in this play than an exact study and understanding of Whig-and-Tory politics or the intricacies of the French Revolution.

The main pattern and design of the play has a dramatic equation which poises self-hood and integrity in balance against calculation and expediency and this modulates, finally, into the ultimate equipoise which, I suppose, lies at the centre of all works of art and at the centre of art itself; namely, the confronting of illusion by reality. 'Real-ness', to *The Marry-*

ing of Ann Leete, subsists in the hard-fought-for, barely-glimpsed, desperately-seized apprehension of life by the lonely, individual soul, the authority of individual revelation despite all official codifications of behaviour or belief. This sense, present throughout the play but revealing itself lightly and gracefully without any heavy-handed urging, is the measure of the work's thorough-going romanticism. It is also a measure, in the way that it is handled, of the play's astonishing modernity – not only for audiences in its own time but for the nineteen-eighties as well. For there is nothing of jauntiness or easy self-confidence in the way the play gives its ultimate authority to the validity of personal revelation. The victory, so to say, is seized from the jaws of defeat; the over-all atmosphere – as Margery Morgan rightly says – is one of melancholy; the diaphanous, translucent texture is full of cloudy hints of half-meaning, a metaphor for life itself. There is a quality of sturdy self-reliance in it all, but it is tempered with a healthy scepticism and doubt. It is this wariness which gives strength to the final scene of the play:

ABUD: Ann . . . we're beginning life together.
ANN: Remember . . . work's enough . . . no stopping to talk.
ABUD: I'll work for you.
ANN: I'll do my part . . . something will come of it.

The element of risk and of facing the unknown is recognized by both of them and accepted:

ANN: Well . . . this is an experiment.
ABUD   (*with reverence*): God help us both.
ANN: Amen. Some people are so careful of their lives. If we fail miserably we'll hold our tongues . . . won't we?
ABUD: I don't know . . . I can't speak of this.
ANN: These impossible things which are done mustn't be talked of . . . that spoils them. We don't want to boast of this, do we?

And a little later, Ann says, more to herself than to him:

Papa . . . I said . . . we've all been in too great a hurry to get civilized. False dawn. I mean to go back. So he saw I was of no use to him and he's penniless and he let me go. When my father dies what will he take with him? . . . for you do take your works with you into Heaven or Hell, I believe. Much wit. Sally is afraid to die. Don't you aspire like George's wife. I was afraid to live . . . and now . . . I am content.

Notice the packed density of this short speech, how it draws together in little space at the play's end many of the principal strands of the pattern and refers them to the eschatological test of final things.

Throughout the play sexuality, and particularly the physical aspects of sexuality, is a dominant motif. Partly, it serves the main central dramatic dichotomy of integrity versus affectation and expediency; partly, it stands as a symbol of an uncontrollable motive power which drives life on without thinking of niceness or niceties. Part of Ann's process of maturing is her perception of the difference between her sister's attitude to the sex/marriage relationship and the attitude towards it which she herself, under the pressure of life and events, is just beginning to develop. And as matters become clearer to her, she more and more rejects the decorations and outward shows of courtly 'romantic' love and treats sex as a plain, dour, powerful but mysterious thing. In that last scene, again, this reaches its summation:

ABUD:	May I come near to you?
ANN	(*in a low voice*): Come.
	He sits beside her, gazing.
ABUD:	Wife . . . I have never kissed you.
ANN:	Shut your eyes.
ABUD:	Are you afraid of me?
ANN:	We're not to play such games at love.
ABUD:	I can't help wanting to feel very tender towards you.
ANN:	Think of me . . . not as a wife . . . but as a mother of your children . . . if it's to be so. Treat me so.
ABUD:	You are a part of me.
ANN:	We must try and understand it . . . as a simple thing.
ABUD:	But shall I kiss you?
ANN	(*lowering her head*): Kiss me.

The political concerns of the early part of the play are summarily dismissed as representative of that outer life which ultimately has neither value nor virtue; the political world in the play is an image of mere artifice and artificiality, not important when it comes to the reckoning of real things. And one of the great strengths of the play is that, looking back over it from the vantage-point of its final scene, we intuitively recognize that the beginning of the play gave us sufficient hints that this dismissal of politics and politicking and the whole political world was to come. It is in this sense more than any other that *The Marrying of Ann Leete* is superior to *Our Visitor to 'Work-a-day'*: it has a dramaturgical pattern and design which develops naturally, organically and which, without either straining or over-simplifying, reaches a resolution which our senses approve.

Both plays are superior to *The Weather-Hen* in that their imagery is more complex, more sophisticated, more interestingly diverse – ultimately more true. But *Our Visitor to 'Work-a-day'* lacks both the momentum and the completeness of design of *The Marrying of Ann Leete*.

Apart from these main, central strengths, *The Marrying of Ann Leete* makes one other great advance over the two earlier plays: its characters are much more fully realized and are, indeed, taken all together, a more interesting collection of people than either of the other plays contains. The growth and development of Ann is a much more extended portrait, much more fully conceived and executed, than any figure in the earlier plays; and Carnaby Leete (as Margery Morgan remarks) is one of the most impressive figures in the whole roster of Barker's drama, either before *Ann Leete* was written or after. The first scene of Act IV contains a whole gallery of grotesques and caricatures of the most striking kind, vivid in themselves and extremely apt as a commentary upon and an enrichment of the pattern of the whole play.

Masefield, in the 1909 letter from which I have already quoted, praised Barker especially for his skill in character-drawing: 'You are such a subtle devil to think, you get all round your people before you begin, and when you do begin, they just walk out of prison and are thenceforth free. I wish I could do that, I grope around, & catch a little bit of a person, & shut it up mighty tight.' The praise was intended to apply to Barker's work as a whole up to 1909 and was not, I think, misplaced. *The Marrying of Ann Leete*, however, is the first of his plays in which Barker's skill in this regard becomes fully evident.

The main senses of the play, obliquely expressed and never risking the banality and diminution of explicit statement, permeate the entire structure of plot, character and dialogue, but it is the last of these elements which binds the structure together, acts as a catalyst for the other elements and finally gives the work its special, indefinable atmosphere and unique quality. What is so extraordinary in this dialogue is the way it manages to combine tautness and economy with a breadth of expressiveness, spareness with richness. It possesses, at one and the same time, the sense of the inconsequentiality of everyday conversation with the sense of measure and control. It is artifice of the highest degree, yet artifice placed at the service of the free expression of a profound spirit. It has, again as Miss Morgan has noted, some of the engaging qualities of a highly-figured dance – though this does not, in my view, warrant the extended and rather strained music-dance analogy in which she indulges.

The whole play has scarcely a speech in it longer than three or four lines (and most of them shorter than that) yet it is full of subtleties and delicious complexities. Take, for example, the following passage from Act III and consider how many things, all of them relevant though not directly related, are going on at the same time:

CARNABY: I'm well enough . . . to travel. This marriage makes us safe, Sarah . . . an anchor in each camp . . . There's a mixed metaphor.

SARAH: If you'll have my advice, Papa, you'll keep those plans clear of Ann's mind.

CARNABY: John Carp is so much clay . . . a man of forty ignorant of himself.

SARAH: But if the Duke will not . . .

CARNABY: The Duke hates a scandal.

SARAH: Does he detest scandal!

CARNABY: The girl is well-bred and harmless . . . why publicly quarrel with John and incense her old brute of a father? There's the Duke in a score of words. He'll take a little time to think it out so.

SARAH: And I say: Do you get on the right side of the Duke once again – that's what we've worked for – and leave these two alone.

CARNABY: Am I to lose my daughter?

SARAH: Papa . . . your food's intrigue.

CARNABY Scold at Society . . . and what's the use?

ANN *rejoins them now. The twilight is gathering.*

CARNABY: My mother's very old . . . your grandfather's younger and seventy-nine . . . he swears I'll never come into the title. There's little else.

SARAH: You're feverish . . . why are you saying this?

CARNABY: Ann . . . George . . . George via Wycombe . . . Wycombe Court . . . Sir George Leete baronet, Justice of the Peace, Deputy Lieutenant . . . the thought's tumbled. Ann, I first saw your mother in the garden . . . there.

ANN: Was she like me?

SARAH: My age when she married.

CARNABY: She was not beautiful . . . then she died.

ANN: Mr. Tatton thinks it a romantic garden.

CARNABY (*Pause*): D'you hear the wind sighing through that tree?

ANN: The air's quite still.

CARNABY: I hear myself sighing . . . when I first saw your mother in this garden . . . that's how it was done.

SARAH: For a woman must marry.

CARNABY: You all take to it like ducks to water . . . but apple sauce is quite correct . . . I must not mix metaphors.

Perhaps the best example in the whole play of this delicate, impressionistic interweaving is the 'dawn' passage which opens the play and which Masefield so much admired. The stage is in almost total darkness: the two figures are only barely visible:

LORD JOHN: I apologize.
ANN: Why is it so dark?
LORD JOHN: Can you hear what I'm saying?
ANN: Yes.
LORD JOHN: I apologize for having kissed you . . . almost unintentionally.
ANN: Thank you. Mind the steps down.
LORD JOHN: I hope I'm sober, but the air . . .
ANN: Shall we sit for a minute? There are several seats to sit on somewhere.
LORD JOHN: This is a very dark garden.

There is a slight pause.

ANN: You've won your bet.
LORD JOHN: So you did scream!
ANN: But it wasn't fair.
LORD JOHN: Don't reproach me.
ANN: Somebody's coming.
LORD JOHN: How d'you know?
ANN: I can *hear* somebody coming.
LORD JOHN: We're not sitting down.

ANN'S *brother,* GEORGE LEETE, *comes to the top of the steps, and afterwards down them. Rather an old young man.*

GEORGE: Ann!
ANN: Yes.
GEORGE: My lord!
LORD JOHN: Here.
GEORGE: I can't see you. I'm sent to say we're all anxious to know what ghost or other bird of night or beast has frightened Ann to screaming point, and won you . . . the best in Tatton's stables – so he says now. He's quite annoyed.
LORD JOHN: The mare is a very good mare.
ANN: He betted it because he wanted to bet it; I didn't want him to bet it.
GEORGE: What frightened her?

ANN:	I had rather, my lord, that you did not tell my brother why I screamed.
LORD JOHN:	I kissed her.
GEORGE:	Did you?
ANN:	I had rather, Lord John, that you had not told my brother why I screamed.
LORD JOHN:	I misunderstood you.

This – and, indeed, the play as a whole – is a piece of astonishingly accomplished writing for a person not yet twenty-two, the more so when one remembers that within a month or two of completing the writing of *The Marrying of Ann Leete* Barker was demonstrating, in his performance of *Richard II*, that he was equally accomplished and equally mature an actor as he was a dramatist. The play he wrote that year has, moreover, not since lost its capacity to command the stage and live in the theatre. Though *Ann Leete* has, like all of Barker's plays, been unjustifiably neglected for many years, the Royal Shakespeare Company mounted a distinguished and successful production of it, directed by David Jones, in 1975. Perhaps the most remarkable thing about that production was the complete absence of any sense of its being an 'old-fashioned' play and also of any sense of its being the work of a novice playwright. Irving Wardle, writing in *The Times* of September 19, 1975, said: 'I cannot imagine a more eloquent opening for a Granville Barker revival than this beautifully articulated production . . .' and adds a little later, 'The fact that Barker wrote *Ann Leete* at the age of 22 is only one of the amazing things about it. His voice, totally different from his ally Shaw's, rings across the 76 years with the same modernity. The stage-craft, treatment of character, attitude towards the audience, all proclaim a man reinventing the art of playwriting and forecasting developments of half a century later.' This contrasts nicely and ironically with the account by one of Wardle's predecessors as *The Times*'s theatre critic: A.B. Walkley, in the issue of January 28, 1902, said of the first performance of the play: 'It must be difficult to write a play in four acts, four fairly long acts, the last in two scenes, and throughout them all to keep your audience blankly ignorant of the meaning of it . . . Granville Barker calls his piece a comedy. It might more suitably be termed a practical joke.' Irving Wardle's article about the 1975 production was headed: 'NEG-LECTED MASTER REVIVED' and Benedict Nightingale, in the *New Statesman* of September 26, 1975, though his admiration for the play is not quite as whole-hearted as Wardle's and is tempered with some element of doubt, nevertheless sums it up in total as '. . . an extraordinarily original and fascinating work. . . .'

Barker, at the age of twenty-two, moved into the new century a fully-fledged playwright and a fully-fledged actor. The two skills were, of course, interrelated and – though play-writing, judging from his many comments about it in his letters to Archer and Gilbert Murray, was always an agony of excruciating doubts to him – he gave, at that stage in his career, equal attention to each of them and regarded it as perfectly normal to practise the two crafts side by side. His letters, as well as the comments we have of others about him, speak of a man of enormous activity, well-organized, moving rapidly from one job to the next, full of an almost feverish nervous energy.

He was already very dissatisfied with the theatre as he found it. He considered its standards of execution generally low and its objectives puerile, childish. Its plays offended him intellectually and its practices offended his sense of justice and individual dignity. In a letter to Archer in April, 1903[14] he said: 'Our actors – and worse still our actresses – are becoming demoralized by lack of intellectual work, the continual demand for nothing but smartness and prettiness.' And later in the same month, writing to Archer again, he returns to the same topic: 'But I do hope the National Theatre will hurry up and that it will fall into liberal or even radical hands and deliver us to some extent from the manager with the wooden head and the stage manager with the iron hand before another generation of actors (mine in this case) has gone to the devil artistically.' He felt that the argument applied to the audience as well as the actor: 'I think there is a class of intellectual would-be playgoers who are profoundly bored by the theatre as it is. Matinée productions don't touch these people (who are all workers) and Sunday evening [production] is expensive and incapable of expansion.'

His own plays written in these years clearly show not only his desire to make the stage artistically more serious and more purposeful but also his search for the best technical means to employ, especially as far as dialogue was concerned. The over-blown rhetorical prose of the popular plays of the time, which he himself had to some extent imitated in *The Family of the Oldroyds*, he rejected outright. Two other ways seemed open to him, clear opposites of each other – at least on the face of it. Each had a major exponent whose plays were recognized as important and were vastly influential in England, as they were in the rest of Europe. Their plays were probably the two principal influences on Barker, both in his play-writing and in his general approach to the theatre, during the closing years of the nineteenth century and the opening years of the twentieth.

And so far as play-writing style was concerned, they tended to drag him in opposite directions. They were, of course, Ibsen and Maeterlinck. His own style, as it emerged, proved to be like neither of theirs while clearly showing the influence of both; but it does seem that they caused him to develop *two* styles and to oscillate between the two. One was the veiled but highly-charged poetic prose which we have been considering in *Our Visitor to 'Work-a-day'* and *The Marrying of Ann Leete*; the other was the flatter, deliberately more bare and austere conversational prose of his next two full-length plays, *Agnes Colander* and *The Voysey Inheritance*. The former has some kinship with the gossamer silences and atmosphere of significance-felt-rather-than-expounded which emanate from Maeterlinck's plays; the latter owes something to Ibsen's method (especially in his 'middle period') of starting in what at first beguilingly seems the most ordinary, everyday way, showing the recognizable surfaces of life and speaking the recognizable, unimaginative language of casual conversation, but going on to explore layer upon layer and depth beyond depth beneath those recognizable surfaces. Between his two 'poetic prose' plays and his two 'realistic prose' plays, Barker – as has been briefly mentioned already – experimented with a short play in formal verse. He was obviously grappling, in his own mind, with the problem of how overt the poetry of the theatre should be, to what extent it should depend upon poetry in the purely literary sense. He had consciously begun that exploration of means which would lead him, over thirty years later, to make that statement to R.A. Scott-James about drama's only incidentally being literature.

Critics in the past have usually taken the position that the chief influence on Barker as a dramatist was Shaw. That Shaw certainly had *some* influence on Barker is undeniable, but it is worth pointing out that in this highly important formative period in which four plays were written (two of them major pieces) and the foundations of much of his method and his approach to play-writing were laid, Shaw could have had little direct influence. Barker may well have been influenced in his opinions of and approach to the theatre by Shaw's general example (through, for instance, the theatre criticisms published in the Saturday Review between 1895 and 1898) but any detailed, technical influence in the matter of the actual *writing* of a play there could scarcely have been. *Plays Pleasant and Unpleasant* was not published until 1898 and the only publication of any Shaw play before that was in 1893, when *Widowers' Houses* appeared. There had, moreover, been very few productions of Shaw's plays in London (or elsewhere, for that matter) before 1897 when Barker and Thomas wrote *The Weather-Hen*. Shaw's real influence on Barker came later and was a modifying influence rather than a formative one. Moreover, it affected Barker's attitude and approach to theatre organization, theatre management, theatre politics and practical procedures rather than his attitude and approach to play writing. It is, I think, a mistake to regard Barker the dramatist either as a muted and minor version of Shaw or as a disciple of Shaw's who introduced some interesting little variations into the pattern. He was a genuine original and one of astonishing precocity. His plays are utterly different from Shaw's, both in style and in *geste*, posture, poetic perspective. Not only do the plays themselves, properly examined, show this, but the timetable of the two dramatists' work precludes the possibility of the kind of influence which has often been assumed.

Ibsen's play writing, on the other hand, was finished by the turn of the century, his last play, *When We Dead Awaken*, being published in December, 1899. And Maeterlinck's most influential plays all belong to the period between 1891, when *The Intruder* was first performed, and 1903, in which year Georgette Leblanc played the name-part in *Joyzelle* which, like *Aglavaine and Selysette* (1896) and *Monna Vanna* (1902), had been especially written for her by Maeterlinck. But the Maeterlinck work which, one might hazard a guess, probably influenced Barker as much as any of these plays was itself not a play at all but a collection of essays about life, art and the theatre. Maeterlinck published it in 1896 under the title *The Treasure of the Humble* and it first appeared in English the following year, in the translation of Alfred Sutro and with an Introduction by A.B. Walkley. To the young dramatist, groping for means and meanings, it must have seemed like a sounding bell or a torch held high. One can see now, with the benefit of hindsight, how the very titles of some of the essays in the book point forward to what will become *leitmotifs* in Barker's work and in his thinking. There are ten essays in all: four of them are called:

Silence
The Invisible Goodness
The Deeper Life
The Inner Beauty

One of the main theses of the book is that the greatest plays are not really, ultimately, concerned with action but with 'states of being' and that the ideal theatre, therefore, would exist in a state of perfect stasis. In the essay called 'The Tragical in Daily Life' ('*Le Tragique Quotidien*') Maeterlinck says:

> I shall be told, perhaps, that a motionless life would be invisible, that therefore animation must be conferred upon it, and movement, and that such varied movement as would be acceptable is to be found only in the few passions of which use has hitherto been made. I do not know whether it be true that a static theatre is impossible. Indeed, to me it seems to exist already. Most of the tragedies of Aeschylus are tragedies without movement.

And at another point in the same essay he compares Hamlet with Othello:

> I admire Othello, but he does not appear to me to live the august daily life of a Hamlet, who has the time to live, inasmuch as he does not act. Othello is admirably jealous. But is it not perhaps an ancient error to imagine that it is at the moments when this passion, or others of equal violence, possesses us, that we live our truest lives?

Maeterlinck's own plays of that decade are admirable demonstrations of the principles he adumbrates in *The Treasure of the Humble*. He strips action down to its barest minimum, reduces it until it is vestigial only, and yet fills his plays with tension, confrontation and expectation. In *Les Aveugles* (translated variously as *The Sightless* and *The Blind*) there is, literally, no overt action at all. Six blind men and six blind women sit on rocks and stones and stumps of trees in 'a very ancient northern forest, eternal of aspect, beneath a sky profoundly starred' (this translation, the first into English, is – interestingly – by Alma-Tadema: it was published by Allen & Unwin in 1895). The men sit together on the right, the women in a group on the left. It gradually emerges that they live in some kind of institution fairly near at hand, that they have been led into the forest by a priest who was caring for them and has taken them out for a walk in the fresh air and that he had left them sitting here while he goes in search of a drink of water for one of the women who is mad as well as blind. But what comes out much more clearly than these fragmentary facts is the terror and melancholy of their situation and their various responses to it, ranging from a fretful fearfulness to a dumb resignation. And as the play develops, their sorrows enlarge these people. They are no longer merely a group of blind beggars waiting for help in a wood; they are humankind, abandoned by God. They wait and wait for the priest to return, only to find, towards the end of the play, that he is there and has been there all the time, seated at stage centre between the men on the right and the women on the left, quite dead. We in the audience have been aware of the stiff, still, silent figure throughout and have no doubt guessed its identity by halfway through the play, or even earlier, but the characters in the play are all blind and so have not known of the figure's presence until, partly by accident and partly by a kind of extra-sensory perception on the part of one of the women, they stumble upon the fact that their leader is dead and is seated in their midst.

These same qualities of stasis, silence and unknowing are exploited even more strikingly in *Interior*, written in 1894 – four years later than *Les Aveugles* – and first published in English in 1894, translated by William Archer, in *The New Review*. In this play the central characters remain silent throughout and are seen only through the windows of their house from the garden outside ('An old garden planted with willows'), where an Old Man and a Stranger watch them and wonder how to break to them the news that one of the daughters of the house has been drowned. A crowd of mourners approaches and the body is borne home, but the bearers take it to the other side of the house so that we, the audience, do not see it. Finally, the Old Man goes in to the family to tell them what has happened, while the crowd of mourners and the Stranger watch from outside:

STRANGER: Hush! He has not told them yet. . . .

The Mother is seen to be questioning the Old Man with anxiety. He says a few more words: then, suddenly, all the others rise, too, and seem to question him. Then he slowly makes an affirmative movement of the head.

STRANGER: He has told them – he has told them all at once!
VOICES IN
CROWD: He told them! He has told them!
STRANGER: I can hear nothing. . . .

The Old Man also rises and, without turning, makes a gesture indicating the door. The Mother, the Father and the two Daughters rush to this door, which the Father has difficulty opening. The Old Man tries to prevent the Mother from going out.

CROWD: They are going out! They are going out!

Confusion among the crowd in the garden. All hurry to the other side of the house, except the Stranger, who remains at the windows. In the room, the folding door is at last thrown wide open: all go out at the same time. Beyond can be seen the starry sky, the lawn and the

> *fountain in the moonlight; while, left alone in the middle of the room, the Child continues to sleep peacefully in the armchair. A pause.*

STRANGER: The child has not wakened! (*He also goes out.*)

CURTAIN

These two plays, and others of Maeterlinck's in the same vein, profoundly influenced Barker's ideas of what theatre could do and ought to do, but Maeterlinck had also a much more direct, technical influence on Barker, namely the influence exerted by Maeterlinck's revolutionary way of writing dialogue. Instead of making his characters speak in large, declamatory, rhetorical ways, or in prose passages of careful explication, Maeterlinck gives them hushed, hesitant utterances born of vague terrors and half-perceived dangers. It is as if all the ordinary and usual gestures of living are simply taken for granted and the dramatic heart of life is shown by allowing the characters to grope for the expression of what they do not know. And always one feels that there are several things going on at once, several differing strands being constantly interwoven. This same quality was noted in the dialogue of *The Marrying of Ann Leete* and can be observed in *Our Visitor to 'Work-a-Day'*, as well as (and increasingly) in some of Barker's later work. It was surely from Maeterlinck that, consciously or unconsciously, he learned this way of writing. From, for example, the following, which comes in Act I, Scene 2 of *Pelléas and Mélisande* (1892):

GOLAUD: Is it long since you ran away?
MELISANDA: Yes, yes . . . who are you?
GOLAUD: I am Prince Golaud – grandson of Arkël, the old king of Allemonde . . .
MELISANDA: Oh! You have got grey hairs already . . .
GOLAUD: Yes; a few, here, at the temples. . . .
MELISANDA: And your beard too. . , . Why are you looking at me in that way?
GOLAUD: I am looking at your eyes. Do you never close your eyes?
MELISANDA: Yes, yes; I close them at night . . .
GOLAUD: Why do you look so astonished?
MELISANDA: Are you a giant?
GOLAUD: I am a man like other men . . .
MELISANDA: Why did you come here?
GOLAUD: I don't know myself. I was hunting in the forest. I was pursuing a boar. I missed my way. You look very young. How old are you?

MELISANDA: I am beginning to feel cold. . . .
GOLAUD: Will you come with me?
MELISANDA: No, no; I shall stay here . . .

(The translation, once again, is by Laurence Alma Tadema)

It would not be true to say that one might mistake this for a passage of Barker dialogue: both Maeterlinck and Barker (even early Barker) are instantly recognizable as themselves. But the generic connection is clearly there, nevertheless.

Other signs of Maeterlinck's influence on Barker can also be seen in the latter's early work. The plot of the short verse play, *A Miracle*, for instance, is very like a Maeterlinck plot (see Note no. 6 of Chapter 3 on p. 338) and the setting of the play in a room in a tower – one of Maeterlinck's favourite symbols – in a mythical mediaeval land is also reminiscent of the Belgian dramatist. And one should remember also that among the very first plays which Barker chose for inclusion in his opening season at the Court Theatre was Maeterlinck's *Aglavaine and Selysette*. He presented it, in the Alfred Sutro translation, on November 15, 1904, with Edyth Olive, Thyrza Norman and Walter Hampden in the cast and with special music by Donald Tovey. But, though the influence was perhaps more pronounced – and certainly more obvious – in his early career, it continued to exercise some hold over him till long afterwards. It is perhaps not too fanciful for one to conjecture that there is something more than mere coincidence in the fact that in the year before Barker completed the writing of *The Secret Life*, Maeterlinck had published a study of mysticism and the occult, called *Le Grand Secret*.

What Barker does, having absorbed the tone and sense and something of the technique of the Maeterlinckian play is to make use of these qualities for his own particular artistic purpose. In one of the two main streams of his work, Barker transfers this mystical treatment and its attendant technique of obliquely allusive language from mediaeval (or pseudo-mediaeval) subjects to modern ones. Beneath the surface of all life, including ordinary, everyday modern life, the same mysteries exist, says Barker. He discards the gothic trappings but retains the heart of the matter. It is interesting to note that he himself commends *Interior* especially because it 'brings us nearer to the work-a-day world'. This comment is in the Introduction which Barker wrote to *Alladine and Palomides, Interior* and *The Death of Tintagiles* when they were published as a collection, called *Three Plays*, by Gowans & Gray Ltd. (London) in 1911. Two other qualities, entirely his own, Barker added to Maeterlinck's view of the world and to the techniques employed in expressing that view – irony and humour. Almost from the start they are present and, though the sureness of his touch and the subtlety of his methods certainly increased in his later work, the irony and the humour are fully there, fully developed and fully mature by the time he wrote *The Marrying of Ann Leete* – and are by no means lacking in *Our Visitor to 'Work-a-Day'*. Maeterlinck made little use of irony and almost none of humour. Barker's view of things was, in fact, more complex and more ambivalent than was Maeterlinck's; but the formative and significant influence of Maeterlinck's work on Barker can scarcely be denied.

Barker's playing of Richard II, under Poel's direction, came late in the year 1899 and by the time it took place, establishing Barker as one of London's best young actors, *The Marrying of Ann Leete* was already completed. Barker's change to his 'other style' of writing would come in the next year, in a new century.

−3−

The Emerging Public Life

Granville Barker, by the time the nineteenth century gave place to the twentieth, was already beginning to be something of a public figure and his letters and his plays from these years begin almost immediately to be haunted by that ambivalence of spirit which he was to display for the rest of his life towards the problem of integrating, in mind and in outward activity, his public posture and function with his private *persona*. It was not precisely a question of personal preference or taste: he was not, if contemporary comment is to be believed, in the least shy or retiring. It was rather that he came gradually to feel that the life one leads in public is not only a false life, but that it betrays and destroys true life, the inner life. On the other hand, the only trade Barker had command of, by which to earn his living, was acting and in order to practise that trade he must actively seek publicity and the public life. The years 1900–1903 see him doing that and doing it successfully, but doing it with increasing reservations. The *kind* of public activity which began to preoccupy him in this period is significant in this context. In 1900 he became associated with the newly-founded Stage Society and before the end of that year was invited to become a member of its Council of Management, which he did. The following year he joined the Fabian Society. The significance, surely, is that both of these were rebel groups, so that by joining them one was, in a sense, simultaneously satisfying the need for association and public recognition (needful for both practical and psychological reasons) and the desire to withhold a part of oneself from the generality of community life. Both these Societies were, also, bodies with challenging and idealist objectives whose members were intelligent and sensitive yet forceful people of a decidedly intellectual cast of mind – people very like Barker himself and certainly the sort of people who would automatically appeal to him. Robert Speaight, it seems to me, is entirely correct when he describes Barker (in *William Poel and the Elizabethan Revival*[1]) as 'that rather rare person – an intellectual in theatreland'.

The Stage Society had been founded in 1899 by a small group of people interested in a more progressive approach to theatre; among them were Frederick Whelen, W. Lee Mathews, Sydney Olivier and Hector Thomson. The new society owed a good deal, especially by way of inspiration and example, to J.T. Grien's Independent Theatre, which had existed from 1891 to 1897 for purposes very similar to those now declared by the Stage Society. The Society's proclaimed purpose, to which it admirably adhered through the forty years of its existence, was to mount productions of plays of worth and merit which seemed unlikely to be considered for production by the ordinary commercial theatre. The plays were given only a few performances (sometimes only a single performance) on Sunday afternoons or evenings or on weekday afternoons. One of the regular commercial theatres was rented for the occasion, rehearsals and performances of the Stage Society production being fitted in round the scheduled performances of whatever play was running at that theatre at the time. The directors and the players for the Society's productions were always professionals, often among the best professionals in London – many of whom were prepared to accept only nominal salaries for these occasions because they enjoyed the challenge of such plays and valued the opportunity of playing parts of more substance than the normal commercial fare could offer. The list of plays thus presented between 1899 and 1940, when the Society finally ceased its activities, is a long and distinguished one, including first productions in English of many foreign plays; Pirandello, Kaiser, Toller, Cocteau, Gorki, Jean-Jacques Bernard, Giraudoux, Afinogenov, Lorca and many others were among the authors represented, alongside such British and American dramatists as Shaw, Barker, Masefield, O'Neill, Odets, Ashley Dukes, C.K. Munro, D.H. Lawrence and John Van Druten as well as occasional revivals of the rarer Restoration or Jacobean piece. Much of this, of course, came long after Barker's time with the Society, but the general principles were the same throughout and this partial list of the Society's choices not only *begins* in Barker's time but also gives a fair indication of what the atmosphere and the function of the Society were like in his time. Although – from sheer financial necessity, if for no other reason – he was still actively engaged in the commercial theatre, he had nevertheless moved, by associating himself with the Stage Society, into a significantly different kind of theatre work as well. In 1900 alone, for example, he directed three plays for the Society and acted in four others. The titles vividly show the way his theatrical interests leaned, as well as aptly demonstrating the Stage Society's objectives; the plays in which he acted were:

Ibsen:	*The League of Youth*	(February, 1900)
Hauptmann:	*Friedenfest*	(June, 1900)
Shaw:	*Candida*	(July, 1900)
Shaw:	*Captain Brassbound's Conversion*	(December, 1900)

And the plays he directed (this was his first directorial assignment and was to lead to spectacular things very soon) were:

'Fiona MacLeod':	*The House of Usna*	
Maeterlinck:	*Interior*	(April, 1900)
Maeterlinck:	*The Death of Tintagiles*	

These three are, of course, one-act plays and were produced together as a triple bill.

It is difficult now to learn much in detail about any of these performances, since the press was not at that time invited to report on Stage Society productions. We do know that it was Barker's performance in *Friedenfest* which persuaded Shaw to offer him the part of Marchbanks in the July, 1900 production of *Candida* (Shaw himself tells us this in an article called 'Granville Barker: Some Particulars by Shaw', in the December, 1946 issue of *Drama*[2]). And we also know, from letters written by Shaw to Barker on December 6 and 7, 1900[3], that Barker's playing of Captain Kearney in *Captain Brassbound's Conversion* left the author of that play far from satisfied: 'Unless you can make the acquaintance of a real American and live with him night and day for the next week, that part will ruin you. It's not a question of acting: it's a question of intonation' says the first of the two letters; the second resignedly says, 'I believe you must play that fatheaded captain after all; but by the Lord it will be a disgraceful outrage on nature. You are about as fit to play him as I am to write Besant's novels. Your divine gifts of youth, delicacy and distinction will be murdered; and so will the part. However, I can't write in another Eugene for you; and you will have to do the captain *with your head* . . .'

In addition to these Stage Society productions in 1900 Barker also, in that same year, played briefly with Mrs. Patrick Campbell's company in a revival of Sudermann's *Magda* (and took Mrs. Pat to court to recover wages which he deemed she owed him[4]) and in a piece of sentimental fluff by Anthony Hope and Edward Rose called *English Nell*. More significantly, alongside his acting and directing in 1900 he continued his writing of plays. C.B. Purdom is, I think, right when he says that Barker's first interest at this time was his play-writing and that he regarded himself primarily as a dramatist, or a would-be dramatist, not as an actor. This is borne out by another of those early letters to William Archer[5], in which he asks: 'Do you think it would be good for me – should the opportunity occur – to try my hand at criticism? I've already done a certain – a very small – amount and naturally there was pleasure in seeing one's ideas in print but I look upon everything at present as to how it will influence my play writing. I know how my acting has helped me and how to a large extent it hinders me and now I'm wondering about this other – at present quite theoretical – point of view and I should be very grateful for your opinion. I think I should always take everything I did more or less seriously and you'll know what sort of habit of brain serious criticism breeds in one – I don't.' A vivid glimpse of this complex and intense young man who, his own letters and the testimony of many contemporaries affirm, was high-spirited, witty, energetic and possessed of a well-developed sense of humour, is provided by that telling phrase, 'I think I should always take everything I did more or less seriously . . .' It is the utterance of one entering upon a religious novitiate and consciously preparing himself for ordination in the faith. And the faith, as Barker here sees it, is not acting or even theatre in general but play-writing. There is a curious and lonely sense of dedication about this obviously private resolve to do nothing that might blur his vision as a dramatist.

The letter to Archer in which this appears is the one already referred to and quoted from in Chapter 2 (see p. 42 and Note 13). This letter begins thus:

> Dear Mr. Archer,
> I am sending you another play to see, though this time only a very little one – the result of two days' work about a month ago.

He then goes on to talk about the play's being in verse, from which we must conclude that it was *A Miracle* which he was sending to Archer, this being – as far as we know – the only verse play he ever wrote. Significantly, his intention was to get the play *published*, not produced. 'I am thinking of sending it to a magazine and I should be glad to know what you think of its reading qualities . . .' he says to Archer. The letter does not, in fact, bear the date 1900: it is simply dated April 9, with no year given. There is fairly strong circumstantial evidence, however, which points to 1900. It cannot be earlier, because Barker's letters to Archer in 1899 begin 'Dear Sir', not 'Dear Mr. Archer'; it cannot be later than 1903, because by March, 1904 the form of salutation has become 'My dear Archer'. This leaves us 1900, 1901, 1902 and 1903. In the last three of these Barker was, we happen to know, heavily engaged in various acting and directing activities in the early months of the year. While it does not conclusively follow that he could not have taken a couple of days off in order to write a short one-act play, it seems less probable than that the play was written in the earlier year when all his concentration seemed to be on play-writing and when he had fewer distractions to cope with. Finally, the place which the letter dated 'April 9' physically occupies in the Archer Archive in the British Library would in itself tend to indicate the year 1900. The letter is in a bound volume and not, therefore, subject to casual re-arrangement of its order in relation to the other letters. The letters in the book appear to be in strict date order and it would, therefore, be strange if this were the only one to be out of order. And this one lies between two letters whose dates are firmly known: before it is one of June 11, 1899, the year being fixed by a reference in it to the production of *The Weather-Hen*, which took place (there was ever only one production of this play) in June of 1899; after the letter of 'April 9' is one dated January 26, 1901 and again the year is unquestionably correct since the letter refers to the typescript of *Agnes Colander* and that typescript, also in the British Library, bears the typist's date-stamp which says 'January 10, 1901'. It is therefore fair, I think, to conclude that during the year 1900 Barker wrote two plays, the very brief verse play called *A Miracle*, written in March[6], and the full-length play in 'realistic' prose, *Agnes Colander*, which occupied him throughout the rest of the year and was ready for typing in January, 1901.

This latter is, again, a play about sex: sex not only as a relationship, with its attendant problems, but also about sex as a mysterious driving force, somehow connected with all the springs of life and energy. The phenomenon of physical sex is more directly approached in *Agnes Colander* than in any other Barker play and its force and fascination is acknowledged by all four of the characters, who all deal with it in different ways. One of these characters is a thorough-going Dionysiac figure, associated with all the god's traditional insignia – red wine, an innocent animality, huge eating which is yet not gluttony and frank sexual desire. Another is an over-civilized (and therefore trivialized) version of *la femme amoureuse*. The third and fourth have jointly tried to set physical love aside in a kind of purity pact between them: this in part is a reflection of the Victorian obsession with the idea of sexual 'purity' but is also an attempt to explore, beyond its conventional applications, the possibility of a real power released by celibacy; an attempt, in fact, to harness sublimated forces and apply them in a nobler cause. Connected with its interest in sexuality, but distinct from it, is the play's concern with marriage as an institution. In this, *Agnes Colander* is most closely akin to *Our Visitor from 'Work-a-day'*, though its links with *The Weather-Hen* and *The Marrying of Ann Leete* are also obvious. Barker was clearly both fascinated and repelled by the whole idea of marriage and by the physical act of sex. His friend Charles Edwin Wheeler was to say to him ten years later, in a letter[7] about *The Madras House*: '. . . as a Puritan you're ashamed of your appetites . . . Because you're not sure of the difference between love and appetite you solve your difficulty by denying any value to love and so get no good of either . . .' And the relation between marriage and work, especially artistic work, was another aspect of the subject which constantly engaged Barker's attention and imagination, as did the possibility of a perfect sexual union as the symbol and the shrine of the highest ideals and principles. It is no accident that, twenty-two years later, *Tristan und Isolde* should be made the basis of his play, *The Secret Life*, nor was it something new in his development which came suddenly to fruition in 1922. The same idea haunts all his work and stands clearly at the centre of his early play, which is concerned not only with sex as an instinct and impulse but with marriage as a compact and an institution. (Agnes, like Vivien in *Our Visitor to 'Work-a-day'*, talks about having 'an ideal of marriage'.)

   Agnes Colander, the central figure, is an artist – a painter – who has left her husband because the marriage was stifling her creative senses and because she felt that this stultification of what she regards as most vital in her was a wickedness. But she finds that living alone is no good to her, either; she still cannot work properly and she feels lonely and depressed. 'Now I seem to be finding that the talent was only his teaching and that I need a lord and master. I'm a nobody', she says. Otho, an artist friend who finds Agnes personally attractive and who also has deep and genuine admiration and regard for her work, asks her to come and live with him and continue her painting. He urges her, in her work and in her life generally, to shun conventionality and to keep in touch with the simple, natural realities:

OTHO:	It is my experience that only by forgetting all one had ever learnt can one learn to live at all. Look, men are taught to work. I would have them taught to play and only let work bubble out from them. Then we should have in the world only geniuses and children. Of course, it is very hard for a good woman to live a natural life. You are all taught false things and then some are left stranded and so many half married –
AGNES	*(with pain)*: I know. Don't you know there are times, Otho, when I want to care for you, loverlike? But circumstances have said no to it and there has been an end.
OTHO:	How much do you fear a scandal and a divorce?
AGNES:	Not a little bit.
OTHO:	Straight out now – you love me?
AGNES:	I tell you I am a dead thing.
OTHO:	But if I could make you live?
AGNES:	Why then I suppose I should belong to you.
OTHO:	Now we are speaking truth.

In parallel with this relationship is another, of a different kind, between Agnes and Alec. This is consciously and deliberately Platonic. They do not ignore the possibility and the pull of physical love between them: they consider it, reject it as something destructive and debased and deliberately foreswear it, making a joint vow of chastity which is intended to apply not only to their relationship with each other but also to the relationships which each may develop with third parties.

The main dramatic dichotomy of the play, therefore, is embodied in Otho and Alec, representing the eternal and inevitable conflict of these two main concepts of human sexuality. But the play also admits of a third concept, mysterious, undefined, the essence of love itself. To this concept Agnes is dedicated, both in the sense of being set up by the play as the symbol of this high theme and also in the sense that, as a character in the play, she consciously and actively associates herself with this third idea of love. About her legal marriage to Henry Verity (who never appears in the play) she says: 'But there was all my maidenhood gone almost before I had been conscious of it. Oh – how I hated him for that. For I have never loved and now I never can. There may be passion for me, or tenderness – some feeling beyond friendship; but never the great beauty – no memory of it even.' Not passion, not tenderness, but some mystical, overwhelming experience that takes possession of the whole personality is what Agnes yearns for and the play seems to suggest, though not altogether consistently throughout its entire length, that Barker himself regarded this as the great ideal at which the man/woman relationship should aim, beyond practicalities, beyond considerations of affection and esteem. It is interwoven with a quasi-mystical idea of 'purity' (Agnes talks, towards the end of Act I, about 'virginity of soul'), which seems to subsist for all practical purposes in chastity, continence, celibacy – though the value of such chastity is in its symbolism, rather than in itself. Barker has, in fact, inherited and given approval to – though with some irony and with some doubts and hesitations – the nineteenth-century version of mediaeval romantic and chivalric love. His artistic exploration is aimed at trying to discover how deeply this quality is embedded in the human psyche (in other words, how 'real' it is, how basic) and how it adapts itself – if at all – to the stresses of urban living in a highly complex, industrialized society. Agnes, like Vivien, is a woman who 'believes in' marriage, in the possibility of a 'true marriage' and tries to define what this should be. Paradoxically, though *Agnes Colander* is expressed in much more down-to-earth language than *Our Visitor to 'Work-a-day'*, Agnes is a much more conventionally 'romantic' figure than Griselda. The latter, who produces a kind of hard but elusive poetry of her own, is the more truly revolutionary figure and *her* play is the more profoundly probing of the two.

The parallel of the two relationships – Otho on the one hand, Alec on the other – provides *Agnes Colander* with its dramaturgic structure, which is neatly and quite powerfully worked out. Each of the three acts has one main duologue between Agnes and each of the men in turn and to Acts 2 and 3 is added the obbligato of Emmaline Marjoribanks, a light-minded but shrewd woman determined to live by the conventional social code but to collect what personal satisfaction she can along the way. Agnes, partly out of weariness and partly because she thinks it may after all be the way to self-integration, allows herself to be persuaded by Otho and Act 2 finds them living in an old farmhouse in Normandy as if married to each other. Indeed, they allow Emmaline to believe that they are, in fact, married. But, before leaving England, Agnes has agreed with Alec that *their* friendship must somehow continue: 'If ever we should slip far apart, Alec, through fault of mine, still I should grieve, so will you stick by me if you can?'

When she decides to go to Normandy with Otho, Agnes does not tell Alec, but he finds out and comes to visit her, chiefly to reproach her for her breaking of the 'purity pact' which they made and to confess that, to get even with her, he has plunged into a sordid and ephemeral *affaire* with a French girl:

AGNES:	Alec – do I know her?
ALEC:	You certainly wouldn't. Mine was an affair of a day or two – a 'little French milliner'. Laugh at that. I have heard you laugh at it in a play.
AGNES:	Those were not real people.
ALEC:	Nor are we, perhaps.

Agnes is disgusted with Alec's pettiness and is on the point of sending him packing and deciding to throw in her lot with Otho once and for all. There is a scene of powerful physicality between Otho and Agnes but during this Otho's latent jealousy, part of his animal nature, becomes dominant and half-intentionally, half by accident, he strikes her, cutting her lip and making it bleed. He is immediately swept by remorse, but the incident has changed Agnes's perspective on things and the next day she tells him that she is leaving him. When she also tells this to Alec he at first rejoices because he supposes that it means that Agnes is forsaking Otho in order to live with him. But she tells him that she has now liberated herself from both of them and that she will live with neither of them. She asks Alec to escort her back to England (as custom and convention – and perhaps personal prudence and safety – demanded), where she plans to return to her art work in London, living alone. Then gradually, she suggests at the end of the play, she and Alec may be able to work out a decent and durable relationship based on mutual trust and friendship:

ALEC:	Perhaps it's for us to discover –
AGNES:	How to love decently. Let's think so.
ALEC:	Of course, it'll be imperfect. One is meant to –
AGNES:	No doubt. But men have muddled the world so and I – and you – for a little while must pay the penalty. It's worth paying.

Agnes is an admirably-drawn character, with real density and complexity and with a real development throughout the play. Without abandoning her ideal of a love which subsumes both passion and tenderness yet transcends both, she changes by the end of the play in a way that enables her to accept the truth of the commonplace as well as the metaphysical ideal. This change and development is convincingly done and is one of the play's main strengths.

Of all Barker's plays, this is the one that, structurally, owes most to Ibsen, though in spirit it is not so close to Ibsen as are *Our Visitor to 'Work-a-day'* and *The Marrying of Ann Leete*. *Agnes Colander* consists

essentially, as do so many of the later Ibsen plays, of a series of interlocking duologues and Barker manages them with considerable adroitness.
They have, of course, little of the complexity and profundity of Ibsen,
but they nevertheless represent a considerable and creditable performance by an emerging young dramatist. They seem to me as good as,
and perhaps better than, comparable passages in the almost-exactly-
contemporaneous plays of Hubert Henry Davies, better than nearly all of
Henry Arthur Jones or Alfred Sutro, not very far short of all but the very
best of St. John Hankin, though distinctly less good than Barker himself
at *his* best (which came later). We have, as it happens, some indication –
though an ambivalent one – of Barker's own view of the matter. On the
front of the typescript there are two notes in his handwriting. One says:

> I suspect this play (I've been glancing into it) to be very poor. It should
> certainly *not* be published. It might well be destroyed.

> H.G.B. August, 1929

The second adds an affirmation:

> It *should* be destroyed.

> April, 1932

Then why wasn't it? It was his own property and in his own possession. He could perfecly well have destroyed it. He didn't: instead, he not
only preserved it with some care for over thirty years; he then gave it to
The Meyer Sassoon Library in Paris, whose imprint is stamped on
several pages of it. In the light of this, the notes he wrote on the front of the
script seem either distinctly disingenuous or the expression of a hesitancy
so deep-seated as to be almost pathological. Certainly the fact that he
wrote these public asseverations about destroying the manuscript
instead of quietly burning it gives us the right to disagree with his
opinion about the worth of the play. At the very least we can be thankful
for its preservation because it provides valuable information about
Barker's development as a dramatist as well as illustrating still further his
enormous preoccupation with the connection between the spiritual and
the physical in the sexual relation. Standing as it does between *Ann Leete*
and *The Voysey Inheritance* – the former absorbed entirely with the
private, secret life, the latter concentrating upon the public, outward
man; and both concerned with the relation between the two – *Agnes
Colander* takes a middle ground between the two extremes. There is in
Act II a brief passage of great significance in this connection. It occurs

after Otho and Agnes have escaped from the grime and stress and frustration of the city to the quiet, ordered, eventless life of the Normandy countryside, which ought to be, for an artist, idyllic and ideal:

AGNES: I know I must be in London among the ugliness and difficulty of things to be able to express myself.
OTHO: Must you still go straining to understand those creatures?
AGNES: Because I love them. And then knowing what is, to paint what might be – fairy tales.

Barker comes back to this idea in drawing the figure of Hugh Voysey two or three years later (and it is especially interesting to note that, in the two subsequent revisions of *The Voysey Inheritance* in 1913 and 1934 Hugh was one of the characters who came in for major attention and relatively major alteration). And the general argument about the place of art amid the squalor and degradation of the city figures again in the last act of *The Madras House* in 1909. So *Agnes Colander* is most germane to a full and final understanding of Barker and its position in the roster of his works is a pivotal one.

Its chief weakness is a certain over-earnestness, unmitigated as yet by the touch of irony which Barker learned a little later to apply both as a theatrical emollient and as an astringent. This tendency towards solemnity, the over-eager desire to explain, makes the play occasionally mawkish and occasionally pompous (inherent and endemic dangers in all realistic-naturalistic plays). In this sense, *Agnes Colander* is something of a retrogression, since it is less assured in its touch in this respect than is *The Marrying of Ann Leete*, which has none of the over-explanatory moments and is shot through with a delicious irony, expertly employed. The reason for the apparently backward step lies, I think, in the change of general style, the move to a completely factual, realist-naturalist technique in *Agnes Colander*. This must surely have been a completely conscious decision, made presumably in response to the prevailing climate of the time and the advice of people like Archer (who warned Barker in 1900 about the dangers of being a crank). It was perhaps a mistaken decision, for though it led to *The Voysey Inheritance* and *Waste* – both of them fine, large, mature plays for which *Agnes Colander* was, technically speaking, a necessary preliminary exercise – it tended to inhibit something of the natural flow of Barker's artistic expression. The assuredness of touch and the poetically ironic overtones which were largely absent from *Agnes Colander* Barker learned to use with great skill, even in spite of the naturalistic style and atmosphere, in *The Voysey Inheritance* and

Waste; but they *had* to be learned, whereas in *The Marrying of Ann Leete* they were entirely natural. The two methods come triumphantly together in *The Madras House* but in a way which even Barker himself found impossible to use again. That play is *sui generis*, one of those works (like, say, *Murder in the Cathedral*) which seem to step aside from the pattern of its author's other works and exist in a brilliance of its own, unrepeatable. The quintessential Barker which first fully showed in *The Marrying of Ann Leete*, and which to some extent was then submerged and obscured, did not fully make its reappearance until *The Secret Life* (1919–22), a play which Barker himself described[8] as 'the "Ann Leete" of my second period'. So the weakness which shows in *Agnes Colander*, the substituting of prosaic explication for poetic insight, derives partly from inexperience but partly from a false decision about which way to go. Even at that, the weakness is partial only and is not ruinous. Barker's already-considerable theatrical skill, combined with his intensity of feeling and his accuracy of observation, saves a good deal of the play.

The very title of the play provides a nice example of this over-earnestness and of the curious mixture of artistic virtue with artistic error. Otho gives us the clue, in the passage just quoted, when he says 'Must you still go straining to understand those creatures?' Now this is exactly right, both for the character and the play. For Otho (in the drawing of whose character Barker surely drew heavily – consciously or unconsciously – on the stories about Gaugin, whose retreat to Tahiti had taken place less than ten years before the play was started) there was something unnatural, strained, in Agnes's rigid determination to be 'good' by sheer intellectual effort. And for the play, the observing of this trait in Agnes (for Otho is right about her in this) not only makes the character more credible as a living person but also gives the general theme of the play – the nature and manifestation of goodness and purity – a complexity, ambivalence and sophistication which increases its reality, too. But the point is over-laboured by the play's title, which bludgeons us with its self-conscious seriousness. 'Colander' derives from *colare*, the Latin word meaning 'to strain'. To it, Barker adds 'Agnes'. St. Agnes was renowned for, and martyred for, her chastity; and her saintly symbol is a lamb (*agnus*), the animal which in several mythological systems connotes purity. So the name Agnes Colander indicates pretty clearly what is intended to be the essential posture of the character. All too clearly, perhaps, for those who might relish a little subtlety. And all too solemnly, too, for those with an irreverent turn of mind and a semantic sense of humour, for 'colander', surely, has irrepressible culinary associations: brussels sprouts in a holey bowl. The ear of the later Barker would have picked up this unfortunate connection and have rejected 'colander', no matter how solemnly precious; but in 1900 he was still a shade too high-minded and a thought too undisciplined to make full use of the cutting edge of his critical faculties. There are signs that he was, in fact, unhappy with the title, but he did nothing about it. The typescript bears on its title-page hand-written notes of three possible alternative titles, all repudiating the sententiousness of the original. They are: 'A Blind Alley and Blue Sky', 'An Experiment' and 'An Attempt at Life'. Barker's decision not to adopt any of these was wise, since they are as bad as the original title; but his decision to give in at that point and retain 'Agnes Colander', with its accidental kitchen reference and its too-deliberate classical one, was not wise. It is a small matter but interesting because it is rather typical of the fault which tends to mar the whole play and because it provides some indication of the kind of thinking which led to that fault. The point must be made, however, that the fault is not all-pervasive and does not negate the solid virtues of the play – the economy of means, the depth and originality of the character drawing, the firmness of control and the deftness of the structural manipulation. To which list one should add theatrical viability. Though it has never been played, the dialogue as it appears on the pages gives the very firm impression that it would play extremely well. It lacks the elusive (and allusive) magic of the talk in *Our Visitor* and *Ann Leete* but it is supple and resilient, telling and (with the exception of the few awkward moments already referred to) speakable. In the ultimate analysis it is not resonant enough to convey with complete success the play's central sense (as I take it) and gesture, but even here the failure is not entire, some scenes working very well towards this end. Within the ambiguities and ambivalence of the sexual theme itself, what the play wants us to understand is that there is an essential purity of soul which can survive physical besmirching and, in surviving, provide a talisman by which the ambivalence can be reconciled, the grossness purged and the whole sexual experience integrated into a deeper sense of a purposeful and noble existence. But this must come through experience and acceptance, not through avoidance:

AGNES: It comes to me – how one hammers eternally at the door of this sex question.

ALEC: I think the door is always open. People who have passed through we annoy. Those who have avoided it we shock. But the question is put to every one of us, so it's no use pretending that it isn't there.

Nor can one come upon the genuine reality by way of polite fictions or conventional attitudes, however heroic. One must struggle to understand, from one's own responses, the actual nature of the experience:

AGNES: I should have considered what a kiss might mean to you.
ALEC: Why more to me than to you?
AGNES: My feelings over such things are coarser than yours.
ALEC: They are not – they are not.
AGNES: They are, dear boy, naturally.

As well as the nature of this essential purity, the play probes other, related, ambiguities – the relationship between sexual energy and artistic energy; the relationship between marriage and friendship; the importance or unimportance of physical love. All of them are questions that crop up again and again in Barker's plays. The prevalence of the idea and possibility of perfect friendship between a man and a woman, especially *after* they are married to each other, is particularly striking. It occurs in *Agnes Colander* not only in the conversations between Agnes and Alec, where it is regarded as an alternative to loving 'in the common way' (Alec's phrase) but also between Agnes and Otho, where 'comradeship' (the word occurs several times) is seen as co-existing with physical passion as a part – the more important part – of marriage. It is a theme to which Barker will return many times. In one of the three different and distinct versions of *The Voysey Inheritance* – the second one, made in 1913 – Alice Maitland says to Edward Voysey in the last scene of the play: 'Oh my dear, don't be afraid of wanting me. Shall we be less than friends by being more? If I thought that, should I ever have let it come to this?' In two of his plays – *Waste* and *The Secret Life* – the passionate and sexual relationship is replaced by making the household consist of a middle-aged man and his sister, who runs the house for him as a wife would and is, in theory, a perfect companion and 'comrade', except that – ironically – the relationship is in both bases completely arid. Perhaps the most significant example of all, however, comes not from one of his plays but from his own life: in 1905, shortly after playing John Tanner to her Ann Whitefield in the first production of *Man and Superman*, and shortly before he asked her to marry him, Barker gave to Lillah McCarthy a photograph[9] of himself, on which was written the following inscription:

To 'Ann' in ransom from 'John Tanner'
To Miss McCarthy in comradeship
                    from
                              H. Granville Barker

Agnes Colander, as well as marking a conscious move towards a greater degree of factual realism, possesses one other stylistic difference that is worth noting: it is worked on a much smaller canvas than any other of Barker's full-length plays. The exercise in artistic discipline must have been a very valuable one for him and he carries it out with considerable assurance, but one is nevertheless left with the impression that some of the thinness of the treatment is the result of the unnatural constriction which the method of the play imposed upon him. His natural *milieu* is a broader canvas, on which the fine balance and exact juxtaposition of figures and themes can produce that unique poetic irony which is his signal contribution to the theatre. Plays as different as *The Marrying of Ann Leete, The Madras House, The Secret Life* and *His Majesty* all strikingly demonstrate this quality – and, ironically, in so doing reduce their chances of production, since their expansiveness of method and spirit translates, when it comes to practical considerations of production, into large casts, complicated stage settings and very heavy production costs. *Agnes Colander* demonstrates the opposite method, of deliberately-limited structure and severe economy of means, but – significantly – Barker used it only once.

On January 26, 1901, immediately the typing of it was complete, Barker sent the play to Archer, saying: 'Is the New Century Theatre still alive and if it is will you consider if this, my latest play, is producible? If it is not will you yet be good enough to read the play.' Archer's reply to this letter has not survived and there is no record of what he thought of the play. The New Century Theatre, one of the smaller 'theatre societies', which had been founded by Archer a few years before, did not produce *Agnes Colander*, nor did anybody else. So far as we know, Barker never offered the play for commercial production.

William Archer has already been mentioned several times in connection with Barker and in view of the friendship which was to develop between these two strangely dissimilar men it might be well at this stage to give some brief account of Archer. By the time Barker began to write to him, Archer was firmly established as one of the two most influential theatre critics in London (the other – Archer's great rival in the Ibsen debates – being Clement Scott). From 1878 to 1881 Archer was the critic for the *London Figaro*; since 1884 he had been with Edmund Yates's *World*, a paper he was to stay with until 1906. He was also, by 1900, famous not only for his fervent support of Ibsen and productions of Ibsen but also for his own translations of Ibsen, several of which had already been produced in London. He was a good deal older than Barker – the same age as Shaw, in fact. His family was Scottish and he himself was born at Perth; but his paternal grandparents had emigrated to Larvik, Norway and much of William Archer's childhood was spent there – so much that, Charles Archer tells us in his biography of his brother, the boy temporarily lost most of his English and spoke only Norwegian. Archer, long afterwards, once described his grandparents' house in Larvik as 'the first place I can remember and the last that I shall forget'. He attended various schools in England and Scotland and in 1872 entered the University of Edinburgh. About his undergraduate days two or three things stand out as having some significance in the light of his later career: he was known, for instance, as a voracious reader; he began, while still a student, to practise daily journalism, writing an editorial column for the *Edinburgh Evening News*; and his consuming interest in the theatre, which had already showed itself during his boyhood, began to dominate his thinking and his writing at that time. Very shortly after graduating from the University, and while he was still living in Edinburgh, he collaborated with two of his friends to produce a pamphlet called *The Fashionable Tragedian: a Criticism*. It found immediate publication in 1877 and went into a second edition before the end of the year, the first edition being published by Thomas Gray & Co., of Edinburgh and Glasgow and the second by George Taylor, London. The critical writing, one gathers, was mainly Archer's, though he had the assistance of R.W. Lowe; the caricature drawings were by G.R. Halkett. The pamphlet was an all-out attack on Henry Irving, who is described as 'one of the worst actors that ever trod the British stage in so-called 'leading characters' . . . a weak, loosely-built figure, and a face whose range of expression is very limited, are the two principal disadvantages under which he has had to labour.' The pamphlet goes on to compare Irving with Salvini, to the great disparagement of the former. The general tone of the writing is extravagantly and mockingly derogatory, as one might expect from a very young critic, but only six years later – by which time he had already established himself in London as a regularly practising theatre critic – Archer published another critique of Irving which was not only much more balanced, moderate and judicious in tone but which showed, in fact, real perceptiveness and critical acuity at a time when balanced judgment about Irving was hard to come by. This short work was called *Henry Irving, Actor and Manager: a Critical Study* (London: The Leadenhall Press, 1883). In it, Archer examines Irving's style and technique and tries to analyse the nature of Irving's extraordinary appeal. In this latter connection, he comes to an important conclusion: 'In all parts he moves them; but he leaves them always conscious of the motive mechanism. He grasps them, but they are not rapt away.' And a little later, talking of Irving's playing of Dubosc in the third act of *The Lyons Mail* (Charles Reade's adaptation of *Le Courrier de Lyons*, in which Irving played both the saintly Lesurques and the devilish Dubosc) he says: 'The scene is a masterpiece, because there is in it no appeal to our higher emotions. Wherever such an appeal is demanded, Mr. Irving indicates rather than attains the highest possibilities. He does not lack skill, he may not even fail in truth: there is only one word for what we miss, and that is inspiration.' Archer has already said, half-a-dozen pages earlier: 'Mr. Irving is, of all distinguished actors, the least inspired. He never carries us away on the wings of his passion or his pathos, to set us down again after a little, wondering through what regions of terror or beauty we have in the meantime been wafted.' He goes on to praise Irving's industriousness, his patience and his ingenuity, saying: 'Burbage and Betterton, relying upon pure convention for their surroundings, bore the whole weight of the drama upon their shoulders. . . . Mr. Irving, with all the resources of absolute scenic illusion at his disposal, wisely shifts upon his accessories more than half the burden.' Most important of all, in Archer's view, are two other qualities of Irving's – his intellect and his 'intensity'. 'It is his face and his brain that have made him what he is', he says: 'his glittering eye and his restless, inventive intellect.' This anticipates, by a dozen years or more, similar criticisms of Irving made by Shaw.

As well as his dramatic criticism, Archer had by the turn of the century a good deal of other literary work to his credit. He had published *English Dramatists of Today* (London: Sampson Low, 1882), *About the Theatre* (London: T. Fisher Unwin, 1886), *Masks or Faces? A Study in the Psychology of Acting* (London: Longmans, Green, 1888), critical editions of the theatre essays of Leigh Hunt, Hazlitt, Forster and G.H. Lewes (London: Walter Scott, 1894–96) and a biography of Macready. As regards the theatre itself he was recognized as a sturdy supporter of the 'new drama' and a constant advocate of the need for supporting and encouraging new playwrights. He approached the theatre with a sense of high seriousness and expected it to respond in like terms. While he recognized the sensuous appeal of histrionic virtuosity as being the essential basis of all theatre, he firmly believed that this virtuosity should not be employed in empty display but in the service of fine and serious ideas. His weakness as a critic, ultimately considered, rests in the way he tended to define 'fine and serious ideas': he looked for them to be intellectually explicit and expressed in purely literary terms; the theatre was to him, in the last analysis, a branch of literature. He lacked Barker's instinctive sense of performance-as-art and was also largely without Barker's poetic sensibility.

But when Barker first approached Archer, in 1898, he did so as the tyro approaching the expert. Attracted, doubtless, by Archer's reputation and by his espousal of causes already dear to Barker's own heart, the younger man was, clearly, appealing to the established practitioner who could – he felt – give him the most help. What is remarkable is the way in which their relationship, once established, developed and endured. From that first letter, beginning 'Dear Sir', in 1898, until Archer's death in December, 1924, their correspondence was continuous and frequent. Though the two men were broadly in sympathy in their ideas about theatre, they were widely at variance as to the practical applications of those ideas. And temperamentally they were utterly different. Archer was a steady, cautious, commonsense man, in a sense rather unimaginative; he was a man of liberal views, strict principles and enormous patience; in the arts he hated sloppiness, slovenliness and illogicality, though his demands so far as poetic sensibility is concerned were modest and his appreciation of that quality, limited. Barker was unsteady, incautious, electrically imaginative and madly impatient; he, too, hated slovenliness, but his poetic sensibility was of a high order and could see far beyond the literal logic of the surface of things. But there is, running through his long correspondence with Archer, a thread of gentleness and affection which only increased in strength as both of them gradually realized – as both did – who was the greater artist of the two. It was a curiously-matched friendship but its warmth and sincerity over a quarter of a century is beyond question, as is the fact that each man recognized and valued the sterling qualities of the other, though different from his own. The style and quality of Barker's relationship with William Archer was quite different from those of his relationship with Gilbert Murray. Both Murray and Archer were appreciably older than Barker but this difference in age was not, after the initial onset, a matter of any significance. Perhaps the main difference between the two relationships could be best defined by saying that with Murray there was something very like ecstasy, at least on occasion; with Archer, there was always a certain reserve, even though the warmth and affection were always there.

When Charles Archer published his biography of his brother in 1931, Barker wrote to the *Times Literary Supplement* about it, a letter which catches very clearly many of the senses of their relationship:

Sir,

Will you allow me to ask the sympathetic reviewer of William Archer's 'Life' to explain what he means by saying in conclusion that the writing of *The Green Goddess* 'contradicted his life-long principles'? I should have thought that the peculiar strength of Archer's position as a dramatic critic lay in his patient willingness to appreciate any play of any kind if he could only discover it to be good of its kind. This certainly was one of the chief grounds of his influence in the theatre. While other literary men were apt to be off-hand with whatever they did not choose to call literature, he was always ready to apply the more purely dramatic, even the purely theatrical, test. Too ready, was the accusation that some of us were inclined to bring against him! It was an ill-considered one. For, coming into the inheritance, which he had done so much to prepare, of a drama and literature made, approximately at any rate (I quote your review), 'one flesh', we too readily forgot the novelty and jeopardy of the union. His complaisances towards the more skittish partner to it were politic. Later there were those who, like your reviewer, would insist on identifying him solely with the sterner side. Again, he refused to be. To quote from the biography and a letter about *The Green Goddess* and its success: 'I was amused by a remark of Desmond MacCarthy's in the *New Statesman*. He said he was glad I was no longer a critic, for this was not the sort of play I would have approved. But I don't know. I always had a weak spot for melodrama.'

That is the Archer of 1923 looking back down the long hill (the road, he feared, now beginning to dip again) which he has climbed together with his beloved English drama, and the 'weak spot' is fatherly affection for the honest simpleton of the family. But, during those fifty years – or nearly – of critical authority, to not the crudest melodrama set before him had he done other than painstaking justice. In one of his earliest books, moreover, we find him urging upon Sims and Pettitt and the 'Adelphi' playwrights of the day the rich opportunities of the melodramatic convention, let but a little more care and common sense be brought to bear upon it. Long after, he successfully translates these precepts into practice. Here, he held, was the sort of play which need not wait for its writing upon inspiration – to which he made no pretence. But he had always extolled good craftsmanship. And he put forward *The Green Goddess* as an example of it; making no higher claim, thinking this, though, by no means a negligible one.

An essential thing to be said about Archer, it seems to me, is that, as single adventurer or pilot, in dramatic matters or in the wider interests of which his life was full (and which helped to keep him so salutary an influence in those dramatic matters), he could hold a course once he had laid it down, even though it seemed a commonplace course, and be turned from it neither by momentary failure nor by distracted enthusiasms. As to the theatre, he thought that it must always be primarily a popular entertainment. But, as a good Liberal, he would never admit that because of this it could not be, in its every aspect, a reasonably intelligent entertainment too. And I really cannot imagine upon what 'principle' your reviewer supposes that he would have struck good melodrama from its canon.

Faithfully yours,
Harley Granville Barker

Conventional melodrama, no matter how 'good of its kind', was not Barker's favourite kind of theatre and he spent, indeed, much of his professional life inveighing against its vapidity and insipidity. But, the letter shows, he must leap to a dead friend's defence when help is needed, setting aside his own preferences and principles (to some extent, at any rate – though there is a sly reservation in that penultimate sentence: Barker, too, had once reckoned himself 'a good Liberal', though when it came to the theatre he never could quite bring himself to accept the idea that a 'popular entertainment' might also be a 'reasonably intelligent entertainment'; and what a guarding of his own personal conviction rests in that one word 'reasonably' – as if to say that from the popular theatre one must not expect too much). This letter, written seven years after Archer's death, vividly reflects both men – the warmth of their friendship and the instinctive differences of their temperaments. There had been many debates between them in the years from 1901 to 1924, but never a cross word: always some slight reserving of the self on both sides, I think (again the contrast with Gilbert Murray springs to mind) but never a hint of animosity or disaffection. But in 1901, all this was still to come. When the young Granville Barker sent the typescript of his new play, *Agnes Colander*, to him, William Archer's star was at its zenith; Barker thought only to get some good advice on his play and also to increase, perhaps, its chances of being produced.

While he had been finishing the writing of *Agnes Colander* he had also been acting continuously. *English Nell*, which had opened on August 21, 1900, ran until February 9, 1901 (and Marie Tempest, who had been playing the part of Nell Gwynn, opened four days later at the same theatre playing the part of Peg Woffington in a play based on Charles Reade's novel). It is well to remind ourselves of the continuousness of his work as an actor. Because we know so well what happened later and where his real importance lay, and because he himself so emphasised that his real work was his writing, we tend now to think of him as a young highbrow actor who played a few matinée performances of a few esoteric highbrow plays, while waiting for his serious work to begin. We overlook the fact that he was, by the time he reached his early twenties, a very competent actor who was continuously in employment and was fully capable, had he been so inclined, of making a respectable living from his acting alone. After his five and a half month run at the Prince of Wales's Theatre in *English Nell* he did three pieces of work for J.T. Grein's Independent Theatre, in February and March of 1901, acting in matinée performances of *Le Monde où l'on s'ennuie,* by Edouard Pailleron (which Grein himself had translated) and Shaw's *Man of Destiny* and directing *The Revolted Daughter,* by Israel Zangwill. He then went almost immediately into the cast of Charles Wyndham's revival of Henry Arthur Jones's *The Case of the Rebellious Susan* (which Wyndham had first produced in 1894). It opened on May 16, 1901 and ran until July 11, when the 'season' petered out. But Barker again found immediate employment, this time in an adaptation by Robert Hichens and Cosmo Gordon Lennox of *Vanity Fair.* Called simply 'Becky Sharp', it opened at the Prince of Wales's Theatre on August 27 and ran until February 22 of the following year. Again the leading rôle was played by Marie Tempest. So, even without counting the special matinée performances of plays whose artistic importance exceeded their commercial viability, Barker had been acting almost uninterruptedly alongside some of the best people in the business (the cast of *English Nell,* for example, had included – as well as Marie Tempest – Ben Webster, H.B. Warner and Mabel Terry-Lewis) for fourteen out of the eighteen months ending in February, 1902. From the onlooker's point of view, his position at this time was that of a young London actor who was beginning to 'make his way', as the saying is, and who did a little scribbling on the side. That, however, was not the way Barker himself looked at it.

In 1901 also, while appearing nightly at Wyndham's or the Prince of Wales's, in another arena another aspect of his many-faceted personality began to assert itself, a curiously ambivalent one and one that would, indirectly, exercise considerable influence upon him during the next dozen or so years. He became a member of the Fabian Society. Barker's socialism has been the subject of ribald comment from time to time, especially in the light of his marriage, after the divorce from Lillah McCarthy, to an American millionairess. But the situation merits closer examination and deserves something better than a cheaply cynical sneer. His concern for social justice was perfectly genuine and Anne Fremantle, in her *This Little Band of Prophets* (London: Allen & Unwin, 1959) is wide of the mark when she describes him, in relation to the Fabian Society, merely as a 'crony of G.B.S.' Though his friendship with Shaw undoubtedly influenced his decision to join the Fabians, he had his own reasons, too, and once in the Society, he addressed himself to its business with characteristic vigour. Edward R. Pease, in his *History of the Fabian Society* (London: A.C. Fifield, 1916 and 1925), says of Barker: 'He served on the Executive from 1907 to 1912 and took a large share in the detailed work of the Committees, besides giving many lectures and assisting in social functions' and Pease uses Barker's record to point up the contrast between new members who joined the Society to work for it and others who joined but made little or no contribution. Judging by his letters, Barker was politically fairly naïve, especially if one compares him with the leading Fabians of his day – Shaw, the Webbs, Sydney Olivier, Hubert Bland, Frank Podmore or Graham Wallas – but his naïveté applied more to methodology than to principles. He saw clearly and felt deeply that the society into which he was born was deliberately founded on inequality and injustice. His response was the same as his response to the evils of the theatre as he perceived them, namely a kind of divine desperation which made him throw himself into the struggle in the belief that there was just a chance, just an outside chance, that, if all men of goodwill nerved themselves and acted together at once, even problems of these proportions could be subdued. But there was always a note of desperation in his energy and optimism; and there was, as most of his plays – and especially *Waste* – show, an accompanying strain of pessimism which would, on occasion, burst out. He was, in fact, to use the now-modish cant term, a manic depressive. I do not think he ever really accepted the Fabian notion of the 'inevitability of gradualness' (the phrase is Sidney Webb's); much more did he see himself as one who had a rendezvous with Death at some disputed barricade. But he joined the Fabians because they were at least doing *something* about it and because their purity of motive appealed to his idealistic spirit. W. Bridges Admas, who knew him, though never on terms of great intimacy, for over thirty years, thought that Barker's political interests were really only a species of self-delusion and that the real motive power lay elsewhere. In a letter[10] to W.A. Darlington, the theatre critic, written on May 12, 1962, Bridges Adams says: 'He may have kidded himself that he felt deeply about politics, but he was an artist with Italian blood in his veins, and I think he would have embraced any creed that served his turn.' This seems to me to over-simplify the matter. It is a welcome corrective to Margery M. Morgan's view that Barker's art was founded upon and almost wholly shaped by political concepts and a political sense, but it leans too far in the contrary direction in suggesting that his interest in practical politics was a mere device designed to serve his own ends as an artist. His art and his politics sprang from the same root, but there was nothing calculating in the relationship between them: rather the reverse; he was, if anything, precipitate in his responses. He was, if the paradox will hold up, a desperate Fabian.

But that was later: in 1901 he joined the Society in good faith and, although busy with his own profession of acting, was prepared to do his share of the donkey-work. A little later, he was to become close to the Fabian Society in another, more literal, sense: when he married Lillah McCarthy in 1906, their first London home together was an apartment at 3, Clement's Inn, the building in which the Society had in 1899 established its offices in two rooms in the basement.

In January of 1902, while still playing in *Becky Sharp* at the Prince of Wales's Theatre, Barker got his first chance to direct one of his own plays. *The Marrying of Ann Leete* was given two performances at the Royalty Theatre under the auspices of the Stage Society and slightly earlier in the same month he was also acting for the Society, playing the part of Frank in two performances (January 5 and 6) of Shaw's *Mrs. Warren's Profession* at the New Lyric Club. This was his fourth Shaw part in the space of eighteen months or so, all of them acted under the direction of Shaw himself. Later in the year he played Osric in a Johnston Forbes-Robertson production of *Hamlet* which was presented for six special matinée performances in July at the Lyric Theatre where, in the evenings, Forbes-Robertson was appearing with Gertrude Elliott in a play called *Mice and Men*. Forbes-Robertson was always one of Barker's heroes: nearly twenty years later, in a letter[11] to Helen Huntington, he said: 'Forbes, when I was first in the theatre, was one of my demi-gods – unapproachable – and to this day I have the old feeling, "What an honour to be spoken to by him!" And when he asks my advice . . .!' The noteworthy feature about all of this activity is that, quite apart from his up-to-now more or less private aspirations as a dramatist and apart, too, from his emerging sense of public conscience, he was during these years continuously working as an actor. Much of this work was artistically insubstantial, but as training in the particular craft of acting and in the general sense of the theatre it was invaluable. Of all the dramatists of his period, Granville Barker is the only one who had had real experience on the stage. It stood him in good stead in his play-writing; his dialogue is lithe and supple, eminently speakable. His own claim was probably a justifiable one when he said to Archer in a letter written on September 22, 1923: 'I protest I never have – *I cannot* –

write an unactable play; it would be against nature, against second nature anyhow: I act it as I write it.'

He did some further work for the Stage Society during 1903 but, much more important, he played again for the Elizabethan Stage Society (a quite different organization) under William Poel's direction and he began the writing of *The Voysey Inheritance*. The Elizabethan Stage Society production was Marlowe's *Edward II*, presented at the New Theatre, Oxford, on August 10, 1903; Barker played the title rôle. It was, Robert Speaight tells us (*op. cit.*, p. 179), the first production of the play since its author's death in 1593. Poel was always adventurous in this regard: two years before *Edward II* he had re-discovered and produced for the first time since the Middle Ages the morality play of *Everyman*, making up a stage script from the manuscript text in the library of Lincoln Cathedral. Indeed, the theatre's debt to Poel is not confined to his revolutionizing theatrical thinking about the staging of Shakespeare but includes also his restoring to the living stage several great standard works such as these. His casting of Barker as Edward, after the latter's success as Richard II, was an obvious and natural thing to do and Barker proved, in the event, no disappointment. It is worth noting in passing, however, how peculiarly apt both of these parts must have been for an actor of Barker's temperament. Richard and Edward are both men who have been thrust, if not against their desires certainly against their temperaments, into blazingly public lives; and both have a marked capacity for retreating into secret kingdoms within the long-corridored silences of their own minds. It is little wonder that the sensitive and poetic Barker found a ready sympathy with each of them and was able to convey that sympathy to the audience. 'His performance,' says Speaight, 'was subtle, scholarly and sensitive, though inaudible in the final scenes'; and C.B. Purdom (op. cit., p. 17) quotes *The Pilot* of August 15, 1903, as saying: 'Mr. Granville Barker, one of the very cleverest of the younger generation, deserves much praise for his careful study of the King . . . He does not so much show physical suffering itself as the effect which intense physical suffering often produces on the mind . . .' Desmond MacCarthy was to say rather similar things about Barker's playing (for the second time) of Eugene Marchbanks in *Candida* the following year. He was obviously that kind of quiveringly vital actor who automatically shows an audience the *inner* life of the character; and he was, equally obviously, the kind of man who lives the bigger – and the better – part of his own life inside his own head.

There is no direct relationship between *Edward II* and *The Voysey*

Inheritance, except the relationship of seriousness of artistic purpose and the originality and sensitivity which informed Barker's performing of the one and writing of the other. The more direct antecedents of *Voysey* lie in *Agnes Colander* and it is this connection which one should bear in mind in beginning to think about the later play. The comparison is wholly to the advantage of *The Voysey Inheritance*, in which the touch is much more assured, the integration of the parts into the whole more thoroughly accomplished – though this is not to deny the virtues already ascribed to the earlier play.

In many ways, *The Voysey Inheritance* is the least typical of all Barker's plays. Though it has some things – and one very important thing – in common with all his work, it also has some things – and one very important one – at variance with the other plays. The main factor which it holds in common with the others is the defence of integrity by secret-ness. It not only shows us the inner life of its central character – any play of worth does that – but it shows that character as being more and more aware, as the play progresses, of the absolute necessity for keeping that life separate from the world and for living it alone and in secret, if its essential nature is to be preserved. The chief variant factor is the absence, in all but a tangential sense, of any treatment of the sexual element: unlike all the rest of Barker's plays, sex is not the mainspring of *The Voysey Inheritance*. It is not ignored and it certainly is not deliberately avoided by the play, but it does not stand at this play's heart in the way it does at the heart of the other plays.

The central issue, the poised dichotomy which provides the play with its main structure, is a balancing of forces between the personal, private idealism which longs for an absolute right, a moral imperative, and the inevitable compromises and half-measures that belong quite unavoidably to the murky transactions of everyday living. The pattern of the play is rich and complicated but all its parts are illuminated by this central theme and they, in turn, give life and authority to it. Its sense, sometimes explicitly expressed, sometimes left to be inferred or to seep into the consciousness of a scene unobserved and unsuspected, is everywhere in the play. 'Fine feelings, my dear, are as much a luxury as clean gloves', says Beatrice to Alice (in the second and third versions of the play: more must be said later about Barker's prodigal habit of writing the same play three times over). And, in another scene, the following exchange occurs:

EDWARD: Alice . . . there's something else I could do.
ALICE: What?

EDWARD   It's illegal.
ALICE: So much the better, perhaps. Oh, I'm lawless by birthright, being a woman.

The natural law, learned by instinct, is seen as superior to man-made statute; the personal perception of moral rectitude is more to be trusted than the conventions of the community or the rules laid down and spelled out by society. But in a later scene between Alice and Edward, she says: 'I understand this temptation to neglect and despise practical things. But if one yields to it one's character narrows and cheapens. That's a pity . . . but it's so.' So, although one should trust one's own sense of rightness, one should not make this an excuse for retreating from the world. Ignore its pronouncements and its chicanery; but do not ignore the world itself. 'Oh, Edward, be a little proud of humanity . . . take your share in it gladly. It so discourages the rest of us if you don't', says Alice towards the end of the final Act (in versions 1 & 2; not in version 3). And the dilemma applies to other characters as well as Edward. The stage direction which introduces Beatrice (Hugh's wife) to us in Act II (in all three versions) says: *'Beatrice is as hard as nails and as clever as paint. But if she keeps her feelings buried pretty deep it is because they are precious to her; and if she is impatient with fools it is because her own brains have had to win her everything in the world, so perhaps she does overvalue them a little.'* And this is not a character speaking but, so to say, the play itself, committing itself to its conviction of the power of and the necessity for the secret life. 'It is surprising', says Margery M. Morgan, 'how often the fact that *The Voysey Inheritance* is primarily a political drama has been overlooked.' (*op. cit.*, p. 89) Miss Morgan goes on to set out an argument which seeks to link *The Voysey Inheritance* with Book I of Plato's *Republic* and Ruskin's *The Crown of Wild Olive*. I must confess that I find her case more ingenious than convincing; and unless one gives to the word 'political' so broad a definition that it ceases to have any particularity of meaning at all, I find it difficult to regard *The Voysey Inheritance* as 'primarily a political drama'. I would, in fact, go further and say that this play is primarily – indeed, almost wholly – a non-political drama, a drama of the private conscience and, so far as it has any political consciousness at all, it is an anti-political play.

Its plot concerns a lawyer who for many years has made a fat living by cheating his clients, using money from trust accounts to speculate in stocks and shares and then taking the winnings, when there were any, for himself. By the exercise of financial wizardry and sleight of hand he has managed to cover his traces, using money from one client's funds to pay debts on another's on those occasions when, in the normal course of business, capital was called in for one reason or another. But the result has inevitably been that, while he has managed throughout the years to pay all his clients the interest which was due to them, in many cases the capital has been 'borrowed', dissipated and no longer exists. At the beginning of the play, he is found breaking the news of the firm's true position to Edward, his son and partner, who will succeed Mr. Voysey as head of the firm on the latter's death. The firm has always enjoyed a solid reputation for impeccable business behaviour and Edward is shattered by his father's revelations. At first he refuses to have anything to do with the matter and announces his intention of leaving the firm. His father manages to persuade him to stay on by pleading that such a step would bring ruin and suffering to a lot of innocent people, including the members of his own immediate family and by pointing out that the decision now facing Edward is the same decision that he himself faced when *his* father died, for the fraud had been passed on from father to son once before. It was not Edward's father who originated it, but his grandfather. Edward's father feels no shame at all in the matter; rather the reverse – through his own financial acumen he has managed to avoid a crash and has preserved the fortunes of his firm and his family by so doing. He feels that his son Edward is deserting his responsibilities, being selfish and cowardly, by refusing to continue the work of reclamation (as he sees it to be). Reluctantly, Edward agrees to stay on and keep quiet, but on the understanding that he will take no part in the current defalcations. A year later, old Mr. Voysey dies and Edward is left as the head of the firm. He immediately calls the family together and tells them the whole truth and says he proposes to turn over the firm's books to the authorities, admit the guilt and stand trial. He points out also that the various bequests which the family is expecting from Mr. Voysey's will cannot be paid, since the funds which stand in Mr. Voysey's name were not rightfully his and therefore must now be applied to the liquidation of some of the firm's debts.

The rest of the play is taken up with the different reactions of various members of the family to the challenge presented by Edward and with the change and growth in Edward's own character in response to the situation as it develops. The Voysey family consists of four sons and two daughters, Edward being the youngest-but-one of the sons and the only unmarried one. Neither sister is married when the play starts; Ethel marries between Act II and Act III and dies in childbirth between Act III and Act IV. Honor remains unmarried and keeps her place throughout the play as the family drudge. There is, additionally, a cousin, called Alice Maitland, who spends a good deal of time with the family at the family home in Chislehurst. Edward has, in the past, several times asked Alice to marry him but she has always refused him. It is Alice who, after the family has stormed and shuffled and in effect declined to give Edward any assistance in clearing up the mess, persuades him to abandon his rigid principles for the sake of a more immediate good, even if only a partial one. At her suggestion Edward agrees to continue the concealment of the firm's defalcations, in the hope that he can gradually, secretly, put things right, at least with the smaller accounts. He succeeds, in fact, in doing so with some of them; but after eighteen months the inevitable happens – old George Booth, the long-time family friend after whom one of the Voysey sons is named, the wealthy bachelor whose private fortune has always been managed and looked after by the Voysey firm, decides to withdraw his funds and take his business elsewhere. He does this not because he has any suspicions as to the true state of affairs but because he dislikes Edward personally and this leads him, quite irrationally, to mistrust Edward's judgment in business matters. The withdrawal of so large an account would precipitate the crisis that Edward has both feared and longed for and he is forced to tell George Booth that a great part of his money has gone. With relief he invites Booth to prosecute, but Booth has a more wily remedy: he will take all that Edward can give him immediately and then, holding the threat of exposure constantly over him, will blackmail Edward into continuing the firm's false life behind a respectable front but now with all the profits being devoted to Booth's account instead of being spread out over all the deficits. Edward scornfully repudiates this and determines once again to disclose the whole matter to the police; and once again it is Alice who persuades him to avoid this, not by surrendering to George Booth's blackmail but by convening a meeting of *all* the clients whose money is involved, informing them of the true position and soliciting for their co-operation. And in the same conversation, while urging Edward to this course, Alice also asks him to marry her. This is where the play leaves them. Barker, wisely, does not finish with a scene of splendid heroics and glib triumph. The main practical issue – the 'smash' – about which the characters have talked throughout the play, remains still unresolved and unrevealed at the end of the play, for the very good reason that, so far as dramatic resolution is concerned, it is not an issue at all: it is merely a mechanism, a means to an end. The achieving of the necessary dramatic equipoise lies elsewhere, namely with the joint realization by Edward and Alice that by subtlety, patience and constant vigilance a balance can be struck between the intensity and purity of the inner life on the one hand and the rough vitality of the ordinary, surface, everyday, communal existence on the other: and this realization carries with it two others – first, that such a balance must be struck, that both sides of the equation are needed if the equation is to make any sense; and secondly, that just occasionally, for a little while, the secret life can sometimes be shared.

ALICE: You couldn't call them all together . . . get them round a table and explain? They won't all be like Mr. Booth and the Vicar. Couldn't we bargain with them to let us go on?

The 'we' and the 'us' come naturally

EDWARD: But . . . heavens above . . . I don't want to go on. You don't know what the life has been.

ALICE: Yes, I do. I see when I look at you. But it was partly the fear, wasn't it . . . or the hope . . . that this would happen. Once it's all open and above-board . . .! Besides . . . you've had no other life. Now there's to be ours. That'll make a difference.

But perhaps, in spite of its slightly cloying flavour and its faint atmosphere of quaintness and heroics, the earlier version (1905 and 1913) of this moment actually catches the sense of the play better:

EDWARD: If they could all meet and agree, they might syndicate themselves and keep me at it for life.

ALICE: What more could you wish for?

EDWARD: Than that dreary round!

ALICE: My dear, the world must be put tidy. That's the work which splendid criminals leave for us poor commonplace people to do.

EDWARD (*with a little laugh*): And I don't believe in Heaven either.

ALICE (*close to him*): But there's to be our life. What's wrong with that?

EDWARD: My dear, when they put me in prison for swindling – (*he makes the word sound its worst*)

ALICE: I think they won't. But if they are so stupid . . . I must be very careful.

EDWARD: Of what?

ALICE: To avoid false pride. I shall be foolishly proud of you.

EDWARD: It's good to be praised sometimes . . . by you.

ALICE: My heart praises you. Good night.

EDWARD: Good night.

Barker has made the young woman – as Shakespeare often did – wiser and more balanced, more in touch with the heart of the true world, than the young man. But it is in Edward's progress towards a state of grace that the movement of the play resides; it is the development and maturing of his character which gives the play its forward thrust and momentum. In the course of that development he moves from a simple, rather priggish position of self-contained virtue and moral principle to a tacit acceptance of Alice's 'lawlessness', the essentially anarchical position of having the courage to defend one's own spiritual territory in one's own way and on one's own terms.

Around this central figure (and in spite of her importance as a catalyst Alice is not drawn fully enough to be considered a part of a central group of two) Barker has assembled a number of striking portraits. Not only are they brilliantly observed and equally brilliantly realized, but their relationships to each other are finely judged and the whole picture is assembled with a tautness, a sense of over-all balance and an economy of means which Barker achieved only once again (in *Waste*). Edward's three brothers, Trenchard, Booth and Hugh, are particularly well done: Trenchard the cold-as-ice egotist, a precise, pedantic barrister with brains but no imagination; Booth the booming, pompous, conventional, assinine Army man; Hugh the over-sensitive but fecklessly irresponsible artist. And brooding through the play, even after his death, is the figure of the father of these – Old Voysey, a slightly-larger-than-life robber baron drawn with theatrical gusto but never caricatured. One of the marks of Barker's skill, superiority and maturity as a dramatist in this play is the way he constantly resists the temptation to reduce his characters to the over-simplified, black-and-white terms of melodrama. The humanizing details are lovingly touched in, making it impossible to treat the characters simply as lay figures in a pre-determined good-versus-bad moralizing tale. Old Voysey is one of the best examples of this: he is a quirky, three-dimensional person, with inconsistencies like the rest of us, fond of his home and his family – for whom he has, in his sense of the word, worked hard; and absolutely devoted to his wife, as she is to him. They have had a marvellously full and happy life together. Neither has any regrets.

Barker uses all this with tremendous irony throughout the play, keeping the ambivalences always before us. At the family conference immediately after Mr. Voysey's death, Mrs. Voysey admits that she has known for years of the state of her husband's business affairs but has kept closely hidden from him, so as not to humiliate him or challenge his dignity, the fact that she knew what was going on. And Edward discovers, in a conversation with Peacey, the firm's chief clerk (whose father passed on to him the secret of how Voysey & Co. was run and who for years has drawn hush money from Old Voysey) that Voysey, having inherited the tampered-with accounts from *his* father, had succeeded once in putting everything to rights, getting all the accounts in order and had then, for no reason other than his own natural gambler's instinct, begun the whole practice (or, rather, malpractice) over again after an interval of several years, (fifteen in the first two versions of the play; six in the third version.)

The Voysey Inheritance is remarkable for the deftness with which Barker positions these pieces of information from the past (he quite consciously and deliberately studied and imitated Ibsen's methods in this); he is able, by this device, to keep Old Voysey living in our imaginations after his death, in the same way as he lives in the memories of his sons and daughters. The feat is a remarkable one. It is also a very necessary one for the play's structural health, since the growing dramatic and moral force of Edward's developing character requires the counter-balancing force of Old Voysey's buccaneering amorality to keep the central column of the play upright and steady. Dramaturgically, the other family characters are not there merely to fill in the background and give authenticity to the picture (though Barker's command of realistic detail in this regard is astonishing) but are there to provide variant responses to the central issue. Trenchard, the oldest son, who quarrelled with his father years ago, has rejected the problem outright: the search for an absolute, though he understands it, has no interest for him since it does not address itself to the immediate issue (for him) of professional success and advancement. Lawyers should be honest, in his point of view; but only because he would hate to be taking part in a competition in which the rules were unknown or set at defiance. Edward's dourly naïve response when first confronted with the issue – 'But it's *wrong*' – has no real meaning for Trenchard. Booth, the second son, protected from any qualms or uneasiness by an invincible stupidity, solves the problem by believing that it does not exist: there is for him no clash between the inner longing for a divine order of rightness and the outer anarchy of greed, selfishness and cupidity, because he quite fails to recognize the bases of society in their true colours and perspective. Gentlemanly society seems to him not only well organized and workable but worthy, laudable and desirable. He grants that his father has broken the rules, but he sees nothing symptomatic, much less symbolic, in the

fact: it is an isolated case, a mere exception to the general pattern. The
pattern itself is good: society is sound: the natural nobility, for which
Edward longs, seems to Booth to be there quite automatically in man's
everyday intercourse, everything clear and obvious and on the surface
for all to see. (The character does not *say* these things – it's a play, not a
debate or a moral discourse – but these are the implications of the
character and of his position in the play.) The most sensitive response and
the one closest to Edward's, is that of Hugh, the youngest son. He is an
artist, filled with an artist's disgust at the tawdriness and chicanery of the
world, raging over his own helplessness either to remedy it or escape
from it. The difference between him and Edward subsists in Hugh's lack
of development or growth. I do not mean that the playwright has failed
dramaturgically: to the contrary, he has succeeded brilliantly in portray-
ing the kind of character who never does develop or grow, in whom the
potential for growth is not present, the sort of person whose early,
instinctive responses, sensitive and real and true, nevertheless fail to
develop the fibre needed to give them any more substance than that of an
angry dream. (Interestingly, the character of Hugh is – along with the
Edward/Alice scenes – the part of the play most re-written by Barker in
his two revisions of the play. Barker was obviously especially interested
in the posture of the artist and was anxious to get it right. The general
drift of his revision of Hugh's speeches, in common with his alterations
to other parts of the play, is toward a more muted, less declamatory style:
and in the case of the character of Hugh, the addition of a certain wry
acceptance of the world and of his own weakness in facing it.)

Of the women in the play the most important, after Alice, is Beatrice.
Like her husband, she is an artist (he is a painter; she is a novelist); unlike
him, she has wit and balance and determination. When they finally agree
to separate, she sums up the situation neatly by saying: 'Hugh's tragedy
is that he is just clever enough to have found himself out . . . and no
cleverer'; and when the foolish Booth blusters and tries to bully her, she
deftly parries:

BOOTH   (*magnanimous but stern*): I will be frank. You have never made
            the best of Hugh.
BEATRICE: No . . . at the worst it never came to that.

This comes from the third version and is an improvement on the first
two, in which Beatrice's reply is: 'I have spared him that indignity'. The
change is typical of the general tendency of the revision: a dryer tone,
more irony, less moral outrage. Gerald Weales has argued, in his

Introduction to his anthology called *Edwardian Plays*[12], that Barker was too prone to revision and that the plays suffered, rather than gained, in consequence. I doubt it. Certainly the point is, at best, debatable, by no means a self-evident, foregone conclusion; and in the case of *The Voysey Inheritance* even less to be taken for granted than in the case of the revisions of *Waste* and *The Madras House*. The third version of *Voysey*, while not altering the general thrust of the play or reducing its stature in any way, does seem to me to have improved upon the original by giving it a dryer tone and a sharper focus. We could use Beatrice again to demonstrate the point. Here is a brief passage between her and Edward towards the end of Act V:

1. *Text of 1913* (which follows the original of 1903–05 except for very minor alterations – all improvements – of odd words within the speeches)

EDWARD	(*with sudden excitement*): Do you know what I found out the other day about (*he nods at the portrait of his father*) . . . about him?
BEATRICE	(*inquiring calmly*): What?
EDWARD:	He saved his firm once. That was true. A pretty capable piece of heroism. Then, fifteen years afterwards . . . he started again.
BEATRICE	(*greatly interested*): Did he now?
EDWARD:	It can't have been merely through weakness . . .
BEATRICE	(*with artistic enthusiasm*): Of course not. He was a man of imagination and a great financier. He had to find scope for his abilities or die. He despised these fat little clients living so snugly on their fattening little incomes . . . and put them and their money to the best use he could.
EDWARD	(*shaking his head solemnly*): Fine phrases for robbery.

BEATRICE *turns her clever face to him and begins to follow up her subject keenly.*

BEATRICE:	But didn't Hugh tell me that your golden deed has been robbing your rich clients for the benefit of the poor ones?
ALICE	(*who hasn't missed a word*): That's true.
EDWARD	(*gently*): Well, we're all a bit in debt to the poor, aren't we?
BEATRICE:	Quite so. And you don't possess and your father didn't possess that innate sense of the sacredness of property . . . (*she enjoys that phrase*) which mostly makes your merely honest man. Nor did the man possess it who picked my pocket last Friday week . . . nor does the tax gatherer . . . nor do I.

2. *Text of 1934*

EDWARD:	D'you know what I think I've found out about him now.
BEATRICE:	Something interesting, I'm sure.
EDWARD:	He did save my grandfather and the firm from a smash. That was true. A pretty capable piece of heroism! Then . . . six years after . . . he started on his own account . . . cheating again. I suppose he found himself in a corner . . .
BEATRICE	(*psychologically fascinated*): Not a bit of it! He did it deliberately. One day when he was feeling extra fit he must have said to himself: Why not? Well, here goes! You never understood your father. I do . . . it's my business to.
EDWARD:	He was an old scoundrel, Beatrice, and it's sophistry to pretend otherwise.
BEATRICE:	But he was a bit of a genius too. You can't be expected to appreciate that. It's tiresome work, I know . . . tidying up after these little Napoleons. He really did make money, didn't he, besides stealing it?
EDWARD:	Lord, yes! And I daresay more than he stole. An honest two thousand a year from the firm. He had another thousand . . . and he spent about ten. He must have found the difference somewhere.
BEATRICE:	There you are, then. And we all loved him. You did, too, Alice.
ALICE:	I adored him.
EDWARD:	He was a scoundrel and a thief.
ALICE:	I always knew he was a scoundrel of some sort. I thought he probably had another family somewhere.
BEATRICE:	Oh . . . what fun! Had he, Edward?
EDWARD:	I fancy not.

Notice particularly the improvement in the one speech of Beatrice's in which she voices her admiration for Old Voysey's toughness and spirit. How much more vivid is her 'One day when he was feeling extra fit . . .' than the earlier 'He was a man of imagination and a great financier . . .'; though it is a pity to lose, in the final version, her speech on the sacredness of property. But the general tone of the 1934 version is better over-all: clearer, sharper, free of the tendency which the first version of the scene has to 'go soft' at some moments.

The Voysey Inheritance has widely come to be regarded as the best and most typical of Barker's plays. In fact it is neither, though it *is* very fine. I suspect that its position of pre-eminence among his plays, in the popular mind, is due to its being the most accessible, so far as subject-matter is concerned, the most 'ordinary', if you will. In a sense, its plot and characters are so good, the details of them so accurate and so instantly recognizable, that they have tended to obscure the deeper purposes and greater scope of the play. Early critics tended to dwell on the social portraiture angle and this very quickly became the generally-accepted estimate of the play's chief virtue. Characteristic of this view is the comment made by Fred Kerr, in his autobiographical *Recollections of a Defective Memory* (London: Thornton Butterworth, 1930). Kerr was one of the two actors who played old Mr. Voysey at the Court Theatre: the part was played originally by A.E. George when the play was presented for six matinées in November, 1905. When it was put into the evening bill for a four-week run, in February 1906, there were several changes of cast (including the taking-over of the part of Edward by Barker himself); it was at this point that Kerr, who was with the company principally to play Brassbound in the revival of *Captain Brassbound's Conversion*, took over the part of Mr. Voysey. About it he says in his book (p. 177): 'Old Voysey was a delightful old rascal – the sort of man you may see any morning getting out of the train at Waterloo with a geranium in his buttonhole, thoroughly respectable and respected, prosperous and opulent, and probably a churchwarden in his own suburban parish. It was one of those curious parts which bring the actor into a kind of friendly intimacy with many of his audience. Everyone seemed to know old Voysey and to have met him . . .' Even Desmond MacCarthy, perceptive critic though he was, saw *The Voysey Inheritance* chiefly in terms of realistic verisimilitude: 'Its second great merit', he says in *The Court Theatre, 1904–1907* (London: A.H. Bullen, 1907), 'is the vividness with which a large family is presented, each member of which is a distinct character.' And he sees as the play's only real defect the fact that the *story* isn't properly finished: 'The interest of the author has been centred entirely on the moral development of the hero, and the growth in him of a new way of life, with the consequence that when this has been accomplished subsequent developments do not appear to the dramatist important. Still, the audience would like to know whether old Booth did prosecute or not; and the fact that the curtain falls at a juncture which rouses curiosity instead of satisfying it is a defect.' (*op. cit.*, pp. 28–29). Ashley Dukes, in his book *Modern Dramatists* (London: Frank Palmer, 1911) takes the same line: 'The play is chiefly remarkable for its extraordinarily vivid portrait of an English middle-class family. Its appearance was a landmark in realist drama.' (p. 137) All these comments suffer from the same fault: they can't see the forest because of the trees. William Archer, in a passage which C.B. Purdom describes as the 'best description of the play's impact', tends to make the same mistake. 'I submit that, in *The Voysey Inheritance*, we have an English family group presented with a mastery of draughtmanship and a depth of colour that remind us of a canvas of Rembrandt or Franz Hals . . .' The statement is true and the praise not undeserved: the danger is in the constant over-emphasis on surface portraiture, mere sociological observation. The passage in question is to be found on p. 129 of *The Old Drama and the New* (London: Heinemann, 1923)[13] and has an interesting and revealing codicil: 'while at the same time the dramatic movement is sustained with subtle and original art . . .' That grand Archerian phrase, 'subtle and original art' is not mere bombast; yet Archer makes no attempt anywhere to define the subtlety or originality; he does not try to explain in what, to him, the 'art' lay. The truth is, I think, that his admiration is perfectly genuine; he felt the size and the power of the play but did not really understand it. He makes the point himself, in another part of this book, that *The Voysey Inheritance* was the first Barker play which he *had* been able to understand. He had read the manuscripts of all its predecessors; he had seen two of them on stage: 'At last, tired of writing plays which were Hebrew to me,' he says of their author, 'he declared he would write down to my intelligence . . .' Somehow, the opinion stuck: *The Voysey Inheritance* was easier than the other Barker plays; it had things more recognizable in it. The view has tended to be perpetuated since and Barker's plays are played so rarely that the chances for first-hand re-evaluation are scant. By the time Archer published *The Old Drama and the New*, within eighteen months of his death, his relationship with Barker was one of very long-standing friendship. They visited each other's homes; they constantly exchanged letters about their work, about plays, about lectures, about books. Archer's respect for Barker was unbounded and he fully recognized Barker's stature as a dramatist, though he never succeeded in defining in what that stature subsisted. (He is charmingly modest – and accurate! – in a letter in which he compares his own simple-minded melodrama, *The Green Goddess*, with Barker's *The Secret Life*.) On p. 358 of *The Old Drama and the New*, he says – talking of the first performance of *The Voysey Inheritance* – 'The high opinion of Mr. Barker's talent which I there and then conceived was more than confirmed when *Waste* was produced in 1907 and *The Madras House* in 1910. I do not hesitate to say that I consider these three plays the biggest things our modern movement has produced . . . each of them is a dramatic creation of the first order.' Yet this was written at about the same time as a lengthy (and fascinating) exchange of letters between him and Barker about *The Secret Life* (which Barker had just at that time finished writing) in which Archer rather plaintively admits that he does not really understand what is going on in the play, though he feels that whatever it is, is sizeable and important. This often-reiterated plaint of Archer's, of finding Barker's plays too subtle, too 'intellectual', too difficult, though directed more particularly against such plays as *The Marrying of Ann Leete* and *The Secret Life*, really applied also to those 'realistic' plays which he thought he *did* understand. He missed, I think, much of their inner significance and right to the end he tended to praise them for the wrong reasons.

Amid this stampede to get *The Voysey Inheritance* firmly ticketed and tidily filed away as a 'realistic play' there appeared, some nine years after its production, one very interesting exception among contemporary criticism. It was in a wittily elegant article[14] in *The Bookman* (the British monthly, not the American one of the same name) in 1914. The article considers four of Barker's plays: *Ann Leete, Voysey, Waste* and *The Madras House*. In relation to the second of these, having quoted the long descriptions, from the beginnings of Act I and Act II, of the Office of Voysey and Son and of the Voysey dining-room at Chislehurst, the article says:

Decidedly, this looks like Reality. No expense has been spared; that is to say, no economy. . . . This is undeniably a nineteenth-century interior. That is an unmistakable top-hat. These are certainly the red-papered walls of old England. And yet – there is something queer about it all. There is a certain strangeness in the air, a lack of nitrogen, a disconcerting quality of dream. If that hat of Mr. Voysey's suddenly began quietly turning somersaults on its little red-curtained shelf, we would not feel tremendously surprised. For in the accentuated realism of these rooms, there is something oddly like the bright veracity of the streets of shops in harlequinade; and although the characters all apparently behave with the most absolute naturalness, we watch them as though they were figures moving in a void. Why should this be so? What invalidates the atmosphere? What can make a grained oak sideboard seem bizarre? Well, put quite simply, it is because these rooms are haunted. There is a skeleton in that sideboard. The characters are under a spell . . . The true Voysey inheritance is something far more fateful that the black bequest that burdens Edward. And it is this lurking legacy, of which they never speak, that secretly moves their minds and plucks their limbs.'

The article goes on to explain that the ghostly influence which pervades the play is the author's sense of vision and design, that we see the characters as themselves, we recognize their vitality and authenticity, but simultaneously we see (or sense and feel, rather than see) behind their reality a larger reality that explores the nature of all humanity. Of the working of artistry on the fabric of the play, the article has this to say: 'Given Mr. Barker's unconquerable flair for shapeliness; given too, his determination to deal with plain reality and 'facts'; we have still to explain why he should have let the first frustrate the second by devoting itself to the careful manufacture of this particularly metallic sort of plot.' And at another point in the argument the plot of the play is described as 'as neat as anything of Poe's or Maupassant's. As ingenious, as artificial, as 'romantic' as that – and therefore absolutely fatal as a mainspring meant to drive a middle-classical clock constructed to tell Chislehurst time with stolid truthfulness. You don't get 'realism' by merely changing centuries, by substituting a deed-box for duels; and it is a fact that if you only move its mahogany furniture aside, the whole of this play will be found to have been laid out as artificially as that seventeenth-century garden at Markswayde.'[15]

It should be borne in mind that 'art' and 'artifice' and 'artificial' are, despite the corruptions of their lay usages, conceptually – as well as semantically – linked; and, in this context, 'artificial' has no pejorative intent. This being granted, the *Bookman* article seems to me to come closer to the truth of *The Voysey Inheritance* than did any other critic of that period (or since, for that matter). Even Max Beerbohm, though he praised the play and obviously liked it, did not really get it right. 'It is always the most obvious and most promising themes that our playwrights most ostentatiously neglect. One of these themes is the fraudulent solicitor. Mr. Barker's mere choice of this theme is laudable . . .': the statement is not so much inaccurate as inadequate; it suggests, once again, that the critic is looking at, and for, the wrong things – surface things. Indeed, it is a little shocking to find a critic of Beerbohm's sensitivity and stature (and standing) referring to a fraudulent solicitor as a 'theme' at all. C.B. Purdom reflects the general critical trend with regard to the play when he says (*op. cit.*, p. 47): 'While the play showed Barker's skill in craftsmanship, it is extraordinarily dry in emotional content . . .' This is the received wisdom of the time and Purdom responds to it. He has, in fact, very few opinions which are genuinely his own where plays are concerned and seems to respond rather to their reputations than to their contents. It would have to be an extraordinarily bad performance, or a very careless reading, of *The Voysey Inheritance* that could give any credence to his statement. The play has authority and conviction and passion, but they are not deployed in obvious ways or devoted to commonplace causes.

It is worth noting, briefly, that the play had some immediate and direct descendants, whether consciously imitated from it or not. One thinks particularly of Githa Sowerby's *Rutherford and Son*, the play for which Bernard Shaw expressed such admiration, and of *Milestones*, by Arnold Bennett and Edward Knoblock. Both of these were first produced in 1912, only seven years after the first production of *The Voysey Inheritance*; both deal with succession and tradition in a family business. So, in a way, does Stanley Houghton's *The Younger Generation*, which also had its first London production in 1912, though it had previously been produced by B. Iden Payne at the Gaiety Theatre, Manchester, in 1910.

The Voysey Inheritance is – if we must wrestle to get tickets and names on living works of art – ironic comedy. It starts with the admirable extravagance – admirable but unsustainable – of an absolute statement; it moves through various stages of dramatic disequilibrium to a state of dramatic equilibrium, hard-won and finely poised. It reflects a complex sense of that segment of human experience which is prodded and prompted into being by the urge, partly intellectual and partly intuitive, towards moral purpose and moral commitment; it celebrates the anarchic moral assertions and moral claims of the individual soul, as opposed to divine decrees on the one hand and communal-political formulations on the other. Richard Ellman, in an essay called 'The Two Faces of Edward', catches much of the sense of it when he says: 'Granville Barker brings Edward Voysey to sudden maturity when, like the hero of that neo-Edwardian novel, *By Love Possessed*, he discovers the world is contaminated and that he may nonetheless act in it.'[16]

The writing of *The Voysey Inheritance* was begun in 1903, at about the time when Barker was playing Marlowe's *Edward II* for William Poel. When he started it he had no definite production plans in mind for it and no production facilities available to him. Both were to develop during 1904, alongside the gradual developing of the play itself, as a part of a much more important over-all development: two developments, in fact: both of the first importance. The first was the famous Barker-Vedrenne management at the Court Theatre; the second, which sprang from the first, was Barker's absolute conviction, which he kept to the end of his life, of the necessity for the theatre to be organized on a repertory basis, rather than a long-run basis, if serious drama of high quality both in its writing and its performance were to survive.

−4−

Director of Repertory

*E*arly in 1904 William Archer, who was already a firm admirer of his
work, recommended Barker for a job. It happened that J.H. Leigh,
a man of independent means with a great love for the theatre but little
talent, had taken the Court Theatre in Sloane Square, Chelsea, with the
intention of mounting a series of productions of Shakespeare plays.
Leigh's motives were mixed: he had recently married a pretty and
talented actress called Thyrza Norman and his venture at the Court was,
at least in part, designed to create parts for Miss Norman. But the
productions were not turning out as well as Leigh had hoped and Archer
suggested to him that, for the next one – which was to be *Two Gentlemen
of Verona* – Granville Barker be engaged and put in charge of the
production. Barker accepted the offer but persuaded Leigh to write into
the contract a clause which would permit Barker also to present six
matinée performances of Shaw's *Candida* at the Court during the run of
Two Gentlemen of Verona, thus enabling Barker to repeat, before a much
wider audience, his performance of Marchbanks which he had originally
done for the Stage Society in 1900. So in April of 1904 Barker directed
Two Gentlemen of Verona and played the part of Speed (not, as J.C.
Trewin aptly remarks in his *The Edwardian Theatre*[1], the most obvious
piece of casting in the world). Later in the same month the six matinées of
Candida began, and ran on into May, in which month Barker was
involved in another startling new project, perhaps the most important of
all his activities at that time. This was a production at the Lyric Theatre of
Gilbert Murray's new version of the *Hippolytus* of Euripides, which

Barker directed and in which he played the part of the Messenger. Barker had met Murray five years earlier when playing in *Carlyon Sahib* with Mrs. Patrick Campbell's company. An instant liking and affinity had sprung up between the two men and it was entirely natural – indeed, almost inevitable – that they should presently think of working together in the theatre, so perfectly complementary were their talents. Both were convinced that the classical Greek dramatist-poets could be treated as modern theatre playwrights and that their plays could, and should, be presented unashamedly as pieces of entertainment. The idea was a revolutionary one at the time: the Greek plays were performed even more rarely then than they are now – and never in an ordinary theatre context. The production of the *Hippolytus*, coinciding as it did with Barker's first, tentative connection with the Court Theatre, was to lead to important results. On June 5, 1904, just after the production was over, Barker, in London, wrote to Murray, in Oxford,[2] to ask to what address some costumes borrowed for the production should be returned. To this letter he added a postscript which said: 'J.H. Leigh has expressed himself bitten with the idea of doing Greek plays. Not a word – but let us talk anon.' That talk led to the idea of using the Court Theatre for a whole series of plays and that, in turn, led to the establishing of the Barker-Vedrenne management which began its operation in October, 1904, with a series of six matinée performances of the *Hippolytus* (substantially the same production which had been presented at the Lyric earlier in the year; there were one or two unimportant changes of cast but Barker again played the Messenger, Ben Webster was Hippolytus, Edyth Olive again played Phaedra and the Leader of the Chorus was again Tita Brand, the daughter of the formidable Wagnerian soprano, Marie Brema – who would the following year herself appear at the Court as Hecuba in *The Trojan Women*; disastrously, we gather from the Murray-Barker correspondence). It is usual to attribute the inception of the Barker-Vedrenne season at the Court to the influence of Shaw and, directly, to the production there in April 1904 of *Candida*, but this really was not the case. Though Shaw became vastly influential later, and though the effect of Shaw on Barker's work and of Barker on Shaw's can scarcely be over-estimated, the beginnings of the scheme sprang not from Shaw or Shaw's plays but from the direct influence of Gilbert Murray and his translations of Euripides. Some such idea had, in any case, been lurking in Barker's mind for some time: it needed only the stimulus of circumstances and the happy coincidence of *Hippolytus* with the Court productions of *Two Gentlemen of Verona* and *Candida* to give it practical substance. Barker had, in fact, written to Archer[3] on April 21, 1903 saying: 'Do you think there is anything in this idea? To take the Court Theatre for six months or a year and to run there a stock season of the uncommercial Drama: Hauptmann – Sudermann – Ibsen – Maeterlinck – Schnitzler – Shaw – Brieux, etc. Not necessarily plays untried in England. A fresh production every fortnight. The highest price five or six shillings . . . I think the working expenses could be kept to £250 a week. I would stake everything upon plays and acting – not attempt "productions".' A week later he wrote to Archer again on the same subject but in a different mood, now with the gloomy side of his nature uppermost: 'I have been meaning to write and thank you for coming and having that long talk with me. It is helpful to me in my impatience to get under the wing of your knowledge and experience sometimes. I don't think my "Court Theatre" scheme will come to anything and it is perhaps better that it should not.' We have no further documentary evidence on the subject, but it is safe to assume that in the year which elapsed between the writing of this letter and the invitation to produce Shakespeare at the Court the idea of making that little theatre a headquarters for a new kind of play and a new kind of approach must have come back to Barker's mind many times. No doubt, given his mercurial temperament, he approved it and disapproved it by turns; but the fact that he accepted with such alacrity the invitation when it came and immediately sought – and successfully, too – to use the Shakespeare production as a lever to put into motion the scheme he already had in mind for the Court Theatre clearly demonstrates the seriousness with which he treated the idea: it was his nerve that sometimes wavered about the matter, not his intellectual conviction. The offer of the use of the Court Theatre, combined with the incidence of *Hippolytus* and J.H. Leigh's sudden interest in producing Greek plays, clinched the argument. The Barker-Vedrenne management became a reality and went on to become a legend. For a little while now Barker was to look upon the directing of plays and the acting in plays as being at least as important to him as the writing of plays – but for a very special reason. He wanted to create (the thought appears many times in his letters and essays and speeches) a stage and an audience which would be worthy of the sort of play that he wanted to write and that he most admired in the writings of other dramatists. Even so, his own writing was never far from his mind. *The Voysey Inheritance* was probably not completed by the time the Barker-Vedrenne management began its operations. The published text of the play, in all its various editions, gives the date of composition as

1903–5 (though in a letter to St. John Ervine[4] written in 1923 Barker says 'I wrote The Voysey Inheritance before I went into management with Vedrenne: it was merely revised for production'). And towards the end of 1904 he collaborated with Laurence Housman in the writing of *Prunella; or, Love in a Dutch Garden*, especially for production in his first full season at the Court, though this was not really a full-scale writing project for Barker, since the dialogue is almost certainly all Housman's: Barker's contribution was probably the devising of the plot and the outlining of the characters.

At the Court, Barker was responsible for the choosing and casting of all the plays, for directing all of them except those by Shaw (who at that time always directed the first production of his plays himself) and for playing in some of them. (Actually, in the three years during which the venture lasted, Barker played eleven different parts, of which seven were leading parts in Shaw plays: this, in a total of thirty-two different productions, some of which were brought back into the repertory three and four times – more particularly the Shaw plays.) John Eugene Vedrenne was the business manager of the venture. He was J.H. Leigh's general manager at the Court Theatre and linked up with Barker when the latter came to the Court. Though his background and training were in commerce, he was sensitive and intelligent about the theatre and was genuinely interested in what Barker was trying to do. Without Vedrenne, certainly, Barker would not have lasted three months in management: his mind was too set upon getting each production just right, and providing for it exactly the right accoutrements, to stop to calculate whether there was enough money to pay for everything. Not that he wanted to make his productions ornate or physically opulent, but he had an exacting eye for the visual rightness of the stage and that could sometimes be as costly as opulence, even if the mode were artistically austere. Vedrenne's contribution to the joint venture was a very important one. Though the two men never became intimate friends, though they disagreed often and though there was often some friction and irritability in those disagreements, they each had a deep and firm respect for the talents of the other and both of them came to recognize the unique nature of the thing they had jointly conceived. During their first season (1904–05) the productions were mounted in the afternoons, while the theatre's own regular programme continued in the evenings. Each production was given, initially, six performances, usually in the space of two weeks. By May, 1905 one or two of the most successful and most popular plays (almost always Shaw) were brought back for runs of three

The presentation studio portrait, in sepia, which Barker gave to Lillah McCarthy at the time of the production of Man and Superman *in 1905. The inscription reads: 'To "Ann" in ransom from "John Tanner". To Miss McCarthy in comradeship from H. Granville Barker'.*

weeks in the evenings, while the new productions still occupied the
matinée slots. And for the second and third seasons, Barker and
Vedrenne took over the evening programme completely, as well as the
afternoons, presenting tried items from their repertory in the evenings
and new productions in the afternoons. A play that did well in its initial
matinée performances was brought back a little later on and offered as
the evening fare: one that seemed artistically unsatisfactory, or very
unpopular, or both, got its initial six matinée performances but no more.
The range of plays was enormous – from *Votes for Women!*, by Elizabeth
Robins to Ibsen's *Hedda Gabler*; and from two new comedies by St. John
Hankin (*The Return of the Prodigal* and *The Charity that Began at Home*) to
three translations of Euripides by Gilbert Murray (*Hippolytus, Electra* and
Troades), as well as eleven Shaw plays (six of them for the first time on
any stage) and first plays by Galsworthy and Masefield.

As well as giving a sturdy and important voice to the 'serious' theatre
and placing a new and welcome emphasis on the playwright, Barker's
work at the Court introduced the repertory system to ordinary British
theatrical life and demonstrated the efficacy and desirability of it, indeed
the imperative necessity of it for theatre's survival as a serious art form. It
took over fifty years, from the time of his experiments with and
passionate advocacy of repertory, for the message to be grasped and the
lesson to be learned, but it is no exaggeration to say that the system on
which Britain's two major theatres, the National and the Royal
Shakespeare, are now run, is founded wholly on the work that Barker
did and the principles he enunciated at the Court Theatre between 1904
and 1907. He also did one other thing, during those three years at the
Court, which has had tremendous influence since: he invented – so far as
the English-speaking theatre, at least, is concerned – the director. He did
not call the position by that name; nor, at that time, did anyone else.
Indeed, the use of the word in that sense developed in the United States,
not in England, and was not general until the nineteen-fifties. But before
Barker's work at the Court Theatre, not only did the name not exist;
neither did the position and function. The idea that there should be one
person whose only job was to co-ordinate the functions of all the others,
to give pattern and coherence to the whole play, to conceive an over-all
interpretation of the piece which would faithfully reflect the author's
intention, was a new and revolutionary one in British theatre and it was
Granville Barker who first developed it. He was probably influenced in
his theatrical approach to this issue by the examples of George, Duke of
Saxe-Meiningen in Germany and André Antoine in France, though the

influence must have been a theoretical rather than practical one, since Barker had been neither to Germany nor France at the time he started at the Court Theatre and he could scarcely have seen the Meiningen Players when they visited Covent Garden, since he was then only four years old. The practical necessity for a director – given his views on the proper nature of plays and the theatre – he discovered for himself, empirically. It is significant, for example, as Anthony Jackson has pointed out[5], that when he began the Court Theatre experiment he was in the habit, quite often (though not invariably) of appearing in his own productions, as did every other producer in London at the time. The practice became progressively less frequent as the operation continued. In 1906 he relinquished his rôles in *Prunella, Hedda Gabler, You Never Can Tell* and *John Bull's Other Island* and in 1907 he did not play once, either in plays which he himself directed or in the Shaw plays directed by Shaw. He had discovered that acting and directing were two different, distinct and mutually exclusive artistic activities and in later years he articulated this idea many times in lectures, speeches, magazine articles and books. To us, now, it is a truism, almost a cliché, but that is only because we have absorbed so thoroughly the lesson which Barker has taught us. To him, and to the theatre of his time, it was an exciting new discovery. And Granville Barker was its discoverer. The example of Shaw was scarcely a parallel, since he directed only his *own* plays: he was there primarily as the author. Barker conceived the idea of being there, whatever the play or whenever it was written, as the author's representative, making sure that all the physical elements of the production, including the acting itself, remain faithful to the play and reflect the sense of experience which first moved the author to write the play. Margaret Webster, in her autobiographical *The Same Only Different* (London: Gollancz, 1969) tells a story which interestingly illustrates the difference between the old approach and the new and the impact of the latter on the former. She is talking about her mother, May Whitty[6], who played the part of Amelia Madras in the first production of *The Madras House* at the Duke of York's Theatre in 1910 under Barker's direction:

> Barker's methods, too, were different. She was trained for difficulty; she had rehearsed on trains or walking down the street with another actor, or while the stagehands were 'setting up', or not at all. She was prepared to 'go on' with only the most elementary direction in the matter of positions and business. But Barker would rehearse nowhere but on the stage itself.[7] (How on earth did the stagehands ever clear the last production and set up the next?) He was a stickler for absolute quiet; the smallest whisper drove him to a frenzy.

Moreover, he supplied the actors with a wealth of psychological background which May found fascinating but alarming. He didn't discuss the play at any length before the actors 'got on their feet'; the instruction was given as you went along. At the first rehearsal of May's first entrance in *The Madras House* he told her: 'From the moment you come in you must make the audience understand that you live in a small town in the provinces and visit a great deal with the local clergy; you make slippers for the curate and go to dreary tea-parties.' She realised the value of these admonitions. But she was used to working through the lines; and the line, in this case, was 'How do you do?'[8]

Note the stark difference in method between the old-fashioned, self-reliant, individualistic, essentially nineteenth-century actress and the probing, intellectual, essentially twentieth-century director. Note also the tone of faint scorn and derisiveness of the former for the latter.

The claim that Barker 'invented' both the position and the function of the director in the English theatre is a large one and should, perhaps, be examined a little further, not allowed merely to rest on a bare assertion. Didn't the great actor-managers 'direct' their productions – Irving, Alexander, Tree? And if one retorts that they were all actors who were merely arranging sympathetic backgrounds for their own performances, then what about Daly, who never himself appeared on any stage but certainly was the one who caused productions to happen? And did Garrick 'direct'? Kalman Burnim actually calls his 1961 study of him, *David Garrick, Director*. These challenges can be answered, I think. First, by pointing out that what Barker did was new in that he conceived the artistic direction of the piece as being (eventually) his *only* job. The financial responsibility lay elsewhere; the scenic and decorative responsibility lay elsewhere; the acting/performing responsibility lay elsewhere: Barker saw his job as the co-ordinating of all these elements in the light of an over-all concept designed to serve not the moment-by-moment effect but the total sense of experience imprisoned within the play as a whole, and he set about the achieving of this through the detailed use of rehearsals. It was the idea of a long (comparatively) series of rehearsals organised and conducted at every turn and at every moment by a *director*, without reference to star performers as star performers, which made Barker's approach unique. It is true that Daly, for example, made a production into an entity, as Barker did, and controlled it, director-fashion, from outside itself, so to speak; but he had none of Barker's respect for the text and no guiding principles except public appeal and a rather vulgar sense of showmanship. Barker, too, was – if report is to be believed – a great showman, but he placed showmanship at the service of an altogether finer and more serious sense of the world and of the theatre. Daly was a great craftsman and a great businessman, but he was an impresario, not a director. The two things are different. The same is true also of Irving, Tree, *et al.* They, too, were really impresarios, with themselves as their chief products: they existed (magnificently!) by the cleverness with which they double-guessed the public's whims and their ability to move so quickly and surely in response to those whims that they were able to give, at least in the short run, the impression of leading when they were really following. But their 'directing', so far as they did any at all (and one should not forget the *normal* rehearsal methods described by people like Margaret Webster and Cathleen Nesbitt – see, for example, pages 107 and 117 of this present book – who grew up under the old system), consisted either of the piecemeal teaching of skills to individual performers or of the organising of complicated traffic control systems. What Barker did with a play, though it embraced these sorts of skills as well, was not just a more thorough example of what had been done before: it was different in kind. What the actor-manager did in rehearsals, both in relation to the play and in relation to the other players, was really a simple extension of his own craft either as an actor or as a manager (and, snared by glamour, posterity has tended to overlook the managerial skill and to over-emphasize the acting skill): what Barker did, and uniquely did, was to invent a new craft. Even Professor Burnim, with the mighty Garrick as his examplar, succeeds only in demonstrating that Garrick did more by way of supervising rehearsals than was the common practice of the time. This demonstration, in *David Garrick, Director* (University of Pittsburgh Press, 1961), is immaculately done; it is extremely well-documented and entirely convincing – but it amounts to a good deal less than a proof that Garrick was a director in anything like the modern sense of the term. A good deal of the book is taken up with Garrick as actor (how *could* one write of Garrick otherwise?), as manager and as text-adaptor. About his rehearsals and his directorial practices Dr. Burnim tells us absolutely all there is to know, but it is far less than would be needed to establish Garrick as an early example of the director in the theatre.

The one real challenge to the idea of Barker as the first director, as such, in the English-speaking theatre comes when one considers the work of William Poel. Barker, as he himself was always happy to acknowledge and reiterate, learned much from Poel; and certainly Poel's sense of responsibility towards a play, and his main ideas about what function the producer/director should perform, were almost identical with Barker's. But he was far too erratic and unmethodical to practise as a professional director. He was essentially the pioneer, the discoverer, whose discoveries needed to be translated into regular, practical terms and built into a system by someone else: Barker was that someone. Not that he added nothing to Poel's original concept: on the contrary, he expanded it greatly. But his great contribution is that he made it into a craft that could be practised systematically and professionally. In other words, one could say that Barker did not precisely invent *directing*; but he invented the director, and certainly the professional director. The difference between him and Poel is hit off nicely by Barker himself in two comments he made in letters to Gilbert Murray. On June 5, 1904, he said:

> But now I've had the letter from Poel which I enclose (and I hope you can read it). I've told him that I see no reason Hippolytus shouldn't be toured so and that he'd better communicate with you direct. If I may advise, I wouldn't let him do it in London, for he may produce it in rather a cracked though clever way, not that this is so much a business reason as that there may well be a London revival in it as done just now. Also, I'd be very sharp over your contract with him, for Poel is one of those limpid-eyed enthusiasts who sacrifices himself body, soul and pocket to his cause, and expects and is absolutely unscrupulous in making everyone else do the same thing.

And on July 9 of the same year, still discussing with Murray the proposal that Poel should be allowed to produce the *Hippolytus* for a tour to various English cities (the production never materialized, in fact), Barker said:

> The only adequate reply to Poel is 'Skittles'. His system of payment may be Elizabethan but it won't do. It reminds one of 'Toe Master Murry for writting ye plaie VIII pence'.

(Both these letters are in the Murray Archive at the Bodleian Library)

Poel, in the final analysis, was a dreamer and a theorist. Barker, in spite of his own blazingly uncompromising idealism, was a practical theatre man. Poel conceived the idea of what the director ought to do; it was Barker who demonstrated how it could be done in the context of the professional theatre and how it could be permanently integrated with that profession. 'In any case,' says Robert Speaight in *William Poel and the Elizabethan Revival* (p. 274) 'Poel did not possess in a high degree the gift of communication. What he possessed was the gift of prophecy; the stark unbending truth proclaimed to the people who comprehended it not.'

The generality of people may not have comprehended it, but Granville Barker did, and quickly taught himself how to put that truth to practical effect. Moreover, he deliberately trained others to adopt and apply his methods and in some cases actually supervised their early productions at other theatres. This was the case, for example, with both Lewis Casson and B. Iden Payne at Miss Horniman's Gaiety Theatre in Manchester. And the same sense of consciously following in the master's footsteps applies to the early directorial work of Norman Marshall and to W. Bridges Adams and Harcourt Williams; perhaps even to Basil Dean in his work at the Gaiety and at the Liverpool Playhouse. Barker was starting a movement and knew that was what he was doing. And the new instrument of that new movement, devised and given organizational standing by Barker, was the director.

What Barker was doing in London in 1904–07 was very similar in general sense – and in some particulars – to what Stanislavsky was doing in Moscow. It is highly unlikely that either influenced the other directly at the time they were working out their ideas since neither had at that time published anything on their new 'methods' and they did not meet personally until 1914, when Barker paid a brief visit to Moscow. (Margaret Webster says, in another part of her book, that Lewis Casson told her that Barker went to Moscow in 1906, but I think this is an error. His time and activities in 1906 are fully accounted for and do not seem to include – so far as any documentation which I can trace shows – a visit to Moscow: indeed, that year was a particularly busy one for him, with eight new productions at the Court as well as several revivals of earlier productions and complicated planning for future productions, including Murray's translation of the *Medea*. 1906 was also the year in which he and Lillah McCarthy got married. His letters to Archer, Shaw and Murray for that year give a very complete picture of his activities, almost day-by-day, and make no mention of Moscow. There is, however, a letter from him to Archer written on February 14, 1914[9], in which he says: 'I will write to you from Moscow and burn a candle for you to St. Isaac.' And to Gilbert Murray on February 10, 1914[10] he wrote: 'I am off I think and hope about Saturday or Monday next to Moscow via Berlin. Why don't you come? After all, what is Oxford, even in term time?') The situation as between Barker and Stanislavsky was of that kind, not entirely unknown also in the scientific field upon occasion, in which two explorers in the same field, responding to the form and pressure of the time, make the same series of discoveries simultaneously, co-incidently, without reference to or knowledge of each other's work, thus corroborating each other's findings without ever having intended to do so. So far as the establishing of the director as a pivotal and essential figure in international theatre is concerned, this achievement belongs more to Barker, Antione and Reinhardt (working independently but more or less simultaneously) than to Stanislavsky. And so far as the English-speaking theatre is concerned, the achievement is wholly Barker's.

The main characteristics of his style and method were these: absolute faithfulness to the text of the play and the discernible intention of the author; insistence on ensemble playing, unity of purpose and effect, elimination of 'stars' and solo display; the abjuring of cheap theatricality and empty histrionics in favour of a quiet intensity of acting style and the portrayal of 'inward' truth. Again, all this sounds rather commonplace to us now: every college manual about the director's craft, so eagerly devoured by countless American university students, cites all of these things as the basic principles of modern directing – elevates them, in fact, into a kind of Hippocratic Oath for professing directors – but this is simply an indication of the extent of Barker's influence. It was he who showed the way and the three years at the Court Theatre gave him his first great testing-ground and his first great opportunity to clarify, practise and demonstrate those principles for himself. It is perhaps worth emphasizing also that these revolutionary ideas were not part of a plan or manifesto which he drew up in advance. They came to him gradually, element by element, as he worked on the plays; and they started, in every case, from the needs of the plays themselves. Barker was both reading and writing plays for several years before he came to the job of directing plays. He believed in the plays themselves and in the theatre's potential for interpreting great plays nobly. His directorial methods grew up gradually as a result of his efforts to find practical ways of implementing those beliefs.

Barker's own statements about what these practical methods turned out to be were made, naturally enough, after the fact. The best and fullest expression of them is probably that contained in his book, *The Exemplary Theatre*[11], and especially in chapter five of that book, 'The Production of a Play'; but in looking at that chapter as a guide to what went on at the Court Theatre, it is important to remember that the book was written in 1922, nearly twenty years after the Court experiment began. That the views expressed in the book result largely from the Court Theatre years there can be no reasonable doubt, for those years represented the longest and most concentrated, sustained experience Barker had as a director. We have, moreover, both the written and spoken testimony of various actors who worked with him at the Court (most notably, that of Lewis Casson, who several times in various places and contexts, wrote of Barker's approach and methods) and this in almost all cases tends fascinatingly to show the gradual putting-together of the elements which would eventually constitute the coherent view which Barker himself expressed in *The Exemplary Theatre*. But that final statement was influenced and refined, of course, by his additional experience and experiments as a director between 1907, when the Court venture finished and 1915, when the First World War and the turmoil in his own life brought his career as a director – for all practical purposes – to a close. Nevertheless, even with this caution in mind, it is safe to look upon *The Exemplary Theatre* not only as the quintessence of Barker's ideas about the function of the director, but also as a summary of what he learned from, in the main, his experience at the Court Theatre between 1904 and 1907.

Interestingly, though the unique product of his work was the establishment of the directorial position, the centre of all his comments, both in *The Exemplary Theatre* and elsewhere, is the actor. His concern as a director (or 'producer', as the position was then called) was first with the author and then with the actor: nowhere in his writings is there a single reference to the authority of the director or to the director's idea of the play or its interpretation, much less his divine right to superimpose some arbitrary meaning of his own upon it. 'To suggest, to criticize, to co-ordinate – that should be the limit of his function', says Barker in *The Exemplary Theatre*. The object should always be to bring the actor to the point at which he can confidently surrender himself to the part he is playing, while enabling him to see with clarity the relationship between that part and the inner life of the whole play. Barker, in discussing this problem, gives us a vivid impression of what it must have been like to work under his direction and what a profound understanding he had of the director's function *vis-à-vis* the actor (and therefore why the theatre, if it were to climb out of the intellectual and artistic triviality in which the nineteenth century had left it, *needed* this new functionary). Here is one of the central passages of Barker's argument:

And so it becomes plainer, perhaps, why in the theatre, where the personal appeal of the actor for the audience is so strong, we need by some means to detach the actor from himself. Efforts to charm us by chorus girl's smile, comedian's wink, or by a tragedian self-centred in the limelight is the demagogy of the theatre, and rightly to be resented. And it is to be the more condemned; for, at least, the politician drags in no playwright as an unwitting accomplice. (Not that one condemns chorus girl or comedian for their goings-on, as long as they made no pretence to be practising the art of the theatre.) To ask for sheer impersonation will not serve; playing at disguises is only a good child's game. We need interpreters, but it must truly be the characters of the play which they interpret. Working in full consciousness they cannot do it; self will be asserted. Identification of the actual with the imaginary, of the actor with his part, asking for a murderer to play a murderer and for a saint to appear as a saint, is as impossible as the fiction of personation is puerile. And so we are brought to the need for a creation in the actor of something like an integral sub-conscious self.

In this creation a double process is involved: first the mental search and the provocative argument into and around the character and the play; then the sensitizing of the actor's receptive faculties, mental and emotional too. It should be a concurrent process; and the argument will promote the mental receptivity – it will, at least, if the parties to it direct their attention more to the play, the third factor, than to each other. The emotional part of this sensitizing process is not so demonstrable. It is difficult enough even to define sympathy, and, in human relations, it is certainly a fatal error to try and cultivate it by prescription. But even in the world of make-believe one can affirm no more than this: let the actor surrender himself wholly to the idea of his part as it forms itself to his apprehension under the spell of this generous study, and there will, by his Muse's grace, be added unto him, as fruit of the personal surrender, this mysterious second personality, which will be not himself and yet will be a part of himself. . . . Surrender to an idea robs no man of his birthright: these wedded beings born of the actor's art live for their one purpose only, and will perish if unsustained by it. While they live, though, their very limitations give them power, and perfection, too, to a degree. In any fine playing of a part – of Imogen, shall we say? – there is a power not the player's own, and a beauty which certainly does not accompany her off the stage. Nor can the complete effect be accounted for by adding together the words of Shakespeare, the woman's looks and voice, the theatre's lights and scenery. Pick the whole thing to pieces, and you'll no more find out that secret than you'll find a soul in the body's anatomy. If it does not lie in the surrendered self, and the possession for the time of the obedient body by the changeling idea, then where?

All this, it will be noted, appertains to the actor, not the director. Barker, indeed, makes the almost automatic assumption that the director's only task is to serve the actor and, through him, the play. What he regards as the director's main function is the creation of a rehearsal atmosphere which allows and encourages the actors to explore together the inner realities of the play and then, by a process compounded of conscious control and intuitive responsiveness, to make themselves the instruments by which the play can play its own tune. He emphasizes that this should be a corporate venture among the actors (with the director as a kind of catalyst), even going so far as to say that individual study of his part by the lone actor can be dangerous and damaging: 'There is much to be said for the method of the seventeenth-century music-teacher, who locked up the instrument upon his departure for fear his pupil might practise. Actors might well leave their books behind them on the table.' In another part of the same chapter he sums the matter up by saying: 'Rehearsals, be it noted, have always this main object of enabling an actor to forget both himself and them in the performance.' Nevertheless, though he sees the actor as the prime instrument and first concern of the director, he also stresses the duty of the director to find unity in diversity (using the over-all, total gesture of the play as his touchstone) and thus enable the play to speak with a clear and undivided voice, yet without suppressing the vitality which springs from its complexity and variousness.

All this, we can safely assume, is the product – generally speaking – of those three years at the Court Theatre and his letters to William Archer, Gilbert Murray and Bernard Shaw during the years 1904–1907 give us fascinating glimpses of the day-by-day details which, in the long run, added together to form the experience which he later set down on paper. Those same letters also give us interesting instances in which the high-minded counsels of perfection did not obtain and in which Barker was being forced by shortages of either time or money (or both) to scramble in desperation for compromises, short cuts and palliatives, just to keep the particular production in question alive and kicking. To Shaw, in a letter dated November 21, 1913, he says: 'I lost my voice yesterday afternoon showing Miss Mary Lawton how to play Julia!¹² Leave her to me and I think I will shake her into something. Incidentally I can broaden Maude into something but really it means my teaching them both a lot of tricks and ways which they ought to know already . . .' To Archer on November 8, 1905 he writes, about the original production of *The Voysey Inheritance*: 'The scene seems long because I cannot knock the point of it into Thalberg yet and therefore he does it wrong . . .' And on November 14, 1908, after watching a rehearsal of *The Bacchae* which William Poel was directing, Barker sends a panic-stricken telegram to Gilbert Murray, in the following terms:

Suggest your seeing Poel, insisting that chorus must be audible and intelligible which means that Fates must speak either a whole line each or some lines all together, that singer must sing or, better, chant articulately to some proper music. Suggest Mrs. Lee Mathews could find enough Mozart for strings without piano in ten minutes. As to end of play, explain precisely to him what it means and give him 24 hours to present you with his modified or new interpretation of that meaning. Accept or reject this. Sorry there's this bother but think if you were Shakespeare.

Barker

His early experience as an actor had taught him the necessity for getting the mechanics of the thing right and his anxiety to give actors enough creative freedom to enable him and them to tap the real sources of their creative vitality did not blind him to that necessity. All the comments one hears or reads from actors who worked with him both at the Court Theatre and later, speak of his endless patience and persistence in rehearsals, his consuming passion for getting every detail right. Most actors – though not quite all – seem not to have minded the long and arduous rehearsing which resulted. Almost all of them speak of Barker's kindness and courteousness when directing a play and also of the personal magnetism which drew them on to follow him. Cathleen Nesbitt, who was the Perdita in Barker's 1912 production of *The Winter's Tale* at the Savoy, speaks in *A Little Love and Good Company* (London: Faber, 1975) of rehearsals which went on until 3 a.m. and stopped then only because Lillah McCarthy – speaking more as Mrs. Barker than as the leading lady – interceded with Barker on behalf of an exhausted company. Barker himself seems to have been, quite literally, indefatigable. Shaw accused him, more than once (there are two or three Shaw letters to this effect), of working actors too hard and of having too little feeling and consideration for them. The accusation, apparently, surprised Barker and genuinely shocked him. 'He always assumed', says Lewis Casson in his Foreword to C. B. Purdom's biography of Barker, 'that everyone was as keen as he on research into and expression of the author's meaning, and the motives, thoughts and emotions of his characters, evoking the actor's enthusiasm and making everyone contribute his utmost.' Casson also comments in this Foreword on Barker's sense of humour and ready laugh: ' . . . my remembrance of him [in the Court Theatre days] is one of vital sensitive youth and energy, a lithe, athletic figure, warm brown eyes, thick red-brown hair, tidily parted till he pushed his fingers through it, and an air of relaxed concentration ready to spring in a flash to action or laughter.' Cathleen Nesbitt, also, mentions the laughter: 'And he would laugh and say, "All right. I'll shut up. I promise I'll go to the dress circle and not utter a *word* till the end of the act." '

Harcourt Williams, an actor with a long and distinguished career, says of Barker, in *Four Years at the Old Vic* (London: Putnam: 1955): 'I had worked with him in many productions, starting at the Court and later at the Savoy, Little Theatre and Kingsway. I have yet to find a better producer.' And Sir John Gielgud, in a long and very interesting conversation with me on the subject said – speaking in tones of obvious sincerity and admiration – 'He was a master: I feel honoured to have known him and worked with him.' Hesketh Pearson, too, who in his days as an actor had several times played under Barker's direction, expresses the same view and gives some interesting amplification of it in his book, *Modern Men and Mummers* (London: Allen & Unwin, 1921):

> Granville Barker is the greatest producer of his time in England. Without people being altogether aware of it, he has revolutionized stage production in this country. . . . His work is always distinguished for its detail. There are no rough edges in his productions, and his companies are always the best for what is known as 'team work' in London. . . . His method of producing is, on the whole, Shavian. He takes things quietly and talks matters over intimately. But he has some curiously anti-Shavian lapses from grace. For one thing, he gets annoyed – and shows it. Shows it in a very terrifying manner. His curses are neither loud nor deep: they are atmospheric. It is what he doesn't say that paralyzes one. He *looks*; and having looked, he turns his back to the stage – and you can still see him looking through the back of his head. You feel that he is saying quite a lot of things to himself, saying them thoughtfully and witheringly – annihilating things. You wish he would turn and say them aloud. You wish he would assault you, with whatever consequences to yourself. You wish he would do anything rather than imitate a potential earthquake. Sometimes he will execute a little dance, a quiet, solitary waltz with ghastly possibilities. . . . It would be a grave mistake to speak to him at those moments. The best thing to do is to hide yourself from him completely until he calls you back. By that time he will have recovered, and will be quite charming . . . Later, you will ask someone what happened after you had gone away. You will be told that nothing happened – nothing whatever! That is the appalling thing about Barker. Nothing happens. But all sorts of things are *going* to happen. He is the supreme artist of Suggestion.

Harcourt Williams, in an earlier book [13] than the one quoted above, also gives some interesting details of Barker's rehearsal methods:

> Youngsters often ask me in what way Granville-Barker was a great producer.

It is not an easy matter to answer that question . . . Roughly one might say that Barker worked from the inside to the outside. He had an exceptional interest in what was theatrically effective, but never got it by theatrical means. It had to be won by mental clarity and emotional truth – in fact the very opposite to the method of most producers. Besides his intellectual attainments he had gone through the rough and tumble of an actor's training and knew to a hairsbreadth what an actor could put up with and how he could best be handled. I have known him change readings and positions from day to day without explaining why he did it, on purpose to break down the inhibitions of some actor, and at last, out of the subconscious if you will, would emerge the right way of doing it. It could be an agony to a sensitive actor, but hard training never hurt anyone. Before my wife, Jean Stirling Mackinlay, left the stage proper to become a diseuse, she played Alice in Granville-Barker's play, *The Voysey Inheritance*. She found the part very difficult, as indeed it is, and Barker dragooned her not a little but finally got the result he wanted; at the end of the last dress rehearsal he kissed her hand with a courteous gesture that seemed to beg forgiveness for the pain and anguish of creation.

It is worth comparing this description with a statement of Barker's own. In a lecture called *The Study of Drama* given at Cambridge on August 2, 1934, he made the comment that 'the producer impersonates the audience; an ideally critical audience.' When the lecture was published a little later, he added a footnote to this comment:

It should be the producer's ideal also, once the production is planned and rehearsals are under way, to be this [*i.e.* 'an ideally critical audience'] and no more. The more he can leave initiative to the actors the better. And, when he cannot, let him emulate the diplomat rather than the drill-sergeant, hint and coax and flatter and cajole, do anything rather than give orders; let them if possible still be persuaded that the initiative is theirs, not his.

Reading contemporary commentary on his productions, both that of other theatre practitioners and that of critics and observers, one is repeatedly struck by the fact that, in addition to the main general principles and objectives of his work, there is constant mention of three technical qualities in the performances. They are these: first, 'naturalness', both of speech and behaviour (Shaw, indeed, several times accused Barker of being so terrified of 'ham' acting that he *under*-played and got other actors, in his productions, to do the same [14]); secondly, the capacity to speak dialogue – and especially verse – rapidly and excitingly without loss of vocal clarity, avoiding the ponderous sonorities of the old actor-managers' style; and thirdly the consistent excellence of the smaller parts (London in 1904 was unused to this: the duty of small-part actors in the commercial theatre of the day consisted of giving cues to leading actors and discreetly keeping out of the way. Nothing more was expected of them either by the actor-manager or the audience. They were about as important as the man who comes on, in full evening dress, and opens the lid of the grand piano for the star pianist at a celebrity concert. Cathleen Nesbitt, in *A Little Love and Good Company*, says: '. . . we just kept out of each other's way. If there wasn't an empty space you sat down on the nearest chair.') Desmond MacCarthy and Max Beerbohm, among many others, commented frequently and approvingly at the time on these three characteristics of Barker's productions.

Hesketh Pearson, in *Modern Men and Mummers*, sums up the Court Theatre venture thus: 'Granville Barker was the directing artistic spirit behind the most famous epoch in theatrical management since the days of the Globe on Bankside. . . . Without him, it is possible that Shaw would never have obtained his English audience. The Vedrenne-Barker tenancy of the Court Theatre is the most shining event in the story of our drama since the time of Shakespeare.' This was in 1921, when the events concerned were still comparatively fresh in men's minds; Barker was still very much alive (was, in fact, only forty-four years old) and had not at that time made it clear that he had adamantly resolved to leave practical theatre work for good: indeed, he had directed a production of Maeterlinck's *The Betrothal* in January of that very year. Pearson was, therefore, expressing an opinion about a living director who, as far as he or anyone else at that time knew, might well go on to other signal achievements in the directorial field. Pearson's testimony so soon after the event (and before the Barker Legend, which Pearson himself would later assiduously propagate) is particularly valuable since it comes from an essentially unsympathetic witness, a man who quite obviously disliked Barker personally and in later years never missed an opportunity to disparage him. When he came to write *The Last Actor-Managers*[15] nearly thirty years after *Modern Men and Mummers*, he included a short chapter on Barker which is almost entirely unsympathetic and is, in places, downright scurrilous; yet even in that chapter he reiterates, more or less, his opinion of thirty years ago about the Barker productions at the Court. The opinion has, by now, been endorsed and re-endorsed many times and yet we have still – and rightly – a strong sense of wonder at what those two young men achieved: for it is well to remember that in 1904, when they first went into business together at the Court Theatre, Barker was only twenty-seven and Vedrenne only thirty-six. W.

Bridges-Adams, director of the old Shakespeare Memorial Theatre at Stratford-on-Avon from 1919 to 1926 (when it burned down) and of the new one from 1932 to 1934, writing in the magazine *Drama* in 1959[16] said of the Barker-Vedrenne regime at the Court:

> It owed its four years' life to the prudent pessimism of Vedrenne, to the abounding output of Shaw and, above all, to the genius and ardour of Barker. It was not long in being before one began to hear it said that under Mr. Barker's firm stage-management (that was still the word)[17] even well-known players seemed to give finer performances than they gave elsewhere. There was no question of the firmness, although he was of course too young, and much too wise, to attempt a quarter-deck manner with his seniors in the profession, particularly when they had come to him, as they often and gladly did, for less than their accustomed salaries. He held his authority in virtue of a clear, cool head and of a sincerity that shone not only from him but through him. Gently, but insistently, he could induce in the dullest member of his cast an awareness that to fall short of the perfection he exacted would be an affront to heaven itself. And this quality in him, potent as it was when he was concerned with the faithful representation of everyday life, became a mighty weapon when he turned his attention to the classics.

Harcourt Williams says the same sort of thing[18]:

> When producing a play he always had the whole thing at his fingers' ends at the first rehearsal. That the stage management was always fixed to the last movement goes without saying, but he also knew the whole background of the play and what each character should have in his or her mind.

All Barker's expertise, already of a remarkable order when he went to the Court and there amplified and developed week by week as production followed production, was engendered by his passion for fine plays. Histrionics as such interested him not at all and stage 'personality', when devoted to no other purpose than its own display, bored and angered him. Solemnity in the theatre he hated also, but he conceived the notion that the theatre could be a *serious* thing (more, perhaps one should say, in the French sense of that word than the English): serious, even in its comic moments, and elevated. Everything, for him, turned on the quality of the play itself and everything should be made to serve the play. Desmond MacCarthy, in his book about the Barker-Vedrenne achievement (*op. cit.* – see p. 93), sees this clearly and in commending Barker's new standards relates them to their real purpose: 'When will the other London managers learn', he asks, 'that the dramatist who is worth his salt needs the co-operation of every part, however small, in order to drive his meaning home; that we want to see *plays*, not to have our attention riveted perpetually on the same personality for three hours at a stretch?' (The added emphasis on 'plays' is mine, not MacCarthy's). Barker was determined that plays they should see: that was the whole object of the exercise. In the three years from October, 1904 to June, 1907 he presented thirty-two, quite half of them major works and almost all of them plays which would certainly not have been produced by the commercial theatre of the time (or, for that matter, by the commercial theatre now – or at any other time in between). The variety was astonishing and so was the fact that the list included half-a-dozen new British dramatists whose work was being presented in the theatre for the first time and five foreign dramatists (two of whom were Ibsen and Euripides) whose work had been seen in London only very rarely before.

This approached, in one way, Barker's other important ideal, though it did not exemplify it fully: the ideal of drama-in-repertory. And if his creating of the modern director was an unpremeditated act but a benefit which gradually evolved as he proceeded, the attempt to create a repertory theatre – insofar as that *is* what the Court Theatre scheme was attempting to do – was thoroughly premeditated. It became the most constant and continuing of all Barker's theatrical ideas and it was there both in his mind and on paper before his work at the Court Theatre began. Earlier in that same year – 1904 – Granville Barker and William Archer had collaborated to write and to have privately printed a short book not only advocating the building of a repertory theatre in London but also demonstrating, with a wealth of practical detail, how such a theatre should be organised and run, what sort of plays it should do, how many such plays it should present in any one week and what it would cost to operate the theatre. The book, known privately between Archer and Barker as 'The Blue Book', was officially called *A National Theatre: Scheme & Estimates*. In 1907 the privately-printed edition was superseded by a published version, for which Barker supplied a Preface, in the form of a letter to Archer. The letter began:

My dear Archer,
   You want a preface from me – do you? – to say how far the three years' experience of theatre management, through which I have passed since this unofficial blue-book was written and printed, has altered, as far as I am concerned, the views expressed in it. It hasn't really altered them at all. The need for a repertory theatre remains the same: no less, and it could not well be greater.

The book advocated a thorough-going permanent repertory of thirty-four plays, of a wide variety of types, all to be kept in production for at least a year, with some of them forming the basis for a *répertoire courant*, holding their places in the repertory year after year on the grounds that they were, so to speak, 'basic English plays' which, in the words of Barker and Archer, should be regarded 'as belonging to the permanent substratum of the repertory'. It was emphasised that no existing London theatre would be adequate to house the project and that, therefore, a new theatre, complete with its own rehearsal rooms, workshops and other facilities, must be built. The company to be engaged would, the book suggested, consist of about forty-two actors and twenty-four actresses, all on three-year contracts. Barker was, of course, far too restricted in his work at the Court Theatre, both by lack of funds and lack of any guarantee of continuity (or even continued existence) to attempt anything as grandiose as this; but he did, nevertheless, attempt – and not without a considerable degree of success – to apply the same basic principles on a smaller scale. Some productions *were* held over from one season to another, or brought back into the repertory later in the same season, when they seemed important enough and popular enough. Often, when this was done, the casts were virtually unchanged, so it really was the same production, with some continuity of playing, not just another new revival of the same play. Actors and actresses *did* get the stimulus of moving from one kind of part to another and, occasionally, of playing two very different parts in the same week. The emphasis *did* rest on the plays themselves, for their own sakes, and not on 'star' performers. In the matter of the choice of plays, though, there was an important difference between Barker's Court Theatre practice and the principles enunciated in *A National Theatre: Scheme & Estimates*. The latter had said: 'It is not an "advanced" theatre that we are designing. . . . The main principles we had in view, in sketching our specimen repertory, were that it should be national, representative, and popular. . . . We have purposely excluded from this specimen repertory all plays of the class which may be called disputable, designing to show that there was ample material at the command of the Theatre without travelling beyond the range of universally accepted classics, and modern work which has proved its attractiveness for the English public. For this reason the names of Tolstoy, Gorky, Ibsen, Björnson, Hauptmann, D'Annunzio and Bernard Shaw do not figure in our list of authors.' (And it is, perhaps, significant that the names of Strindberg and Chekhov do not even figure in the list of exclusions!) When he came to plan the Court

Theatre repertory, Barker abandoned the broader 'national' and 'popular' principle in favour of deliberately choosing 'advanced' plays, plays that otherwise would have virtually no chance of production – and certainly no chance of such careful, painstaking and good-quality production as he was determined to give them. However, though he changed his approach in this regard, he retained – so far as the physical circumstances would permit – both the theory and the practice of the repertory idea. And after the Court experiment ran out of steam, he continued his ardent advocacy and, on one or two occasions, demonstrations of that idea.

The ending of the Court experiment (or, rather, of the extension of it to the Barker-Vedrenne management of the Savoy Theatre from September 1907 to March 1908) was curious and is still curiously interesting. Shaw, in his 'Granville Barker: Some Particulars By Shaw'[19], describes it with a fine sense of finality and romantic flourish, but this gives, in the light of all the other evidence which is available, so over-simplified an account of the matter as to be downright inaccurate:

> At last we were in debt and had to put up the shutters. Having ruined Vedrenne in spite of his remonstrances we could not ask him to pay the debts; and we were bound to clear him without a stain on his character. Barker paid all he possessed; I paid the rest; and so the firm went down with its colours flying, leaving us with a proved certainty that no National Theatre in London devoted to the art of the theatre at its best can bear the burden of London rents and London rates. Freed from them it might pay its way under a director content to work hard for a modest salary. For the evidence read the book Barker wrote in collaboration with William Archer.

In fact, there were other disintegrative forces at work as well as – and probably more powerful than – the financial factor, all of them centred on Barker, some of them temperamental, some circumstantial, and some a combination of the two. The move from the Court to the Savoy, which was made in September 1907 was, in a way, both a cause and an effect of the impending disintegration. The move was made mainly at Barker's instigation because he felt that their work needed not only a bigger theatre, where they could be artistically more expansive (and that not only in mere physical size) but also where they would be closer to the theatrical heart of London and more in the public eye. The Savoy seemed from this point of view ideal. Barker's plan was clear: he would expand the concept which had evolved at the little Court Theatre and turn the Savoy into his longed-for National Theatre by main force. He proposed

(Right) Barker as Keegan in John Bull's Other Island *(1904)*

(Below) Barker as General Burgoyne in The Devil's Disciple *(1907).*

to open at the Savoy with *Peer Gynt* and in a letter to William Archer[20] he said: 'I wanted to open it [*i.e.* the theatre] on better music, better designs for the scenery and, for instance in the Dovre scene, perhaps designs for the dresses. In fact I wanted to behave for that production as if I were for once working under an endowment. Were I a Tree I should be ashamed to tell you this, but I do not think I should be merely extravagant.' He was frustrated in his desires both to work as if 'under an endowment' and to open his new theatre with the first British production of *Peer Gynt* (Richard Mansfield had done the first production of this play in English in New York just one year before). Instead, the management's Savoy venture opened with a rather tame revival of *You Never Can Tell* in the evenings and a series of matinée performances of John Galsworthy's new play, *Joy*. These were followed by a revival of *The Devil's Disciple* (with Barker playing General Burgoyne) in the evening bill and first performances of Murray's translation of the *Medea* of Euripides in the afternoons. While *The Devil's Disciple* was still in rehearsal (just a week before it opened, in fact) Shaw had occasion to write to Gilbert Murray about the theatre censorship row which was just then blowing up; in passing he made this comment about Barker[21]:

> The D's D. revolts Barker's soul: he strives earnestly to crush the cast and get a delicate galsworthy result. Then I sail in and turn the whole thing into a blatant Richardson's Show. Between us, we shall pull it through; but his loathing of the stage and of the vulgarity called acting is getting serious; so keep plenty of oxygen playing on Medea or he will mix it with hydrogen and apply it cold.

This could be dismissed as one of Shaw's customary hyperboles were it not substantiated elsewhere, but Barker himself confessed to Helen Huntington, in a letter written some years later (in June, 1918): 'I do believe my present loathing for the theatre is loathing for the audience. I have never loved them.' 'Loathing' is a strong word for an actor-director to use about a theatre and an audience; and 'never' is a very long time. But this same distaste and unease shows over and over again in Barker's letters to Gilbert Murray, especially during the months of the Savoy Theatre productions. The Bodleian Library has, in the Gilbert Murray Archive, a couple of dozen or so letters from Barker to Murray written during this period and, while there are no overt and explicit statements of disillusion, the general tone is often a good deal more sombre than in earlier exchanges between the two. The enthusiasm for plays still shows through fairly often and so does his abounding sense of fun, but not with the irrepressible high spirits formerly in evidence. And I take this change to be of particular significance since Murray was probably the person who, of all his friends and acquaintances, was closest to Barker. Their correspondence over the years – and it is mountainous in volume: I myself have examined over two hundred letters which passed between them and I feel fairly certain that there are many others still extant but which have not yet come to light – indicates quite clearly that there was from the first an instinctive sympathy between these two: each recognized and respected the very considerable talents of the other and both obviously felt that, in their theatre work together, their skills and their contributions were complementary. There is a sustained tone of gaiety, warmth and confidence, on both sides, in their correspondence and of Barker it can undoubtedly be said that he was probably more at ease with Gilbert Murray than with anyone else in the whole course of his life. This is clear throughout the correspondence (which begins in 1904 and extends to 1945) but, as it happens, there is one particularly striking example of it in the middle of the 'Savoy period' which we are here considering. In December, 1907, Barker wrote to Murray as follows:

Savoy Theatre
Thursday night

My very dear Friend,

I won't sit down to tell you – describe to you – the joy that your Xmas letter gives me, nor will I go putting on paper the love I have for you – it's a particular sort and kind that I haven't for anyone else in the world – though this is a time when one is allowed to come nearest to saying these things. I'm sure you know; you know so many things that can't just be learnt by rote. But just this: it is very much that you have a corner in your heart for me.

I like much the bookcase – I wish it meant I was to travel for a whole year. There is to be a photograph of me for you; it hasn't come in time for Xmas, though. Lillah asked today if I hadn't written you a love-letter in its place. I can now reply that I have.

I have been owing you a letter about 'Waste' for more than a month: it has not been the letter that was difficult but the subject. I've not been able to look at it since it was done. With the new year, though, I must get at it. I hope for a talk with you instead of a letter. May I come down to Gilmuire just for lunch one Sunday? If the roads would behave I'd bicycle over from Windsor. My love, till then, and a good new year.

Yours,
H.G.B.

Notice the phrase 'I wish it meant I was to travel for a whole year': many of his letters to Murray about this time contain similar asides indicating a sense of restlessness and discontent in him. Some of this was due to professional frustrations and to his consuming impatience over the slowness with which his schemes for a true repertory theatre advanced: but some of it was due simply to his own temperament. He veered violently and rapidly and often from resolution and optimism to doubt and despair. There were, however, also two other particular, practical causes for his restlessness at this time. One of them is mentioned in the New Year letter to Murray: namely, the fact that he had been busy ever since May with the writing of another play. He himself later confessed, in the letter written to St. John Ervine on October 2, 1923: 'Absenting myself to write Waste, and the general strain of that affair, were among the chief causes of the breaking of that management.' The management in question is, of course, the Barker-Vedrenne management and the issue had been raised by St. John Ervine's taking upon himself to remonstrate with and reproach Barker for having 'deserted' the theatre. Ervine's argument, which was presented publicly in his regular weekly column in *The Observer* (Sunday, September 30, 1923), made the point that Barker's desire to devote himself to the writing of plays need not have prevented his continuing in active theatre management and directing, since he had plainly demonstrated in the past that he could cope with both simultaneously. Barker was rebutting this point with a flat 'No, not so.' The truth of the matter seems to have lain somewhere between the two extremes. Barker's writing did not come easily and Ervine was mistaken in supposing that the plays were, or could have been, written in odd moments in between managerial and/or directorial duties. On the other hand, Barker's 'absenting' himself to write *Waste* was neither total nor prolonged. He began the play while he was still busy with the final productions at the Court Theatre, in May and June of 1907: 'The truth is that for the moment I'm giving my best energies to the play that I'm a-chewing of . . .', he says in a letter to Archer, in May. He finished it some time in November, for on November 30 he says in a letter to Murray: '*Waste* has wasted me, and I am finding it difficult not to leave undone the things that I ought to be doing . . .' So he must have been working on the play through September and October when the season at the Savoy was just beginning and there would have been a mass of organizational details to attend to, in addition to the directing of three plays and the acting in one of them. Small wonder that he felt himself under some pressure! Whenever he could, he would get away to his cottage in Fernhurst, between Haslemere and Midhurst, for a day or two at a time, to get on with his writing. But though he did not 'absent' himself entirely, he is doubtless right when he says to St. John Ervine that the general strain set up by this division of his attention, interest and energies helped to contribute to the break-up of the management. The thing that had carried the Court triumphantly along in its early days had been precisely the whole-hearted sense of commitment on the part of everyone involved, a whole-heartedness which Barker himself was largely responsible for inspiring, both by example and by exhortation. To an extent sufficient to be damaging, both these elements were absent at the start of the Savoy venture. And a further element of unrest was introduced in connection with *Waste* when, as Barker had predicted would happen, the Lord Chamberlain refused to license the play for public performance.

The other unsettling practical matter that intervened was a suggestion which had been put to Barker early in 1907 to go to New York as the artistic director (as we should now say) of a brand-new repertory theatre, being built especially for the purpose, designed to be run on the lines Barker and Archer had advocated in their 'blue-book'. Barker evidently took the suggestion very seriously and obviously felt, at least in the early stages of the negotiations, that this New York theatre might well be the natural base for the development of true repertory for the first time in English and the rather half-hearted developments at the Savoy must have seemed somewhat pale and tame by comparison. In that same letter to Archer, in May 1907, he had said: 'America looks rather real at moments and it would be the correct sequel to the blue book if we went together.' His idea was that Archer should become the dramaturg for the new theatre and should also be offered a professorship at Harvard or Columbia University. The matter was very actively in his mind throughout the whole period of preparing for and carrying out the short season at the Savoy. In August, 1907 he said in a letter to Murray:

> I'll own that if I am going to do the Millionaire's Theatre I should like to get in first with Euripides-Murray. But I think the chances are I'm not and anyhow I shan't know till April. Though again, I have it in my mind, if I don't take over the whole job, to propose to them to go over and play my best cards for them, which would include E–M . . .

So the debate continued in his mind and he constantly changed sides in it, lending neither stability nor real momentum to the Barker-Vedrenne management of the Savoy. The fact is that after the three years' frantic activity at the Court Theatre, which by 1907–08 Barker viewed rather in the light of an apprenticeship or a 'pilot programme' intended as a prelude to something much more comprehensive, his imagination was dominated by two images, at war with each other – the one was of a fully-fledged Repertory Theatre, ready for immediate use; the other was of a quiet, withdrawn, secluded life devoted to the writing of plays. The Savoy offered neither; and while the experience at the Court Theatre had been invaluable to him (having connections, in a sense, with both of his dominant ideas), there seemed by the end of 1907 no special reason for repeating it and certainly not for repeating it *ad infinitum*.

With *Waste* banned by the censor, he allowed circumstance to dictate his choices. As soon as the Savoy season ended, in March 1908, he and Archer went to New York, hoping to find there an immediate way of putting their blue-book into practice. They found that the new theatre which was being built was well endowed, was in the hands of a committee which was entirely serious-minded about repertory theatre and recognized the need for subsidising it. As if to dramatize this, the theatre was being built well away from Broadway, on Central Park West between 62nd and 63rd Streets. Everything was right – except the theatre itself. It was far too large for the purpose, with an enormous, gaping, cavernous proscenium, fit only for old-fashioned, nineteenth-century spectacle. Barker, not without some hesitations and regrets, turned down the offer and returned to London. He had the gloomy satisfaction of seeing his judgement vindicated. The New Theatre in New York opened in 1909 under the direction of Winthrop Ames and lasted as a repertory theatre for only three years. Then, re-christened the Century Theatre, it was handed back to commerce and became a musical comedy theatre (mainly) until it was demolished in 1930.

Barker, though he continued for six more years as a very active director, got only two chances to run seasons of repertory, both very short: one was at the Duke of York's Theatre in 1910 and the other at the St. James's Theatre in 1913. In the between-times he directed a number of distinguished productions at various theatres, but always on the old basis of assembling a cast of whatever actors happened to be available for a particular production. His correspondence in those years shows that he took endless pains over his casting but almost always had to settle for compromises of one sort or another and was almost always disappointed with the results, artistically speaking. But he did not waver in the standard of play he chose: though they were of many types and though some, quite naturally, were better than others, none was less than

*Lillah McCarthy and
Godfrey Tearle in*
The Sentimentalists
*(Meredith)1 — Duke of
York's Theatre, 1910.*

O. P. Heggie and Phil Dwyer in
Androcles and the Lion –
St. James's Theatre, 1913.

interesting, original and challenging. He had no use at all for the 'popular success' and he never once directed such. He once said to Gilbert Murray that it was no use his trying to direct rubbishy plays because all he did was to show up their essential meretriciousness. Between 1908 and 1914, apart from his two short repertory seasons and his brief but glorious 'Shakespeare period', he chose and directed things as various as Masefield's *The Tragedy of Nan*, Galsworthy's *Strife*, Schnitzler's *Anatol*, Ibsen's *The Master Builder*, a stage version, prepared by himself, of Hardy's *The Dynasts* and *Iphigenia in Tauris* (Euripides–Murray).

As to the two brief attempts at 'true repertory', the former, at the Duke of York's Theatre in 1910, was sponsored by Charles Frohman, the American impresario, who was persuaded to it by J.M. Barrie. From the start the combination of talents and interests was an uneasy one. Frohman was a commercial manager who spent a whole lifetime being dazzled by the theatre's glamour. His theatrical vocabulary consisted, really, of a single word: 'star'. Though he respected the repertory idea in theory, he did not really understand it or its aims, much less its plays: what he understood was the glitter of big, public personalities and he thought that the names of Shaw, Barrie, Galsworthy, Barker and Pinero – let alone a list of some of the best actors in London – would give him this. He found that though these names guaranteed a high degree of artistic distinction, they did not provide full houses; and the production of ten plays in four months was immensely costly. When Edward VII died in May of that year, Frohman seized the opportunity to close down the repertory season as a mark of respect – and then keep it closed.

Though Frohman was the producer, Barker was the real moving spirit behind the venture. It was Barker who chose the plays and who arranged the order of them in the repertory; he directed six of the ten plays himself; he wrote one of them. And it was, of course, Barker who had advocated the whole idea of repertory in the first place. The new plays included in the programme were: *Justice* (Galsworthy), *Misalliance* (Shaw), *Old Friends* (Barrie), *The Twelve-Pound Look* (Barrie), *The Sentimentalists* (Meredith), *The Madras House* (Barker) and *Helen's Path* (Hope & Cosmo Gordon Lennox). The revivals were: *Trelawney of the Wells* (Pinero), *Chains* (Elizabeth Baker) and *Prunella* (Housman & Barker). The two Barrie plays and the unfinished fragment of Meredith's were all one-act pieces and were presented as a triple bill. These three, together with three of the new full-length plays, were all presented in the first three weeks of the programme, in the following order:

Monday, February 21	*Justice*
Tuesday	*Justice*
Wednesday	*Misalliance*
Thursday (matinée & evening)	*Justice*
Friday	*Misalliance*
Saturday (matinée)	*Misalliance*
Saturday (evening)	*Justice*
Monday, February 28	*Misalliance*
Tuesday	Triple Bill
Wednesday	*Justice*
Thursday (matinée)	*Justice*
Thursday (evening)	Triple Bill
Friday	*Misalliance*
Saturday (matinée)	Triple Bill
Saturday (evening)	*Misalliance*
Monday, March 7	Triple Bill
Tuesday	*Misalliance*
Wednesday	*The Madras House*
Thursday (matinée)	*Misalliance*
Thursday (evening)	*Justice*
Friday	*Justice*
Saturday (matinée)	*The Madras House*
Saturday (evening)	Triple Bill

It was an immense and most laudable effort. It was not a failure in any sense but the commercial-popular sense and that is of no significance in the long run. Four of the productions (*The Madras House, Trelawney of the Wells, Prunella* and *Chains*) were, apparently, extremely good and one (*Justice*) was superb, if contemporary account can be relied on. Though the season had proved, as Shaw pointed out at the time, that it was hopeless to try to run a repertory theatre with a commercial management and retaining the 'star' system of casting, it also proved that the repertory idea was basically sound and that there was no intrinsic reason why it should not work in English as successfully as it already did in French and German.

One of the plays proposed for production in this repertory season, and then abandoned when Frohman got cold feet, was the subject of an interesting exchange of letters which provides at least a glimpse or two of Barker's idea about how a repertory theatre should work and the practical methods he adopted in the running of it. The play was Gilbert Murray's newly-completed translation of the Euripides *Iphigenia in*

Tauris and the letters are between Murray and Barker. The first is a brief note of November 27, 1909:

> Dear G.M.,
> Can I have the cast of Iphigenia, and when can I have a copy of the play? And will you suggest any people you want. Here are those already engaged to be used up more or less if possible, and the others to be more or less ad hoc for the actual plays to be done.
>
> > Yours,
> > H.G.B.

And with the letter was the list of actors. It read as follows:

Engaged for the Repertory Theatre
Sydney Valentine
Dennis Eadie
O.P. Heggie
Charles Bryant
Edmund Gwenn
Charles Maude
Lillah McCarthy
Dorothy Minto
Florence Haydon
Mary Barton

Barker was attempting not only to present the plays in true repertory fashion, but also to establish a permanent repertory company, capable on its own of carrying a complete repertoire of plays. He has another comment on this in another letter to Murray, written on March 12, 1910, after the season has begun:

> . . . But, for the rest of the cast: I have no Orestes; Bryant would be hopeless in it – he is rather a disappointment to us so far; Valentine could play Thoas and Casson one of the Messengers, but – here is the real point – if it were to mean special engagements outside the Company for Iphigenia, Orestes, one Messenger, perhaps Athena, and at least two thirds of the Chorus, it makes it very expensive at two performances a week, which is what it might average.
> A little shifting is going on in the Company which might make matters easier, but it hasn't so far. My hope is in the autumn when we shall have one or two robuster plays to do that we may have collected more likely people; the only way of forming this Company (it isn't really formed yet) not quite ruinously, is to engage people for two or three plays.
> I write this at great length and rather confusedly. I wish I could talk to you,

for there are many complications and I am not, of course, in any absolute
authority.

That question of 'absolute authority', the necessary control needed to
weld the company together into a cohesive entity, was obviously a sore
and delicate (and crucial) point. He had already referred glancingly to it,
earlier in the same letter, in discussing a suggestion that the proposed
production of *Iphigenia* should perhaps be preceded by the revival of one
of Murray's earlier translations which Barker had directed:

> Yes, I rather think with you, I'm afraid, that the revival before *Iphigenia* is bad.
> The notion sprang from several rather confusing currents of events; one thing
> that was in my mind was, as we had Casson in the Company, to let him repeat
> for a few performances his production of *Hippolytus*. I very much want to get
> in some other producers than myself. But there's the casting difficulty again
> and the powers that be didn't jump at it.

There are sufficient indications in this brief exchange of letters alone that,
though he was glad of the opportunity to experiment with the
presentation of a repertoire of plays, Barker did not find the circumstances ideal and was irked by the complexity of the organization, the
dominance of commercial considerations and the personal remoteness
(often literally, geographically) of Frohman, who divided his time
between London and New York and usually acted through minions and
intermediaries.

As between Barker and Murray another interesting artistic–procedural
debate was going on in these same letters. Barker had written to Murray
suggesting the revival not of *one* of the earlier productions of Greek plays
but of several. He had also suggested that, partly for economy's sake and
partly for reasons of artistic unity, a single stage setting be devised that
would serve all the plays. On March 11, 1910, Murray replied:

> My dear Barker,
>   I do not think there would be any difficulty in having one scene for Hip.,
> Med. and at a pinch Iph. and Tro. and El. But the three last would want
> modifications, obviously. On the whole I do not much like the idea, as there is
> after all only one scene wanted for each play as it is. And the one scene would
> have to be rather colourless. One set of dresses would do all right, with slight
> variations. Chorus dressed like the *Medea* chorus. Also we could use one
> method for all choruses.

Barker replied to this the next day, in the letter from which I have already
quoted[22], saying:

Dear G.M.,

I go back, I think, on my idea of one scene – well, I go back I think to this extent: could we have one platform and one set of seats for the chorus and then vary the background? This is not so much for the sake of cheapness as in order to standardise the arrangements, for I am convinced that there is only *one* best way, and I am trying to wipe my mind clear of what we've done before in order to discover that one. At present I incline to setting them up and down stage on either side, like the stalls in the choir of a cathedral.

Then ought there to be an altar in the middle of the stage? This seems more or less indicated in *Iphigenia*; it could be used in *Hippolytus* with effect I suppose, but there is nothing to it in *Electra* or *The Trojan Women*, is there? I do believe it would be a magnificent effect to have a life-size bit of the Temple of Paestum as a scene. I shall part from this idea with great reluctance.

In those first months of 1910 his mind was filled, obviously, with the day-to-day mechanisms of running a complicated programme of repertory – dovetailing of casts, overlapping of rehearsals, combining of settings, and so on. We still do not know all the details of what his approach entailed or what a permanent repertory theatre under Granville Barker's direction would have been like, but some fragments of information and some contemporary documents such as the Murray letters do give us a shrewd idea both of his objectives and of his methods. They give us also a vivid impression of the extreme precariousness of such ventures and of the ambivalence of Barker's responses to the situation. As the March 12 letter shows, he was – in spite of the difficulties – confidently expecting at that time that his repertory season at the Duke of York's would continue into the autumn and would by then have expanded and strengthened. The innate compromises of the system under which it was operating, however, combined with Charles Frohman's sudden loss of enthusiasm, denied the fulfilment of that expectation. It was three years before Barker got the chance to try again.

The second repertory attempt, at the St. James's, was produced by Barker himself, with financial assistance from Lord Howard de Walden. It began on December 1, 1913 and lasted, as true repertory, only six weeks. Lillah and Harley Granville Barker had control of the St. James's Theatre for about six months, from August, 1913 onward. The brief attempt at repertory presentation in December had been preceded by short runs of a new Shaw play (*Androcles and the Lion*) and a revived Masefield play (*The Witch*). Barker directed both of these and went on to direct six others to make up the repertory programme. *The Witch* was retained in the repertory; *Androcles and the Lion* was not. The additional six plays were: *The Wild Duck* (Ibsen); *Le Mariage Forcé* (Molière); *The Tragedy of Nan* (Masefield); *The Doctor's Dilemma* (Shaw); *The Silver Box* (Galsworthy); *The Death of Tintagiles* (Maeterlinck). All, except the Molière, Barker had directed on previous occasions: three of them had first been done at the Court Theatre between 1904 and 1907; the other two elsewhere. In other words, during this season at the St. James's his whole concentration was primarily upon the repertory experiment, not upon the finding and producing of new plays. All the indications are that he was viewing this occasion as a last chance to break through into the only system of theatre presentation that by then seemed to him viable, if proper artistic standards were to be maintained. Two days before the three-week repertory at the St. James's ended and the company was to transfer to the Savoy Theatre once again for further performances of the repertory and a production of *A Midsummer Night's Dream* (which Barker hoped – vainly, as it turned out – to make the basis for a renewed and enlarged repertory programme) he made a speech to the audience after the performance of *The Death of Tintagiles* and *The Silver Box* (which were given on the same evening). Here, in part, is what he said:

> . . . Many of our audience tonight are here not for the first time in these three weeks. For we have been doing repertory, real repertory. I own I take a certain pride in the very word . . . Let me apologise for our shortcomings. We have given you no Shakespeare, and without Shakespeare English repertory is, as Mrs. Jones puts it, 'not quite itself' . . . . We have been conscious sometimes, as I am afraid you have, of a certain lack of complete preparation in the performances; incidental, some critics have suggested, to any repertory theatre. No, it is not. Performances in repertory could be more perfect not less than other performances. But incidental to our setting out upon this adventure without adequate resources and equipment, relying on the loyalty of our staff and the enthusiasm of our Company. Not in vain. . . . But I know I did not prophesy falsely to myself when I thought that doing our work in the right spirit any little shortcomings in the letter would be forgiven.
> Well, ladies and gentlemen, is this repertory to continue? . . .

He went on to appeal for a thousand people each to subscribe £25 (not a negligible sum in those days) to a trust fund for the support of a permanent repertory theatre in London and to be willing, if needed, to subscribe a further £25 per year for the next three years. Three weeks later, in January, 1914, he embodied this appeal in a formal document and had it fairly widely distributed not only in London but in other parts of the country, too. Both the after-curtain speech and the printed appeal were widely commented upon in the press, most of the comments – though not quite all – being sympathetic and supportive. 'I hope Mr. Barker will get the money he wants. Yet somehow I do not think he will', said *The Scotsman*, the Edinburgh daily, on January 10, 1914. There was, however, stout support from the *Western Morning News* (Plymouth) and the *Yorkshire Post* (Leeds). And in London, *The Observer*, under the fiery and emphatic lead of its editor, J.L. Garvin, waged a vigorous campaign in Barker's favour. And the *Evening Mail*, in an article which began 'London is the only European capital of any importance that does not possess a repertory theatre . . .', said 'People who do not care for the idea of a State-supported theatre that would be rather academic and official in its methods ought to support Mr. Barker's scheme. Mr. Barker is the right man to carry it out and if only he reorganizes his methods of appeal so as to include all playgoers, and not merely a wealthy section of them, he ought to make a huge success of his scheme and give us a repertory theatre within the next twelve months.' *The Era*, on December 24, 1913, had this to say: 'Mr. Granville Barker's appeal at the conclusion of the performance of *The Silver Box* at the St. James's on Wednesday for assistance in establishing a permanent repertory theatre has been widely discussed. He is looking for a thousand individuals willing to subscribe £25 a year for three years. Within 48 hours of making his appeal Mr. Granville Barker had received a number of handsome cheques, and every day brings in a further list of subscribers.'

It really did look, in the early months of 1914, and especially after the success of the production of *A Midsummer Night's Dream* at the Savoy in February/March, as though the optimism of the press comments was going to be justified. Money continued to come in and three Trustees – Lord Howard de Walden, Sir James Barrie and Professor Gilbert Murray – were appointed to take charge of it and administer it. Clause 2 of the formal, printed appeal-agreement had said: 'If by the 31st day of July, 1914, the money contributed shall not amount to £10,000, my £25 is to be returned to me.' But it had not proved necessary to invoke this clause: the limiting amount had been exceeded before the deadline was reached. Even as late as December 1914 (by which time the country was beginning to realise that the War was not going to be 'over by Christmas') Barker was still in fairly good heart about the prospects. On the first day of that month he wrote to Archer, saying:

Dear Archer,
    In December last when we made our appeal for a London Repertory

Barker (right) in the title-rôle of Anatol *(Schnitzler), with Nigel Playfair. The play, which Barker had translated with the help of C. E. Wheeler, is really a series of short sketches, the one illustrated being called* The Farewell Supper.

Theatre you were good enough not only to give us your support but to send in earnest of it the first cheque for £25. Many excellent suggestions and some guarantees of substantial help brought about modifications of the original scheme. These were still proceeding when the outbreak of war stopped everything. At present there is very little to be done. But once the war is over I shall be more confident, not less, of the chances of bringing into being a serious theatre in London. No use of course has been made of the money. It is on deposit in a Repertory Account at the London County and Westminster Bank. I shall be glad of your consent to leave it there until the moment comes when we can make a move; we shall choose the earliest.

> Yours sincerely,
> H. Granville Barker

P.S. This is the formal letter I'm sending round. And if you want the cash (and who doesn't!) of course claim it at once.

But two months later Barker's mood and mind had changed. Whether in response to the grim realities of the war or to the flux of his own mercurial temperament or a combination of these and the play of the former on the latter, is impossible to say. Whatever the reason, on February 4, 1915 he wrote to Archer again, returning his donation:

> My dear W.A.,
>   Someday we 'a-meet' and I'll tell you whys and wherefores. Meanwhile, £25 – the first subscription to that scheme. Well, that has gone by the board with many other things and someone else will now do the job.
>   Do you know W.A. if the millionaires had taken up that Blue Book of ours when it was written I'm not sure we shouldn't have found it a little easier (we, the B.P.[23]) to win this war.
>   I was so glad of your message the other day.
>
> Yours,
> H.G.B.

Even allowing for those wild fluctuations of Barker's spirit, it does seem that, but for the war, 1914 might have brought forth a permanent repertory theatre in London, with Barker – who was surely the man eminently suitable – in charge of it. In January, 1912 he had written to Murray revealing different plans and a different mood. His letter then ends on a wistful and melancholy dying fall:

> . . . But I want these matinées [of *Iphigenia in Tauris*] to be as good as I can get them, for I mean them to be my last. It's nine years since I started with Hippolytus and it's good and appropriate to be finishing with Iphigenia. After

this – whatever evening bills I must; one snap at William S.; but for the rest –
other people must get on with it.

But by January, 1914 the mood and the plan had changed once more.
Again he writes to Murray:

> . . . We simply must pull this repertory through; it is now or never. One thing
> else you could do and, if you please, you really must. Masefield has a brilliant
> idea that during one week of the repertory (which will last at the Savoy for
> another three) we shall each of us take a performance, in this sense; after it,
> come in front of the curtain and make a short but moving appeal to the
> audience. Really, my speech was a good tip. It affected people in a way that
> letters to the papers don't. . . .

But the ambivalence was always there, even in a matter as dear to him
as the repertory theatre idea. Remembering those years afterwards, he
wrote in that 1923 letter to St. John Ervine:

> As to the producing of plays, I made up my mind sometime before 1910 that it
> was futile to plough the sand: i.e., in this connection, to make a production
> and then disperse it, the play to semi-oblivion, the actors to demoralisation.
> On the personal count I made up my mind even earlier to give up acting when
> I was 30 and producing when I was 40. I made – or contributed to – one
> attempt after another to create a theatre which should be an institution of
> some permanence. In 1914 this seemed on the verge of accomplishment (I
> calculated that by 1919 it might have developed a life of its own, so that I could
> go free.) Then came the war. . . .

For ten years, from 1904 to 1914, he had been, with only very brief
breaks, in continuous production, sometimes as actor, sometimes as
director (accepting from that position the new burdens which he himself
had laid on it), sometimes as both. The furthering of fine plays had,
throughout, been his first concern and part of that concern had been to
create a physical environment which would support and foster those
plays. In the pauses between frantic bouts of practical activity he had
written two major plays himself and joined with collaborators in the
writing of two minor ones – *Prunella*, with Laurence Housman and
Harlequinade with Dion Clayton Calthrop. Throughout the whole ten
years there was a constant tugging and division in his mind between the
two activities, writing and producing. They are, as near as makes no
matter, mutually exclusive (St. John Ervine's argument notwithstanding). Barker knew this – and drove himself and everyone around him

half-frantic trying either to make up his mind between them or to invent a way of living that would somehow manage to reconcile the irreconcil-ables.

(right) Barker about the time of writing The Madras House.

(below) Barker in his garden at Stansted, Kent.

Major Plays

Prunella and *Harlequinade* hardly count, except for us to note their presence in passing; the former in 1904 and the latter in 1913. And perhaps to note also three other relatively minor but not uninteresting things about them: (1) Barker's fondness for the theatricality and the theatrical metaphor of the *commedia* figures (though in their nineteenth-century, sentimentalized form), which shows not only in the choice of subject in these two plays but also, a little later, in his translating of Sacha Guitry's *Debutau* into an English play; (2) the touches of irony and melancholy and a sort of resigned bitterness which are almost certainly, along with plotting and ordering of events, Barker's total contribution to each of the plays – the dialogue, in each case, was almost as certainly the work of his collaborator; (3) the popularity not only of the pieces themselves but of a whole *genre* which they established; *Prunella*, in particular, gave rise to many highly derivative works, especially in the then-rising one-act form, Oliphant Down's *The Maker of Dreams* (1911) and Frank Sladen-Smith's *Polonaise* (1941) providing two striking examples. *Polonaise*, in particular, is downright imitative, plot and metaphor and symbolism and all. Its author once told me how, in his little upstairs sitting-room in Rusholme, Manchester, he was at his desk one quiet evening in 1941, writing this little play about unruly life's intrusion into a Watteau-esque garden, withdrawn from the rowdy world, when a German incendiary bomb plunged through the roof and had to be smothered with sandbags before it burned the building down.

But neither *Prunella* nor *Harlequinade*, charming though they still are in their slight ways, represent for us anything very significant in relation to Granville Barker's work as a whole. The other two plays of that period, *Waste* (1906–7) and *The Madras House* (1909–10) are a different story.

One might almost take as an epigraph for *Waste* the lines which concluded the first Act of *Agnes Colander*, only six years before:

AGNES: It comes to me – how one hammers eternally at the door of this sex question.

ALEC: I think the door is always open. People who have passed through we annoy. Those who have avoided it we shock. But the question is put to every one of us, so it's no use pretending that it isn't there.

Waste is – so far as any major play can be reduced to an over-simplified formulation in this way – a play about sex, especially about how sex fits into the private experience of the individual on the one hand and the structure of society on the other. Marriage concerns this play not at all; what holds it in fascinated thrall is the crude and often destructive power of physical passion and the intricate and mysterious relationship between this and other human creative impulses. Or, to put it in another way, *Waste* is about the clash, at the very centre of life, of the natural forces of creation with the natural forces of destruction, which bafflingly co-exist in one life, in all life. But that is only to say again that this is a play about sex. The play is – if one makes due allowance for its author's growth in maturity and experience in the intervening years – a logical extension, thematically speaking, from *Agnes Colander*. It has, of course, *learned* a lot from *The Voysey Inheritance* but it does not really continue the exploration of experience begun in *Voysey*; its lineage goes back, rather, to the earlier piece. There are, however, two prime influences which should be noted before *Waste* is discussed further. In 1905, the year immediately before he began the writing of *Waste*, Barker had read, for the first time, Shaw's *Man and Superman* and Gilbert Murray's translation of the *Bacchae* of Euripides: the former he had played the lead in and helped to produce; the latter he had already planned to direct (though in fact he never did) and had begun to study it with production in mind. Murray had published it towards the end of 1904, but he had lent Barker a copy of it, in manuscript, before publication. In his correspondence with Murray during 1905 and 1906, Barker frequently mentions the *Bacchae*; the play had quite obviously made a profound impression upon him. Not only the sexual elements from the *Bacchae* reflect themselves in *Waste*; so does the theme and idea of religious possession, which is in its turn mysteriously and complexly connected with the sexual connotations. Barker himself makes reference to these connections in a letter to Murray written in September 1909[1]: referring to a review of the published text of the play, which Barker had included in *Three Plays* (London: Sidgwick & Jackson, 1909), he said:

> I think what Butler says about Waste is most just and right. The worst of it is, it is faults of execution not conception. I have him all right in my head. The man of no religious ideas who, when he gets one at a great crisis in his life, is so superstitiously possessed by it that it drives him monomaniacal and kills him. That's all right, I believe – but I've not *done* it!!!

The description – 'so superstitiously possessed by it that it drives him monomaniacal and kills him' – fits Pentheus in the Euripides play as closely as it fits Trebell, the central character in *Waste*; and it fits the Trebell of the second version of *Waste*, which was completely re-written in 1926, better than it fits the Trebell of the original 1907 version.

The central confrontation in *Waste*, the clash which gives energy to the whole piece and which produces the final moment of dramatic equilibrium, is no less an issue than that of life-wish *versus* death-wish. In the first version the actual term 'Life Force' is used and there are multiple echoes from the Shaw play of a year before, though they echo sombrely and run in reverse directions from their bounding high spirits in *Man and Superman*. In Barker's play the dominant image is that of barrenness (the word 'barren' itself occurs several times at crucial moments) and sexual barrenness and the wilful refusal of life is overtly and explicitly equated with spiritual barrenness. 'I've stood for success, Fanny,' Trebell says: 'I still stand for success. . . . But suddenly I've a feeling the work would be barren. What is it in your thoughts and actions which makes them bear fruit? Something that the roughest peasant may have in common with the best of us intellectual men; something that a dog might have. It isn't successful cleverness.' The whole process of ratiocination is especially stigmatized as a barren one.

The plot-line of the play is a simple one. Trebell is a brilliant, forceful, egocentric barrister who has gone into politics and has quickly made his mark. He is ambitious and, in a sense, ruthless; but he is not dominated by mere careerism. Lately, he has embraced, from sincere conviction, the cause of Disestablishment – the breaking of the ties which bind the Church of England to the state apparatus and make it, in effect, into a mere state department, a state church. Trebell wants to divest the church of its vested interests, take its endowments away from it, compel it to act from conviction alone. His intention is to change the very nature not only of the church but of religion itself. There will be a good deal of surplus money released by disestablishment and the dissolution of official church properties and this Trebell proposes to use for the establishing of a new system of colleges and universities. (It needs to be remembered that the play was written in 1906, before the development of a universally-available higher education system.) His expressed hope is that men with a true sense of vocation, who would formerly have taken vows and entered the priesthood, will – after Disestablishment – dedicate themselves to teaching and regard it in a religious light. 'I'm offering you the foundation of a new Order of men and women who'll serve God by teaching his children', he says in the first version of the play. He is utterly absorbed in the task he has set himself, spiritually devoted to it as a *cause*, the cause of promoting a true sense of education in the land: knowledge and the natural search for knowledge are sacred things and he means to use Disestablishment as an instrument to erect an educational system in which men and women will *believe*, with a religious fervour. In the second version of the play Trebell describes his position and his state of mind in a way which not only places it accurately in the right category of experience but also carries a great deal of ironic significance in view of what happens to him in his personal life. He says: 'I found I've fallen in love. No, not with a woman, you old sentimental-ist! With this job. I am in love with a Bill for the Disestablishment of the Church of England – and for doing sundry other more interesting things. And I mean to make an honest Act of Parliament of the little darling.'

Trebell's position in the House of Commons is that of an Independent (he was elected as such) who has, on the whole, normally associated himself with and voted with the Liberals. To further his Disestablish-ment Bill, he deserts the Liberals and makes common cause with the Conservatives. (The politician who changes sides had, it would seem, a special fascination for Barker: Carnaby Leete, in *The Marrying of Ann Leete*, is such another – though for baser motives.) A general election is approaching and the Conservatives, it is confidently predicted, will win. If they do they are committed to some kind of disestablishment measure. The only person with the skill, courage, knowledge and imagination to draft a Disestablishment Bill acceptable to all parties in the House and to all sections of the Church and the religious community generally, is Trebell. It is all but inevitable that he will be invited to become a member of the new Conservative Cabinet when it takes office. To ensure that nothing goes wrong and that all the diverse factions of the Conservative

Party are brought to accept Trebell (who has in the past been a scourge to them from the Liberal benches), the wife of one of the Conservative leaders, Julia Farrant – a woman given to political intrigue and to operating as 'the power behind the throne' – gives a weekend house-party to which all the relevant people, as well as one or two others intended as catalysts, are invited. The weekend is almost over – it is Sunday night – when Trebell, answering a sudden, unguarded whim, suddenly responds to the flirtatious advances of Amy O'Connell, a frivolous and discontented married woman. Swept by a gust of physical passion which was premeditated by neither of them they spend part of the night together. To Trebell it is a passing moment and he walks away from it the next day without giving it a second thought. But to Amy, frivolous and shallow though she is, it has come (she herself is surprised to find) to mean much more. She is separated from her husband and is lonely. She desperately wants someone to take her seriously and pay attention to her. Trebell's indifference, after his suddenly allowing himself to be attracted, hurts and angers her. This is the state of mind she is in when she discovers a much more immediate complication: she is pregnant. On the very morning when he is to meet with Lord Charles Cantelupe[2], a prominent High Churchman whose support for the Disestablishment Bill is vital, Amy comes to tell Trebell about her pregnancy and to ask his assistance in seeking an abortion (again, let us recall that this is 1906, not 1983). He refuses to help in this regard, not because of any automatic conventional or social response on his part but because he is genuinely shocked at the suggestion that a new life should be arbitrarily eliminated. He does not even, at first, object because it is *his* child which is being destroyed: that reaction comes later. His first, spontaneous, instinctive response is revolt against the idea of turning against life, of becoming a life-denier. The personal involvement takes hold of him later in the play, increasing in intensity and becoming clearer and more explicit as he himself gradually recognizes its nature. At the beginning of the final act, in the first version of the play, the following passage occurs:

TREBELL: Was she so very mad? I'm not thinking of her own death.
WEDGECROFT: Don't brood, Trebell. Your mind isn't healthy yet about her and –
TREBELL: And my child.
WEDGECROFT: Is that how you're thinking of it?
TREBELL: How else? It's very inexplicable – this sense of fatherhood.

Amy O'Connell has died as a result of an abortion operation performed by some back-street quack. There is the danger that if, through the inquest which must inevitably be held, Trebell's involvement becomes publicly known, his work on the Disestablishment Bill will be jeopardized, as will his seat in the new Cabinet. Those members of the Cabinet who support him, and who regret the possible damage to his work, eventually persuade Justin O'Connell, Amy's husband, not to make at the inquest any statement that will implicate Trebell; but the one member who has all along resented Trebell's inclusion manages by skilful argument to persuade the Prime Minister that Trebell will now be a liability in any case and should be dropped. The Prime Minister reluctantly agrees and writes a note to Trebell telling him so. After receiving the note, Trebell shoots himself. The reasons for his suicide are complex ones: not that he fears the scandal (that danger is past); not because of any disappointment at losing a Cabinet post and a career opportunity (he has plenty of those, in two or three different directions); but because he has begun to equate the destruction of this one particular piece of work, the Disestablishment Bill, which he had taken on for its own intrinsic worth and not for its possible influence on his career, with the destruction of his unborn child. He seems all at once surrounded by death; the whole path of his life has led him, he feels, into an arid and a barren place; in these circumstances his own physical death seems the only logical outcome. 'And if this new power coming to birth in me has been killed now', he says to his sister Frances on hearing of his exclusion from the Cabinet, 'as wantonly as she denied life to that child . . ! I'd rather like to think Fate could be so subtle in revenge.' His sister's reply to this is: 'This isn't sane! It isn't sane!' And to this he makes rejoinder: 'By other measure than our thrifty sanity my life may well be of no more account than that balked scrap of being was.' This is from the second version of the play which is, for most of the play, both surer and subtler than the first: but this particular conversation, towards the end of the play, has parallel passages, in the first and second version, which are fascinating to compare. Take, for example, the following:

1st version (1906–07)

FRANCES: Is your mother the Wide World nothing to you? Can't you open your heart like a child again?

TREBELL: No, neither to the beauty of Nature nor the particular human animals that are always called a part of it. I don't even see them with your eyes. I'm a son of the anger of Man at men's foolishness, and unless I've that to feed upon . . .! Don't you know that when a man cuts himself shaving, he swears? When he loses a seat in the Cabinet he turns inward for comfort – and if he only finds there a spirit which should have been born, but is dead, what's to be done then?

FRANCES: You mustn't think of that woman. . . .

TREBELL: I've reasoned my way through life. . . .

FRANCES: I see how awful it is to have the double blow fall.

TREBELL: But here's something in me which no knowledge touches – some feeling, some power which should be the beginning of new strength. But it has been killed in me unborn before I had learnt to understand – and that's killing me.

FRANCES   (*crying out*): Why, why did no woman teach you to be gentle? Why did you never believe in any woman? Perhaps even I am to blame. . . .

TREBELL: The little fool, the little fool . . . why did she kill my child? What did it matter what I thought her? We were committed together to that one thing.

2nd version (1926)

FRANCES: But this one piece of work – had it come to mean everything to you?

TREBELL: More.

FRANCES: More?

TREBELL: Yes. I'd never, so to speak, given myself away before. It's a dreadful joy to do that – to become part of a purpose bigger than your own. Another strength is added to your own: it's a mystery. But it follows, you see, that having lost myself in the thing – the loss of it leaves me a dead man.

FRANCES: Yes, I understand. But these are only words.

TREBELL: D'you think so? Death is a fact to be faced. And what is it that dies? One may be dead for years – and who'll notice, if one keeps up appearances? It's not good manners to notice. I once heard four doctors disputing the moment, the exact moment, when they'd a right to say: this is death. I thought the corpse ought to know. And after some days – and nights – of consideration, I'm of the opinion that in all that matters to me I'm a dead man.

FRANCES: You're a sick man. And suffering is so strange to you.

TREBELL: I'm not suffering – far from it. While one suffers, one lives, I suppose.

The particular segment of experience which holds the play – and especially the end of the play – in an enthralled fascination and which produces both the final turn of the plot and the poised equilibrium, the tragic stasis, of the ending, is the realization of the interlocking nature of the pattern of the forces of creation and destruction; both sexually and spiritually (and those two aspects of experience are not separate) the force that renews life also destroys it; ecstasy, exaltation and despair are part of the same impulse; tenderness and savagery are mysteriously intertwined. The influence of the *Bacchae* is very clear in all this (though whether Barker himself was in any way conscious of that influence is, of course, impossible to say – and fruitless to pursue: his awareness of it, or otherwise, is in any case irrelevant to our understanding of and sense of the finished work). The wonder is that, in a play replete with so much accurately-observed detail of the matters of everyday (the *political* detail, for example, is astonishingly accurate, as are the intricacies of the whole Church question) it is possible to erect a larger-than-life yet vitally life-like figure capable of sustaining a convincingly autonomous existence while at the same time bearing the weight of existential and eschatological implications. Trebell, I am prepared to assert, is a full-scale tragic figure in the classic mould, powerfully equipped to move us, first to that baffled state of spirit in which the ambiguities and ambivalences of the human condition play oppressively on our senses and on our image of the world and then to the Miltonian 'calm of mind' in which we are enabled to realize that the hero-figure has outsoared the shadow of our night and, free from the contagion of the world's slow stain, exists timelessly in a new dimension. From the very start he has all the marks of the tragic hero upon him: he is, at the beginning, impressive, appealing, but over-assured; frighteningly self-confident; over-reliant on pure reason; packed with the nervous energy of life but somehow, even at the first, intimate with death. No man could fly so high and so strongly and not be cut down: he has the fatal flaw of *hubris* stamped upon his forehead. But he also has the one virtue without which a tragic hero cannot exist: courage. And it is, moreover, the courage to out-face the very god that strikes him down. This quality comes out much more clearly in the second version than in the first:

FRANCES:	. . . Very well. Don't work, though – or sit and think. I'll choose you a book.
TREBELL:	My mind was never clearer.
FRANCES:	The rest of you is the more tired. Mark Twain?
TREBELL:	Good – not a woman's choice, either. 'Huck Finn', please. Mark was a sound fellow. He had comic courage. A gift. I'd

Granville Barker, about the time he wrote Waste.

choose it, I think, before any. Man's last weapon against the
gods. When he's at his puniest he can still laugh them into
littlenesss – and come to his own standing again. Thank you.
I'll give Mark his chance to stop me thinking – if he can.

FRANCES: But I can't help?

TREBELL: No.

Two other traits, also, distinguish Trebell and identify him as one of the
chosen: his instinct for absolute truth and his thirst for the ideal. Like all
tragic figures, he insists to himself and others that mankind was created
to behave perfectly and the falling-off from perfection, though through
universal, and even forgivable, faults, drives him to destruction. And like
all tragic figures he comes to see that mankind's faults are *his* faults also,
that he must answer for them not only at the personal level and in his
own behalf but also as mankind's paradigm: all are sinners and he is a
sinner and he is at one with all sinners. Hence, of course, the frequent
invocations of images of natural forces, with which the play abounds.
Hence, also, statements like 'I am a son of the anger of Man at men's
foolishness . . .', statements which effectively expand the ambience of
the play from the personal to the universal, from the temporal to the
eternal. The inevitability of the reckoning is also strongly insisted upon
and convincingly conveyed by the shape of the play and by the tone and
texture of the last act: he *must* answer – no amount of rationalizing or
gainsaying or equivocating will now avail. From the common plane of
political manoeuvring and political necessity, the play moves to a plane
upon which stratagems and evasions are no longer permitted. The
experience, in other words, is a species of religious experience and is seen
by the central character as such; he kills himself, finally, not out of
despair, or out of a desire to spite his enemies, but out of simple, common
honesty (not that honesty *is* simple, or all that common).

The cumulative and mounting effect of the play is much more
cunningly contrived and is much more persuasive in the second version
than in the first. Indeed, Barker's self-criticism in that 1909 letter to
Murray ('That's all right, I believe – but I've not *done* it!!!') is, in relation
to the first version of the play, well warranted: the potential is there but
not the full realization of it. The 1926 version remedies this fault, largely
because three key scenes are much more clearly, cleanly and profoundly
written than they were the first time. The first of these scenes is a brief
confrontation between Trebell and Justin O'Connell, Amy's husband,
during the discussion at the Prime Minister's house of the strategy to be
adopted at the inquest the next day; the second is the wily conversation of

politicians which takes place, after Trebell has left, between those who are likely to constitute the next Cabinet; and the third is the passage, already discussed, between Trebell and his sister immediately before the final catastrophe. To these, one could also add mention of the scene between Frances and Julia Farrant, the scheming politician's wife, which takes place after Trebell's suicide: this scene is not a part of the rising action; it does not – and is not intended to – add to the cumulative and mounting effect; but it does, chorus-like, serve to cement and secure that action at the end of the play, to bring it into a final equilibrium in its right perspective; and it does this much more finely and firmly in the 1926 version of the play than in that of 1906.

The fault with the O'Connell-Trebell scene in the first version is a slight over-aggressiveness, too great a desire to justify and explain: Trebell comes out of it as being rather shrill and gratuitously callous and rude; his stature is diminished thereby. The scene has a certain coarseness and a faint hint of melodrama (tragedy's bastard cousin) about it. In the second version the scene is kept shorter – hardly a dozen lines in all – with all the emphasis falling upon the one essential: that O'Connell is the only one who understands Trebell and who shares his horror of a civilisation which, by implication at least, values sterility more than life. 'The two ignore the rest', says the stage direction: '*They might be alone together. The Irish voice keeps its level irony.*'

O'CONNELL: What then can I do for you?

TREBELL: What she was to you – you know. Tell the truth of it tomorrow. She has had to die to trap me. I'll tell the truth of that if need be.

If no one else understands, O'CONNELL *does; and he blazes into a white fire of passion.*

O'CONNELL: Yes, indeed . . . yes, indeed . . . a worthless woman! Had she borne you your child I could better have forgiven her. She could cheat me of mine and leave me. Is the curse of barrenness to be nothing to a man? God forgive her now. What have I left to forgive? I think we are brothers in misfortune, sir.

In the first version, Trebell argues this last point, saying that his state is worse than O'Connell's, his problem the more severe. In the second version he makes no rejoinder but simply accepts O'Connell's view and definition of the situation. The effect is to make him more sensitively perceptive than in the earlier version and, more important, to alert us earlier in the play to his growth towards tragic stature. Notice also, in this connection, the significance of 'She *has had* to die to trap me.' (The added italics are mine, not Barker's.) It is the first announcement of the theme of inevitability and it was not there in the first version.

In the long 'Cabinet discussion' scene, the second version gains by its sheer virtuosity of exposition. In it, Trebell's eventual exclusion from the Cabinet is made to result much more inevitably from his paltering with the forces of aridity and destruction and it also makes it plain that Trebell himself is aware of this and is, even at that stage, already acknowledging the justice and propriety of it at levels other than political ones. The in-fighting is also more clearly and more intricately represented in the re-written version, especially the way that Lord Blackborough, the pragmatic industrialist who has always opposed Trebell's inclusion, seizes opportunities in the twists and turns of the conversation's revelations and finally brings Lord Horsham, the Prime Minister, to a position in which he has no choice but to drop Trebell. The earlier version leaves one with the impression that, once the question of a possible scandal is disposed of by O'Connell's promise not to mention Trebell at the inquest, the rest of the argument could equally well have taken place even if Trebell had not been involved with Amy O'Connell at all. But in the second version this is not true: Trebell's involvement with death has somehow released other death-dealing forces; the argument about his exclusion from the Cabinet proceeds *because* of this involvement of Trebell's. Several times there is, in the conduct of the argument, the suggestion that, even if there were to be no breath of scandal at all, Trebell is now seen as the wrong kind of person to handle a 'Church Bill'. This point of view, though it represents no more than a mere truckling to the mindless, conventional view of such matters (especially at that time), is a very powerful one. Ironically, it uses the same equation as Trebell does, but in reverse. Where he sees the advancing of a philosophical–religious ideal as a symbol of life and birth, and the counterpart of the birth of a son, his opponents see his breaching of the social code by committing adultery as the equivalent of his entering the Cabinet (for whatever reason – and the reason, namely the Disestablishment Bill, has no intrinsic value for them) 'under a cloud'. Trebell reads their minds and intentions and is scornful of them. There is more than a faint suggestion that *he* has decided to reject *them*, even before he gets the Prime Minister's note of apologetic dismissal.

But Trebell's real offence, the duologue with Frances makes plain, is not the breaking of social codes or conventions: it is that he, who has the potential for creation in him (in his inspired view of education and his plan to wed this view to the process of Disestablishment), abdicates his authority and his rational control in a careless moment and, for mere appetite, puts himself at the mercy of the forces of destruction. Why the lusty passion – which is after all, as Trebell points out, perfectly natural and in itself both innocent and harmless – should lead with such seeming inevitability to destruction, is the irreducible mystery at the heart of the whole experience, but the play makes it clear that it does not view this as an accidental irony but as an existential anomaly, an intrinsic part of the phenomenon of physical passion. Enough has already been said, perhaps, about the two versions of the final duologue between Trebell and Frances to demonstrate the superiority of the second version. In many ways this scene is the acid test of the quality of the whole play and in its second version it is not only more assured in its touch, it is also subtler, profounder, more resonant. And it is now entirely free from the slightly overblown, faintly melodramatic tone which occasionally touches and mars the first version.

The immediate occasion for the re-writing of the play was the prospect, after a twenty-year delay, of a public production. The immediate *reason* for the re-writing was the change in, at least, the surface and the vocabulary of British politics caused by the intervening years and, especially, by the War. Among other things, a new political party had in this meantime arisen, one that was obviously moving toward power and one whose views, if the picture of politics was to be anything like complete, must – at the very least – be sketched in, added to the background. The old, simple division between Conservative and Liberal could no longer represent the political sense and climate of the country. However, given this occasion and this reason for re-writing, Barker took the opportunity to do much more than the mere surface demands of verisimilitude would have required. Keeping the plot structure entirely unchanged, he completely re-wrote the dialogue, deepening it and giving it a surer touch and a dryer tone as he went. He himself gave a brief account of the process when the revised version was published in 1927. In a dedicatory letter he said:

My dear H.M. Harwood[3],

You are responsible, though unwittingly, for this revision of *Waste*. When we agreed you should revive it, I never thought of reading it through. Did you? I said lightly that one or two alterations might be needed. Then, later, I turned to the job – and this is the result. I doubt if one scrap of the old dialogue survives[4]; the story and the characters are here, that is all. So it is a thing I had –

dramatically – to say twenty years ago, said as I'd say it now. But now I'd have something different to say.

> Yours very gratefully (if I ought to be!)
> Harley Granville-Barker

When the play was first written, in 1906–7, Barker had intended to include it in the new repertory of the Barker-Vedrenne management on its removal to the Savoy Theatre. This was prevented at the very last minute by the intervention of the censor, who refused to license the play for performance in public unless Barker agreed to omit all reference to the abortion operation. Since this would have made nonsense of the play, Barker refused to make the required alterations.[5] Instead, he presented the play for two private performances sponsored by the Stage Society at the Imperial Theatre on November 24 and 26, 1907, playing the part of Trebell himself at rather short notice, since Norman McKinnell, who had rehearsed the part, was refused permission to play it by Lena Ashwell, to whom he was under contract at the time. It was 1920 before the censor finally licensed the play for public production. In the meantime it had been published and had gone through eight impressions in less than four years, its first appearance in print being in a collection called *Three Plays* in 1909 (the other two plays were *The Marrying of Ann Leete* and *The Voysey Inheritance*). *Three Plays* was repeated three times by August 1913 and, in addition, *Waste* was published separately and also had three further impressions by 1913. It was H.M. Harwood's offer to produce the play at the Ambassador's Theatre which led to its re-submission to the censor in 1920 and to the subsequent lifting of the censorship ban. The proposed production did not materialize, however, and the play had to wait another sixteen years before receiving its first public production. Meanwhile, Barker had fully re-written it and, in 1927, published the new version. Finally, the play was produced at the Westminster Theatre in December, 1936, jointly directed by Michael MacOwan and Barker himself. The part of Trebell was played by Nicholas Hannen, an old friend of Barker's who had worked with him often before. Barker at first felt that Hannen would be too gentle for the part. Writing to him on August 13, 1936[6], Barker says:

> Much as I should want you in *any* play of mine and would like to be having another 'go' at you, Trebell, in his bitterness and hardness, spiritual egoism and blindness of heart, you would have to put on like a wig . . . You'd understand it all, of course, and *know* what to do; but temperamentally it would be so against the grain with you that you'd never be able to relax for a

second from *doing* to being – and I shouldn't credit that suicide. Or *have* you hardened up in these years? No; it's not possible.

Michael MacOwan's first choices for the part were Ralph Richardson, Raymond Massey and Robert Donat (whom Barker described as 'one of the people who thinks he can sell *half* his soul – to the cinema'). None of these three proved to be available at the right time, however, and MacOwan made a special journey to Paris to plead with Barker to reconsider Nicholas Hannen. On October 5, Barker writes to Hannen again:

> However, as Trebell is a devil of a temptation (I know how much I get out of you in whatever you do) I wrestled with it when MacOwan came over. I am wrestling with it as I write; and if, after carefully – but carefully – looking at the thing again you say you *can* do it, I shall have yet another wrestle. But *face* what is against the grain in it. Trebell has no *sunshine* in him. That is his tragedy; that is why he kills himself. Can you come on the stage and *not* impart an extra cheerfulness to the proceedings? I doubt it. But tell me what you think.

In the event, Barker was fairly happy with Hannen's playing of the part and, immediately after the play opened, he wrote to him saying: 'I owe you much, and shall owe you more. Feel your audience. Keep them with you and carry them forward as swiftly – not hurriedly – as you feel they can understandingly go. Dare to be a devil. Never be merely 'sad'. And may heaven prosper you.' There was, however, a half-joking, half-serious afterthought three weeks later when, writing from Paris (on the backs of three picture postcards), Barker says:

1. You don't deserve a Xmas card, so you don't: when a man can write to me and say – after, what, 20 performances? – 'When Trebell was making love to Amy . . . he . . . swayed on his feet . . . it made me wonder if he . . . was quite sober . . .' Curse you: may you have a miserable Xmas and a blighted
2. New Year. Do you expect me to be sitting in front night after night to throw boulders at you? Hopher Wheeler says you are first-rate and have now got the whole thing right. I don't believe him. But another thing is clear. Repertory and National Theatre is the only salvation of
3. my sort of drama.
   I'd have sent you a copy of my Hamlet if I could think you'd read it. But you're like Edward VII – in this only – 'Men are your books': for which I don't blame you.
   Well, you may have as good a Xmas as you deserve.

H.G.B.

The whole correspondence with Nicholas Hannen is interesting. Barker has a number of comments on casting and on interpretation which throw some revealing light on his own ideas about the play. These are too detailed and too numerous to be quoted here in full, but his analysis of the character of Amy O'Connell is sufficiently important to warrant quoting. Talking about the casting of the part, Barker says:

> . . . *Now be careful*; for if you go wrong you can completely wreck Act II and go far towards wrecking the whole play. She is the *femme amoureuse*; but she is not common or vulgar (no polite cockney accents, please), not the peroxide blonde. She is pretty and witty besides; very amusing company, or she would not find herself in that society. She dresses very well, and has enough money to entertain in a 'chic' way. Lady Julia thinks her 'cheap' but that is the worst that can be said of her. What she tells Trebell about herself in Act II is probably quite true. Frances (I think) says that there is 'Something of the waif about her'. That should help you a little. But what is vitally important to the play – I repeat: you may wreck it if this goes wrong – is the balance of sympathy in her case. We must feel that beside Trebell's future career and the Disestablishment Bill and a fresh start for the Church of England she is a worthless little thing; but we must also feel enough pity for her fate to understand why Trebell – just because he *cannot* feel it, did not love her and yet begot a child on her, and has seen both die and still can feel no remorse – shoots himself. *So be careful*; and in consulting me tell me just the qualities your candidates have and have not.

Barker's sense of character, as this passage shows, was very acute and *Waste* is a veritable gallery of closely-observed and cunningly-drawn portraits of a whole class – the ruling class of Edwardian England. But as well as all belonging to one class, these are portraits of *individuals*, all with foibles and idiosyncrasies of their own. Barker misses nothing of this and reproduces the personal variations brilliantly in a group of finely-differentiated portraits: the Shadow Cabinet in Act III is, especially, a piece of craftsmanship of the highest order. The style and language are the style and language of naturalism, stemming from *Agnes Colander* and *The Voysey Inheritance*, and used with great accuracy, assurance and imagination. There is, however, a danger in the very virtuosity of this naturalism: it tends to lead people to look for, and find, the wrong things. Over and over again one encounters critical comment on this central group of Barker plays which assumes that their main (or, in some cases, sole) function is that of social protest – the same mistake that was, and to some extent still is, made over middle-period Ibsen plays. Writing in *Radio Times* on December 2, 1977, for example (to introduce what turned

out to be stunningly-good television production of *Waste* by the BBC),
Michael Billington said:

> But what makes the play so rich and topical is the way it brings together all
> Granville Barker's favourite themes: English hypocrisy, women's liberation
> and, above all, the emotional sterility of many social reformers.

The statement is not exactly untrue; its danger is that it is only part of the
truth – and not the most important part. These 'themes' are, indeed, what
makes the play topical; but these are not what make it rich; its real
richness lies beyond them. The statement gives the impression that this
depiction of social evils is the play's main purpose, which I think is
untrue. It also gives the impression of far too conscious and deliberate a
decision, on Barker's part, to set about some items of much-needed
social reform. Both the tone and the substance of Barker's letters,
especially those to Murray and Archer, tend to militate against such a
view. Eighteen months or so later, in another *Radio Times* article – this
time introducing a BBC television production of *The Voysey Inheritance*
– Billington followed the same line again: 'One of his [Barker's]
favourite themes was the gulf in Britain between morality and practice:
and it is this which animates *The Voysey Inheritance*.' It is not: what
chiefly animates *The Voysey Inheritance* is the anarchistic discovery that
the chief source of power and energy for the real life of the individual
comes not from any compact with society but from the individual's
secret compact with mysterious and ruthless forces beyond himself and
bigger than himself. The same is true of *Waste*: far from condemning
hypocrisy, the play virtually endorses it as the necessary mask behind
which the fully-living, creative self must hide from the trivializing
depredations of the world. Political life is shown as *necessarily* debased:
that is its intrinsic nature. Trebell becomes a brilliant politician because
that is the only way to defend his ideals, but he despises the methods he
has to use; the play is strewn with ironic and cynical comments by him
about both his political associates and his political opponents. What is
more, the play makes it clear that this is not meant to be a condemnation
of politicians in particular: it is mankind itself which is fatally flawed.
Take, for example, the following:

BLACK- BOROUGH	Horsham has called some of us here to discuss the situation. I am considering my opinion.
TREBELL:	You are not, Blackborough. You haven't recovered yet from the shock of your manly feelings. Oh, cheer up. You know we're an adulterous and sterile generation. Why should you cry

out at a proof now and then of what's always in the hearts of
most of us?

(1st version)

Trebell knows that the political defence of ideals, presented to the
political world with the design of fending it off, is a mere façade behind
which the real battle for defence goes on. And this realization, on the part
of both Trebell and the play, forces the play to an altogether higher level
than that of socio-political protest. The issue becomes a spiritual one.
The real power to carry on the battle of defence comes from the secret life
and part of the reason for Trebell's suicide (and part of the entity of
tragedy in the play) is his feeling that he has betrayed his trust precisely
by allowing Amy – who has no title to his heart – to breach this defence
and invade the world of his secrecy. Trebell also recognizes, however
(and here the play moves even further from the sphere of everyday
practical problems and deeper into the complexity and mystery of the
immutable nature of things), that it is not poor, silly, little Amy who is to
blame, but the misdirected sexual urge, which is basic to the nature of
man and which afflicts him as well as her. He is a sacrifice to Dionysus, or
perhaps to that older and more primitive god, Priapus. It is noteworthy
not only that Amy and Trebell do not care for each other but also that
neither of them much likes the opposite sex at all. 'I don't really like men
– that's the silly thing', Amy says to Trebell in Act II when she tells him
of her pregnancy: 'But you've to fool them or they'll fool you.' And in
Act IV, Frances says to him: 'You hate women. . . I've heard you say . . .
when you can't altogether despise them.' So Trebell, who has 'reasoned
his way through life' is caught by Dionysus, the god of high spirits,
quivering nerves and torn flesh, the god of *excess*, excess of eating, excess
of drinking, excess of mating, excess of breeding, excess of killing, excess
of feeling, excess of noise – a pure extravagance; the opposite but twin
master-spirit of the cool Apollonian reason, joint governors of Man,
both rooted inherently in Man's very nature. But Trebell is all
Apollonian, stubbornly denying one half of nature, flying in the face of
the terrible god and being, like Pentheus, destroyed for his pains. It is a
measure of the stature of the play and of the stature to which the central
character attains by the play's end, that he comes to recognize and to
accept the spiritual necessity of his sacrifice. The variant texts of the two
versions are both remarkable on this point. Just before he leaves his sister,
knowing in his heart by now that he will kill himself, the following
occurs:

1st version

TREBELL: Disestablishment. It's a very interesting problem. I must think
             it out.

FRANCES: What do you mean?

             He gets up with a quick movement of strange strength and faces her.
             His smile changes into a graver gladness.

TREBELL: Something has happened – in spite of me. My heart's clean
             again. I'm ready for fresh adventures.

2nd version

TREBELL: And whatever our failings, Frankie, we've meant to live, you
             and I, in the large freedom of the mind. So let's be true to it. My
             faith – a man needs one when he faces the ignorance of death –
             is that Nature is spendthrift: yet the God to whose creating we
             travail may be infinitely economical and waste, perhaps, less of
             the wealth of us when we're dead than *we* waste in the
             faithlessness and slavery of our lives.

Note especially that 'we've meant to live' (not 'we're meant to live')
and that 'God to whose creating we travail . . .' The essential instruments
in the struggle towards a sense of the infinite and the absolute are man's
own sensibilities and his willingness to tune his own nature to the whole
vast mystery of all Nature. Trebell, in saying this, has achieved that
moment of quiet understanding and acceptance which is the mark of and
the reward of the truly tragic figure. This is a deeply religious play.

Perhaps the final word on *Waste* should be this: in the hands of a
playwright only slightly less gifted than Barker, the play's burden of
circumstantial detail and everyday (relatively) conversation would have
dragged it down to the level of an ordinary, decent, drama of political
and social problems. What would have been important in it would have
been a series of questions such as 'Is the disestablishment of the Church of
England a good idea?', 'Should successful politicians sleep with other
men's wives?', 'Should society censure them if they do?', 'Is abortion a
bad thing?', and so on. The genius of the play is (as it is with *A Doll's
House* or *Rosmersholm*) that it makes use of these questions without
dishonouring them and yet rises far above them, to create for itself a
world in which there are new perspectives: practical questions appear
puny and some part of the central mystery is celebrated. There are three
main factors which contribute to this. One is the construction of the play
which, taut as a barrel, rescues us time and again from the shallows of

sociological considerations and propels us firmly into the deeper waters. The second is the dialogue which, while staying firmly (and properly) within the convention of realism which it has set for itself, nevertheless has the capacity – so finely is it modelled – to lift the play above the level of the everyday. Charles Morgan, who was the theatre critic for *The Times* from 1926 to 1939, reviewing the Westminster Theatre production of *Waste* in that journal on December 2, 1936, talked about 'the unhurried distinction of its dialogue' and went on to say: 'As soon as conversation begins one is struck by its point, its careful lightness, the shrewd restraint by which its meaning is declared.' The third element in the elevation of the play to heights beyond the ordinary is the stature and the dynamism of the central character. Morgan again: 'Through it all Mr. Hannen carries the weight of the play. He has the fire to suggest Trebell's imaginative power and a balance which enables him to distinguish Trebell, as Mr. Granville-Barker has distinguished him, from the common political dreamers of the stage.'

We could do worse than take one of Charles Morgan's more general comments, on the play as a whole, for our summing-up: 'The pleasure it gives', he said 'is of a kind nowadays rare.' Rare at any time: but the quality which makes it so also gives it the power to survive in days other than its own. It is only two years younger than *Man and Superman* and three years younger than *The Cherry Orchard* and, while not as mighty as either of them, it *is* still today as living and lively as either of them and is of their quality, if not quite of their stature.

For about a year after completing *Waste*, Granville Barker had no play on the stocks. Then early in 1909 he began the writing of *The Madras House*. He had just returned from his first visit to New York, having turned down the offer of the directorship of the 'millionaires' theatre' – the proposed new repertory theatre. He was busy in the early part of that year directing the first production of Galsworthy's *Strife* at the Duke of York's Theatre, Charles Frohman's theatre. Later in the year he was actively planning, with Gilbert Murray, for a production of the latter's newly-finished translation of *Iphigenia in Tauris* and also, possibly, a revival of the *Hippolytus*. The former, as things turned out, did not take place until 1912 and the latter failed to materialize at all. There were also in that year meetings and campaigns and protests about the Lord Chamberlain's power to censor plays and Barker, both in his capacity as theatre manager and as author, was deeply involved in these. Meanwhile, whenever he could, he retired to the country and got on with *The Madras House*. 'Oh, my poor new play!' he moans to Murray in one letter, when progress was not as fast as he would like. By July, however, he was able to write to Murray saying:

> Dear G.M.,
>
> I have this day done the last bit of a new play – and there's lots wrong with it: principally I know that its philosophic flats are not joined. I seem to have said something quite different from what I had set out to say. And I'd rather like to inflict it on you – if you'd bear it and that were possible – and get your sentiments.

And a little later, in another letter to Murray, he touches on the subject again: 'Well, when will you hear that play, I wonder? It is not what it should be and it certainly does want the light of your intellectual morality and moral intellectuality turned on it.' Long afterwards, his opinion of his play, we find, had improved considerably. Writing to William Archer on May 13, 1921, he said: '*The Madras House* is the best play I've written yet – dialogue almost equal to Dekker.' The claim is not entirely unwarranted.

In broad, general terms *The Madras House* is the comedy counterpart of the tragedy of *Waste*. The twin themes of the power of sex and the possibility of idealism, which were given tragic treatment in *Waste*, are accorded comic treatment in *The Madras House*. And *The Madras House* has a subsidiary theme also which indirectly links with both the main ones: it is money. A brief opening duologue announces the themes firmly and succinctly. Philip, who is the play's central character, says to his friend Hippisly Thomas: 'Well, my dear Tommy, what are the two most important things in a man's character? His attitude towards money and his attitude to women.' And a moment later:

PHILIP: It is quite impossible for any decent man to walk with his eyes open from Waterloo to Denmark Hill on a Sunday morning without wishing me to stand for the County Council.

THOMAS: You've got what I call the Reformer's mind. I shouldn't cultivate it, Phil. It makes a man unhappy and discontented, not with himself but with other people, mark you – so it makes him conceited and puts him out of condition both ways. Don't you get to imagine you can make this country better by tidying it up.

After this exposition, the rest of the play is a set of quite brilliant variations on the two themes; and at the end there is a recapitulation (not altogether satisfactory) and a coda.

The play, on the face of it, looks like a play about the position of women in society. I think it is not. It seems to me, rather, to be a play about *sex* in society: it simply happens that Barker has juxtaposed – and most artfully – a number of situations involving women and society's varying attitudes to them as a way of adumbrating his major theme. But to praise the play – as some have done, both at the time of its first production and since – for its support of the women's liberation movement, is to miss three-quarters of its point. The play is concerned with the freedom of the human spirit, but not in any narrow political sense: and not the female spirit any more than the male. The juxtaposed situations aforementioned each occupy one act of the play. They are linked together by the slenderest of plot-lines but are very firmly unified by the central themes: sex – money – idealism. The first two acts deal, in a manner of speaking, with women in prison, all their creativity – sexual and otherwise – suppressed. In Act I the prison is a Victorian–Edwardian family; the prisoners are the six unmarried daughters, varying in ages from twenty-six to thirty-nine: the case of Honor Voysey is, as it were, extended to its logical conclusion and becomes, though frighteningly, a *reductio ad absurdum*. In Act II the prison is a draper's shop and the prisoners, both men and women, are the employees who not only work in the shop but are victims of the 'living-in' system: they live on the premises, sleeping in supervised dormitories. The third act deals not so much with imprisonment as commercial exploitation. The victims, who are also in a sense the predators, are mannequins who work for an expensive West End gown shop, using their sexual attractions and allure but not for any proper sexual purpose. The fourth act considers women – and one woman in particular – in marriage, and here the play looks half-hopefully at the possibility of comradeship, companionship and real partnership in place of the constant ploys and stratagems of the sexual game. Philip says to Jessica, his wife: 'But I do so hate that farm-yard world of sex – men and women always treating each other in this unfriendly way.' Jessica's reply is: 'I hate it, too – but I happen to love you, Phil.'

The drapery shop of Act II is that of Roberts & Huxtable and is in Peckham. The gown shop of Act III is the Madras House and is in Bond Street. These two establishments are both owned jointly by two inter-related families. The Madras House was started thirty years before by Constantine Madras, who married Amelia Huxtable, sister of Henry Huxtable, owner of the drapery establishment of Roberts & Huxtable. The six unmarried duaghters, living in the large family house on Denmark Hill, are Henry Huxtable's daughters. Constantine many years ago deserted Amelia, became a Mohammedan (which Barker always spells 'Mahommedan') because he thought the Muslim treatment of women more dignified and went to live in Southern Arabia. Amelia, meanwhile, has remained what she calls 'faithful' to him so as to be in the position of best advantage to reproach him the more. Philip, Constantine's son, is now part-owner of both businesses and is disgusted with the dreariness, grubbiness and crass commercialism into which they have turned his life. He contemplates leaving the business world, no matter how lucrative, and finding some more meaningful way of living. His opportunity comes when an American millionaire, Eustace Perrin State, indicates an interest in buying-up both the Madras House and Roberts & Huxtable. That is the extent of the main plot of the play. There are two sub-plots, of sorts. One concerns Amelia's efforts to get Constantine to return to her, on the simple grounds that it is his moral duty to do so. The other concerns Miss Yates, an employee in the drapery shop who inconveniently (considering that she is unmarried) becomes pregnant and refuses to be repentant about it. After some threatening misunderstandings about 'who the man was' and some false accusations against a mild-mannered and henpecked married man who also works at the Roberts & Huxtable shop, it transpires that the father of Miss Yates's child is Constantine.

So far as actual happenings and occurrences are concerned, that is the entire play. We gather that the sale of the two businesses is to go through, but it does not happen during the play; we gather that Philip will stand for the County Council and will devote himself to good works, but it does not happen during the play. Constantine reluctantly consents to meet Amelia, at her urgent request, talks with her for a few minutes and then returns to his Mohammedan life in Hit, Southern Arabia. Everything remains *in statu quo ante*.

Clearly, we are dealing here with a design quite different from the tightly-knit and event-full structure of *Waste*. *The Madras House* utterly rejects the notion that a play must tell a story and that the only kind of forward movement it can possibly have is from one more or less exciting incident to another. The forward movement in *The Madras House* is a movement through a range of passionately perceived ideas. It begins at the point of ordinary, normal complacency – that we're really not such a bad lot and that our institutions and society are really pretty civilized, taken all in all. Take this sex question, for example: we've tamed the tiger and taught him manners; men and women rub along (if you'll forgive the expression) pretty well together these days. . . . It proceeds through the hypocrisy, sterility, barrenness and aridity of all the chief centres of our civilization (family, local commerce, big business, marriage). It arrives with a tentative hopefulness at the possibility of a kind of aristocracy of the spirit promoted by the diligence, compassion and sensitivity of individual relationships. The dominant imagery of the play, as in *Waste*, is barrenness,[7] but since it is treated comically instead of tragically there emerges from the work the possibility of an eventual fecundity. Or perhaps one should put that the other way round and say that because the vision of life in *The Madras House* is, though ironic, a more hopeful one than it is in *Waste*, seeing the possibility of humanity's overcoming its spiritual barrenness, *The Madras House* becomes a comedy while *Waste* is a tragedy.

Just as the plot of *The Madras House* is deliberately reduced to vestigial remains, so the characters are deliberately drawn without any kind of development during the play. They are whole, complete, entire at their first appearances and they remain unchanged. To refer to them as 'portraits', indeed, has a particular and pointed significance in this play, for they come to us like pictures in gilt frames, fixed forever in their perfect postures. And in saying so, I intend no derogation: given the kind of play this is, it is perfectly proper – absolutely necessary, in fact – that the characters should have this fixed, deliberately static, quality. In the case of three of them there is the suggestion of the *possibility* of movement, though that movement does not occur – nor should it – during the play: but in these three instances it is right and proper that the play should suggest the presence of a potential for development in the character. The three are Miss Yates, Philip Madras and – highly controversially – Jessica Madras. (I say 'controversially' because I can find no other critic to agree with me and several who write at some length about Jessica in ways with which I find I cannot agree: I will develop this argument and difference of opinion a little later on.) Apart from the question of mobility and development, the characters of *The Madras House* have another special quality peculiar to themselves (or, rather, peculiar to this particular play): they are intriguingly placed – by the *play*, I mean: I do not imply a deliberate and schematic decision on the part of the playwright – on a sliding scale which ranges from the detailed naturalistic–realistic portrait to the out-and-out, larger-than-life caricature. In fact, this might with usefulness be rendered graphically, as follows:

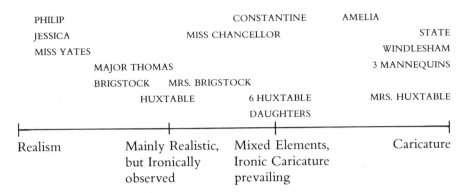

PHILIP		CONSTANTINE	AMELIA	
JESSICA		MISS CHANCELLOR		STATE
MISS YATES				WINDLESHAM
	MAJOR THOMAS			3 MANNEQUINS
	BRIGSTOCK MRS. BRIGSTOCK			
	HUXTABLE	6 HUXTABLE		MRS. HUXTABLE
		DAUGHTERS		

Realism	Mainly Realistic, but Ironically observed	Mixed Elements, Ironic Caricature prevailing	Caricature

In a less well-constructed and less firmly-controlled piece this breadth of stylistic approach might well result in a mere patchwork effect or, worse still, downright disintegration: in *The Madras House* the result is an astonishing richness of surface and depth of observation, held in place and relation by the multiple strands of imagery running through the play and the sheer intellectual force and integrity with which the central experience of the play is approached.

(Of course, no literary or dramatic portrait is *absolutely* realistic, a mere photograph's reproduction devoid of all comment; and no real play or novel is just a documentary record, or it would be just that – a documentary record and not a work of art at all. All the characters represented, if they have any quality, contain some element of *generality*, of extrapolation from the individual figure to the great bulk of mankind, though this does not imply, of necessity, any suggestion of caricature. Nevertheless, that process of extrapolation, of generality, is the beginning of the road towards caricature, satirical portraiture. The nature of the work, if the work is organically sound, will control the *extent* of this process and will decide how far the process is to be allowed to go. The striking feature of *The Madras House* is its capacity to extend that process much further in some characters than others without sacrificing the essential unity of the piece: it contrives to maintain unity, in other words, without the necessity for homogeneity.

The two figures which most completely exemplify the satirical mode of the play, Mr. Windlesham and Eustace Perrin State, are worth a special word. Mr. Windlesham is the manager of Madras House, Philip's employee, organizer of the mannequin parade which is presented for the delectation of Philip, Constantine, State and Huxtable in Act III: Eustace Perrin State is the rich American who comes to buy up the two businesses of Roberts & Huxtable, drapers and Madras House, *hauts couturiers*.

Even their names make fun of them: 'State', as the name of a domineering American, is obvious enough; 'Windlesham' is subtler and more interesting. 'Windle' is an old Scots dialect word meaning thin, dry, wasted: the word is never found now except in the combination, 'windlestraw', which is the dried stalk after the flower and the seed-pod have fallen. So, 'Windlesham' – a man of straw, desiccated, barren: and only an imitation, a sham, even at that.

(Shaw, of course, often named his characters – in the fashion of the seventeenth and eighteenth centuries – by names which suggested their functions or characteristics and Barker sometimes followed suit. *The Madras House* is full of this device and it is especially appropriate that it should be so: it is an anti-naturalistic signal which helps to prevent our thinking of the play as a piece of Edwardian 'social drama', a stuffy study of 'conditions'; and it is especially suitable for a play which is an important and distinguished example of a species of comedy of manners. 'Madras' itself is, in the trade, a name for a kind of cloth. 'Huxtable' derives from 'huxter', an archaic form of 'huckster', the meaning of which is given by the Oxford English Dictionary as 'a retailer of small goods . . . a broker, a middleman . . . a person ready to make his profit of anything in a mean and petty way'. 'Constantine' is surely intended to have for us suggestions both of the imperial and of the Byzantine: vaguely Middle-East connotations at the very least, perhaps with ironic overtones when one discovers that this Constantine is, in reversal of the example of his Imperial namesake, a convert *from* Christianity. And we note in passing that the person appointed by the supreme authority to exercise deputed jurisdiction over the household of Roberts & Huxtable, is Miss *Chancellor*.)

Mr. Windlesham is caricature at its purest (and funniest): a cross between an eighteenth-century French dancing-master and an Egyptian eunuch, he is a person whom the system and the situation have entirely emasculated, leaving him fit for nothing but to be laughed at. Nor need we pause to waste sympathy on him as a pathetic figure (indeed, the play's authority is firmly set against such a response), since he is a willing party to his own debasement; he *likes* it; he is a part of the very system which demoralized him. Barker's description of him in the stage directions, when he first enters, catches his image exactly:

> He is a tailor-made man; and the tailor only left off for the wax modeller and the wigmaker to begin. For his clothes are too perfect to be worn by anything but a dummy, and his hair and complexion are far from human. Not that he dyes or paints them; no, they were made like that. His voice is a little inhuman, too, and as he prefers the French

language, with which he has a most unripe acquaintance, to his own, and so speaks English as much like French as his French is like English, his conversation seems as unreal as the rest of him. Impossible to think of him in any of the ordinary relations of life. He is a functionary.

This figure – and, for that matter, the whole of Act III – is enough to correct any mistaken impression that the central concern of the play can be reduced to anything as simple as the victimization of women by men. It is not a heroines-and-villains melodrama, giving us a simple-minded invitation to take sides. Rather, it reflects in terms which are comic at first impact and fraught with unease in their final effect the sense of modern western urban society's (I almost wrote 'civilization's', but thought in time of the two-edged irony of such a usage) awful proclivity for willingly and wilfully rendering itself barren, for refusing to see in the sexual relationship a metaphor for both the force of life and the danger of death, not merely for the individual but for the race as a whole. Just short of the tragedy of seeing the Life Principle itself give up and surrender to an eternity of non-being is the comedy of seeing dead things pretending to be alive; and of the latter phenomenon, Mr. Windlesham is a prime and beautiful example.

Mr. State is a potent and dangerous variant of the same theme: over a ruthless and predatory commercial instinct he has spread a veneer of cultural highmindess. He maintains – and apparently actually believes – that his principal motive for wanting to buy up the Madras House is a wish to make a significant contribution to what he calls 'the Woman Question'. He sees female adornment and allure as a selfless, high-minded thing quite devoid of any implications of physical sexuality, a 'beautiful' and 'poetic' thing, an extension of what, in his cosy, over-heated, highly sentimental way, he regards as being true cultural values. His conversation is larded with literary references and quotations, scraps of popular Latin and second-hand philosophy. If he were not funny he would be loathsome: actually, he is *very* funny: the whole concept of him is brilliantly original and is brilliantly executed. He explains how he bought up the millinery business, Burrows & Co., in Nottingham and hit on the splendidly simple device of having women shop assistants to serve in the men's clothing department and men to serve in the women's department:

Athletes everyone of 'em . . . not a man under six foot . . . bronzed, noble fellows! And no flirting allowed . . . no making eyes . . . no pandering to anything Depraved. Just the Ordinary Courtesies of our Modern Civilization

from Pure Clean-minded Gentlemen towards any of the Fair Sex who step in
to buy a shilling sachet or the like. And pay, sir . . . The women come in
flocks!

Though he deceives none of his listeners, either among the characters of
the play or among the audience, he does deceive himself. His pursuit of
profit is, for him, completely masked by what he genuinely regards as
noble motives:

> It is but six months ago that I started to study the Woman Question from the
> point of view of Burrows and Co. I attended women's meetings in London, in
> Manchester and in one-horse places as well. Now Political Claims were but
> the narrowest, drabbest aspect as I saw it. The Women's Movement is
> Woman expressing herself. Let us look at things as they are. What are a
> woman's chief means – how often her only means – of expressing herself?
> Anyway . . . what is the first thing she spends her money on? Clothes,
> gentlemen, clothes.

Notice the capital letters which Barker uses to delineate State's subject
headings: Woman Question, Political Claims, etc. Even the printed page
satirizes this most egregious of pretentious self-deluders, who sums up
his view of the progress of woman in the following way:

> And now that the Seed of Freedom is sown in their Sweet Natures . . . what
> Mighty Forest . . . what a Luxuriant, Tropical, Scented growth of Woman-
> hood may not spring up around us. For we live in an Ugly World. Look at my
> tie! Consider your vest, Major Thomas! This is all the Living Beauty there is.
> We want more of it.

The 'Living Beauty' is the mannequin display, which is being presented
by Mr. Windlesham at the time: but by 'Living Beauty' Mr. State does
not mean the young woman who is wearing the dress, but the dress itself.
He actually says a moment later, about the young woman: 'You clean
forget they're there. We gave some time and money to elaborating a
mechanical moving figure to take the place of . . . a real automaton, in
fact. But sometimes it stuck and sometimes it ran away . . .'

One of the twentieth century's more dubious contributions to the
pattern of human activity is the invention of the advertising man, the
public relations officer, the purveyor of half-truths whose profession and
craft (in both senses of the word) depend, consciously or unconsciously,
upon misrepresentation. Even lacking modern, sophisticated examples,
Barker caught the breed to the life and fixed it accurately for ever in the
satirical figure of Eustace Perrin State, who takes the easily acceptable

cliché elements of the Victorian attitude to women, coarsens and sen-
timentalizes it, clothes it in high-flown, specious, spurious language and
uses it to cloak his own commercial rapaciousness from others. His
posture and his actions are both meretricious and deadly – in the most
precisely literal sense of both of those words – but he is, nevertheless, not
a villain; he is not a cause of the disease but a symptom of it: the cause lies
deeper, in the way society has structured itself; and perhaps even deeper
than that, in the basic, essential nature of the humanity which makes up
that society. For it is humanity's tendency to deny its own potential and
to commit spiritual suicide by cultivating sterility and the deathly forces
within itself that the play is concerned with. And Constantine's easy
argument for encouraging mere physical self-indulgence by organizing
society in such a way as to treat sex as a play-thing, a toy, sequestered
from the serious work of the world. is no adequate response. Spiritual
barrenness demands spiritual regeneration; mere physical fecundity is
not the answer.

Act III of *The Madras House* is the comic focus of the play and the
work's true centre of gravity. But because Act III represents the nadir,
the bottom of the spiritual pit, though the zenith of theatrical energy and
high spirits, Act IV becomes all the more necessary to restore the
spiritual balance. From the first production of the play in 1910 onward,
many critics of the rare revivals of the play and of the published text have
stigmatized Act IV either as an anti-climax or even as an irrelevance.
Barker himself was dissatisfied with his writing of this Act and for the
revival of the play at the Ambassador's Theatre in 1925 (when Nicholas
Hannen played Philip Madras and the Jessica was Cathleen Nesbitt) he
re-wrote the long, final duologue between Philip and Jessica, and greatly
improved it. (His slight adjustments of the rest of the text were relatively
unimportant and all the foregoing quotations from the play have been
taken from the original 1910 text.) But even in the original text the
intention of Act IV, and especially of its final duologue, seems to me to be
clear, though sometimes a little clumsy in execution and sometimes a
little too earnest and over-heated – too anxious, in fact, to *tell* us what the
play is about. These were the faults which Barker contrived to correct in
the 1925 version. Clumsiness apart, however, the real crux of the matter,
so far as the effectiveness of Act IV is concerned (and its effectiveness
ultimately depends upon its capacity to bring the play into a state of
dramatic equilibrium in an established and recognizable conclusion
rather than allowing it to drift off the stage in an indeterminate sort of
way), is the position to be occupied by Jessica. Philip, too, presents some

questions of balance and emphasis, but the real problem is Jessica.

We have seen her briefly before, in Act II, where she is introduced to us by a long and highly important description in the stage directions. It says:

> *Philip's wife is an epitome of all that aesthetic culture can do for a woman. More: she is the result not of thirty-three years but of three or four generations of cumulative refinement. She might be a race horse! Come to think of it, it is a very wonderful thing to have raised this crop of ladyhood. Creatures, dainty in mind and body, gentle in thought and word, charming, delicate, sensitive, graceful, chaste, credulous of all good, shaming the world's ugliness and strife by the very ease and delightsomeness of their existence; fastidious – fastidious – fastidious; also in these latter years with their attractions more generally salted by the addition of learning and humour. Is not the perfect lady perhaps the most wonderful achievement of civilisation, and worth the cost of her breeding, worth the toil and the helotage of – all the others? Jessica Madras is even something more than a lady, for she is conscious of her ladyhood. She values her culture and fosters it. It is her weapon, it justifies her. As she floats now into the ugly room, exquisite from her eyelashes to her shoes, it is a great relief – just the sight of her.*

Is this description intended ironically? Is it meant to imply that fine breeding only creates parasites? Is it saying that 'culture' – refinement, delicacy, beauty, sensitivity – is only one more of the prisons in which we entrap the human spirit (or, if you like, one more of the self-indulgent escape-routes from the grim realities of the world to a warm, clean, scented never-never land)? This is the way the character of Jessica and the place she occupies in the play have often been read. (It was, for example, the way the part was played in the magnificent revival at the National Theatre in 1977.) Approached thus, Jessica necessarily becomes one of the static, satirical figures in relation to whom we are not invited (by the play) to consider even the possibility of movement or character development.

There are three difficulties about such a reading. One is that it seems to run counter to some of the things Jessica is given to say, especially in the final duologue (and more especially in the revised version of that duologue); the second is – it seems to me – that a negative Jessica of this sort, no matter how brilliant the caricature, makes it very difficult to bring off the ending of the play, where a sympathetically-considered Jessica, the female counterpart of Philip's male character, is needed; the third difficulty is that a mocked Jessica seems, when one really gets down to it, to contradict the sense and spirit of that long stage direction in Act II, which, though it has – and is meant to have – a touch of irony and an ambivalence of tone, is nevertheless genuine in its admiration of Jessica.

As to the things Jessica herself says in the play, the clearest picture of her position can be obtained by putting together a line or two of dialogue from the 1910 version with a line or two from the 1925 version. Indeed, Barker should perhaps, for clarity's sake, have somehow worked both into the final version. In the first, the passage reads:

PHILIP: . . . And with each other. . . why not always some touch of the tranquil understanding which is yours and mine, dear, at the best of moments?

JESSICA   (*happily*): Do you mean when we sometimes want to shake hands?

PHILIP   (*happily too*): That's it. And I want an art and culture that shan't be just a veneer on savagery. . . but it must spring in good time from the happiness of a whole people.

JESSICA *gives herself one little shake of womanly commonsense.*

JESSICA: Well, what's to be done?

PHILIP: I've been making suggestions. We must learn to live on a thousand a year . . . put Mildred to a sensible school . . . and I must go on the County Council. That's how great spiritual revolutions work out in practice, to begin with.

JESSICA   (*as one who demands a right*): Where's my share of the job?

A Jessica fixed in the amber of satire or caricature would be incapable of suggesting the sympathetic development implied by her 'What's to be done?' and 'Where's my share of the job?' Similarly in the second version:

PHILIP: . . . Our fireside problem is the world's in a sense . . . since male and female created He them, leaving us to do the rest: though men and women have been long enough in the making . . . for we two do sum up most of the differences in life between us. And we don't shirk them.

JESSICA: I do, often.

PHILIP: Then don't you dare to.

JESSICA   (*with a little secret sigh*): I always shall. It's easier for you to face things and not fear if the truth will hurt. You are free. You weren't brought up to think you must be either good or bad . . . and wondering whether you'd turn out pretty or plain. Yes, you let me forget I'm a female. And I see your vision, too . . . I think I do . . . when we've been frank and friendly with each other . . . when we feel we want to shake hands.

PHILIP: Yes, that's the good moment.

JESSICA: But you can't be wise for us.

PHILIP: I know.

JESSICA: I suppose we've still to set ourselves free.

Here, Jessica is even more feeling, though less confident of her ability to turn feeling into action. But here again, a hard, unsympathetic or carica- tured Jessica could not possibly carry the point of the scene, which surely is that civilization's proclivity for spiritual suicide can be checked and reversed, that sex need not become, as it seems in modern urban society to have become, a symbol of death instead of life. Jessica's daintiness, exquisiteness, refinement and withdrawal from the ugliness of the world can – and should – be glanced at in the earlier parts of the play with a touch of ironic amusement: it is deserved. But she must not be pilloried or ridiculed (which Windlesham, State, Constantine and Mrs. Huxtable should be) because the play needs her at its end to seal the bargain with Philip – and with us. If one approaches her in this way and then goes back and reads the Act II description of her again, its implied admiration of her becomes clearer. When it asks 'Is not the perfect lady perhaps the most wonderful achievement . . . and worth the cost of her breeding, worth the toil and the helotage of – all the others?' the sociological answer must be 'No, she isn't.' But the answer is given only after a long hesitation – for she stands not just for refinement of manners but refinement of spirit, too: and for the creation and preservation of that, the payment of a large price would seem warranted. And there is implied in that question of cost – of toil and helotage – another, similar question. For the same sort of reckoning applies to great art and great artists: were Aeschylus, Sopho- cles and Euripides worth the price of Greek slavery? Or Beethoven and Goethe the price of the downtrodden German peasant? For that does seem to be the bargain that Nature offers us – the highest achievements of a few great spirits rest on the non-entity of the great mass of mankind and the development and preservation of the former is achieved by the sacrificing of the latter. The alternative seems to be some sort of levelling process which raises the lowest levels a very little but reduces the highest points a great deal. So before we confidently throw all aristocracy overboard (and I do not mean the aristocracy of money or of social class, which *should* be thrown overboard) we need to pause and wonder, not whether the great aristocrats of the spirit are worth the price, but whether we think that life without them is worth the living. The temper of our present egalitarian times tends to dictate the answer to this question, too, but in spite of our temptation to assume that every idea and every activity is just as important and valuable as every other idea and activity, we should not too readily plunge for the obvious, anti- aristocratic reply, unpopular though the alternative may be. This is the dilemma that is built into the end of *The Madras House*. Barker deals fairly with it: he does not cheat by superimposing his own personal view upon the play, but allows the intrinsic, inherent conflicts and contradictions to assert themselves. In the first version he makes Philip say:

PHILIP: And yet we have to teach Mildred what love of the world means, Jessica. Even if it's an uncomfortable business. Even if it means not adding her to that aristocracy of good feeling and good taste . . . the very latest of class distinctions. I tell you I haven't come by these doubts so easily. Beautiful sounds and sights and thoughts are all of the world's heritage I care about. Giving them up is like giving up my carefully created soul out of my keeping before I die.

JESSICA: And into whose?

PHILIP: I'm afraid into the keeping of everybody we are at present tempted to dislike and despise. For that's Public Life. That's Democracy. But that's the Future.

Here was an aspect of the political and social upheavals of the day to which not much attention was being paid in 1910, but seen in retrospect from the vantage point of 1983 the pronouncement is as prophetic as anything in Gorky or Chekhov. Barker's own personal convictions on the question were narrower and more rigid than Philip's. Writing to Sir Cuthbert Headlam on June 7, 1928, he said:

And all the bright young men (of whom you are still one) are going into the City now. Good for the City. In fact, it is going to solve the social problem by making commerce and finance public spirited – aristocratic. If we don't keep an aristocracy of some sort alive we're damned.[8]

His faith in High Finance and the City seems a little naïve, but his leaning toward aristocracy (and the word should not be misinterpreted in this context) is clear enough. His artistic instinct, in the play, is subtler, more profound, more perceptive than his political and social instinct and he gets into *The Madras House* much more of the ambivalence and Janus-quality of the issue than he does into his slightly sycophantic approach to Headlam. None of this is to argue, however, that the ending of *The Madras House* should be treated ponderously and solemnly. It needs a light touch, taking itself seriously but simultaneously realizing the enormity of the proposition. The burden of this falls chiefly on Philip, who needs to be not too intense about his reforming zeal and his divine mission. The London County Council as a symbol of the Kingdom of Heaven on earth is hard to take and Philip, the character, should know that, too, and be prepared half to laugh at himself, rather as a Chekhov character would (Sonya, at the end of *Uncle Vanya*, saying 'We must work . . . we shall rest'; or Gaev in *The Cherry Orchard*, saying 'I've got a job in a bank now: I'm a financier!') Surely Philip, with at least a part of his mind, looks on the County Council as a bit of a *joke*? What right-minded man could possibly do otherwise? And the part of the mind that sees the joke is the creative part, the part that humanity relies on to provide its progress and keep its sanity for it. But this does not mean that when the C.C. does something brutal, mean, self-serving or foolish the other part of that same mind will not be angry. It will be – and should be – blazingly angry. Though fiendishly difficult to play, the final duologue of *The Madras House* seems to me to be finely and correctly conceived. It moves the dramatic action of the play to a point of balance, it brings Jessica into her true focus – with Philip at the centre of the play. He has been, throughout, the central pillar of the whole structure and has come to represent the life-embracing principle, the need for courage in accepting life wherever it leads and whatever it brings; most of all the need for seeing things clearly and facing them honestly. But these virtues are not enough: there is the need, after the acceptance of life, for a refining of its essence until mankind has produced the very best, the very highest, he can produce. At the symbolic level, it is Jessica's task to represent this refinement, not without acknowledging both its dangers and its ironies, but nevertheless tipping the final balance modestly in the positive direction. At the personal level of character-drawing, she is an entirely credible creation – a sensible, sensitive person with high standards, sure of herself but just beginning to realize that her sureness may be ill-founded, just beginning to see that she stands on the edge of new and far-reaching discoveries that will change the balance of her whole outlook and, with it, her whole life. Her immediate, overt response to this discovery is a defensive one; she feels threatened (which, indeed, she is) and she instinctively musters her weapons, one of which is a certain ladylike arrogance. But this is not the only element in her response; nor is it the one which finally prevails. Hesitantly, half-fearfully, she accepts the challenge and agrees to face the new future. I cannot agree with Margery Morgan when she says of Barker:

> Something still prevented him, as it prevents Philip, from coming out against Jessica, recognizing her clearly as perhaps the most negative and cold-hearted character in the whole play, and recognizing the thoroughly unsatisfactory character of Philip's marriage.[9]

What prevents Philip from coming out against Jessica is his instinctive sense that she is half-right and that their two halves of the truth are thoroughly complementary. I think his instinct in this is well-informed and well-founded and I think Barker's instinct, in following Philip, is equally in touch with the realities of things. Philip's marriage to Jessica, far from being 'unsatisfactory', seems to be represented as being sturdy, resilient, wholesome and capable of an even greater growth in stature in the future. But all this is sketched in very warily, with a shrug of self-doubt and a hoping-against-hope: no fine rhetorical flourishes or perfervid asseverations: and all the better for that. (The play is, in this regard, an astonishingly modern one.)

I felt, as I have already hinted, that the mis-interpreting of Jessica, especially in this final scene, was the one flaw in an otherwise almost flawless production of the play by the National Theatre in 1977. About the production, Irving Wardle said, in *The Times* of June 24, '[it] will go down as one of the great performances of the decade' and in the main I would agree. But the Jessica of Helen Ryan was far too trivial, too self-indulgent, too petulant: and, I fear, too coarse-grained. Nothing of the over-bred race horse here; nothing of grace or fastidiousness. She moved lumpishly, spoke sharply (of which Barker's Jessica would surely be incapable) and with the dialect vowel sounds so popular on the guilt-ridden modern British stage, which remembers the etiolated speech of the run-of-the-mill RADA trainee of the 'forties and 'fifties and flees in horror from it. But Jessica should speak perfectly – as she does everything else. Miss Ryan (or her director, William Gaskill) made her into a common flirt with a selfish temperament and too much money. And the costume designer, Deirdre Clancy, made her slightly gaudy to look at, over-dressed. All the descriptions in the text suggest that her visual taste is exquisite and that its keynote is restraint. (Cathleen Nesbitt, who had played Jessica in the 1925 revival under Barker's own direction, told me that Barker had absolutely insisted upon an *austere* costume for Jessica, even commanding that a flower be removed from the lapel of her jacket in Act II.) It was, I think, Jessica's flippancy and hardness in the 1977 National Theatre production which drove Ronald Pickup's Philip (a beautiful study, otherwise) into too earnest and hortatory a style in the final duologue. With a more sympathetic and responsive Jessica, he could have afforded to do much more by hint and suggestion and muted playing and much less by way of rhetorical thumpings. The danger *is* one to which the scene is particularly prone; Bridges-Adams commented upon it in his article on 'Granville Barker and The Savoy' (see footnote 16 of Chapter 4: p. 118), in which he attributed it to the influence of Barker's membership of the Fabian Society: but it is one which must be circumvented if the unity of the play is to be preserved. It really does go back to that question of where one places Jessica on the realism-caricature scale; and for the critical life of me I cannot see either how the play will survive in one piece if you make a caricature of her or what warrant there is in the text for doing so. The play absolutely must have the real man and the woman – in contrast to all the sham ones we have seen in the earlier Acts – together in productive harmony at the end. This is needed, among other reasons, to preserve the integrity of the sexual metaphor. If the play is one 'about sex', and if the sexual relationship is made by the play into a metaphor for spiritual increase (and, therefore, the misuse of the sexual relation becomes a metaphor for spiritual sterility), then the balance is far better, the statement a much more positive one, and the common truth of life more truly rendered, if the ending of the play reflects the aspect of experience opposite from the cynicism and aridity of the earlier scenes.

Seen thus, *The Madras House* is a comedy in the great tradition, for comedy has always been associated with the celebration of fertility, renewal, regeneration. True, this is wryly and indirectly approached in *The Madras House*: it hardly has that full-throated shout of triumph that rings from the end of, say, *As You Like It*. Yet the play has both the stature and the bent to be regarded as belonging to the high comic tradition, which celebrates a mystery and reflects a positive response to life. Perhaps Barker's comparison of *The Madras House* with Dekker – a strange comparison at first sight – does have, upon more consideration, a special significance. It shows, at any rate, that he was clearly thinking of *The Madras House* as belonging to the purely comedic *genre* and not to the didactic, 'problem play' category, for Dekker, surely, was the least doctrinaire, the least schematic and didactic, and the most spontaneous of all the Jacobean writers of comedy. We must be careful, however (if we are in this comparison to do full justice to Barker) to limit the comparing, as he himself does, to the *dialogue*, for in some other departments – most notably that of character-drawing – Barker is Dekker's superior. And Dekker's sentimentality, which Una Ellis-Fermor compares with that of T.W. Robertson or Henry Arthur Jones[10], is a weakness of which Barker would have been quite incapable. On the other hand, Barker has nothing of that sudden, intense *sweetness* of Dekker, nor of Dekker's insouciance; the sheer, happy unconcern of the dawn of a summer morning. But there *is* a certain correspondence of feeling between the two in *The Madras House's* plea for the life-enhancing qualities.

Irving Wardle (to return for a moment to his review of June 24, 1977) sums up a good deal of the play's virtue when he says:

> Over-fastidiousness has always been held against Barker: but what emerges from *The Madras House* is his triumphant conversion of a temperamental limitation into a dramatic strength. If nothing happens in the play apart from a business sale and the hero's decision to quit the firm and join the LCC, it is because Barker recognised that life consists mostly of non-events; and his art consists of dramatizing the habitual and establishing telling social connexions towards which respectability generally turns a blind eye.

To this may be added the conclusion of Benedict Nightingale's laudatory review of the same production of the play. Writing in the *New Statesman* of July 1, 1977, Nightingale says of Philip Madras: 'This is a particularly tricky rôle, partly because it tends rather further towards priggishness than Barker seems to have realized, and partly because it's burdened with "solutions" that could seem awfully banal, given the complexity of the debate.' Then he goes on:

> But Mr. Pickup anticipates the dangers, and manages to make us feel he's earnestly tracking down inconclusive truths, perplexedly hewing out a moral path for himself: which, come to think of it, is precisely what Barker makes us feel he, too, is doing with the help of this earnest, perplexed, fascinating play.

The play had had to wait until thirty years after its author's death before getting reviewers who understood it and audiences who appreciated it. When it was first performed, at the Duke of York's Theatre in 1910, A.B. Walkley, the *Times* theatre critic of the day, said – among other things – 'It seems as though Mr. Granville Barker, with all his cleverness, were lacking in all sense of proportion and never knew when to stop.' And further on in the same notice, this:

> But what a strange, amusing, suggestive, disconcerting, sometimes boring play. Its author dazzles you with his brilliance and annoys you – whether deliberately or unconsciously we cannot guess – by too frequent passages of ugliness and, now and then, bad taste.
>
> (*The Times*, March 10, 1910)

He saw the play again when it was revived in 1925 and offered similar comments:

> . . . There seems to be no reason why *The Madras House* should ever end at all
> . . . The ideas with which *The Madras House* is stuffed are all good fun, but the

puzzle is why the author should have chosen the play form to exhibit them. A novel, an essay, or a lecture would have served just as well . . .

(The Times, December 2, 1925)

There is no attempt at a constructive account of the play in either review and it is clear that Walkley simply did not understand what was going on. One can see why Barker was particularly irritated by Walkley as a critic. 'That popinjay, A.B.W.', he once called him (though not specifically in relation to the review of *The Madras House*). But Walkley's notices were, as a matter of fact, fairly typical of the critical reception accorded the play both in 1910 and in 1925. Barker, in a rueful joke to Murray after the 1910 production, said he was surprised that even the 'Mean Sensual Man' (the phrase is a joke from the play – at Eustace P. State's expense) could have contrived to misunderstand the play so thoroughly. Desmond MacCarthy, reviewing the 1925 production, was more respectful of the play and was, indeed, genuinely admiring of it – but even he is very vague about the play's essential posture and meaning.

The Madras House was, quite simply, a play before its time. Seen now in perspective it is obviously a major work: probably Granville Barker's best play, with the possible exception of *The Secret Life*. And considering the stature of *Waste* and *His Majesty*, to describe *The Madras House* as his best play is to rate it very highly indeed – but not too highly, I think.

–6–

Minor Plays and Two Stories

At about the same time that he was working on the writing and the production of *The Madras House*, Granville Barker wrote two short stories with themes and imagery closely related to the themes and imagery of the play. Each of the tales has as its central character a married man who is genuinely fond of his wife but who nonetheless establishes a more-or-less permanent, parallel relationship with another woman and tries to maintain both relationships at once. The stories are curiously complementary: the first, which is the longer and more complex one, tries to show the effects of the double situation, the deceit and the clandestinity involved, on the three people concerned, especially the 'other woman'; the second more simply tries to explain, from the point of view of the man, how the situation arose and developed. In both, there is a system of antithetical images: imprisonment and escape; sterility and fulfilment; fantasy and reality. The styles of the two stories are quite different – each in its own way effective – but the central senses of the two are very closely linked. The stories are *Georgiana*, which was published in two parts in the *English Review* of February and March, 1909 and *The Bigamist*, which has never been published. In relation to the second of these – having confidently stated that Barker wrote it during the period 1909–10 – one must briefly justify the dating of the piece, especially since its theme would seem to establish for it some connections with *The Madras House*.

The typescript of *The Bigamist*, which is now owned by the

c 1907.

c 1904.

Humanities Research Centre of the University of Texas, has the following on its title-page:

PRISON STUDIES

No. 1 (1910)

THE BIGAMIST

But this is deceptive. It could not possibly have been typed in 1910, because the typed text, when one examines it, is taken almost word for word from a much rougher *manuscript* version which is in the possession of the British Theatre Museum – and about half of this manuscript is written (the handwriting is indisputably Barker's) on the printed letter-head of the British Red Cross and Order of St. John. Now Barker had only one connection with this organization and that was in 1915 when he went to France on its behalf to write a book about Red Cross work at the battlefront. His letters from France at that time – to Shaw, Archer, Murray and others – were written on letter-head paper identical with that used for parts of the draft of *The Bigamist*. The other parts of the draft are on *plain* paper and were, judging by the handwriting, written a few years earlier. The numbering of the pages, moreover, indicates that those pages written on the 1915 paper were intended for insertion into an already-existing manuscript and that they fit into the story and the pagination of the earlier-written pages. Both the earlier-written pages and the 1915 pages are heavily revised, especially the former. Words are crossed out, phrases amended, new material scribbled in margins, and so on. And virtually all of these emendations are incorporated in the typescript, as in a fair copy of a rough draft. Then the typescript itself has been further amended by Barker, handwritten corrections being inserted into the previously-typewritten text; but none of these emendations of the typescript are copied into the manuscript version, which seems to indicate conclusively that the Texas typescript must have been made *after* the Theatre Museum manuscript. The indication is, in fact, of a four-stage process:

    a) a first draft, written some time before 1915;
    b) extensive handwritten emendations and new material written in 1915;
    c) typed fair copy prepared in 1915 or later, but dated 1910;
    d) typescript again amended, but not re-typed.

Barker had a passion – a very commendable one – for dating all his work. All his published plays, for example, have the dates of their composition printed directly beneath their titles. The first manuscript draft of this short story has on its title-page, in the handwriting of the earlier period, the following:

Stories from Prison
(1)

This is crossed out and underneath it is written, in the handwriting of the later period:

Prison Studies (1910)
No. 1. The Bigamist

In other words, in 1915 Barker wanted to make his earlier idea clearer. So he moved the date, 1910, from the first line to the second to show that *Prison Studies* was a generic title under which, at different times in the future, other examples would be added, but the first example – *The Bigamist* – was to be understood as belonging to 1910. (As a matter of fact, only one other *Prison Studies* story was ever written. It was called, strangely, *Out of these Convertites: or, Richard Goes to Prison*: it is undated, but was certainly written after the War, since it refers to 'the long-ago pre-war days'; a probable date is 1923.) It is fair to treat *The Bigamist*, therefore, as having been written, or at least conceived, in 1910, in close juxtaposition with *Georgiana* and *The Madras House*.

Georgiana is an interestingly-constructed piece. The story is told by an older man to his son-in-law who, so to say, passes it on to the reader. The two men are conversing as they stroll round a moonlit garden, late on a summer evening: above them, a light comes on in an upstairs window and the son-in-law says, 'Mary has gone to bed without forgiving you.' 'Children,' replies the father-in-law, 'daughters especially, are always offended by their parents' heterodox opinions. Yes, we secretly admire revolution in a younger generation, it encourages us to think that the world is not ossifying after all, as we feel it to be; but in our fathers and mothers – no, no – indecent!' And a moment later he goes on to add: 'Women would always rather that a woman broke the law and suffered than that the law were called in question. So would the woman herself in nine cases out of ten. A woman takes punishment as no man will. A man spends ingenuity proving that he is right to yield to temptation. A woman will tell you quite plainly that she is going to do wrong and is prepared to suffer for it. I could tell you an interesting story to exemplify that. Shall I?'

The story he tells is about Georgiana, a woman a few years older than himself, whom he had got to know when he himself was a much younger man, thirty years before. He was the junior partner in a law firm and had been married nine years. Once a quarter it was his duty to go down to Wiltshire to look after the affairs of some trust property there and, because the property was in an isolated country spot, the two sisters who managed the estate would put him up at the farmhouse for two or three nights on each of his quarterly visits. One of the sisters was, when his visits began, a semi-invalid, recovering from a nervous breakdown which had been caused by the breaking-up of a disastrous marriage. All the work of the estate falls, therefore, on the other sister, Georgiana, and all the business dealings are consequently with her. Gradually, from purely business dealings, a bond of friendship develops between Georgiana and her lawyer visitor, valued by both of them for its open-mindedness and intellectual stimulation:

> Our talks would be primarily of business but they were illuminated by the sense of humour we had in common; and, business disposed of, they would take now one turn, now another. I wonder if there is anything more delightful in the world than good conversation. It is at its best between two, and between a man and a woman. Though then it is so seldom at its best. For there is apt to be that little cloud of sex attraction blurring the fine outlines – like pink water-colour smudged over a silver-point drawing.

For two years the relationship remains on this basis: then suddenly, there is a change:

> After dinner we sat and talked until Mrs. Meridale, as was her wont, went off to bed about half-past nine. Georgiana and I sat on and talked keenly, irresponsibly, until I suppose it must have seemed quite late. And then she got up and said good-night and I got up too and we shook hands as usual. But suddenly she put her arm round my neck and kissed me full on the lips. Then she drew back a step or two, breathing rather quickly, her eyes wide. Then she turned and went out of the room, shutting the door sharply behind her.

Thinking over the incident afterwards, he muses to himself: 'I wasn't the least bit in love with Georgiana and somehow I didn't believe that in any mawkish or uncomfortable sense of the word she was in love with me. But we had been mentally attracted towards each other and had not feared to show it. And now she had felt physically attracted to me and had not been ashamed to show that either.' This is really the crux of the story – the question of ignoring conventions and fearlessly admitting how you feel: not necessarily admitting it to everyone, but to the other person concerned. The first necessity is to be uninhibited and fulfilled. The second is to be honest. The irony and the difficulty comes when the first of these has to be defended by secrecy, which is a kind of deceit, and ultimately by outright, direct deceit. For how can one enjoy the freedom of honesty with one person if one is involved in deceiving some other person? And there is a secondary irony: so long as one can accept the necessity for the deceit and can live with it day by day, the third party suffers nothing, is not hurt or damaged, is – in fact – as well off as she was before the secret liaison started: so is it right to tell her of it, or not? (This same argument, in exactly the same form, is introduced into *The Bigamist*.)

After discussing it very carefully and objectively, they become lovers, Georgiana and the lawyer. 'I don't believe in the beauties of virginity, of self-limitation,' Georgiana says: 'I don't want to become fastidious and thin-lipped. Some people are afraid of their natural appetites. I'm not. I want to realize all I'm capable of – good or bad; and I will. What's the use of half a woman in this world?'

The second part of the story begins with a re-affirmation of this: 'She was right. It seemed to complete our friendship, not to destroy or supersede it. For three years and more the days that I spent with her were the wonderful days of my life. Nothing ever fretted our relation to each other. It was very normal, but keyed to a high pitch.' Gradually, however, they find the situation changing, especially so far as Georgiana's own feelings are concerned. Though at the start she has been quite prepared to say: 'I own that I am ready to do wrong. I wish it were not wrong. But for everything I have ever wanted there has seemed to be the risk of unhappiness to some person in getting it', yet later on she finds the deceit and concealment oppressive and finally she faces her lover with the choice of telling his wife openly and fully of the up-till-now clandestine relationship or breaking that relationship off altogether. He not so much chooses as prevaricates into a situation in which *she* makes the choice. He ceases to visit her and hears later that she is to marry. Her husband is a very young man, much younger than she; the marriage turns out badly. Georgiana, who had earlier confessed that she married only because she wished to have children, finally arranges to separate from her young husband. There are no children. The narrator finishes his story thus:

> Lord, she's nearly seventy now! Some years ago I came across her photograph in a man's house; white-haired, the forehead creased and the eyes dim, but the firm, fine mouth unspoiled. How many women would have given in to either of her chances of going under – broken their hearts or their health, or taken to drink or religion. Not she. Though I've had no word of her for years, I know she's as serene and as clear-hearted, her nature as well salted with humour as ever; and so it will be till she dies and when she dies. What was that fine old

thing Huxley used to say to us? 'Never regret experience'. Georgiana was worthy to shake hands with him on that. She was one of those who can pay scot and lot without flinching as they go on through life.

Here and there throughout the story, and again at the very end of it, there are brief reminders that this is a tale within a tale; it is being told by a father-in-law to his son-in-law in the wake of some unspecified family disagreement involving the woman who is the teller's daughter and the listener's wife. So there is, throughout, an extra dimension to the story: it is particular to Georgiana but it is presented as illustrating a general case. The lighted window above the lawn, as the two men pace below, keeps this connection before us; and at the end of the story, the window is darkened:

> 'Perhaps I'm not to be forgiven tonight either', I said; 'We must learn not to advocate lawlessness in women.' 'It's getting chilly,' said my father-in-law. 'Let's go in.'

The emphasis throughout is on the woman and on her capacity to break through conventional forms and modes of thought to a fuller, freer and more natural expression of her potential. She is seen, moreover, much more than is the man, as the guardian of the true spirit of life. And the essence of that spirit is not wilfulness or self-indulgence but fulness, honesty, a sense of responsibility and a refusal ever to compromise.

The second story, begun – apparently – less than a year later, uses the same general plot outline (the living of a double marital life) but with three major changes of intention: first, the emphasis is almost entirely on the man; secondly, the main concern is with the causes which led up to the dual arrangement rather than with the effects which sprang from it; and thirdly the question of self-fulfilment is linked with that of rôle-playing and a fantasy-life. Though the man strongly makes the point – as the man in the first story did – that the liaison with the second woman did not damage his love for the first, neither of the relationships in the second story assume the intrinsic importance which they have in the first: the most important thing is the chance to live two quite separate lives. The committing of bigamy is presented almost as incidental to this and the fulfilment of the self, seen through the eyes of the man, comes from the broadening experience of living the two relationships, not from the deepening of one of them. Again, however, conventional behaviour and beliefs are represented as stupid and negative: *both* the 'marriages' would have worked perfectly well simultaneously – all three people concerned were content (two of them, of course, in partial ignorance) – if busybodies from outside had not interfered. It is the blundering of the inept, insensitive (and, on the whole, malevolent) outside world which destroys the individual: this point is much more central in *The Bigamist* than it is in *Georgiana*, where the unease which leads to the final dissolving of ties comes much more from the woman's own subjective response than as a result of overt and conscious outside pressures. On the other hand, those subjective responses are a direct result of Georgiana's concern to preserve her inner integrity. In other words, both *Georgiana* and *The Bigamist* are explorations from different angles, almost from opposite points of view, of the secret life, of the necessity for finding oneself in secret and preserving one's soul alive in secret and for jealously guarding the secret. The teller of the story in *The Bigamist* describes how he first perceived the need for such a secret life. Talking of his marriage and his home, he says:

> I don't know now what put me against it all, for it was as nice as could be – homely and all that. But it grew that sometimes I'd sit there wishing the end of the world would come just for a change. I'd get out of temper over nothing and speak sharp to the children. But she'd taught them never to answer back so that was worse. It wasn't like it every Sunday of course; but, say, once every four or five.
>
> I used to find it did me good to get a walk in the country. I'd go away for all day by myself and if I could get properly tired and enough beer in me to make me sleepy it was nice enough having the missus and supper to come back to. But it was those walks started me taking serious notice of myself. For being alone most of the time I'd get to thinking in a sort of way. And I do believe the whole mischief really began because one morning, without ever having planned to or anything, I got pretending I was somebody else. I was having bread and cheese at a pub and there was an old chap there, a kind old sort, but curious. He started asking me questions. I don't know what made me do it, but up I spoke as ready as anything and not one word of truth did I give him. I told him a wrong name and trade, said I came from Burton instead of Leicester – you couldn't call it lying because it had nothing to do with facts at all.

He finds this acting of a part so exhilarating that he begins to do it regularly, planning it now in advance and putting a little money aside for the purpose. It tones up his whole system, makes him better tempered and more attentive with his family and more assiduous at his work. This leads to promotion and to his being given a job which involves a certain amount of travelling – which in turn gives him greater opportunity to pursue a 'second life'. And this leads to his meeting with Lizzie. They become fond of each other and he gets so involved with her family that he is gradually edged into a position of being expected to marry Lizzie. Frantic now, he tries to find a way out but cannot: in desperation he decides to risk it and goes through a second form of marriage. Then for two years he settles down to two homes, two wives and two marriages. Rather to his surprise he finds that it works rather well and that he himself is no longer nervous and anxious about it, nor restless and discontented about life generally. Only by a silly and trivial accident is he 'found out' and imprisoned for bigamy.

A special feature of *The Bigamist* that should be remarked is Barker's switching from the upper middle class 'professional' characters who form the backbone of most of his writing to working-class figures, a switch which he accomplishes with a good deal of skill. His central character, especially, is very vividly drawn. The dialogue given to him – which is, in fact, the whole body of the narrative – is easy and natural, without either a trace of parody or condescension on the one hand or a ponderous or explicatory falling out of character on the other. And this story, *The Bigamist*, even more than *Georgiana*, shows at every turn the dramatic sense of its author. Shapely and delicately poised, it is couched in terms of antitheses and confrontations. Though there are no exchanges of dialogue written into it, the only direct speech being the narrative of the story itself (which really amounts to a monologue), the story sticks in the memory as a series of 'scenes' with several participating characters.

Both *Georgiana* and *The Bigamist* are, perhaps, more significant for the light they throw on Barker's further exploration of that group of subjects and images which obviously possessed and obsessed him than for their intrinsic merits as literary pieces, though having said this one must add that they are both more than merely competent and that *The Bigamist*, in particular, is striking and memorable. Ironically, it was *Georgiana* which was published, not *The Bigamist*, but both were worthy of publication and would, indeed, still be worth publication now, in my view: perhaps in a collection of Barker's forgotten or previously unpublished pieces. Sexuality stands at the heart of both stories and it comes as no surprise that they were written alongside *The Madras House*. But Barker is not especially interested in the purely physical manifestations of sex or in its purely sociological implications. Not that he shirks or ignores either of these, but two other aspects of sex dominate his imagination. One is its power to *drive* people, to take command of them and direct and shape them: the other is its capacity, artistically speaking, to stand as metaphor for so much else of the vivid and vital parts of life. Both of these interests

are present in these two short stories and what is particularly interesting –
and makes the stories particularly interesting, too – is that what he does
with the stories is no simple repetition of what he has already done in the
plays; nor is it the excuse for mere narrative, interesting though that may
be. The stories – unlike each other in any case, as I have tried to indicate –
are each of them explorations of new aspects of the sexual phenomenon
which do not appear in either *Waste* or *The Madras House* (the plays which
are nearest to them in time) or in any of the earlier plays. True, there are
kinships: Georgiana, in particular, is related to one or two of the women
of the plays – especially to Ann Leete and Agnes Colander. But the story
which contains her pursues a quite different line of enquiry from that
followed either by *The Marrying of Ann Leete* or by *Agnes Colander*. And
similarly with *The Bigamist*: none of the plays reflects quite the sense of
things which this story captures. There is a particularly significant
moment in the early part of the story:

> So there I was, in that sort of fix, almost before I knew it. I swear I'd never
> meant anything of the kind to happen. I never was one to be always after girls.
> If it hadn't been for the habit of it and other chaps doing the same I believe I'd
> always sooner have been without 'em. Now and then, I suppose, any man that
> is a man can't keep away. But I fairly tumbled into it with Lizzie. Mind, I liked
> her from the first and her uncle and her mother saw I liked her and they didn't
> discourage it, oh no! And then suddenly we seemed to be always meeting and
> being left together. It was just the same when I was courting the missus. I'm a
> bit soft about women when I do get with them I daresay, and that's the truth.

At first sight this might be thought to recall Trebell in his relation to
Amy O'Connell, but a moment's thought dismisses such a comparison
as invalid. Trebell – vigorous, ambitious and demanding of life – was
suddenly overpowered by a physical passion, a strong lust which owed
its force to the force of his own personality. Edward, the man in *The
Bigamist* is not especially prone to physical passion, but drifts more or less
by chance into a relationship where a display of passion is tacitly
expected of him. The dominating force in Trebell's encounter with Amy
is physical passion itself; the dominating force in Edward's case is habit
and social pressure. Not that social pressures are wholly absent in Trebell's case; not that physical passion is wholly absent in Edward's; but the
balance of forces is quite different in the second case from what it was in
the first. A different range and segment of experience is explored; and
this is the ultimate justification for the story's having been written at all.
    We have a tendency now, in retrospect, to say: 'Granville Barker? I

didn't know *he* wrote short stories', and to dismiss them accordingly. They are, of course, minor work, but ought not, I think, to be dismissed out of hand as entirely negligible. At the very least they are valuable in that they help to fill a few gaps in our knowledge of the way in which his creative mind was working. But there is really rather more to it than that: they have intrinsic value as autonomous works, though modest in scope. And the fact that Barker himself took them seriously can readily be seen, in that – for example – after a gap of five years he took up the unfinished *The Bigamist* in the middle of a war and within sound of enemy guns and proceeded to work on it again in great detail, not desultorily, polishing, improving, completing. Manuscripts or typescripts (or both) of six of his stories are known to exist. There may, of course, be others which may yet come to light, for he was an author whose papers, after his death, were treated in a very cavalier fashion. Of the six known stories, three are known to have been published; the others, so far as we know, never were. This total of six includes the two discussed in this present chapter; the other four are (in order of composition, as nearly as that can be determined) *Souls on Fifth, The Fire that Burned in the Corner, The God of Good Bricks* (which in its first draft was called *The Bricks of the Temple*) and *Out of these Convertites; or Richard Goes to Prison.*

The year in which Barker wrote the first draft of *The Bigamist* – 1910 – was a busy one for him. The first four months of it were taken up with the repertory season at the Duke of York's Theatre; the middle of the year was occupied with complicated planning for a production of Gilbert Murray's translation of *Iphigenia in Tauris* and, a little later, with further plans for a possible production of Murray's translation of *Oedipus Rex*, which Barker read for the first time in manuscript in October. As things turned out, Barker's production of *Iphigenia* did not take place until 1912 and the *Oedipus* he never did direct. But the work on the planning was done, nevertheless. (Murray and Barker, for instance, were at that time trying to get Granville Bantock, who was then a busy, rising musician, to write special music for both these plays and train the singers for the Chorus. Bantock was enthusiastic and at first undertook the commission, but later found himself unable to carry it out. His place was taken, for the *Iphigenia*, by Percy Pitt.) In October, Barker was acting again, playing Tanner in a revival of *Man and Superman* which he directed for the Royalty Theatre in Glasgow, for whom he was also directing the first production of *The Witch*, by John Masefield – an adaptation made at William Archer's suggestion of a Norwegian melodrama called *Anne Pedersdotter*. From Glasgow, after these two productions, Barker went straight to Berlin to see some of Max Reinhardt's rehearsals for his production of *Oedipus Rex* and immediately upon his return he played William Shakespeare in the first production of Shaw's little, one-act, *jeu d'esprit* called *The Dark Lady of the Sonnets*. And in the middle of this year, working round and in between these practical theatre commitments, he began the writing of another full-length play. Its title, when he started work on it, was *The Village Carpenter*.

'How are you? How is the play?' asks Murray in a letter dated September 2, 1910. But the play was going only very slowly. In point of fact, he never did finish it. His massive production programme of 1912 and 1913, which included *Iphigenia*, the St. James's repertory and the three great Shakespeare productions, interrupted him and it was not until the middle of 1914 that he was able to get back to it. By that time, the title had changed: it was now called *The Wicked Man*. On August 26, 1914, John Masefield wrote to him saying: 'What work is taking you to Stansted? Is it Charley again?' (Charles is the strange, disaffected, unworldly young man who is one of the chief characters in *The Wicked Man*.) And on September 19, 1914, Masefield mentioned the play again in another letter: 'Mind you come down & bring Charles. We've a room for you.' Margery Morgan, in *A Drama of Political Man*, gives some interesting details of the gradual transmutation of *The Village Carpenter* into *The Wicked Man*. The papers to which she refers are, apparently, in private possession and I have not had the good fortune of being able to consult or refer to them, but they consist, according to Miss Morgan, of the following:

a) Three versions of the opening of *The Village Carpenter*.
b) Two versions of the beginning of Act III of *The Village Carpenter*.
c) 30 large sheets of notes for *The Village Carpenter*.
d) Some 'scraps' towards *The Wicked Man*, written on notepaper with printed headings, '17, John Street, Adelphi' and 'Kingsway Theatre' (both of which addresses dates the notes in 1911–12).
e) Two completed Acts of *The Wicked Man* in manuscript, 42 leaves in each Act.

My own knowledge of the play comes only from the typescript, now in the possession of the British Theatre Museum, of two completed acts of *The Wicked Man*. This has forty pages in each Act and is presumably a fair copy of item (e) above: or it could be a copy of item (e) with refinements and emendations made in the process of typing. Only in about half-a-dozen places is this typescript itself amended by handwritten notes and then only an odd word or two is altered.

What one first notices about *The Wicked Man* is the sharp change in the style of its dialogue from that of *The Madras House*: *The Wicked Man* reverts to a close-knit, dense, highly allusive style, similar to that of *The Marrying of Ann Leete*, though now more tightly controlled, more ironic and even more gnomic in tone. And the second striking thing, as prominent and as immediately to be discovered as the first, is the thematic continuity displayed by *The Wicked Man* when one thinks of it in relation to *Waste, Georgiana, The Madras House* and *The Bigamist*. On page 31 of Act I this is announced almost as a motto or emblem:

ELISABETH: Why did you get engaged?
CHARLES: My dear, one must make love . . .

The play's intention was to have been, apparently, to explore the very nature and essence of womanhood: these two existing Acts are strewn with lines that amount often to epigrams on the subject. 'That poor pleasured-out woman dying on the edge of the wood there', is Elisabeth's description of Mary, the woman who has lived as a wanton. Several times Elisabeth, the woman trapped in respectability and ladyhood, compares herself with Mary and tries to define the essence of both their beings: is their womanhood, *essentially*, any different? And which of them has squandered and wasted it the more prodigally? Immediately one is reminded of Philip's saying to Jessica in the last scene of *The Madras House*: 'Jessica, do you feel that it was you shot that poor devil six months ago . . . that it's you who are to be hanged tomorrow? That it's your body is being sold on some street this evening?' And Elisabeth, again, says: 'I'm a revolutionary at heart' and reminds us instantly of Georgiana, and Alice Maitland and Beatrice Voysey. After visiting the dying Mary, Elisabeth says to Hugo, her husband: 'I believe that womanhood is all alike except in the use you put it to. I know that what she was once . . . generous of her love, unashamed . . . every woman has once wished to be.' But the investigation of the nature of woman is neither clinical nor sociological: it is poetic. Beyond it is the attempt to discover a metaphor apt enough and powerful enough to embody and celebrate the mystery of reality's meaning, to find a way of winnowing the few grains of wheat from the mountains of chaff. 'It fades from us inevitably I suppose', Elisabeth says, 'the happy unconscious living and loving . . .' and then, a little later – contemplating her married life and her husband's successful career – adds bitterly: 'What shall we get on to when we get past getting on?'

As the two existing acts stand, Elisabeth is very firmly the focal figure, though judging from the comments in Masefield's letters, Barker was thinking more of Charles as the central character. Charles has been brought up by Elisabeth:

ELISABETH: Your mother left you to me . . . I was so proud of that . . . I worshipped her . . . not much more than a child myself . . . she knew I'd no worldly wisdom to help you with.

CHARLES: But what you believe at twenty is right and true . . . no matter the foolish things one does.

As a child he formed a deep and lasting attachment for her which has translated itself into an adult passion as he has grown up. Her marriage to Hugo, the successful politician, Charles has bitterly resented.

CHARLES: I used to feel wonderfully about women because I loved you.

ELISABETH: You were a child.

CHARLES: Doesn't matter. Then you jilted me . . . for I'd had your promise.

ELISABETH: You weren't twelve.

CHARLES: I've a soul as well as a body . . . and in spite of it. That made me a blackguard in thought. Most men feel wrong about bad women. I'm too dainty for that. I feel wrong about good ones.

So the relationship of Charles and Elisabeth is, from the start, 'other-worldly' and is pitched dramatically against its antithesis, Elisabeth's marriage to Hugo. Charles is the very figure of Edgar O'Shaughnessy's 'world-losers and world-forsakers': 'this damned machine of a world', he calls it. He has been educated at Oxford (at Hugo's expense) and says now that he wants to be a writer. Hugo is urging him to get 'a regular job' and then to marry. The antagonism between these two, representing as they do two diametrically opposed views of the world and senses of life, is sharp and total; yet it is always expressed in polite terms and, moreover, in rather abstract, general terms which never issue into action. The effect of this is not, as might at first be thought, to reduce the dramatic tension or to blunt the sharpness of the confrontation, but rather to move it to a different, and higher, plane. Freed of the dangers of becoming a merely personal quarrel about some more-or-less sordid practical issue, the Hugo-Charles confrontation becomes an epitome of the battle for our loyalties between the spiritual and the temporal. At the personal level of the characters-as-people, there is implied hostility, but no overt dislike, even. Certainly no hint of violence, though the whole of both Acts as we have them broods with a sense of *incipient* violence: the play has a very uneasy (and brilliantly conceived and evoked) quality about it, as if some strange and violent eruption were imminent. Margery Morgan tells us that among the rough sketchings for the play, somewhere in its process of transition between 1910 and 1914 and between *The Village Carpenter* and *The Wicked Man*, is a note which outlines one crude act of overt physical violence which was designed, probably, to be the climax of the play. It involves Hugo but not, however, Charles. The other party to this one act of violence is John Abud, another of the rejecters of the ordered, tamed and 'civilized' world. His name is the same as that of the gardener who married Ann Leete in the earlier play and Barker envisaged him, apparently, as a grandson of the earlier John Abud. He has the same sturdy (and prickly) independence as his ancestor, but where the earlier Abud was wary of the world but cautiously optimistic about it, this John Abud is bitter and violent. Hugo has found him living, Timon-fashion, in a cave in the woods of the country estate, and has installed him rent free in a small cottage, in return for modest services on the property. Abud is presented throughout as an image of cleansing violence. He has served a prison sentence for robbery with violence, but his motive for the crime was not personal gain. In fact, he paid over to the Government, as conscience money, the £25 which he had stolen. He explains to Charles that the money was taken from a well-to-do stranger as an act of vengeance, rough justice, because the son of a widow in the tenement where he lived had died of tuberculosis due chiefly to neglect. The stranger had, in any practical or personal sense, nothing to do with the young man who died – but the argument of the play is not a personal one: its implications are wider than that. Abud himself explains it thus: 'That was logic. Logic of doing things . . . not talking them. For see a foul thing and not show you're angry . . . bend you head to wickedness . . . can you ever hold it up again?' Charles, listening to him, continues the same theme: 'Abud, I make a discovery. Elisabeth, it's a great discovery. Feel deeply enough to do desperate things – whether they're silly or whether they're mad – we could alter the world by Wednesday week.' Abud had visited a just vengeance upon society for the wrong it had committed against its weaker brethren.

Abud was married, long ago, to Mary and was much in love with her. But she had found him hard and cold and left him for other men. He did not protest at her going or try to revenge himself upon her. In fact, he used his meagre savings to arrange a divorce for her so that she could marry someone else. After living the life of a wanton, she has indeed married again, but now has run away from this second husband and has come back to Abud 'to die'. She is not suffering from any specific illness, nor is she very old: she is dying because her life is, so to speak, used up. Abud understands this, welcomes her back and vows to protect her: 'Husbands and doctors and lawyers be damned', he says: 'She's tired . . . and I'll see she goes unhindered to her death.' Mary's present husband, Owen, comes to the village, having heard of her whereabouts, in an effort to get her to return to him, but she not only refuses – afraid that he will try to abduct her by force, she runs away. Abud, Charles and Hugo – each of them concerned in their different ways – try individually to find her (and it is at this point that the text as we have it breaks off). It is important to emphasize that both Owen and Hugo are perfectly well-intentioned in their attitudes to Mary and to Abud. Yet they are seen as negative figures and forces. Hugo's offence is spiritual blindness; Owen's is spiritual cowardice. The play's irony is directed against both, the handling of Owen being especially savage: he is mocked out of court, in effect; not by any of the characters but by the play itself. Abud, on the other hand, is invested throughout with a kind of primitive dignity and truthfulness of soul. There is a strange passage toward the end of Act II which emphasizes this metaphysical dimension and makes quite clear the level at which the play intends to operate. Owen has just departed, having told Hugo that Mary has run away into the woods. Hugo, Charles and Elisabeth are discussing the best course to take next:

HUGO:	The poor soul can't have got very far . . . let's think what she's likeliest to have done.
ELISABETH:	You'll be very gentle with her, Hugo . . . bring her to the house if you can.
HUGO:	No good rushing about . . . we'd better get the men up to beat the copses.
CHARLES:	Good sport! . . . here's a symbolic ending . . . well, better hunt her to death than pack her back to her husband.
HUGO:	My dear boy . . . what on earth's the matter?
CHARLES:	Elisabeth . . . I've been spending the day with you in the wonderful world . . . you and I and our children . . . John Abud and Mary . . . a glorious company.
HUGO:	Whose children?
CHARLES:	We stood upright before God – for evil and good were under our feet, neither could the wicked man harden his face against us.
HUGO:	Don't stop here talking nonsense.
CHARLES:	Elisabeth . . . will you elope with me? Is the flesh never one with the spirit? Don't say I didn't ask you.

ELISABETH: Where and when?

CHARLES: Yes . . . that's the earthly answer . . . meaning never and nowhere.

More than in any other of his plays, in this one Barker externalizes and separates the 'secret life' from everyday living, even giving it, in *The Wicked Man*, a separate physical location of its own. The ordinary, decent (and damned) world of Hugo, Owen, Charles's fiancée Ottilia and Ottilia's father (neither of whom had made their appearance by the end of Act II but were to come into Act III) belongs partly to the city and partly to the complicated rituals and sophisticated organization of the big country house; the other life, the inner, secret life (not only of the individuals but of the world), belonging to and epitomized by Elisabeth, Charles, Abud and Mary, is inseparably associated with woodland, open country, simple cottages, wild creatures and natural things. In none of the other plays is this separation so complete and so symbolically underlined. Indeed, Barker's more usual technique is to emphasize the closeness and the interdependence of the two states, showing the strange, secret life as co-existing with the mundane but preserving its own integrity by its secrecy: in this one play he seems to be moving deliberately to widen the gap between the two and to represent that breach physically upon the stage. This is pressed so far as to affect quite radically the actual dramaturgical structure of the piece: the texture, as a result, is much more loosely woven; the tight-knit, interacting group of characters of, for example, *Waste* or *The Secret Life* is abandoned in favour of a series of intimate conversations (often duologues) taken first from one 'world' and then from the other, rather loosely connected and following each other in a simple procession of confrontations, one world against the other. And the main link between the two (at least as the unfinished script now stands) is Elisabeth and, so to speak, the palpable presence of Elisabeth's womanhood. For it is, once again, sexuality which provides the play with its cohesive force and its most potent metaphor. The continuation of the scene from which I have just quoted makes this clear: after Charles has departed, Hugo says to Elisabeth:

HUGO: Elope with Charles?

ELISABETH: Why not?

HUGO: He was joking.

ELISABETH: Am I so impossibly old and perished?

HUGO: My dear . . . this is neither very sane nor very pleasant.

ELISABETH: Perhaps womanhood is neither. Men's aspirations are the law

ELISABETH: of the land, aren't they? Oh . . . but I warn you . . . keep us in your waistcoat pockets if you can.

HUGO: You can't frighten me. When the choice comes men and women of self-respect do what the world most wants of them . . . that's the point of honour.

ELISABETH: So I married you and bore my children.

HUGO: We also happened to love each other.

ELISABETH: The mere excuse . . . does a woman sacrifice her life for that any more than a man does? And now does the world want nothing more of me except what you think it ought to? Wicked man . . . don't harden your face.

The two separate worlds face each other here, their separate positions clearly defined, and the wickedness mooted by the play's title and glancingly referred to by Charles is now identified and named: it is the wickedness of turning fruitful things to barrenness, of misinterpreting fecundity to mean mere physical fecundity, of supposing that the preserving of ourselves and our own petty interests can legitimately be substituted for a proper caring for all of life: it is the wickedness, ultimately, of turning one's back, of becoming through selfishness, cowardice or (worse) sheer insensitivity a life-denier. In the process of this confrontation, 'Womanhood' has become almost a creature in its own right and the exploration of its nature leads Barker straight to his beloved cave of secrecy: once again he sees the mystery of sex as being the mystery of life itself; sexual force should be a liberating force if only the relations between the sexes could themselves be freed from cant and cruelty. And Womanhood is seen as the source of wisdom, compassion and courage. An earlier conversation between Hugo and Elisabeth has already evoked these images for us and centred them firmly upon Elisabeth:

ELISABETH: But I'm so proud of my womanhood . . . I don't want it wasted. Hugo, when you've had your little House of Commons group down here and I've sat there too canvassing this reform and that.

HUGO: And as clear-headed as any of us when you chose.

ELISABETH: One easily picks up the trick of thought. But when my head ached enough I've gone to my room to look out, and listen – in a west wind I can hear these beeches . . . a deeper voice than all the other trees . . . and I've asked why our cleverness only begets more cleverness and our riches and comforts more riches still. Down below you'll be talking of thrift and the

	birthrate while I pray God to tell me why when Nature's had
	her crudest use of us our joy in life should no longer overflow
	. . . when our bodies have been fruitful, why should our souls
	be barren . . . and deep as the voice of the wind in the beeches
	my womanhood gives me the answer.
HUGO:	What answer?
ELISABETH:	Oh . . . if I could find words for it my way of life'd be clear.
	You believe, don't you, this world would be a perfect place if
	everyone in it behaved properly . . . and you had a year or so to
	tell them how to behave.
HUGO:	I own up . . . in my heart I do.
ELISABETH:	I know it wouldn't be . . . lacking this power.
HUGO:	What power?
ELISABETH:	Can't you always feel when it's lacking in things and in people?
	. . . I can . . . and I catch the queerest glimpses of it.

It is impossible to judge from the incomplete play, as we have it, whether Barker could have succeeded eventually in pulling the scattered images together into a coherent and dynamic whole. Certainly the two completed Acts, though they are smoothly constructed and fluent enough, give more the impression of a number of brilliantly evocative, but separate, elements than of an organically developing entity: the connective bonds seem rather arbitrarily devised. On the other hand, there can be no denying the power of Abud or the appealing quality of Elisabeth, even in their unfinished state. But the most remarkable thing about this unfinished play is its dialogue. The return which it represents to the style of language of *The Marrying of Anne Leete* makes of *The Wicked Man* a clear link that connects the earlier play with *The Secret Life*, which was to be written in 1919–1922. And *The Secret Life* would also prove to contain re-worked versions of some of the themes and some of the characters of *The Wicked Man*. (Elisabeth, for example, is an early sketch for Joan Westbury of *The Secret Life*.) And, quite apart from technical considerations of style, *The Wicked Man* is very valuable in showing us the continuity of the basic elements of Barker's vision of things. Though in no sense a repetition of those plays and stories which had immediately preceded it, and though it explores other aspects of the same central response which motivates them, its close kinship with the works immediately adjacent to it is obvious. However, it represents an approach to that vision which is, at one and the same time, both more subtle and more extreme. *The Wicked Man* shows us, more clearly than any of the completed plays do, the growing conviction in Barker's mind

that good works are not enough, that 'goodness' ultimately lies elsewhere, that its recognition and pursuit and celebration is one of humanity's central experiences (and that, therefore, the serious artist cannot but
be concerned with it). The observation, on our part, of this movement of
his mind – and the gradual discovery, on his part, that it was occurring –
have technical and stylistic implications as well as purely interpretative
ones. With *Agnes Colander* and *The Voysey Inheritance* he had moved into
the orbit of the realistic–naturalistic drama. Technically, he stayed within
this mode for *Waste*, though the play transcends the mode, especially in
its last Act. *The Madras House*, though it marvellously harnesses some of
the elements of realism–naturalism for its own use, is really a kind of
satirical fantasy which shows every sign of wanting to burst the bonds of
naturalism completely. (Even the scenes that seem, on the face of things,
scenes of detailed realism turn out to have strong anti-realistic factors in
them – all those orchestrated and almost choreographed 'How d'you do'
and 'Goodbye' sequences, for example, in Act I.) Coming only a few
months later – in its original conception, anyway – *The Wicked Man*,
while still ostensibly using, as *The Madras House* does, the realistic prose
of everyday conversation as its medium for dialogue, increases significantly Barker's move away from the realistic–naturalistic school towards
a less restrictive style. The truth is that he never was a realistic-
naturalistic dramatist at all and what *The Wicked Man* represents is the
beginning of his return to his own proper style. His realism of the years
1900–1910 had been, it seems to me, the result of three things. First, it
was a genuine artistic experiment, part of the normal exploration which
any artist must undertake of the proper relationship between matter and
method, between sense and style. Secondly, it resulted to some extent
from the pressure of the examples and arguments around him, especially
during the Court Theatre days. And thirdly, it represented a false equation between acting style and writing style: as an actor and director he
had been from the very start of his career an opponent of the 'high style'
of the late nineteenth century, the rolling, empty rhetoric and bombast of
the actor-managers' typical performance; in getting rid of this in his own
performances and in those of the actors he directed, and in 'reducing'
these performances (a reduction in physical scale, not in artistic truth) to a
style of quiet intensity, clarity, thoughtful truthfulness, he fell at first, I
think, into the error of supposing that, because artistry had been misused
and inflated into an empty hot-air balloon, one must, for the sake of
truth, avoid artistry altogether: and he extended this argument from
acting to writing (*via*, perhaps, the plays of John Galsworthy, four of

which he directed between 1906 and 1910); for a play to speak true it must – so the argument developed in his mind – speak literally; and for that truth to be truly a part of the common experience of humanity, it must be seen to relate directly to everybody's everyday experience. Translating this idea into terms of the writing of plays, he had for a while moved toward the naturalistic style. Now, in *The Wicked Man*, we see him instinctively confirm and increase the move in the opposite direction which began in *The Madras House*. It is worth noting that in all three of the greatest of the realistic-naturalistic dramatists – Ibsen, Strindberg and Hauptmann[1] – precisely the same kind of movement of style can be observed: all three, after embracing a supremely realistic style as the only way of giving truth-with-urgency to their plays, found the mode too limiting and, each in his own way, forged a hybrid style which would better serve his artistic purpose. I am not suggesting that the stylistic inventions to which they came were in any way similar to each other (they were not) or that Granville Barker's final solution resembled theirs (it did not); but the impulse which motivated the shift of styles was the same in each case and the movements were in the same general directions: first toward realism and then away from it – in Barker's case to that indirect dialogue, the dialogue of the glancing blow, the turned head, the half-formulated doubt, the half-assumed conclusion, the dialogue which performs its poetic mission by subtly insisting that the particular be related to the general, time to eternity. There are short passages in *The Wicked Man* in which he handles this technique more surely than he does anywhere in *The Marrying of Ann Leete* and in ways that, even though *The Wicked Man* came to nothing, would be valuable to him as exemplars when he came to write *The Secret Life*.

During the four years covered by the composition of *The Wicked Man*, as far as it went, Barker was immensely busy also with production work of various sorts. This is the time of his three Shakespeare productions (which are dealt with in the next chapter), of the St. James's repertory experiment and of the seasons which he and Lillah McCarthy ran at the Little Theatre in 1912–14 with productions of *Fanny's First Play, The Master Builder, Iphigenia in Tauris*, a revival of *The Tragedy of Nan*, Schnitzler's *Anatol*, Bennett's *The Great Adventure* and a stage version of Hardy's *The Dynasts*, among various other plays. In between-times during all this furious activity, Barker wrote two more plays, both quite short, one-act pieces: one is a farce, the other an ironic little comedy. *Rococo*, the farce, was performed almost immediately; *Vote by Ballot* has never had a professional production. The published text of *Rococo* (in

Rococo and Two Others, published by Sidgwick & Jackson in 1917) gives the date of its composition as 1912 but it was, in fact, written in 1911 and produced by Barker in that same year, first at the Little Theatre in October and then at the Royalty Theatre, Glasgow, in November. It is a well-crafted little play without a care in the world, and very funny. It is about a family quarrel over a legacy. The item in question is a two-feet-tall rococo vase of more than ordinary ugliness. It had been given to a now-deceased member of the family by the German Emperor and the question at issue is, in view of some haziness in the wording of the will, who should have the honour of possessing this precious family heirloom now. When the play begins the family is locked in combat – quite literally: a niece pinned against the wall by an aunt, a nephew kneeling on the chest of an uncle, a brother-in-law hiding under a table. The indignity of this situation is increased by the fact that the uncle who has been subdued by his nephew is a Church of England vicar. Upon the required word of apology's being given, the physical combat is abandoned and the contestants return to their seats, dusting themselves off (and the brother-in-law from under the table readjusts his toupee). The battle then continues in verbal form until the insults, suspicions and accusations become unbearable again, when personal assault breaks out once more. In the resulting melée the swaying knot of combatants reels against the table on which the object of contention has been mounted for display. For a moment it sways precariously – then crashes to the floor and disintegrates into a thousand pieces. Curtain. The argument which occupies the body of the play is ingeniously and amusingly worked out and, in the published version of the play, the stage directions which describe the action and its participants are almost funnier than the dialogue and action itself; the sign, I take it, of a born writer at work.

Vote by Ballot is, in its small way, a play about the imprisoned spirit. Lewis Torpenhouse is the managing director of a small but prosperous boot and shoe factory. He has been a life-long friend of the owner of the factory, Mr. Wychway, and, since the latter long ago developed political ambitions (though more as an extension of his commercial enterprise than from any heartfelt conviction), Torpenhouse agreed to assist him in them. He has for many years been chairman of Wychway's election committee, has conducted all the local organization efforts and has duly got his candidate elected as Liberal member of parliament. But here rests the irony of the matter, for through it all he has been secretly, silently, at heart a Tory. In due course of time, Mr. Wychway – who by now is very rich, owns half the town and regards the parliamentary seat as his private property, is elevated to the peerage as Lord Silverwell and his son, Noel, is automatically put up as the next Liberal candidate. The election is a very close one; in fact, on a re-count it is discovered that Noel has been defeated by one vote. And that is the moment which Torpenhouse chooses to confess to Wychway and his son that the one vote is *his* and that for all the years during which he has, for reasons of professional prudence and because, at the personal level, he was fond of Wychway, openly supported the Liberal cause, he has secretly voted Tory. There is little more to the play than this: its modest virtues lie in the lightly sardonic observation and drawing of character, the pleasantly ironic invention which is its central situation and the sureness of touch exhibited in the smooth and easy-flowing dialogue. The play is also an obvious-enough example of Barker's use of characters' names to delineate their salient characteristics: a politician whose name is Wychway hardly needs further comment; nor does the title he chooses upon elevation to the peerage – Lord Silverwell – especially since the town in which he has made his name and his fame (and his money) is called Cuttleton. And Lewis Torpenhouse has all his life been a person of intellectual inertia – torpor, in fact. It could just be noted, however, that Barker is not savage or denunciatory about either the situation or the people: the play is handled with a light irony and the characters with a kindly tolerance. Here, for instance, is Barker's stage-direction description of Lord Silverwell when he first appears:

> *He is sixty and his country riding clothes are smart. They are his armour, for beneath a quite harmless pomposity one may discern a slightly apologetic soul. A man, one would say, who has been thrust willy-nilly into importance. Nor when we learn that he is a wealthy manufacturer, a self-made man, a petty prince of commerce, need we revise this judgment. Mostly such folks are left wondering, after the first few years, how on earth they did get rich. In their hearts they are sometimes a little ashamed of it.*

The play was written, the published text says[2], in 1914 – after the third and last of the Shakespeare productions, therefore, and at about the time that Barker resumed his work on *The Wicked Man*. This congruence is not altogether without its point. Both plays, in a manner of speaking, are concerned with public success (represented, as so often in Barker, by politicans) and private conscience. *Vote by Ballot* stays firmly on the surface of the question, looking at it in terms of ordinary, decent, everyday behaviour. *The Wicked Man* sets out to explore its metaphysical implications, looking beneath the temporal surface for the eternal realities. The difference in artistic purpose would naturally argue a different technique, as between the two plays; but there is no difference in craftsmanship. *Vote by Ballot* is theatrically entirely sound and is written with the same skill and care for detail as is evinced by Barker's more complex and serious work.

He has one other one-act play, but though it was written not very long after *Vote by Ballot* – in 1916, to be precise – it belongs to a different phase of his work and should be considered later. It has, in view of Barker's personal history, a title of quirky significance: it is called *Farewell to the Theatre*.

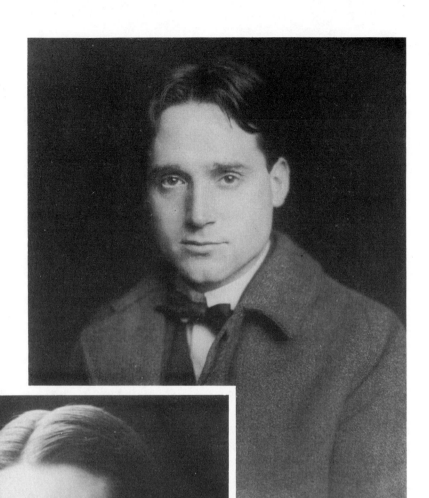

*Barker in
1914.*

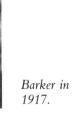

*Barker in
1917.*

Barker and Shakespeare

‘ . . . one snap at William S.; but for the rest – other people must get on with it’, he had said to Gilbert Murray in the letter written in January, 1912. As things turned out, it proved to be rather a long 'snap'. In effect, it began in 1912 and ended with his death in 1946. For the whole of Barker's major Shakespeare criticism, written between 1924 and 1946, is not only the natural extension of his work as a director of Shakespeare in the years 1912–14, but is also written entirely from the point of view of performance-as-artefact. The famous *Prefaces* and his essays and lectures on Shakespeare are all of a piece with his stage productions of Shakespeare and are, moreover, part of a *continuous* task which he set himself, starting with the production of *The Winter's Tale* at the Savoy in September, 1912 and going on, occasionally interrupted (by the 1914–18 War, for instance) but in an essentially unbroken line, to the *Coriolanus* preface in 1946. There has been some attempt to characterize his written comments on the plays as becoming more and more 'academic' (intended by its users in this context as a pejorative term) as it went along. The criticism seems wide of the mark. Throughout the *Prefaces*, up to and including *Coriolanus*, there is not only the very vivid sense still of a lively mind at work but, more specifically, of a mind which saw the plays always as things to be performed. There is much in his analyses of the plays which is debatable; there are some things with which one would want to disagree outright; but there is no point – even in the most abstruse discussion of character or the most technical consideration of verse forms – at which one feels, I would submit, that he has lost touch with the stage, much less that he has done so wilfully.

Barker approached Shakespeare in rather the same spirit in which he had approached Euripides nearly ten years before: he wanted to rescue him from his own reputation and restore him to the theatre as a writer of living plays: Barker's aim, in both cases, was to take the playwright off his pedestal and put him on the stage. In both cases this would mean, Barker well realized, the inventing and gradual developing of new techniques both of acting and of stage presentation. There was, though, one important difference. In the case of Euripides, Barker had the field to himself: in the case of Shakespeare, he had to live down an already-existing tradition which, though we now recognize it as a thoroughly bad tradition, was in Barker's day the accepted and virtually unquestioned norm. It had the blessing of the best and best-known actors in the country and it was immensely popular. Beerbohm Tree, who was its high priest and chief celebrant, makes the point in a quaint, pompous, affected and rather silly book, called *Thoughts and Afterthoughts* (London: Cassell, 1913): on page 46 he says, of his own productions at His Majesty's Theatre:

> In London alone two hundred and forty-two thousand people witnessed *Julius Caesar*, over one hundred and seventy thousand came to see *King John*, and nearly two hundred and twenty thousand were present during the run of *A Midsummer Night's Dream* – in all a grand total of six hundred and thirty-two thousand visitors to these three productions. And no doubt my brother managers who have catered for the public in this manner could, with the great successes they have had, point to similar figures.

A little further on, on page 51, he coyly remarks:

> Again I apologise for intruding the results of my own experience, but I feel bound to state – if only for the sake of encouraging others to put Shakespeare on the stage as bountifully as they can afford – that no single one of my Shakespearian productions has been unattended by a substantial pecuniary reward.

Tree sets out, in this same volume, the essentials of the tradition. His argument is that, since the modern stage has all that lovely, illusion-making machinery at its disposal, it would be a slovenly discourtesy not to place it at Shakespeare's disposal: 'our great poet' (the phrase is Tree's own and he uses it several times) would have approved, Tree asserts, and for proof points to the opening speech of Chorus in *Henry V*, to show that Shakespeare was discontented with the crudities of the Elizabethan stage. Sir Herbert takes the gist of this speech to be that Shakespeare,

being an artist and therefore more or less clairvoyant, had some prescience of the fact that the stage would one day improve and would
gradually become worthy of his plays and capable of staging them
properly – by which he means with lavish and detailed naturalistic
settings ('the scenic embellishment should be as beautiful and costly as
the subject of the drama being performed seems to demand', he says).
And speaking of the stage methods of the Elizabethan and Jacobean
theatre he says: 'Whatever was the case then, there is no reason that we
should continue in imperfections which may be supposed to characterize
Shakespeare's stage mounting.' From this, by an easy step, he passes to
the second part of his argument, which is that, since elaborate scenery is
now an absolute essential you must have time to manipulate and man-
oeuvre it and to make the necessary time you will naturally have to
dispense with some of the text. The process does not seem to disturb him
at all:

> In regard to this cutting of the text, it is only fair to point out that the process
> to an extent is necessary in the present day. It would be impossible otherwise
> to bring most of Shakespeare's plays within the three-hours' limit which he
> himself has described as the proper traffic of the stage. In times gone by when
> there was practically no scenery at all, when the public were satisfied to come
> to the playhouse and remain in their seats without moving from the begin-
> ning to the end of the performance a much lengthier play was possible than in
> these days; but to perform any single one of Shakespeare's plays without
> excision at all would be to court failure instead of success.

Sir Herbert is generous: he gives Shakespeare a whole hour longer than
Shakespeare himself allowed in his talk, in the Prologue to *Romeo and
Juliet*, of 'the two hours' traffic of our stage'; but even with this conces-
sion, Sir Herbert finds, not all of the prolix poet's effusions, together
with the several tons of scenery which the poetry quite obviously
demands, can be accommodated in a single performance. So the obvious
solution is to cut out some of the verse – heaven knows there's enough of
it! Nowhere, so far as I know, does Tree explain in any detail how he
decides which pieces to cut out and which to leave in. One gets, indeed, a
quite strong feeling from *Thoughts and Afterthoughts* that it doesn't much
matter: all of it is 'sublime', so all you need is the right *length* of it,
provided that it doesn't get in the way of the scenery. He returns over and
over again to the necessity for *illustration*, of a very literal kind, of the
verse. He begs his readers 'carefully to read the stage instructions in *The
Tempest, Henry VIII* and *Pericles* and ask yourself why, if Shakespeare

contemplated nothing in the way of what we call a production, he gave such minute direction for effects which even in our time of artistic and scientific mounting are difficult of realization.' In a later chapter of the book he illustrates this point further by quoting (among other things) the opening stage direction of *The Tempest*: but he virtually invalidates his own argument by quoting not the Shakespeare version but Pope's editorializing of it. The First Folio says bluntly 'A tempestuous noise of lightning and thunder heard' – the noise, combined with the dialogue which follows, being enough in Shakespeare's theatre to suggest the place and the circumstances: Pope did, in his editing, what Tree was wont to do on the stage – add a note of pedestrian literalism. The stage direction in Pope's edition reads: 'On a ship at sea. A tempestuous noise . . . etc.' What Beerbohm Tree never came to understand was that this kind of literal descriptiveness in the theatre (as elsewhere in the arts) tends always to imprison the imagination rather than to liberate it.

This, then, was the general state of Shakespearean production when Barker came to it. Tree, though a bit more flamboyant and assertive than some of the other actor-managers, was fairly typical of the commonly-accepted approach to Shakespeare on the stage: he simply carried to its logical conclusion a movement that was already there. Tree himself, as well as being a very kindly, witty,[1] charming man off the stage and the possessor of an absolutely spell-binding personality on, must also have been in many ways a rather simple-minded man and – more important in this context – a very literal-minded man. Verse obviously appealed to him almost wholly for its rodomontade: of sensitivity to poetry as such he had hardly a trace.

Barker, as one could have guessed from everything else about him, was from the start instinctively opposed to the standard, current method of producing Shakespeare. He was not the only rebel, of course, or the first. Shaw's mockery of Irving and Tree dates from his *Saturday Review* articles of 1895–98; Craig's advocacy of abstract settings on a non-representational stage is first fully expressed in *On the Art of the Theatre*, published in 1911; William Poel's work on Shakespeare, from which Barker had learned so much, began in the 1890s. But Poel was an amateur, Shaw was a critic and Craig was a drop-out; Barker was the only truly professional theatre man among them and he wanted to challenge Tree and the rest on their own professional territory ('pretentious', Tree called him, in a letter to his daughter Viola, dated October 4, 1912 – just after the opening of Barker's production of *The Winter's Tale*). The essence of that challenge, crudely stated, had four constituent elements: first, that the text of the play should be, with a few specific and minor exceptions, uncut; second, that the verse should be spoken crisply, incisively and *rapidly*; third, that the stage setting should be non-localized and non-representational; fourth, that the stage should be handsome and decorative to look at, but not obtrusive; and that the physical relation-ships of its acting areas should reproduce the essential relationships of the stage for which that particular play was written, whether the Globe or the Blackfriars or one or other of the great private halls of Elizabethan and Jacobean times. He had not, it is important to emphasize, enunciated and articulated these principles in advance in any sort of manifesto: the principles evolved from the practice and were enunciated later. But it is convenient now, in considering Barker's actual productions, to tabulate those principles in advance, so to speak, so as to be able to gauge the extent to which these productions represented a challenge to the estab-lished order of the day. The extent is considerable: the challenge is, in fact, total. *The Winter's Tale*, the first of the three productions which were to embody the challenge, opened at the Savoy Theatre on Sep-tember 21, 1912 and A.B. Walkley's review of it, in *The Times* of September 23, gives a fair idea of the response it elicited from a good many of those in its audience. He begins:

> It was bound to come. Here, like it or lump it, is Post-Impressionist Shakes-peare. Mr. Granville Barker tells us that the costumes have been designed by Mr. Albert Rothenstein after Giulio Romano, 'that rare Italian master', to whom Paulina's Steward attributed the supposed statue of Hermione; but this is only Mr. Barker's (or Mr. Rothenstein's) fun. The costumes are after Beardsley and still more after Bakst; the busbies and caftans and deep-skirted tunics of the courtiers come from the Russian Ballet, and the *bizarre* smocks and fal-lals of the merrymakers at the sheep-shearing come from the Chelsea Arts Club Ball.

A little further on in the review he comments in similar vein upon the stage setting:

> There is no 'scenery' in the modern sense of the term, but, as Mr. Barker calls it, 'decoration'. For the Leontes-Hermione section of the play Mr. Norman Wilkinson has provided a simple harmony of white pilasters and dead-gold curtain which we like; but his bungalow in the rustic part strikes us as a joke, and not a good one. . . . (there are no footlights, but search-lamps converging on the stage from the dress-circle.)

On the play itself and the acting, his main comment is as follows:

> If he is a little too freakish, you are ready to forgive him because this queer

Shakespeare of his has the sovereign virtue of being alive . . . It must be added that, with all Mr. Barker's exertions, some parts of *The Winter's Tale* are less alive than others. The least alive are the crowned heads. . . . Leontes is 'tearing and raging' with life; but he only illustrates the truth that it is possible to be at once violent and dull. Hermione is virtuously long-suffering and dull. Mr. Ainley and Miss Lillah McCarthy try hard to make out that they are not really as dull as they seem, but it won't do. Neither the infinite variety of Mr. Ainley's 'business' and gestures and poses, his crouching upon couches and grovelling in corners, nor Miss McCarthy's exercises in 'living statues' can hoodwink us into the belief that this Royal pair are not dull.

'Post-Impressionist Shakespeare is distinctly amusing', is Walkley's final summing-up: like that whole review, this final remark is designedly off-hand and a little condescending, though not so much as one might at first think; one needs to bear in mind that 'amusing' was one of Walkley's favourite words and was intended as commendation – the function of theatre, as far as Walkley was concerned, is to amuse: an amusing play is a good play. He prided himself upon his status as an amateur and a gentleman, for whom it would be demeaning to become too involved or intense.

Some of the other critics were more severe than Walkley, especially in regard to the speaking of the verse, which they said was 'gabbled'. Barker defended himself against the charge in a letter to the *Daily Mail*, dated September 26, 1912. In it he says '. . . I am grateful, too (and again so should we all be), to Mr. William Poel . . . who taught me how swift and passionate a thing, how beautiful in its variety, Elizabethan blank verse might be when tongues were trained to speak and ears acute to hear it.' In the same letter he also takes up a more general point:

> See *The Winter's Tale* at the Savoy Theatre. Spend the evening in a dispute with yourself or your neighbour as to whether this is right or wrong, ugly or beautiful, whether that is as you last saw it, or as you never thought it could be – why, you may well go away worried and confused. But sit there at your ease to listen and watch, and only ask yourself, when the curtain has finally fallen: was I stirred and amused, has it been enthralling to hear and beautiful to see? – and by the answer to that question we will abide, as indeed we must. I make the challenge with the more confidence, as by the behaviour of the audience these last two or three performances, mouselike while the play proceeded, more than generous of their applause at the end, I have no great doubt of the issue.

The Winter's Tale ran for six weeks and Barker followed it almost immediately with a production of *Twelfth Night*, using substantially the same company. Leon Quartermaine, who had played Clown in *The Winter's Tale*, became Sir Andrew Aguecheek, Lillah McCarthy moved from Hermoine to Viola, Henry Ainley exchanged Leontes for Malvolio. A.B. Walkley was won over entirely: his review of the production, in *The Times* of November 16, 1912, is almost entirely free from the condescending, patronizing tone of his review of *The Winter's Tale*. He describes it as '. . . the most enjoyable performance of *Twelfth Night* that we have had the fortune to see.' And at one point he addresses himself specifically to one of the most contentious issues raised in connection with the earlier production:

> Though the people say virtually all that Shakespeare set down for them to say, they do not gabble it: they can all – or all that matter – be distinctly heard. It is a most agreeable sensation to feel that for once you are listening to Shakespeare as he wrote: to a Shakespeare who is being allowed to have his say out: and to perceive that you are enjoying it, in a simple, natural, childlike way, without any need for make-belief or for appeal to the 'historical sense'.

For this production, Norman Wilkinson designed both the stage setting and the costumes. The set consisted of a main permanent stage suggesting, in formal, semi–abstract terms, Olivia's garden, an inner stage which was used for the drinking scenes and the prison and a wide apron built out over the orchestra pit where, against a traverse curtain of an abstract black and white design, the scenes in Orsino's palace, and some of the shorter, linking scenes, could be played. As will readily be seen, this arrangement of the stage represents, in one respect, a compromise on Barker's part – and the same thing had happened in *The Winter's Tale*: the set is non–representational but it is not entirely non–localized. Barker has not quite had the courage of his convictions: particular decorative elements are permanently attached to and identified with particular locales. On the other hand, since these elements do not consist of huge masses of realistically painted scenery the visual imagination is not inhibited by them and the physical flow of the play is not impeded. The action was, in fact, played continuously, without breaks or pauses except for two official 'house' intervals, one at the end of Act II Scene 3 and one after Act IV Scene 1.

Not only in the matter of staging but also as regards character interpretation Barker had innovative ideas. And again, his ideas stemmed from two sources – the text of the play and such knowledge as we have of Elizabethan stage conditions. In the preface to an 'acting edition' of the play published by Heinemann to coincide with the production,[2] Barker considers in particular the playing of Viola:

The most important aspect of the play must be viewed, to view it rightly, with Elizabethan eyes. Viola was played, and was meant to be played, by a boy. See what this involves. To that original audience the strain of make-believe in the matter ended just where for us it most begins, at Viola's entrance as a page. Shakespeare's audience saw Cesario without effort as Orsino sees him; more importantly they saw him as Olivia sees him; indeed it was over Olivia they had most to make believe. One feels at once how this affects the sympathy and balance of the love scenes of the play. One sees how dramatically right is the delicate still grace of the dialogue between Orsino and Cesario, and how possible it makes the more outspoken passion of the scenes with Olivia. Give to Olivia, as we must do now, all the value of her sex, and to the supposed Cesario none of the value of his, we are naturally quite unmoved by the business. Olivia looks a fool. And it is the common practice for actresses of Viola to seize every chance of reminding the audience that they are girls dressed up, to impress on one moreover, by childish by-play as to legs and petticoats or the absence of them, that this is the play's supreme joke. Now Shakespeare has devised one most carefully placed soliloquy where we are to be forcibly reminded that Cesario is Viola: in it he has as carefully divided the comic from the serious side of the matter. That scene played, the Viola, who does not do her best, as far as the passages with Olivia are concerned, to make us believe, as Olivia believes, that she is a man, shows, to my mind, a lack of imagination and is guilty of dramatic bad manners, knocking, for the sake of a little laughter, the whole of the play's romantic plot on the head.

Desmond MacCarthy, in the *New Statesman* for January 4, 1913, praised particularly Lillah McCarthy's playing of the part:

Miss Lillah McCarthy's performance is one of the best, if not the very best, pieces of acting she has done. Her gestures and carriage have added for the future a new vibrating note to the very mention of the name Viola. Her gallant and youthful poise in the scenes with Olivia, her easy alertness and her remarkable gift of remaining *still*, the pretty boyish docility of her hero-worship for the Duke Orsino, are points which the critic may single out, if he keeps his best praise for the discretion with which the supposed 'Cesario' played her part as a youth. Mr. Barker has insisted how important it is that the actress in the scenes with Olivia should do her best to make us believe her a man. We could not believe that, nor do we want to, but the part can be so played that we can imagine it being believed on the stage, with Viola in this case acted with an animation which made Olivia's mistake imaginatively conceivable.

H.M. Walbrook, the theatre critic of the *Pall Mall Gazette* enjoyed the play so much that he not only visited it a second time, he also wrote about it a second time: on January 8, 1913 the following appeared in his paper:

'TWELFTH NIGHT'

REVISITED

*

The Success of the Savoy
Revival

After a brief absence, Miss Lillah McCarthy reappeared as Viola at the Savoy Theatre last night, and was received with the heartiest applause after each of the three acts into which the comedy is here divided. Her performance, always able, impassioned, and eloquent, has improved with many repetitions, and last night she both acted and spoke the whole of it quite beautifully. The revival is now nearly through its second month, yet last night the theatre seemed full in every part, and never have we seen an audience more visibly fascinated. It was most interesting to glance round the house for a moment while the play was in progress and see how the whole attention of everyone was concentrated on the stage. Good, also, was it to hear the peals of laughter over the scenes of the Aguecheek challenges and the duel; and better still, perhaps, to note the perfect stillness in which the wonderful rhetoric of Viola, Olivia, and Orsino, and the quite exquisite singing of Mr. Hayden Coffin in the part of Feste were listened to. Best of all was it to hear people whispering as one scene opened, 'this is a charming scene,' or, as another began, 'This is most amusing.' It showed that there were many in the house who were seeing the performance, perhaps, a third or fourth time. And, assuredly, of all the good things to be seen in London playhouses just now, there is none that has the magic of this almost perfect rendering of a play written by Shakespeare three hundred years ago.

Critical sentiment had obviously swung very rapidly in Barker's favour: Desmond MacCarthy concluded his January 4 review by an explicit articulation of that very point. 'For years', he said, 'the Elizabethan Stage Society and Mr. William Poel have been undermining contemporary Shakespeare productions, which have only held their ground thanks to an invariably lavish and often disinterested expenditure on gorgeously unimaginative scenery; for years the critics have impotently complained. But a few more productions like this of *Twelfth Night* and the public taste itself will alter, and then – fly away into space poor hierophants of costly fiascos.' I doubt whether even Desmond MacCarthy realized in 1913 how quickly his prophecy would come true or how complete – in the space of only one year and two productions – Barker's victory had been. He had, virtually single-handedly, demolished in that one year the wealthy and powerful tradition of almost a century's standing. Not that there were not still some dissident voices: there were, but they were now in the nature of peripheral guerilla attacks on the edges of the main battle; the central force of the foe was already broken, though the day had not yet been officially conceded. One such isolated pocket of resistance was the critic who wrote for *Play Pictorial* (not a journal which was noted for its advanced views or its intellectual grasp). Barker replied to the criticism in a letter to the editor which was published in the magazine in November, 1912, during the run of *Twelfth Night*. Barker, in this letter, argues his case so reasonably and touches upon so many of the central issu⌐ ⌐ that the letter is worth quoting in full. It reads as follows:

> Savoy Theatre
> November, 1912

Dear Sir,

Does it come to this, that you enjoyed the performance mightily, but that now you doubt gravely whether you ought to have enjoyed it? Make reasonably sure, one is tempted to reply, that it was Shakespeare's play of *Twelfth Night* – veritably that – which you enjoyed, and, if so, be dashed to your doubts. But I know where your critical, next-morning conscience pinches; not over the acting, not even the costumes, but over that confoundedly-puzzling scenery. Well, this has an importance, I think, beyond its own merits or demerits.

Something may be gained by discussing the question. For there is a question, a problem, and very glad we should be for a little assistance in solving it. Why does one so often look for that in vain, even from the friendliest critics? Tell me how much you admire, or how utterly you detest Norman Wilkinson's pink pillars, and, as privately and politely as possible, I yawn, and so does Wilkinson. I ask you, when you yourself are trying to set down something important, to have your handwriting admired, or to be tripped up over a mistake in syntax – what are your feelings?

Indeed, as such things go, it is important – this problem of Shakespearean scenery. And, as a new formula, a new convention, has to be found, the audience must learn to see, even as we learn to work in it. And the ideal audience (you, yourself, the dramatic critic) might even now begin to cultivate the eye, if not of faith, of prophecy. We need help; I assure you that such experiments aren't easy.

I postulate that a new formula has to be found. Realistic scenery won't do, if only because it swears against everything in the plays; if only because it's never realistic; I can't argue that point now, even if there's need. So we begin again at the beginning.

What are the conditions? We must have a background. What sort? Any sort? But if we have our choice? Well, we want something that will reflect light and suggest space; if it's to be a background permanent for a play (this, for many reasons, it should be), something that will not tie us too rigidly indoors or out. Sky-blue then will be too like sky; patterns suggest walls. Tapestry curtains hung round? Well, tapestry is apt to be stuffy and – archaeological.

We shall not save our souls by being Elizabethan. It is an easy way out, and, strictly followed, an honourable one. But there's the difficulty. To be Elizabethan one must be strictly, logically or quite ineffectively so. And, even then, it is asking much of an audience to come to the theatre so historically-sensed as that.

But a curtained background of some sort? Excellent as a background, if a simple background were all that is wanted. But what about a play's demand for houses, with their doors and balconies, gardens with hedges, a forest with trees? Here is the problem. I state it; its solution does not lie in words but it is an attempt at a solution that we have been making at the Savoy Theatre.

There was much praise, I think, for the palace of Leontes. But – six pillars and curtains to bridge them, granted their proportion and colour needed to be simply right – what could be easier of solution? I see little difficulty where architecture is concerned. The cottage of the shepherd was much blamed. Rightly or wrongly? – I'll offer no opinion. But I doubt if many of the scolders began to know where the rights and wrongs of the matter lay.

The play demanded a cottage, to be put in conventional surroundings, and, therefore, a conventional cottage; to stand against the simplest background and to remain in the nature of a background itself; solve that.

Now Olivia's garden, which needs for the play's purposes at the very least a box hedge to be placed against that same conventional background – that or another. A box hedge truly, when well gardenered, is one of nature's most conventional works. Nevertheless, try the closest-clipped of them in its actuality against curtain or canvas – it will suit about as well as a brier path in a bed of tulips.

To invent a new hieroglyphic language of scenery, that, in a phrase, is the problem. Come to the more difficult aspects of it. What about a forest of Arden? As I hope never to produce the play[3], my proposal is sufficiently disinterested. Let the *Daily   *, that organ ever in the vanguard of theatrical progress, offer a prize of £50 for the best design for the Forest Scene in *As You Like It*, to set against some conventional background, to be decorative, therefore, not realistic, and to be uncumbrous. Trial and Error is the quickest road forward.

My space is filled. I have not dealt with the minor problems of the traverse-scenes, front-cloths, or front-curtains – call them either of the three – but that is but a shadow of the other.

Faithfully yours,
H. Granville Barker

'But a few more productions like this . . .', Desmond MacCarthy had said. The sentiments were echoed a little over a year later by A.B. Walkley, who concluded his review of Barker's next Shakespeare production with these words:

> If only he can keep it up! If only he can run through all Shakespeare in the spirit of daring artistic adventure with which he has turned the fairy-land of *A Midsummer Night's Dream* into gold.

But MacCarthy and Walkley were not to get their wish: the production of *A Midsummer Night's Dream*, which opened at the Savoy on February 6, 1914 and was repeated a year later at Wallack's Theatre in New York, was, as things turned out, Barker's last Shakespeare production. But the battle was won, nevertheless, without any further blows being needed. Barker had revolutionized our concept of what Shakespeare in the twentieth-century theatre should look like and sound like. And, having demonstrated the main principles in a practical way, he went on to refine them and apply them to other of Shakespeare's plays in a set of writings about Shakespeare which are quite unique.

For the production of *A Midsummer Night's Dream* there was again an 'acting edition' published by Heinemann in parallel with the production: in this edition Barker says:

> Then come the fairies. Can even genius succeed in putting fairies on the stage? The pious commentators say not. This play and the sublimer parts of *King Lear* are freely quoted as impossible in the theatre. But, then, by some trick of reasoning they blame the theatre for it. I cannot follow that. If a play written for the stage cannot be put on the stage the playwright, it seems to me, has failed, be he who he may. Has Shakespeare failed or need the producer only pray for a little genius, too? The fairies are the producer's test. Let me confess that, though mainly love of the play, yet partly, too, a hope of passing that test has inspired the present production. Foolhardy one feels facing it. But if a method of staging can compass the difficulties of *A Midsummer Night's Dream*, surely its cause is won.

His way of meeting the challenge of the fairies was a highly original one and was the element in the production which provoked the most comment – not all of it favourable. But all of it proved Barker's point that the practical problem of presenting fairies on the stage was the *central* problem of the play: the play is a fairy play; the essence of its spirit lies in the magic and mystery of the woodland. Find a way of reaching the audience with that magic, convince the onlookers of the *power* of the fairies, the natural dwellers in the misty twilight, and the play comes magically to life. To do this, Barker jettisoned all the traditional cargo of sentimental prettiness that the play had acquired on its voyage through the nineteenth century: his fairies were adults, not children; they were strange, other-worldly, slightly sinister; they were unaccompanied by Mendelssohn; and they were gilded – all gold, from head to foot; faces, hands, everything. The forest was represented largely by flowing draperies in purple and various shades of green and the great visual beauty of the mass of gold against this shifting, diaphanous background was much commented on. Walkley described it as 'something to strike us all with wonder and delight . . .' and said, of the fairies themselves, 'they look like Cambodian idols and posture like Nijinsky in *Le Dieu Bleu*.' His review contains one passage of quite striking description:

> In the end the golden fairies play hide-and-seek round the columns of Theseus's palace. Gradually their numbers dwindle. At last only one, a girl, is left – the last patch of gold to fade from the sight, and to leave on the mind the strange, new impression of the play as golden, a 'golden book of spirit and sense'. Who is the magician who invented these golden faires? Is it Mr. Barker or Mr. Norman Wilkinson?

He goes on to criticize the 'bewitched quartet of lovers' and says of them: 'The difficulty is that they are often in imminent danger of becoming bores.' But he returns to his former theme:

> But it is not of these [the lovers] one thinks in the end. The mind goes back to the golden fairies, and one's memories of this production must always be golden memories.

The rapid speaking of the verse still occasioned some comment, though not by any means as universally adverse as had been the case with *The Winter's Tale*. The *New York Times*, pursuing a middle course in its mainly complimentary review of February 17, 1915, said:

> The delivery represents an open and welcome rebellion against all the pomposities of Shakespearean declamation. The mood of the comedy is capitally served by the swift, rhythmic utterance of the verse in clear, fine head tones. The price is not small. The lines of Oberon and Titania fare well, but, while Titania's voice is lovely, her fancies are often indistinguishable and Puck is spiritedly unintelligible much of the time.

(The Oberon and Titania in New York were Horace Braham and Isobel Jeans; in London the parts had been played by Dennis Neilson-Terry and Christine Silver. Puck was Cecil Cameron in New York and Donald Calthrop in London.)

One needs to remember that of Barker's three Shakespeare productions during 1912–14, *A Midsummer Night's Dream* was probably the one that would shock the audience and critics most, partly because this play, even more firmly than the others, was most firmly associated in their minds with extravagant visual spectacle. It was, of all Shakespeare's plays, the one upon which the actor-managers of the nineteenth century had lavished their most extravagant and literal-minded scenic illustrations and this would mean at first, as Desmond MacCarthy acutely pointed out in the *New Statesman*, that the stage setting of Barker's imaginative non-scenic production would divert attention from the play's real significance, distract from the true values, as much as the old, painted, picture-scenery did. But, added MacCarthy, pay a *second* visit to the production and note how the previously-disturbing novelties fall into proper place and perspective, how they seem to release and serve the real spirit of the play, previously smothered by staging and now set free for the first time in over a hundred years.

William Archer, who did not write a public notice of the production, made some interesting points about it in a private letter to Barker.[4] 'On the whole I was charmed: the spirit is right, the decoration right, 99 details out of 100 absolutely right.' He felt that both Puck and Bottom (Nigel Playfair) were mis-cast; he found Theseus' voice 'untuned'; and he wondered whether 'in attaining distinction you miss something of delightfulness.' I suspect that this last comment may be due to the fact that Archer, an older and – on the whole – less imaginative man than the other critics, still had a secret hankering for the old, pictorial production: he does actually say that he had 'seen infinitely more faulty performances that gave me acuter pleasure'. That word 'delightfulness' is a little disturbing, I think: 'delight' in the theatre has altered its sense since the days when Dryden used it with such beautiful exactitude; as an adjective to describe a work of art, 'delightful' is now distinctly uncomfortable – it can so often and so easily mean either 'very pretty' or 'mildly titillating'. Archer does, however, have one other comment that is of distinct interest:

> It is a great pleasure to hear scores of lines restored that Daly & Co. used to cut; but I think you go to the opposite extreme. There are a few lines – perhaps not fifty in all – that have 'gone dead' & would be better away.

In a reply written three days later, Barker answered this criticism, as follows:

> I do agree with what you say about the dead lines, and if I felt that the non-cut,

play-straight-through battle was really won I should have been tempted to take out a few; but it is not and we have nailed Shakespeare un-cut to the mast. Also it is a tricky business to cut. One is so apt to take things out because you don't understand them. But there are about 20 lines that I feel hang heavy. I do not think that they will make the real difference to the play though. What does is that the character drawing is very poor, very, and if the actors (Demetrius and Lysander especially) are not all the time better than their parts it is dull, dull, dull. It is a poor play from this point of view and there is an end of it, and I cannot afford young Gods at fifty pounds a week apiece, even if I could get them.

In London, the production of *A Midsummer Night's Dream* ran for ninety-nine performances. The following year in New York it lasted less long, partly because it was one item of a repertory of four plays, partly because American taste was then – as it still is – far more conservative than British taste and partly because Wallack's theatre was scheduled for demolition and had to be vacated. By April of 1915, Granville Barker's Shakespeare productions had come to an end. And the world was deep into a war so vast that no imagination could compass it and no individual life escape its awful, searing touch. It seemed time to call a halt.

Artistically, Barker's mind went elsewhere for a space: in America he directed two of Gilbert Murray's translations of Euripides (*The Trojan Women* and *Iphigenia in Tauris*); he wrote a short play and a short story; he began work on a critical treatise which was to become *The Exemplary Theatre*; he translated Sacha Guitry's *Deburau* from the French; he wrote, after the war was over, an important full-length play (*The Secret Life*). Much of this, especially the earlier part of it, was carried out – if his letters to Shaw from America are anything to go by – in an increasing atmosphere of unreality, as if the sense and meaning of any artistic work could be retained only by effort of the conscious will. And artistry apart, his personal life fell, during the same period, into chaos. It was a full eight years before he got back to his Shakespeare work again.

In 1923, Ernest Benn Ltd. launched a major Shakespeare publishing project. They proposed to publish the whole Shakespeare canon in separate volumes, under the general title of the Players' Shakespeare, using the text of the First Folio, with a fairly detailed study of each play, from the director's point of view, by Granville Barker and with costume and stage designs by various artists under the general art editorship of Albert Rutherston (*i.e.* Albert Rothenstein who for fairly obvious reasons changed his name by deed-poll early in the War). *The Exemplary Theatre* and *The Secret Life* both recently completed and published,

Barker set about the new task with a will. 1923 saw the appearance of no less than three of the new series: *Macbeth, The Merchant of Venice* and *Cymbeline*. The artists concerned, in these three cases, were Charles Ricketts, Thomas Lowinsky and Rutherston himself. What Barker did with his prefaces was, in effect, to imagine that he was himself preparing the play for production and then write, under separate section headings, notes on all the things that struck him as problems in bringing the play to life on the stage. So these prefaces are, in fact, like more elaborate, more detailed versions of the ones he wrote after the event for the 'acting editions' of 1912–14, which dealt with the three plays that actually *were* produced. The headings, though not standardized from preface to preface, are things like 'The Text', 'Staging and Directing', 'Music', 'Costume', 'The Casting of the Parts', etc.

A Midsummer Night's Dream, with illustrations by Paul Nash and *Love's Labour's Lost*, illustrated by Norman Wilkinson, followed in 1924; *Julius Caesar*, illustrated by Ernest Stern, came in 1925; and *King Lear* (Paul Nash again) in 1927. Here, the series petered out. The books $12\frac{1}{2}''$ × $9\frac{1}{2}''$ and bound in vellum, printed in very small editions, simply could not be made to pay for themselves, beautiful though they were. But though the series petered out, Barker's writing of prefaces did not. In that same year, 1927, he extensively revised and lengthened the prefaces to *Love's Labour's Lost, Julius Caesar* and *King Lear* and published them as a collected volume under the title of *Prefaces to Shakespeare* (London: Sidgwick & Jackson). Three years later he was ready with a second volume dealing with four more of the plays. The prefaces to *The Merchant of Venice* and *Cymbeline* were revised versions (very thoroughly revised) of the Players' Shakespeare prefaces of 1923; the *Romeo and Juliet* and *Antony and Cleopatra* prefaces were based on lectures given at University College, Aberystwyth. The *Times Literary Supplement* of January 2, 1930 greeted this second set of Prefaces by saying: 'One can only hope that these Prefaces will go on until we have, as it were, a complete "Granville-Barker Shakespeare". Such a book, when completed, should be a permanent part of our Shakespeare literature; among commentaries it would stand out always, we think, with a character and force of its own; and it would not, this is worth emphasizing, be a work for theatrical producers and actors only.' Barker had obviously set himself a mammoth task and seems to have been prepared to carry on with it for the rest of his life if need be, taking Shakespeare's plays in turn and commenting upon them, in great detail, from the point of view of the stage interpretation of them. Whether he really ever intended to deal with the whole canon in this way we don't, of course, know. There is no documentary evidence either way on the point but it seems reasonable to doubt whether there was ever such an intention in his mind. For one thing, the Prefaces got longer and more complex as he went along; for another, his plans – whatever they were – were again disrupted by the outbreak of war. It was seven years after the second volume before its successor appeared: Sidgwick & Jackson published *Prefaces to Shakespeare: Third Series* in 1937. The volume contained one play only: it was a book-length study of *Hamlet*. Then followed a gap of eight years before *Othello* appeared; this, which was based on lectures given at Harvard in 1941, was also a single-play volume, which was called *Prefaces to Shakespeare: Fourth Series*. The final volume, containing *Coriolanus*, was published posthumously in 1947; Barker had based it on a series of lectures which he gave in 1942 at University College, Toronto. Some time in the late nineteen-thirties he had also begun a preface on *Macbeth* – a new piece of work entirely, we gather, which had little or no connection with the brief Players' Shakespeare preface of 1923. He mentions this new *Macbeth* preface briefly in a letter written from New York to Sir John Gielgud on October 27, 1940, when he says: 'As to *Macbeth*, I fear I can't be very helpful. I have a five-year old draft for a 'Preface' here – a solitary copy which I managed to bring away. But when I shall be able to return to it I don't know.' Apparently, he never managed to get back to it; and after his death in 1946 the draft he mentions was not found among his papers.

Implicit throughout these thirty years' writings about Shakespearean production and explicit at many points, from the earliest to the latest of these *Prefaces*, is the group of severely practical problems which Barker saw as the central issue when he approached his first Shakespeare production (not counting the 1904 *Two Gentlemen of Verona*, that is) in 1912. Though it is obvious, as one reads the *Prefaces* now, that some of the issues involved have no longer any power to plague us (and this fact in itself is due in no small measure to Barker's work), it is also clear that they were all real enough and urgent enough in Barker's day and that they vitally affected the practical question of putting Shakespeare on the stage. They are not vague or general issues, but precise and specific ones, interconnected, all being concerned ultimately with the integrity of the play and the propriety of playing it in the theatre. They can be simply stated and tabulated and there might be some virtue and usefulness in so doing. They are:

a) the question of whether and when to cut the text, and how much;
b) the question of a non-localized stage, as opposed to 'realistic' scenery;

c) the question of how to speak the verse;
d) the question of ensemble playing as opposed to the deliberate exploitation of the play as a vehicle for a 'star' performer;
e) the question of whether the plays should, in fact, be presented in the theatre at all.

The last of these seems the oddest of all to us now, but it was a very real issue in the first decade of the century. There was a not inconsiderable body of opinion which held that the true beauties of Shakespeare's plays could be realized only in the quiet of the study and that to put the plays on the stage of a public theatre was automatically to rob them of half their poetry and all their subtlety. The very first sub-heading in the Introduction to Barker's first volume of prefaces in 1927 says 'The Study and the Stage' and Beerbohm Tree, in *Thoughts and Afterthoughts* says, in a chapter called 'The Living Shakespeare' and devoted to a consideration of some of the adverse criticisms levelled at his own productions of Shakespeare: 'I have said that I could understand such writers as Hazlitt, Lamb and Emerson declaring that they preferred that Shakespeare should not be presented on the stage at all, for there is undoubtedly a tendency in performances other than those of the first order to destroy the illusion of the highly cultured; and I can conceive that such a one would say to himself, "Why undergo the unnecessary discomfort and expense of a visit to the theatre when I can read my Shakespeare at ease in my arm-chair?" ' Theatre people of every stripe, when it came to Shakespeare, felt under the obligation of having to *justify* the acting of him. For so long his plays had been written about, in slightly awe-stricken tones, as Great Literature that to the late Victorian and Edwardian mind it seemed proper and necessary to make some *excuse* for tinkering with him in so frivolous a place as a theatre. So Barker, who insisted right from the start that the 'text of a play is a score waiting performance' and applied this dictum to Shakespeare just as much and just as necessarily as any other playwright, had two different sorts of adversary: a first group who thought Shakespeare too sacred to be submitted to the sacrilege of the stage, and a second group who almost justified the strictures of the first by doing violence to the plays in the process of staging them. Having both of these difficulties to deal with proved, in the event, to be a very apt and happy stimulus to Barker in the writing of the *Prefaces*. Convinced as he was, both intellectually and intuitively, that the only ultimate aesthetic justification for the plays was the theatrical performance of them, and that only in such performance were the plays themselves complete, he was compelled in his thinking and writing about them always to distinguish sharply between a legitimate theatricality which supported and furthered the plays' true, artistic ends and a meretriciously false theatricality which had on occasion been superimposed upon the plays for adventitious ends and had succeeded in smothering the plays in the process. This need for distinguishing true from false methods forced Barker back to a very close and detailed study of the texts of the plays and led him to look for (and often to find) another and profounder kind of distinction – that between theatrical and dramatic values. To be able to assert that some kinds of theatricality were valid while others were not, it was incumbent upon him to demonstrate the deeper cause which the theatrical method was called upon to serve and this called for the examination of intrinsic *dramatic* values in the plays themselves. Though he was perhaps unduly influenced by the 'character-drawing' school of scholarly criticism (of which A.C. Bradley was the most skilful and distinguished exponent), Barker nevertheless became one of the leaders of and chief influences within that movement which, in the first thirty years of the twentieth century, began to move Shakespearean criticism in the direction of seeing the plays primarily as artistic artefacts with shape, form and completeness of their own, poised structures controlled to a nicety by their own systems of dramatic dichotomies whose strength, importance and artistic effectiveness derive from the fact that they spring from and are rooted in those facets of human experience which see life and the world as held in eternal but uneasy balance between equal and opposing forces. This discernment of the dramatic heart of the plays shows repeatedly in Barker's writing, more particularly in his detailed consideration of individual plays in these *Prefaces*. It is noteworthy also that, whereas Barker had been greatly influenced at the start of his work by the academic and scholarly critics of Shakespeare (a fact which made many theatre people of the day, with their instinctive mistrust of any kind of intellectual process, deeply suspicious of him), his *Prefaces* were, at least in part, instrumental in starting a new and fruitful trend in Shakespearean criticism and did themselves exert a considerable influence upon Shakespearean scholars and scholarship of the middle of the twentieth century: the admirable work of Dr. M.C. Bradbrook, for example, who refuses to divorce text from stage and, while studying the text very perceptively and in great depth, sees it always as the text of a play for acting and not just as a poem for reading. Her book, *Elizabethan Stage Conditions*, appeared only five years after the first volume of *Prefaces*. It is still very lively reading as well as being very accurate scholarship and very imaginative criticism: and it contains multiple examples of the intelligent application of our hard-won knowledge of the Elizabethan-Jacobean stage to problems of interpretation in the plays themselves – exactly the kind of thing, in fact, that Barker advocates, demonstrates and practises in his approach to all the plays he treats of in the *Prefaces*. Similarly, as J.L. Styan has pointed out in Chapter 6 of his *The Shakespeare Revolution* (Cambridge University Press, 1977), Barker's influence shows markedly in the work of scholar-critics such as S.L. Bethell and Anne Righter, not only on the matter of the effects on the plays of precise details of stagecraft, but also as far as more general considerations are concerned – the realization, for example, of the crucial part played in the actual *meanings* of the plays by the fact that Shakespeare's chief stage instrument was aural, not visual; and the even more complex consideration of the effect on the writing and structure of the play of Shakespeare's automatic assumptions about the attitudes (which were extremely sophisticated ones) of an Elizabethan audience in a theatre. Incidentally, one of the more recent critics to respond sensitively and perceptively to that general line of thought which Barker launched in the *Prefaces* is J.L. Styan himself, as his *Shakespeare's Stagecraft* (Cambridge University Press, 1967) shows. Barker himself never saw the gap between study and stage as an unbridgeable abyss: in his Introduction to the first volume of *Prefaces* in 1927, talking of true and false theatricality, he says:

> There is hardly a theatre in the world where masterpiece and trumpery alike are not rushed through rehearsals to an arbitrarily effective performance, little more learned of them than the words, gaps in the understanding of them filled up with 'business' – effect without cause, the demand for this being the curse of theatre as of other arts, as of other things than art. Not to such treatment will the greater plays of Shakespeare yield their secrets. But working upon a stage which reproduced the essential conditions of his, working as students, not as showmen merely, a company of actors might well find many of the riddles of the library answering themselves unasked. And these prefaces could best be a record of such work, if such work were to be done.

And in the very next paragraph, eschewing pedantry and indicating what kind of approach the study of the play should take, he has this to say:

> We cannot, on the other hand, begin our research by postulating the principles of the Elizabethan stage. One is tempted to say it had none, was too much a child of nature to bother about such things . . .
> Shakespeare's work shows such principles as the growth of a tree shows. It is not haphazard merely because it is not formal; it is shaped by inner strength.

He goes on to emphasize that, because of this growth, it is impossible to generalize about the plays and that the original stagecraft *of each play*, so far as it can be inferred from the text, should be carefully examined, since it will differ from that of other Shakespeare plays as well as from other Elizabethan and Jacobean plays. The differences will depend in part upon which of the Elizabethan theatres it was written for, whether the Globe or the Blackfriars or one of the other private theatres; but they will also depend upon the increasing skill of Shakespeare's craftsmanship and the increasing profundity of his art, both of which developed with amazing rapidity over the relatively short space of his writing career. In order to see the shape and the stagecraft of the play more clearly, Barker advocates reading it from its Quarto, so as to free it from the act and scene divisions and from the topographical editorializings, of seventeenth- and eighteenth-century editors. It seems to me that this is excellent advice and I cannot help feeling that it probably shows the influence upon him of his work on Gilbert Murray's translations of Greek plays. These, too, came to Barker almost devoid of stage directions, depending entirely upon the words to be spoken from the stage by the characters. Frightening for a timid or an incompetent director, a script in this form becomes a challenge and an inspiration to an imaginative director, liberating him from set customs and preconceived ideas and compelling him to design movements, groupings and acting areas in such a way as best to serve the text and the text alone.

Along with considerations of stagecraft (in its most narrow and precise sense – the actors' use of the physical stage), Barker's other major critical contribution in the *Prefaces* is concerned with the one other great organizing element of the plays – the verse. In play after play he analyses specific passages, using to tremendous advantage not only his actor's experience in a general sense but also, in particular, the delicacy and accuracy of his actor's ear which, judging from these writings alone, must have been of a remarkable order. His analysis of the verse is detailed and technical – by which I mean that he examines both the techniques of the *writing* of the verse and the techniques of speaking it – but is aimed always at elucidating the sense of the speech: not the literal sense of the words; not merely the plot-sense or character-sense of the whole passage; not even the imagistic sense of the poetry; but the *dramatic* sense of the passage, seen in relation to the shape of the whole play. There are many examples of this throughout the *Prefaces*: one must here serve for all. In discussing, very fully and very excitingly, the verse in *Antony and Cleopatra*, Barker quotes the very famous 'The crown o' the earth doth melt. My lord! O, withered is the garland of the war . . . etc.' and then says of it:

> This, in analysis, is little better than ecstatic nonsense; and it is meant to sound so. It has just enough meaning in it for us to feel as we hear it that it may have a little more. Art must by so much at least improve on nature; in nature it would have less or none. But it gives us to perfection the reeling agony of Cleopatra's mind; therefore, in its dramatic setting, it ranks as supreme poetry.

Barker has used an argument similar to this before. In discussing, in his Introduction to the First Series of *Prefaces* in 1927, the general question of the speaking of the verse, he cites by way of an example of especial difficulty the speech of Leontes, in *The Winter's Tale*, which begins:

> Affection! thy intention stabs the centre;
> Thou dost make possible things not so held,
> Communicat'st with dreams; – How can this be?
> With what's unreal thou coactive art,
> And fellow'st nothing; . . .

About this speech Barker makes the following comment:

> The confusion of thought and language is dramatically justified. Shakespeare is picturing a genuinely jealous man (the sort of man that Othello was *not*) in the grip of mental epilepsy. We parse the passage and dispute its sense; spoken, as it was meant to be, in a choking torrent of passion, probably a modicum of sense slipped through, and its first hearers did not find it a mere rigmarole.

The mind of man, in other words, sometimes utters – and *thinks* – that which by rational standards is nonsense; but even nonsense can be turned into powerful poetry; and the rational world is not the only world which man inhabits.

Barker's analysis of the verse in *Antony and Cleopatra* is singled out by J.L. Styan as 'perhaps Granville-Barker's most subtle piece of writing'[5] and he praises the whole of the *Antony and Cleopatra* Preface as 'perhaps Granville-Barker's greatest achievement in dramatic criticism'[6]. I would agree with his judgment in both respects. Styan, in fact, has a brief but vivid and penetrating commentary[7] upon each of Barker's essays in the first two volumes of *Prefaces*. He expresses the view (again, accurately, I think) that Barker misunderstood *Cymbeline* and quite failed to come to terms with it but that the six other plays were all – and in particular *King Lear* and *Antony and Cleopatra* – greatly illuminated by his commentary. Talking of *Antony and Cleopatra* Styan says: 'Granville-Barker conveyed a sense of the play which passed beyond mere stagecraft to what enthralled its audience when "there is nothing left to stand between us and the essential drama", when we are "at one with its realities" '[8]. And he sums up his whole chapter in this way:

> In these remarkable *Prefaces* Granville-Barker was attempting a new descriptive dramatic criticism, fine in its particularity, and yet aiming at something more. He had left the closet far behind and moved his criticism on to the stage itself. Now he seemed to be straining to work out in each essay an ideal production, at once reaching backwards to Shakespeare's first intentions, and forwards to the realized essentials of each unique creation.

Styan regards the seven *Prefaces* which are contained in the First and Second Series (1927 and 1930) as the formative ones, the liveliest and most influential ones. He comments only glancingly, in occasional scattered remarks, upon the others, one of these passing comments being to the effect that 'the *Hamlet* volume, which did not appear after much labour until 1937, already showed signs of academic atrophy and his divorce from stage experience'. In this he follows – though not necessarily deliberately or consciously – the views earlier expressed by C.B. Purdom and Wilson Knight[9]. I find it hard to agree. The *Hamlet* essay *is* long – the longest of the lot: but there is much matter to discuss and more verbiage of dead criticism to clear away with this play than with any other in the world. Barker's tests still seem to me to be the right ones: will it work in the theatre? *how* will it work? what is its intended meaning when it *does* work in the theatre? Discussing – for example – the recurrence of certain images in the verse of *Hamlet* and the implications this has for the actor, Barker says:

> But will the ordinarily attentive listener seize on this connection, spaced out, as it is, across more than half the play's length? That is the test of its dramatic validity. It is hard to say positively. But the image is initially very strongly stressed; and no more notable place could be given it than it has; in Hamlet's first soliloquy (when we are all curiosity about him), where too it follows immediately upon the initial emotional outburst (when our attention is well held).

His interest and imagination here is, surely, fixed and focussed as it always was in the earlier *Prefaces* on a sort of ideal stage performance which he vividly sees and hears in his mind as he writes. And, apart from one or two forgivable longeurs (who is there who does not at some point wax a little expansive about *Hamlet*?), I cannot see that this is not typical of the whole essay.

In a general comment upon Barker's method, Styan says[10]: 'It is true that, as his biographer C.B. Purdom says, he devoted too much of his energy to scholarly issues of little account, like the discussion of the time-scheme in *Othello*, or act-division in *Hamlet*, or the separation of Shakespeare's hand from a collaborator's.' Even looked at from the strictest of practical stage viewpoints, only the middle one of these three instances seems to me to be an issue 'of little account'; the other two, surely, have immediate and important implications for the interpretation and the playing of the play and should properly be among those matters to which a director of the play ought to address himself. Barker's essay on *Othello*, as a matter of fact, has always seemed to me one of the best of his pieces[11] and one of the ones most strictly relevant to the play in the theatre. There are many striking instances of this, not least the discussion of 'Double Time', to which Styan refers.

This theory, which accounts for the complex rhythms of the middle acts of *Othello*, was not Barker's own invention. It was first propounded by Professor John Wilson, writing under the pseudonym of 'Christopher North', in three articles published in *Blackwood's Magazine* in November 1849, April 1850 and May 1850. What Barker did – and it was both important and characteristic – was to examine the idea of the theory in great detail and relate it very closely, through a discussion of stage techniques, to the theatrical situation. He shows us 'how it works' and by showing us this makes us all the readier to accept it as a legitimate artistic convention, rather than regarding it as a 'problem'. Having explained how Shakespeare, through sheer dramaturgical virtuosity, writes Acts II, III and IV in 'Double Time', keeping 'Short Time' and 'Long Time' going – and both making sense – alongside each other, Barker then asks and answers the crucial question[12]:

> Why, however, does he neglect the obvious and simple course of allowing a likely lapse of time between the night of Cassio's disgrace and the priming of Othello to suspect Desdemona and her kindness to him – for which common sense, both our own, and, we might suppose, Iago's, cries out? The answer is that there has been one such break in the action already, forced on him by the voyage to Cyprus, and he must avoid another. The bare Elizabethan stage bred a panoramic form of drama; the story straightforwardly unfolded, as many as possible of its incidents presented, narrative supplying the antecedents and filling the gaps. Its only resources of any value are the action itself and the speech, and the whole burden, therefore, of stimulating and sustaining illusion falls on the actor – whom once he has captured his audience, must, like the spell-binding orator he may in method much resemble, be at pains to hold

them, or a part of his work will be frequently to do again. Our mere acceptance of the fiction, of the story and its peopling – we shall perhaps not withdraw; we came prepared to accept it. Something subtler is involved; the sympathy (in the word's stricter sense) which the art of the actor will have stirred in us. This current interrupted by the suspension of the action is not to be automatically restored by its resumption. Our emotions, roused and let grow cold, must be roused again.

This is typical of all his work on Shakespeare. Barker was not himself a great, original scholar: indeed, he was not a scholar at all, nor did he claim or aspire to be (though in some instances his textual study and criticism amounts to scholarship – and scholarship of a very fine kind). But what he does for us over and over again is to take the product of scholarship, which he assiduously studied, and relate it to the artistic realities of the stage, demonstrating its practical implications for the actor and the audience. In the case of this matter of 'Double Time', it seems to me that both J. Dover Wilson and M.R. Ridley, in their respective editions of *Othello*[13], owe at least as much to Barker as they do to the original scholar and theorist, 'Christopher North'.

Barker's *Preface* to *Othello* also provides us with an excellent example of this imaginative yet practical use of scholarship when applied in more general terms in order to deal with a wider issue. This is in his discussion[14] of what one might call the dramatic heart of the play, the confrontation of two mighty opposites, on which both the energy and the form of the play depends. Barker was always very clear and precise in his use of the term 'dramatic'; he never confused it with 'theatrical'; he knew the exact difference between the two and he recognized the absolute need, in any play of merit and stature, for a central dichotomy, stated or implied, which is large enough, complex enough and, in a sense, mysterious enough to inform the whole play and give energy and vitality to it; most of all, to reflect the play's central sense and to draw on the observed dichotomies of real experience. In the case of *Othello*, Barker sees this central division as 'not of action, since the story forbids that, but of the very essence of the men' (of Othello and Iago, that is). 'Shakespeare gives us then', he says 'in place of conflict of action, conflict of being'. This is no idle theorizing, fit only for the study armchair: it affects from the very start, as Barker points out, the whole approach of the two principal actors in the piece.

In his approach to character-analysis in the plays, perhaps Barker was – as several critics have suggested – over-influenced by Bradley. Certainly Bradley's thoroughly psycho-analytical approach has the effect of divorcing the character from the form and frame and structure of the play and giving him or her a posited existence in some other, quite extraneous, context – almost as if what was being discussed was a character in a Dostoievsky novel or even a person in the everyday, actual world. More recent Shakespeare scholarship has largely rejected this approach but, when Barker began the writing of the major *Prefaces* in the nineteen-twenties, Bradley's 'practice of character-extraction' (to use Anne Ridler's phrase)[15] had scarcely been challenged. Yet even so, Barker's slightly-too-Bradleian approach produced character studies that were still conscious of their part in a stage-pattern and responded to the design of the play as a whole, a design compounded from and ultimately dependent upon a concatenation of bright images struck off by and reflected in performance before an audience. Dover Wilson questions this in regard to Othello[16], wondering whether Barker has not fallen into the same error as T.S. Eliot or F.R. Leavis, who both tend to follow Bradley too far along the route of psychological causation. Wilson, I think has misread Barker's description[17] of Othello's entry in Act V Scene 2, of which Barker says:

> He is as calm as water is when near to boiling, or the sea with a surge of storm beneath. Exalted in his persuasion that it is justice he deals and not vengeance, he regains a satanic semblance of the nobility that was.

The key-word in this passage is that 'regains'. Wilson seems to read this to mean 'regains by conscious effort of will', which he then extends a little further in meaning to imply 'puts on the appearance of', for he says:

> I would even dare to suggest that the criticism by Granville-Barker, actor, producer and dramatist as he was, is open to the same objection as Eliot's. For though I have no doubt that, impersonating Othello himself, he could have acted the suppressed passion or leashed insanity he writes of, he would surely have been hard put to it to *act the acting* of a regained nobility, satanic or otherwise.

But that is not what Barker means: he means, surely, not that Othello *pretends* to regain his nobility, but that, in an ironic and horrible way ('satanic', in short) he really *does* regain something which chimes with and is related to his old nobility. And, in Barker's submission, this baleful echo of a departed nobility *is what the audience actually sees* at that moment. It is a thoroughly theatric image, genuinely stageworthy. Barker is saying that, as he reads the text, this is what it seems to mean in terms of performance. The whole passage, in the Barker *Preface*, contains multiple references to physical mien and posture, the use of stage properties

(Othello carries a candle with naked flame, Barker suggests, partly so that his face is lighted and partly so that the stillness of the unwavering flame will emphasize his praeternatural calm), gesture, costume and so on. Moreover, Barker seems to me to be supremely aware of the scene as the final and climactic scene in a stage tragedy – a celebration in public of a metaphysical mystery, aesthetically conveyed.

This quality is the real strength of all the *Prefaces*, this and Barker's obvious and tremendous enthusiasm over and love for the plays. And his achievement is all the more impressive because, though it exists in truly theatrical terms, it springs from the naked text. There is one point in the discussion of Double Time at which Barker talks about Shakespeare's 'confident, reckless, dexterous way'; Dover Wilson rather primly rebukes him, saying: 'Dexterous and confident, no doubt; but I feel sure not reckless.' Neither could possibly prove his case, of course: but there is something very attractive and right-feeling about Barker's intuition – the intuition of an artist – that there must have been times when Shakespeare the artist metaphorically closed his eyes and gritted his teeth and said to himself, 'Oh, damn: let's risk it.' There is some danger in assuming that an artist – even a great artist – is always calm, assured and completely clear and convinced about his work and the nature of his vision. The exploration of doubt is one half of art's main function and a man who has doubts – as which sensitive man has not? – should also have moments of blind faith, moments when his deepest intuitive senses tell him that the unproven way may yet be the right way. At those moments, recklessness becomes an artistic duty: and Barker, who had been in that position more than once, both as director and as dramatist, found instinctively in Shakespeare's plays those moments of urgency and desperation which he well recognized and with which he automatically sympathized. And always he sees them in stage terms and he firmly believed that Shakespeare did the same. In the second of his *Prefaces*, the seven-page introduction to the performances of *Twelfth Night* in 1912, he says:

> The Winter's Tale, as I see its writing, is complex, vivid, abundant in the variety of its mood and pace and colour, now disordered, now at rest, the product of a mind rapid, changing, and over-full. I believe its interpretation should express all that. *Twelfth Night* is quite other. Daily, as we rehearse together, I learn more what it is and should be; the working together of the theatre is a fine thing.

And in his last *Preface*, the one-hundred-and-forty-eight-page study of *Coriolanus* written in 1942–1947, he has this:

The Stage Directions

Some of these are among the play's most notable features. Incidentally, their dramatic value apart, they stand among the items of evidence of a retirement to Stratford and the writing of the latest plays in a semi-detachment from the theatre. Such evidence is, of course, inferential, no better than guesswork if you will. But *Coriolanus* at least speaks in this respect pretty plainly of a manuscript to be sent to London, and of a staging which the author did not expect to supervise himself. The directions are always expert, devised by someone who has visualized the action very clearly. They may be such a mere memorandum as a prompter might write in, as where, in the passage covering the battle for Corioles, after the customary indicative

The fight is renewed. The Volsces retire into Corioles, and Marcius follows them to the gate.

comes for Marcius the mandatory

Enter the gate.

One builds nothing on that. But

Enter Cominius, as it were in retire, with soldiers.

and later

Enter two Officers, to lay cushions, as it were, in the Capitol.

– these 'as it weres' are, so to say, 'advisory'; the actors must devise their expression for themselves. On the other hand, action of dramatic importance may be underlined, though the spoken text indicate it clearly enough:

Enter Coriolanus, in a gown of humility . . .

and the next words spoken are

Here he comes, and in the gown of humility . . .

And later – though nothing will be plainer than the sight itself –

Enter Coriolanus, in mean apparel, disguised and muffled.

Here is the author, stressing these effects upon the actors, for his own satisfaction, to make sure they miss none of them; for his own great satisfaction, one feels, when it comes to

Draw both the Conspirators and kils Martius, who falles, Auffidius stands on him.

And

Enter Menenius to the Watch or Guard.

'*Watch or Guard*'; whichever you please, it comes to the same thing.
But the direction to be valued most of all is that given to the actor of Marcius
himself. Before he yields to Volumnia he

Holds her by the hand, silent.

–for an appreciable moment, it must be. Had Shakespeare had his actors at
hand to direct should we now ever have had that?

Always that patient attention to stage detail! It never once occurred to
Barker that what Shakespeare is writing is a novel or a case-book; or even
simply a poem (except in the sense in which Dryden and the seventeenth
century used the term): Shakespeare's works, as far as Barker was
concerned, were *plays* – and that meant that they should be acted, or, at
the very least, read with actors and acting in mind.

There is a good case to be made for a thorough and detailed examination of the inter-relation between Barker's unique kind of critical commentary on Shakespeare and the more conventionally scholarly criticism. Such a study, so far as I know, has never been made, except in a
glancing, passing way. And it would take much more time and space
than this present book can afford. But someone in the future might like
to undertake it: it could well prove both valuable and interesting.

Scattered here and there throughout Barker's writings on Shakespeare
are hints of subjective responses which interestingly connect this aspect
of his theatrical life with the rest of that life. Midway through the British
Academy Annual Shakespeare Lecture[18] on May 13, 1925, discussing
Hamlet he had this to say:

> And I think we can hear Shakespeare, the poet, saying, 'Yes, I know now what
> my theatre can do and what it can't. I know at least what *I* can do. Agincourt
> and its heroic swashbuckling – no! The stoic Brutus with his intellectual
> struggles? That was better, though it made hard going. But the passionate,
> suffering inner consciousness of man, his spiritual struggles and triumphs and
> defeats in his impact with an uncomprehending world – this may seem the
> most utterly unfit subject for such a crowded, noisy, vulgar place as the
> theatre; yet this is what I can make comprehensible, here is what I can do with
> my art.'

'The passionate, suffering inner consciousness of man' was never far
from Barker's mind or from his idea of what all art was really for. It is
only another way of talking about that secret life which to Barker was the
real centre of all life. Two years later, when he came to write his

Introduction to the First Series of *Prefaces*, he returned once more to the topic and to the way that, for him, Shakespeare seemed to echo Barker's own sense of the world. 'All great drama', he said, boldly setting Aristotle aside, 'tends to concentrate upon character; and, even so, not upon picturing men as they show themselves to the world like figures on a stage – though that is how it must ostensibly show them – but on the hidden man. And the progress of Shakespeare's art from *Love's Labour's Lost* to *Hamlet*, and thereafter with a difference, lies in the simplifying of this paradox and the solving of the problem it presents; and the process involves the developing of a very subtle sort of stagecraft indeed.'

He is writing about Shakespeare and he is, as always, making automatic connections between the sense of life to be expressed and the technical means best suited to its expression. But he is writing about himself as well, both as man and as artist. It is well to remember that the British Academy lecture on *Hamlet* was given only two years after he completed the writing of *The Secret Life* and the above-quoted Introduction only four years thereafter.

'. . . not upon picturing men as they show themselves to the world . . . but on the hidden man . . .'

Granville Barker at about the time of his second marriage (1918).

Barker and Women

'Granville Barker has not – as I'd heard said that he had – lost his charm and personality – how could he?' Thus Lady Cynthia Asquith, J.M. Barrie's private secretary for a number of years, in her book *Portrait of Barrie* (London: James Barrie, 1954). She was by no means alone in finding Barker charming. Most women, apparently, did. And though the inferring of autobiographical details from an artist's purely creative writings is a dangerous game, one is not taking any very great risk in saying that all Barker's plays and stories would seem to indicate that he was obviously fascinated not only by the general question of the relation between the sexes but also by women themselves. That fascination was not always, by any means, of a comfortable or pleasurable sort, but comfortable or not it shows consistently and forcefully through all his work. Exactly what roots it may have had in his own ordinary life it is now impossible, I think, to say. Of his casual relations with women (there must surely have been some) we know nothing: no letters, no reminiscences, no scandal, have survived – or if they have, they are a very well-guarded secret. Norman Marshall, the director, with whom I talked about a year before his death, thought that Barker was not interested in women at all and that his natural sexual leanings were homosexual. (One or two other people have also privately expressed this same opinion to me.) Marshall, whose career was just beginning when Barker's was at its height, nevertheless knew Barker fairly well, was on terms of personal friendliness with him (I am trying to choose my words very carefully so as not to exaggerate or distort) and owed some of his own early opportunities to Barker. His opinion, therefore, though obviously not conclusive, should be seriously regarded. Frances Briggs, who was the British Drama League's Assistant Secretary for many years and who worked very closely with Barker during the twelve years for which he was the Chairman of the B.D.L., told me, in a conversation in 1978, that she considered Barker 'very attractive' in the B.D.L. days (Barker was then in his forties). She described him as handsome, tall, dark auburn (she wondered if he dyed his hair) and with a 'husky voice'. W. Bridges-Adams, in the 1953 radio talk called *The Lost Leader*, commented thus on Barker's personal appearance and personal magnetism: 'It was as Marchbanks in *Candida* that I first set eyes on him. He was twenty-seven . . . He moved with the slightly dangerous grace of a very high-bred wild animal.'

The evidence of his plays seems to indicate that he regarded physical passion and sexual desire as a quite separate, and less estimable, part of the relationship between a man and a woman. In *The Weather-Hen* it is a sign of flightiness and unsteadiness; Ann Leete, who asks Abud to regard her not as a wife but as a mother of his children, seems to look on it as a disagreeable necessity; in *Agnes Colander* Otho is frankly sensual but is relegated by the play to an inferior status as a result and the play's authority is lent to Agnes's hopes for a purely Platonic relationship with Alec; in *Waste*, physical passion is not only a destroyer but a symbol of ideals betrayed; in *The Madras House* it is treated ambivalently – Miss Yates's sturdy insistence upon her right to be loved is approved of, but Philip says, 'I do so hate that farmyard world of sex'. Only in *Our Visitor to 'Work-a-day'* is sexual passion seen as a possibly constructive part of the pattern of a noble and vital existence; and only in *Georgiana* (with, perhaps, a faint echo of it in *The Bigamist*) is the physical relationship seen as a source of beauty and ecstasy (though in *The Secret Life* there is a sense of infinite regret over a lost and neglected ecstasy). It may well be that this mistrust of, or distaste for, the physical nature of sex comes directly from Barker's own personal predilection: certainly that is what is suggested, for example, by C.E. Wheeler's letter to him of September 30, 1909 from which I have already briefly quoted (see Chapter 3, p. 64): '. . . I'm not sure that you yourself understand properly either Love or Beauty or Art', says Wheeler: 'Why are your heroes and heroines all *afraid* of love? Ashamed to live almost?' And, as I have already noted in Chapter 3, Wheeler also says, '. . . Because you're not sure of the difference between love and appetite you solve your difficulty by denying any value to love and so get no good of either . . .' This is from a man who was one of

Barker's greatest friends and who knew him extremely well. Over and over again in the plays and the stories there is the suggestion that physical sexuality is a blemish on marriage and that the true ideal of marriage is comradeship, especially comradeship in *work*. This idea is very clearly there in the duologue between Philip and Jessica at the end of *The Madras House* and it seems likely that Barker himself approached his own first marriage in this way. Let us remember that inscription on the photograph which he gave to Lillah McCarthy in 1905 (see p. 103). They married in 1906 and their whole married life was spent as a working partnership in the theatre, both of them equally ambitious and with ambitions which tended sometimes to divide them rather than bring them together. Ten years later, when he wrote to her from New York asking her to divorce him, Barker said:

> I did you a very great wrong in asking you to marry me at all. Though I explained at the time how mixed my feelings were and you said you understood nevertheless I should not have let you accept the risk that someday there might happen what has happened now. Though I was willing to accept such a risk as far as you were concerned that does not much affect the matter. For I never loved you as I know – and I knew – that I ought to love a woman to want to be married to her.[1]

This certainly seems to suggest that, even in 1906, comradeship stopped well short of ecstasy – on his part, at any rate. And though Lillah afterwards claimed that the letter came as a great shock and surprise to her, there are indications in it that the subject was not an entirely new one between them. At the beginning of the letter he says:

> I could not lie to you about it, but as you would not believe what I did tell you it became difficult to tell you any more. I should have done so. I would have done so – but you must remember certain things you did and threats you made. In the face of these it seemed to me wiser to let matters rest where they were and, as I had all along intended, to let the thing itself have its test. I am very sorry for any blunders I made in June. Suffering there must always be over a matter of this sort to everyone concerned, but it should not have to be suffering at such cross purposes as that.

Unless the alleged conversations and attitudes of 1906 and 1915 are pure inventions on Barker's part, designed simply to provide him with an excuse for leaving Lillah in 1916, it would appear that the marriage had been much more by her wish than his. (Considering that their closeness had largely been promoted by their collaboration in the first production of *Man and Superman*, in which they played Tanner and Ann

Lillah McCarthy, about 1909.

together, there is a certain pawky irony in this.) And while Barker may well have exaggerated in his letter to Lillah, wanting to make the best case he could for himself, it hardly seems likely that he was fabricating entirely: it seems more probable that the assertion that he went into his first marriage with distinct reservations – reservations which, in one way or another, he expressed at the time – is correct. This does seem to be borne out, moreover, by a curious, pencil-written document in Lillah's handwriting which is now in the collection of the Humanities Research Center at the University of Texas. Written in December, 1915 in a child's 'exercise book', it is what was apparently intended as the first draft of a play. Its title is 'Progress' and its two central characters are perfectly obviously modelled upon Barker and Lillah herself. A stage direction, for example, describes Matthew Brodie as 'a tall, slim, clean-shaven man of 37, with loose brown hair, boyish smile, attractive personality, eloquent in language, never at a loss for words. Dressed in khaki tunic, red cross armlet, breeches and leggings & brown boots.' The description fits Barker exactly, especially as he was in 1915. His age *was* 37 in that year. Even the costume description is right, since in that year Barker had been in France writing the commissioned book for the Red Cross – and in the play Matthew Brodie explains that he has been in France writing a book for the Red Cross. The dialogue, which is almost entirely devoted to discussions of marriage and ideas on marriage, puts quite beyond doubt the fact that the parallel was undoubtedly intentional. Considered as a potential play, of course, the thing is downright embarrassing; but looked at as an indication of what was going on between Barker and his wife and what the latter thought of it and, in particular, of her husband, it is a very useful and revealing document indeed. The speeches assigned to Brodie sound oddly like a combination of two things – over-simplified versions of things Lillah had heard Barker say; and deliberate distortions invented by her to show him how unfair, in her view, he was being to her. Brodie is listed in the *dramatis personae* as 'author'. Mary Vaughan, the central female character, is, at the start of the play, one of a group of young women who are just finishing their schooling at Miss Beardsley's college. They are listed, complete with clichés, as follows:

Mary Vaughan	– English, strong, progressive
Sadie Van Buren	– American, keen, practical
Agnes Serle	– English, wild, ill-regulated
Isabelle de Vigne	– French, pretty, vivacious
Pia-Marie	– Spanish, imaginative, spirituelle
Vittoria	– Italian, narrow, superstitious

Nadine   – Russian, brilliant, affectionate
Sophie   – English, duller, plain, spectacles, large flat feet
Ramabai   – Brahmin, silent, philosophic

Mary, in her strong, progressive, English way, becomes a social worker, reformer and political agitator and it is this work which brings her into contact with Brodie, a playwright with socialist sympathies. Act II of the play contains a long duologue between Mary and Brodie which is perhaps worth quoting *in extenso*, since it gives so vivid a sense of how Lillah saw Barker and since it is the only actual document available to us that comes directly from Lillah. He was away from home at the time, fulfilling lecture engagements in America. She was to have accompanied him but was taken ill and was unable to travel. He had written to her in September, 1915 during the trans-Atlantic crossing. Only part of the letter has survived but in view of the dialogue which Lillah was about to write in December and the other letter which Barker would write to her in January, this fragment[2] is both ironic and poignant. It reads:

> . . . work – and am not months behindhand and irritable to get back to it – and when will that be?
>
> Meanwhile I'd go to the country and breathe air and cogitate.
>
> You're with Charlotte at the Albert Hall tonight – that's an interesting show, I expect. I perceive this voyage is going to make me double-chinned and liverish – there's too much to eat and a beastly orchestra. However, I've a table in my cabin and I'll get through some work if I can.
>
> Bless you, dear Lillah – my dear wife – I love you very much if you please and I'm not far from you. Distance doesn't mainly count.
>
> Get a healthy time; breathe air – and I'll be back soon.
>
> Bless you – I love you, my dearest.
>
> H.

In Lillah's play, Brodie and Mary are not yet married, but Brodie suggests that they should be. The scene reads as follows:

BRODIE: We have known each other for nearly seven years. Our interests and our sympathies have brought us into close companionship. You have been of service to me too, you have encouraged me in my work and appreciated my efforts to create a new school of thought and a higher idea of drama. I think too I have been of material assistance to you in your work. I want you always near. I think we had better marry. I have often thought that I should not marry. I loathe the idea of bondage but I think you and I have enough common sense to be able to enjoy each other's society even if we were legally tied.

MARY:	Why a legal tie? Do you love me?
BRODIE:	Love you? I doubt if I can really love anyone in what is generally accepted as the meaning of the word. In my own way – Yes – but fundamentally I want to be alone. I hate contact with things. My body is a nuisance, it won't do what my mind and spirit desire of it. My ideas mean so much to me, I live almost wholly for them.
MARY:	I should like to hear exactly what are your ideas about marriage.
BRODIE:	You must not expect me to be more than a 'weekend' husband – not even every weekend. I must be unrestricted, unshackled, for something in me shrinks from being held. An all-embracing love always signifies possession. We should have to be married so that we could sometimes go about together and live together occasionally without public disgrace, but neither love nor married life are necessities to me.
MARY:	There are two sides to matrimony – what about the woman's ideas and feelings?
BRODIE:	I think relations between man and woman can exist in a variety of ways. One need not necessarily feel as the other does. You and I ought to pull along better than most married people as we have each got separate interests. I – my writing, you your propagandist work. The creations of my brain are everything to me. I may be egotistical over my work – I daresay you think so.
MARY:	I don't think it – I know it. But you will never do really *great* work until you sink your individuality and let your subject speak through you.
BRODIE:	I can only live my life in the way that is right to me. The important thing in life is to know oneself.
MARY:	*Do* you know yourself – I wonder!
BRODIE:	I think I have explained clearly my views on marriage. Shall we consider the matter settled?
MARY:	Wait a moment – shall our marriage be blessed by the Church?
BRODIE	(*disgusted*): The Church? – Good Heavens No! Have I not told you that I hate bondage, pledging oneself to vows one cannot always keep. We will be married at a Registrar's office.[3] That is the legal form necessary. When shall we take the plunge? Next week?
MARY:	No.
BRODIE:	No? Is that too hurried? Well, the end of this month then. What do you say to that?
MARY:	I still say No.
BRODIE:	What do you mean?

MARY:	I mean I will not marry you at all.
BRODIE:	Why not? Have I not explained my ideas on the matter?
MARY:	My dear Matthew, you have talked of nothing else but yourself and your ideas, but I will not marry you.
BRODIE:	Why not?
MARY:	Because you do not really want a *wife*. You only desire a legalised 'week-end' mistress. One who will wait patiently till you feel inclined to spend a few hours with her. You would make a selfish, irresponsible, blindly cruel husband.
BRODIE	(*virtuously surprised*): I am not cruel or coarse or wanton. I do not think I am unreasonable, even.
MARY:	Oh! I quite acknowledge that you have many good and excellent qualities. You are thoroughly honorable and honest. You are amiable and refined. You would never be coarse or violent. But your selfish blind egotism is worse than any ordinary vices. You *can't*, you never will, see that your calm, unruffled belief in your own superiority, your sense of your excellence is unhuman. If you could only fly into a passion. swear, be angry, even violent, one could come to grips with you! But even now you are not really distressed, only surprised at my bad taste in refusing you. If I married you, the next day you would be reciting these lines to me (*quotes*):

> I said I splendidly loved you – it's not true;
> Such long swift tides stir not a land-locked sea.
> On gods or fools the high risks fall – on you
> The clean clear bitter-sweet that's not for me.
> Love soars from earth to ecstasies unwist,
> Love is flung, Lucifer-like from Heaven to Hell.
> But there are wanderers in the middle mist
> Who cry for shadows, clutch, and cannot tell
> Whether they love at all; or, loving, whom –
> An old song's lady, a fool in fancy dress
> Or phantoms or their own face on the gloom,
> From love of love or from heart's loneliness.
> Pleasure's not theirs, nor pain, They doubt and sigh
> And do not love at all – of these am I.

Oh, Matthew, take my advice – don't try to get married for ten years. You are 37, man's divine age, but you were always slow in maturing and you will not reach divine maturity until you are 50 – if by then your faculties haven't gone rotten, eaten into themselves and left nothing but fatuous decay.

BRODIE	(*Listless with an amused air of boredom shrugging his shoulders*):

Well! You may think better of it! If you change your mind, let me know. I shall be in town for a few days before I go over to France to finish my job. I won't forget to take the chair at your meeting at the Kingsway Hall.

MARY: Thank you, Matthew. Of course we will continue friends – you know I like and appreciate you as a comrade and helper in my work. I hope I have not hurt or wounded you? (*breaking into laughter,* MATTHEW *stares wondering at her*) Oh, Matthew, Matthew, you are hopeless! You would break a wife's heart, smash her life, kill her soul distroy [*sic*] her faith, her trust, her love, crush her to the earth, outrage her tenderest feelings, disert [*sic*] – her – and say amiably, bending to kiss her fingers – 'I hope you are not vexed; I didn't mean to hurt you!' It is no use trying to explain, you can see nothing beyond your own 'creative brain', understand nothing beyond your own 'ideas' – Goodbye.

Lillah gave herself the dismissive 'Goodbye' line in the play but when it came to the point in real life and the lines were the other way round, she fiercely resisted. Reading over the letters on the subject, from Barrie and Shaw to Barker, from Barker to Shaw and from Shaw to Lillah, the impression is all but irresistible that it was not Lillah's heart that was broken but her pride which was badly hurt. She was overtaken by a bad attack of self-pity and this was complicated by a virulent vindictiveness towards her wanting-to-be-ex-husband. She took at first the familiar revenge of simply refusing to divorce him. Though there was money available (on both sides) to arrange for the discreet farce by which the mediaeval divorce laws of the time were customarily subverted, Lillah refused to join in. In vain did Shaw, even as late as August 1917, assure her in a letter that, even though one felt humiliated by such things, 'there is no real humiliation involved, because people do not change on reasonable grounds and often change from better to worse'. In September he had twice to write to her again, the first time to beg her to see that there was no point in refusing the divorce, that Barker would not change his mind and that all she was doing was making everyone very miserable, including herself; the second letter, on September 12, 1917, was to assure her that Barker had made proper financial arrangements to enable him to begin making alimony payments. Finally, Lillah gave in, though with a very bad grace. She engaged Sir George Lewis to act for her and the necessary polite fictions were put in place. The divorce was made absolute in May, 1918.

Lillah was two years Barker's senior. While perhaps not a really *great* actress, she was certainly a very fine one and during her ten years with Barker she rose to be recognized as one of London's leading players. She had, according to contemporary accounts, a voice of great beauty and expressiveness and she was praised also for her commanding stage presence and the beauty of her face and figure. Cathleen Nesbitt, who played Perdita to Lillah's Hermione in the 1912 *The Winter's Tale*, told me she found Lillah warm and friendly and charming and a fine actress – but not very intelligent. She also expressed the view that Barker knew exactly how to direct her in order to get the very best out of her and that it was the absence of his direction, after their divorce, that brought Lillah's career as an actress to a close. Whatever the reason, she certainly made no headway at all after 1917 and in the early 1920s she re-married and retired from the stage, though she was still, rather pathetically, trying to 'make a come-back' as late as 1933 and 1934 (in both of these years she wrote to Shaw about the possibility of her playing in various revivals of his plays and in 1930 she had approached him with a request that he try to persuade Sir Barry Jackson, at the Birmingham Repertory Theatre, to revive Masefield's *The Tragedy of Nan* with her in her original rôle of Nan. Sir Barry refused, on the grounds that he 'loathed the play': Shaw said it was 'that unlucky putrid pie' which revolted him. Whether the fact that Nan is supposed to be seventeen and Lillah was fifty-five at the time had anything to do with it, the correspondence does not show.) But in her day – and her day had been during her years with Barker – she had been an admirable and much admired performer and Barker himself thought very highly of her. He was genuinely fond of her, too, as is shown by the few letters which have survived from the early years of their marriage. But he was not in love with her; their sometimes conflicting professional ambitions unquestionably put a strain on their marriage[4]; and, finally, early in 1915, when they were in New York together for the repertory season at Wallack's Theatre, Barker met and fell violently in love with someone else. '. . . the Italian volcano in him had erupted unexpectedly and amazingly. He fell madly in love – really madly in the Italian manner . . .', says Shaw in the obituary article in the Winter 1946 issue of *Drama*. The lady in question was Helen Huntington, wife of a multi-millionaire (who, ironically, had put up some of the guarantee fund which had enabled Barker to undertake the season at Wallack's). Mrs. Huntington was forty-seven when she met Barker: he was thirty-seven. Norman Wilkinson, the stage designer – and again I am indebted to Cathleen Nesbitt for my information – brought back to London from New York a

Design by Robert Edmond Jones for the setting of The Man who Married a Dumb Wife *(Anatole France) – Wallack's Theatre, New York, 1915.*

A scene from Barker's production of The Man who Married a Dumb Wife: *Lillah McCarthy is on the extreme left.*

Helen Huntington
– a New York
magazine photograph
about 1910.

Her passport photograph
in 1940.

story of Barker's standing beneath the windows of the Huntington house on East 57th Street every night until the light in Helen's room was put out and then blowing a kiss to the darkened window. The story may well be true, too: in a short story called *Souls on Fifth* which he published in America in 1917 (Boston: Little, Brown) Barker describes in great detail how the central character of the story walks nightly along Fifth Avenue, very late, night after night. The description may perhaps reflect a personal experience.

Helen Huntington could scarcely have been more different from Lillah McCarthy, either in background or in temperament. Where Lillah was impulsive and outspoken, Helen was reserved and withdrawn (though not, I think, shy); where Lillah was extrovert and self-confident, Helen was introspective and unsure of herself. She was born Helen Manchester Gates, in 1867 in Beaver Dam, Wisconsin[5]. Her father was Isaac Edwin Gates and her mother was Ellen Maria Huntington, youngest sister of the redoubtable C.P. Huntington. Since her position as his niece was one of the most significant influences on Helen's life – perhaps the most significant – a word had better be said about Collis Potter Huntington.[6] He was born in 1821 in Connecticut. He began his working life as junior partner (his elder brother being the senior partner) in a small hardware business in Oneonta, N.Y. Early in the 1860s he went out to California to seek his fortune – and found it. The basis of his operation in San Francisco was still a hardware store but by a series of astute and none-too-scrupulous financial shifts he made himself the leading promoter in the building of the Central Pacific Railroad, the first railway to reach the west coast from the eastern states. From this and his subsequent 'deals' he amassed an immense fortune and when he died in 1900 he owned a dozen or so railroad companies in various parts of the United States, a major ship-building yard in Newport News, Va., a city which he founded, a large mansion which he had built for himself in New York City, another in Throgg's Neck, Westchester, innumerable smaller pieces of real estate in New York, San Francisco, Sacramento, Lexington (Kentucky) and an immensely valuable collection of famous paintings and water colours. He is reputed to have bought Gainsborough's 'Blue Boy' three times – two forgeries and, the third time, the real thing. Whether the story is true or not I cannot say: certainly the 'real thing' now hangs in the Huntington Library at San Marino, California. The Huntington Library, built by C.P.'s nephew, Henry Edwards Huntington – a man who worked for his rich uncle all his life and had the presence of mind, when he was sixty-three, to marry the said rich uncle's widow – was one of the good works spawned by C.P.'s bad money. (Dirty money gets clean very quickly: money is the most anonymous of all man's products.)

Isaac Edwin Gates, Helen's father, who had originally trained for the ministry (which is why he was in Beaver Dam, Wisconsin in the 1860s), was persuaded by his wife and his masterful brother-in-law to forsake his calling in order to become C.P.'s confidential secretary and office manager: from about 1870 onward he meekly and faithfully guarded C.P.'s interests and fortunes in the New York Office, leaving C.P. free to spend most of his time in San Francisco, developing the western end of the business. Their letters to each other, which are preserved in the George Arents Research Library of Syracuse University, mix the details of business and high finance with enquiries about family affairs. They always begin with 'Dear Brother Huntington' and 'Dear Brother Gates'.

So Helen grew up in a very closed, very wealthy, patriarchal atmosphere, with Collis Potter Huntington as patriarch. The word of 'Uncle Collis' was law. To do her justice, Helen did show, from her early twenties onward, some faint signs of sensitivity and unrest with her too-assured, too-comfortable position, though she had neither the intellect nor the strength of character for open revolt. There are, however, in the Huntington Library, San Marino, some letters from her to Caroline Densmore Huntington, a cousin six years older than herself, and these give us faint glimpses of an awakening mind and a quite lively intelligence at work. Helen's father, when he left Wisconsin to work for his brother-in-law, settled in the town of Elizabeth, New Jersey – an easy train ride from the city of New York, where he journeyed every day. Helen's girlhood was spent in Elizabeth but when she was about sixteen the family moved to Orange, an adjoining township. There she met Thomas Ball Criss. How she met him or what the connection was we don't know, since he was carefully expunged from the family records. His name does appear in two places, however. He is mentioned a good deal in the letters to Caroline; and he actually *writes* a few of the letters emanating from Isaac Gates's office in New York. In other words, when he joined the family in 1889, C.P. took him also into the family firm. Thomas Ball Criss and Helen were married in Orange on December 4, 1889: she was twenty-two; he was twenty-nine. The marriage lasted only five years. There was one child, a daughter named Mildred, born in 1892. By the end of 1894, Helen had been packed off with a chaperone to live at the Cataract Hotel in Sioux Falls, South Dakota while C.P. brought his money to bear on the question, got rid of Mr. Criss and made other suitable arrangements for Helen. The arrangement he hit upon was to detail his adopted son, Archer Milton Huntington, to marry Helen and for this purpose he removed himself, his wife, his adopted son, Helen and his entire entourage from the United States to England in the summer of 1895. The change of country was probably undertaken for reasons of discretion: the matter had been dealt with in almost indecent haste (as late as April of that year Mr. Criss was still signing letters on C.P.H's behalf in the New York office and the legal niceties of his departure must, therefore, have been pushed through at a tremendous rate). It seems possible also that the actual arrangements for disposing of Mr. Criss were not entirely such as to bear very close inspection and the change of venue to a distant and foreign one was probably considered wise. Helen, in writing to Caroline from St. Paul, Minnesota (to which city her exile had been transferred from Sioux City) in April or May, says – about the impending change in her estate – 'Mr. Criss consents to an absolute and final decree of separation'. Nowhere is the word 'divorce' mentioned. Whether the 'decree of separation' was really a divorce and whether Helen was legally entitled to re-marry might just possibly have been open to some question and C.P. evidently felt that things would be more comfortable with the wide Atlantic between him and such unpleasant queries. Helen and Archer were married in London on August 6, 1895.

Archer Milton Huntington was at that time twenty-five years of age. He was the son, by her first marriage, of C.P.'s second wife[7], Arabella D. Worsham. Collis Potter Huntington had married Mrs. Worsham on July 12, 1884, his first wife, Elizabeth Stoddard – to whom he had been married for almost forty years – having died in 1883. Upon marrying Arabella Worsham, C.P. adopted her son and made him his heir: when C.P. died in 1900, the adopted son inherited a great part of the huge estate. Helen, accustomed all her life to having enough money for a leisured life and all her wants, suddenly found herself with a good deal more than enough.

She had been married to Archer Huntington almost exactly twenty years when she met Granville Barker. During that twenty years she had, by dint of a lot of hard work and the application of a modest talent, turned herself into a minor novelist and poet. Judging from the letters to Caroline, it had been her ambition ever since girlhood: judging from the work itself, the ambition was centred more on a desire to be published than on a passionate urge to write. Her poems are almost wholly imitative – full of tired locutions and jaded images (though she did manage to get into Bartlett's *Familiar Quotations* for two successive editions with two simple quatrains, then lost her place when the thirteenth edition was published). Her novels are a little better: indeed, some passages of some of them are really quite fresh and lively still, more particularly in the later ones, and she has one short story, called *Retired*, in a collection called *Wives and Celebrities* (London: Collins, 1926) which is in my view quite brilliant. However, that was later work: at the time she met Barker, in 1915, she had published four novels and two books of verse and was working on a fifth novel, called *Eastern Red*. The titles of the earlier ones were *The Sovereign Good* (1908), *An Apprentice to Truth* (1910), *The Moon Lady* (1911) and *Marsh Lights* (1913).

Except for another visit to France to complete the book for the Red Cross, Barker remained in America for the whole of 1916, living partly in New York City and partly in Williamstown, Massachusetts. He saw Helen Huntington only infrequently during that time but they wrote to each other – according to Barker's letters to Shaw in that year – quite frequently. Their letters, however, have not survived, or have been suppressed. In 1917 Barker became liable for military service under the new conscription laws in England and he therefore returned to London. He enlisted at first as a cadet gunner but shortly thereafter secured a commission in the Intelligence Corps. and spent the rest of the war as a second lieutenant doing office work at the War Office in London. In April, 1918 Helen Huntington, having started the legal proceedings needed to divorce her from Archer Milton Huntington, followed Barker to England. She was accompanied by a friend of her girlhood, Helen (Nellie) Dickinson, who acted as part-servant, part-chaperon, part-companion. For propriety's sake and discretion's sake and to avoid the danger of upsetting the double divorce proceedings by putting themselves under the suspicion of 'misconduct', Barker arranged for her to live not in London but at the Earl's Court Hotel in Tunbridge Wells. He visited her there, on the properest of terms, every weekend from April to June and in between the weekends he wrote to her every day, sometimes two and three times in one day. Sixty-two of these letters have by some strange chance survived and are now in the collection of the Texas Humanities Research Center. They settle for ever at least one of the questions about Barker which has puzzled many. He has been held by some to be a very 'cold' man, incapable of real affection or personal commitment (both Sir John Gielgud and Miss Athene Seyler, for example, told me that they had this impression of him). While it may well have been true of his relations with the generality of his acquaintances, the letters to Helen certainly show very clearly that it was not because he lacked the capacity for loving. These letters are most movingly devoted and tender. He describes for her the minutiae of his life in London, wishing that she were there to see with him the pigeons on the office window-sill and the dogs he meets in the park. He speaks with impatience of the time that must pass until they next meet. He tells her what he thinks of the war news and how the conversation went at an official luncheon with an Italian, an American and a Russian emigré. Almost every day there is a comment on the weather and on the stage of the last big German offensive: the fact that the summer is late in coming and that victory and defeat are finely poised in France assume in the letters – and, I think, in Barker's mind – a symbolic significance and become a kind of nervous obbligato to his own impatience and anxiety about the divorce proceedings: a cold day or a wet one sets him wondering gloomily whether he and Helen will ever be together permanently; the report of a French or British retreat of a few yards throws him into despair about his own life as well as that of the world.

There is a good deal in the letters about his work and about the fact that presently they will be able to work usefully and fruitfully together. By 'work' he always means writing, not producing or directing. In one of the letters of late April he says:

My Helen: I have been thinking much about *our* work. I get depressed too, primarily at all the unfinished things that lie around me – though I could well be depressed at what they'd be like and worth in these days if they were finished! Never yet have I learnt to say the simple direct things that want saying, that sink home. But our work beloved is our vitality – our mental vitality, certainly when we are most 'alive' we do it and the more alive the more unquestioningly. Not that I cavil at questionings, at incidental questionings about it, but to question *it* – itself – is somehow to question life and that one mustn't do. Our writing *is* our unconscious activity; with you, darling heart, even more than with me.

. . . No, I don't say that we won't question the *sorts* of work we'll do – but we'll never question our work. For to write happily is to write well. We'll dig deeper then into our life. Happy, oh we know – but that's not the phrase for life itself: vital and alive, we'll be that, please God.

A few weeks later, he comments again about his own work:

Knoblock has finished a play since he came back from France, sitting up at night to do it. This gives me rather a shock. But I cannot conceive it to be a very good play. However, that is false comfort for the fact that I haven't written really a line these last months. Oh Helen, I *hope* it isn't that I'm lazy. I really don't think it is. But the faculties I write with are not on the surface, somehow. I have to dig down. But there is always that scarifying dread that I *am* lazy – not a 'sticker'.

The letters clearly indicate that he saw his relationship with Helen as something quite different from that with Lillah. The 'working together' has moved from being a simple matter of comradely partnership to something with a much more private and intimate sense about it, almost something mystical. There is a dimension of genuine ecstasy now in his feelings, though only rarely expressed in terms of physical desire. Just occasionally that is there in the letters, too, however. One of the letters towards the end of her stay at Tunbridge Wells (she moved to the Hyde Park Hotel in London late in June, 1918), begins:

Wednesday, 11 p.m.

My darling love,
   Not much *head* to write to you with – your dear love is tired. He did as you said and took a walk right over Rusthall – a wonderful night, belonging to such blessedness as ours: darling, darling. And I took you with me: my love for you took all the spirit of you. But the rest you took at once to bed (I saw the light up in your room: did you feel my kisses on your pillow – four kisses there were?) and to sleep. Oh, you must take care of my Helen *please* until I can, and not give me frights – but real care of her. I shall sleep now. But such a *heart* full to write to you Helen, beloved.

Another letter, early in May ends thus:

Oh my sweet, such love for you – filling me – warming me – life blood. But that's your love for me, I'd say. Except what's the difference – it is all one and we thank God. Oh, thank God: near now to being one in all things. My own, my sweet, you're never afraid, are you? Never afraid of happiness and completion? Never be, for I am yours – all of me – and all the best of me you have made out of what was there. Oh yes, but dead before. You have made it live, so yours. And bless God for you, my Helen.

My dear, my own.

The signature-symbol of intertwined Hs was one which they had invented for themselves. They both used it in letters (there are letters from Helen to Barker written in New York in 1942 – twenty-five years later – in which it still appears) and a formalized version of it appears, from 1918 onward, at the front of all the books published by them, whether jointly or separately:

Pausing at the 'Rose and Crown' in Tonbridge for dinner one Sunday evening, on his way back to London after spending the day with Helen in Tunbridge Wells, he scribbles a note to her at the dinner table and posts it at the station when he goes to catch the express up to town. The note ends with:

> *Great* care of my Helen please. Darling – darling – darling – I hold you very close – my arms round you; feel them. And I love you, I love you – mind and body and heart and soul – all – all of me loving you. My *darling*.

Barker's divorce from Lillah was made absolute in May: it took until late June for the final decree to be issued in Helen's case. When the complicated details had been settled, however, it became clear that Archer Huntington had been extremely generous. He established a trust fund for Helen's benefit which produced an income of over $10,000 per annum (a considerable sum, in those days) and which also gave her, according to the records of Messrs. Cadwalader, Wickersham & Taft of New York (to whom I am greatly obliged for their kindly help in establishing the actual figures), 'the right to dispose of principal in excess of $300,000.' Judging from the occasional references to money in Barker's letters to Helen in 1918, neither of them was expecting the divorce settlement to be as generous as this. Helen was already – before Archer's generosity over the divorce settlement – quite comfortably placed, although not downright wealthy, since she was one of the beneficiaries under C.P. Huntington's will (he had died in 1900). But the divorce settlement meant that Barker and Helen were suddenly rich.

They married on July 31, 1918 at King's Weigh House Chapel, Duke Street, Grosvenor Square. On the marriage certificate, Helen lied about her age, presumably to make it appear, for sentimental reasons, that they were closer together in age than they really were. She said she was forty-three when she was nearly fifty-one. (This seems to have been a permanently sensitive issue with Helen: years later, when she applied for a visa to re-enter the United States as a British subject in 1940, she gave her age as sixty-one – two years less than Barker's – though she was, in fact, nearly seventy-three: when she

Helen Huntington at about the time of her marriage to Barker.

applied for renewal of the visa a year later, in 1941, she still gave her age as sixty-one.)

Throughout the turmoil of comings and goings between England, France and the United States during the years 1915–1918, in spite of the distractions of the war and of his personal affairs, Barker had tried very hard to follow what he by that time regarded as his main occupation. Writing to Shaw[8] from New York on November 19, 1915, he says:

> But remember that now I must pot-boil for my living as well as write decent plays. And don't you boast to me. Since August, though my mind hasn't been quite free from distraction, I have done 30,000 words for the Red Cross, Souls, adapted a three-scene play from Meredith, done two scenarios, an article, two more short stories and got 12,000 words along with a book on the theatre. I don't say it's all first-rate, but still.

Not all of these items are now identifiable, but some are. The 30,000 words for the Red Cross is the beginning of his book on the Red Cross work on the battlefields of France; 'Souls' is the short story, called *Souls on Fifth*; the 'two more short stories' are *The Fire that Burned in the Corner* and *The God of Good Bricks*; the 'book on the theatre' is presumably the beginnings of *The Exemplary Theatre*, finally published in 1922. I cannot place the 'two scenarios' or the 'three-scene play from Meredith': all three have disappeared without trace. And I cannot identify the one article he mentions. *Souls on Fifth* was published as a longish short story, alone, in a very slim book of sixty-one pages, by Little, Brown of Boston in 1917, Norman Wilkinson providing a frontispiece for it. It also appeared, in two parts, in successive numbers of *The Fortnightly Review* in the same year. Barker describes it, in the letter to Shaw, as a 'moral tale'. It really is not very good – is, in fact, rather embarrassingly coy. The other two short stories are better, though very slight. *The God of Good Bricks* was published in the *Century Magazine* (New York) in May 1924.[9] All three, however, share one significant feature – a discontinuity with all his previous work. None of the familiar Barker themes is there: nothing connects these three stories with *Georgiana* or *The Bigamist*, let alone with the plays. They exist in a curious vacuum, apart from all his other writing. Perhaps the explanation is to be sought in his comment about 'pot-boiling'. Perhaps he consciously and deliberately put aside anything which he connected with 'decent plays' in an attempt to write popularly. If so, the moral would appear to be obvious. The following year, however, in 1916, during that time of strange limbo for him in Williamstown, he returned to his more usual and more fruitful vein. It was at this time that he wrote the one-act play, *Farewell to the Theatre*.

The play has two characters only: Dorothy Taverner, a famous actress who, at the age of fifty-eight, finds her work empty and longs to get out of it but cannot summon up the courage to retire; and Edward, her lawyer, who has all his adult life been in love with her and is so still. When they were young she refused his offer of marriage and persuaded him to marry someone else. Throughout his married life, however, Dorothy and he have remained the best of friends and he has always served her faithfully and well as her legal adviser. Now his wife is dead and once again, acting on impulse during a business talk to which he has summoned her to try to persuade her finally to retire, he asks her to marry him. Again, she refuses.

The whole tone of the play is autumnal. Dorothy talks about a sudden moment of realization – the realization that she was 'dead'. 'What did happen so suddenly?' Edward asks her. 'What happens to the summer?' she replies: 'You go walking one day and you feel that it has gone.' The title of the play surely has, without any question at all, a direct and explicit significance in regard to Barker's own personal position: he had made his mind up by 1916 that, whatever else happened, he was not going back into the theatre as a performer or director. Line after line which Dorothy speaks sounds like Barker speaking for and about himself: 'Do I hanker for the old thrill . . . like wine bubbling in one's heart . . . and then the stir in the audience when . . . in I come' she says, but then adds in a moment: 'My well-known enthusiasm . . . it seems to me it rings more tinny every day.' But more than this direct personal reference to Barker's present situation vis-à-vis the theatre is the relevance of the tone of the play, in more general terms, to his state in other ways. The play talks about the death of the one way of life and the hope of being 'born again' to a greater sense of reality and beauty. Barker must, I think, have been thinking of his position with Lillah and Helen as he wrote the play. Living alone in Massachusetts, having recently written the letter to Lillah asking her to divorce him, forbidden by protocol to see Helen for the time being, though still able to write to her and to receive letters from her; the feeling of limbo (or just possibly purgatory?) must have been complete. This perfect little play is steeped in it: undemonstrative, quite without polemic or protest, a lovely example of 'atmospheric' writing for the stage – gentle, contemplative, regretful, but with a wan hopefulness.

There are multiple echoes in the play of Barker's own situation, spiritually (so to say) as well as physically; but they are neither insistent nor obtrusive and he does not allow them either to pollute or to divert the play's main stream. There is, blessedly, not a trace of self-pity. But the echoes are there, all the same, and are interesting. 'I've sometimes thought', Dorothy says, 'since I can't act any longer, I might show the dear Public my rehearsing. That'd teach them! But there . . . I've come down to wanting to teach them. Time to retire.' By 'can't act any longer' she does not mean that she has literally given it up, but that she knows in her heart that when she does it, it is hollow, empty, meaningless. And the alternative looks infinitely attractive to Dorothy – and to Barker:

EDWARD: Do you decide to close the theatre after the next play?
DOROTHY: I decide not to ask man, woman, or devil for another penny.
EDWARD: Then you close.
DOROTHY: But if it's a success?
EDWARD: Then, when it's finished you may have a few pounds more than four hundred a year.
DOROTHY: I don't want 'em.
EDWARD: But you'll close?
DOROTHY: I will. This time I really will and never, never open again. I want my Abbey. I want to sit in the sun and spoil my complexion and acquire virtue. Do you know I can have fourteen volumes at a time from the London Library?
EDWARD: Yes . . . don't spoil your complexion.
DOROTHY: Well . . . when it is really *my* complexion and no longer the dear Public's I may get to like it better. To acquire knowledge for its own sake! Do you never have that hunger on you? To sit and read long books about Byzantium. Not frothy foolish blank-verse plays . . . but nice thick meaty books. To wonder where the Goths went when they vanished out of Italy. Knowledge and Beauty! It's only when you love them for their own sake that they yield their full virtue to you. And you can't deceive them . . . they always know.

The ambivalence of attitude as between public life and private life shows very clearly, too, in this play. Talking of their past, when Edward several times asked her to marry him, they say:

DOROTHY: . . . so we must seem to choose the cat-like comfort of the fireside, the shelter of your cheque-book and our well-mannered world. And, perhaps I should have chosen that if I could have had my choice.
EDWARD: Dorothy!

DOROTHY: Had not some ruthless windy power from beyond me . . .
                blown me free.

And a bit further on in the conversation:

EDWARD: But sometimes I've wondered . . . what we two together
                might have done. Oh, Dorothy, why didn't you try?
DOROTHY: Not with these silly, self-conscious selves. Poor prisoners . . .
                born to an evil time. But visions do come . . . of better things
                than we are . . . of a theatre not tinselled . . . and an office not
                dusty with law . . . all rustling with quarrelsome papers.

The thought here is very similar to that of another one–act play, written
at almost exactly the same time by John Drinkwater, who was part of
that same theatrical-dramatic revival as was Barker. (Indeed, Drinkwater's father, A.E. Drinkwater was for several years Barker's stage manager and company manager at the Little Theatre and the Kingsway.)
Drinkwater's play, written for the Birmingham Repertory Theatre in
1917, is $X = 0$: *A Night of the Trojan War*; in it, two of the young soldiers
are artists (one a poet, one a sculptor) and the other two dream of
becoming great law-givers in cities cleansed of cant, humbug and corruption.

The influence of the inner life upon the outer is invoked throughout
the play, but delicately, glancingly. Nevertheless, it is all the time recognizably there, a familiar Barker leitmotif. Speaking of the woman he did
marry and of her taking up various eccentric kinds of philanthropic work
late in life, Edward says: 'If there had been any genius in my love for her
. . . would she have had to wait till forty-five and then find only those
crabbed half-futile shoots of inner life begin to show? While her children
were amused . . . and I was tolerant!' This sense of what the creative rôle
and creative power of love should be is an aspect of the general theme to
which Barker will return later, in *The Secret Life*.

Dorothy Taverner, in *Farewell to the Theatre*, is another example of the
fascination, almost bewitchment, which beautiful women exercised
over Barker. Note, for instance, the final stage direction:

> *With three fine gestures she puts on her hat again. Time was when one would sit
> through forty minutes of a dull play just to see Dorothy take off her hat and put it on
> again. Much less expressively he finds his and they go out together. The clerks all stare
> ecstatically as she passes.*

The sense which moves behind this description is the same as that behind
the description of Jessica in *The Madras House* (see p. 170). It is not
altogether approving, but it *is* altogether overwhelmed. And it repres-

ents the civilized, cultured (using the word rather carefully) aspect of the same natural phenomenon which shows itself in Amy O'Connell, whom Barker describes as '*a charming woman, if by charming you understand a woman who converts every quality she possesses into a means of attraction and has no use for any other*' or in Vivien, in *Our Visitor to 'Work-a-day'*, whom one of the other characters describes as 'pampered and furnished in sexual tricks; little green apple' and 'lapped in ease'. Dorothy and Jessica are the obverse of the coin which has the stamp and imprint of Amy and Vivien on its reverse. The truth is that Barker was more than half afraid of pretty women.

The use he makes of this obsessive fascination-fear is subtler, more complex and more ambivalent in *Farewell to the Theatre*, structurally slight though it be, than in any of his earlier plays in which it shows itself; the time of its writing, therefore, between the breakdown of his first marriage and his hopes for his second, acquires a special significance. But that significance, though striking, is not the whole story. This play, or something very like it, would have come at this stage in his career whether Lillah and Helen were there or not; for it marks the end of one phase of his artistry and would have been needed to do that in any case. Without the presence of Lillah and Helen, the play would doubtless of expressed itself in other terms, but the theme of the need for a voluntary death, and with it the hope of a re-birth, would have had to be expressed in any event. *Farewell to the Theatre* and 1916 were, both jointly and separately, turning points: the marriage with Helen Huntington, which followed, altered him and not necessarily for the worse or for the less happy.

–9–

The Lost Leader?

'**H**is death was a heavy loss to Shakespeare criticism and to the drama; but to us of the theatre, and especially to those of us who worked with him and for him and who learnt from him what the theatre meant and drew inspiration from his dazzling imagination and intelligence, the blow fell thirty years earlier when he gave up the struggle, threw off the dust of battle, and became a mere professor. To us it was almost a desertion, and we found it hard to forgive him. Always we would have left all and followed him if he had returned from his self-banishment. . . .' This is Lewis Casson, in the Foreword which he wrote in 1955 for C.B. Purdom's biography of Barker: notice the near-quotation from the New Testament which by implication casts Barker in the Messianic rôle. What Sir Lewis is doing is echoing what I have elsewhere called The Barker Legend – of which, as was mentioned in Chapter 1, he was perhaps the main originator. Hesketh Pearson, inveterate gossip that he was, helped, as did Shaw with his jealousy of Helen Huntington. Shaw is reported by Pearson[1] as having said about Barker and Helen:

> He was completely dominated by her, ceasing to be the independent human being we had all known. She made him throw over Socialism as well as Shaw; she made him do translations of Spanish plays, or put his name to her translations; she cut him off from all commerce with the theatre; she tried to turn him into a country gentleman, but as he could neither hunt, shoot nor fish, it was a hopeless proposition . . .

This is Shaw at his least attractive and the only thing that can be said in its defence is that it was not published until all three – Shaw, Barker and Helen – were dead. It was, however, assiduously promulgated by word of mouth in the early nineteen-twenties, until it became the accepted and automatic view of most actors and theatre people – Granville Barker had allowed his new American wife to buy him out of the theatre. I do not know who first cited the Browning poem by way of parallel:

> Just for a handful of silver he left us,
> Just for a riband to stick in his coat.
>
> . . .
>
> We that had loved him so, followed him, honoured him,
> Lived in his mild and magnificent eye,
> Learned his great language, caught his clear accents . . .

Geoffrey Whitworth, in a radio talk about Barker in 1948 refers to it, saying: 'His professional colleagues are dumbfounded, upbraiding him for desertion. They remember Browning's poem "The Lost Leader", and abandon themselves to grief.' And, as has already been mentioned in earlier chapters, W. Bridges-Adams, in *his* radio talk of 1953, actually used (though ironically) the Browning title as the title of his talk. To some extent, however, both Whitworth and Bridges-Adams dismiss the charge of desertion. Bridges-Adams, in fact, started off thus:

> If, towards the end of his life, you looked up Harley Granville-Barker in *Who's Who*, it would tell you that he was a playwright, a Doctor of Law, a Doctor of Letters (twice) and a Fellow of the Royal Society of Literature. Not one word about more than twenty years of struggle, and endurance, and triumph on the stage – almost as if this was a youthful indiscretion he preferred to forget. When we come across this sort of self-obliteration somewhere east of Suez, and not in a flat in the Etoile, we may be forgiven for imagining we are on the track of a Joseph Conrad hero who is trying to trample on his past. That was not so. Barker always loved the theatre. But in my belief – and I knew him for many years – he became what he had always intended to be.

Certainly the evidence of his letters to Archer in the early days, to Murray just after the Court seasons concluded, to Shaw from New York during the war and to St. John Ervine in the nineteen-thirties – all of which have already been referred to in this present book – would seem to support Bridges-Adams' contention. Barker, from the very start, meant to be a writer and he held to his aim with remarkable consistency. I do not think he denigrated or repudiated the work he had done in the theatre, but he outgrew it and moved on to other forms of expression – though the theatre and its metaphor still remained at the centre of his thinking as an artist. In a sense, he never left it: he simply moved into a different department of it. Purdom thinks otherwise: his view is that Barker's *real* work was his practical work in the theatre, partly as an actor but mainly as a director. As for Purdom's views about Barker's desertion of the theatre, whether he inherited them from Lady Keeble or not, I find it extremely difficult to reconcile them either with Barker's own statements about the theatre and his own artistic aims or with an objective appraisal now, in retrospect, of his various written works (and, most especially, of his plays). My own feeling is that, brilliant though his work as a director had been (and I yield place to nobody in my admiration of it), the instinct which drew him away from it and into half-a-lifetime of writing for and about the theatre was a true instinct and he did well to follow it. His genius was of a more complex kind than Purdom sees or allows and it would have been a stultification of a part of it to foster only the other parts. In any case, the love–hate relationship (and I apologise for the cliché) with the theatre which his career as a whole adds up to is a not invalid representation of his true feelings and the feelings of many great theatre-artists; perhaps, indeed, of every kind of artist toward his art (surely Purdom's 'he reaped no harvest of internal harmony. His contradictions were not reconciled' is too naïve a test). And it is mistaken, it seems to me, to see the gesture of Barker's last twenty-five years as a negative one. It was, in fact, astonishingly rich and astonishingly positive, though filled with frustrations from his own point of view. But the frustrations were simply the result of his consuming impatience that everything he dreamed of could not be done at once. Much was done, in spite of his frustration and doubt; and what was done was of the right kind and bore – and still bears – the imprint of a vital and genuine life.

During the four months of waiting, in Tunbridge Wells and London, in 1918 Barker and Helen had talked constantly of acquiring, when they were married, a house in the country where they could not only live peacefully together but where they could also work together. The letters which he wrote to her in those months contain dozens of references to this. ('*No*, we don't want a ballroom and a minstrels' gallery – though I agree that a pink–blue bathroom at 30 guineas a week . . .' he says in one letter in June: Helen had begun to make enquiries of estate agents and was being shown various possible properties.) They discussed various houses which were suggested to them, the favourite idea for a long time being to rent Groombridge Place, four-and-a-half miles south-west of Tunbridge Wells, which was available at that time. Its accessibility to London was one of its attractions – this point is repeated in several of the letters ('As to the house, it must be in a backwards and forwards place – let us say Groombridge is the limit of *in*-accessibility; and it must be easy to run and ready to run') – and renting, rather than buying, is what they had in mind then. Barker says to her in a letter written about the middle of May: 'I want to be sitting in the wood with you and I think tea in the Groombridge garden with no one near but the peacocks would be as near heaven as on the whole I want to get!' And the same pleasant fancy still haunts his senses a month later: 'But give me the Groombridge garden and the peacock shall stand on a wall and keep off the sun with his tail.' Just before their marriage in July, however, they found out that Groombridge Place was unavailable after all; and at about the same time they also found out that, under the terms of Archer Milton Huntington's divorce settlement, Helen was a lot richer than she had expected to be. Their plans changed somewhat: instead of renting a house near London they decided to buy one rather further away. After some searching in Berkshire and Oxfordshire, they lit upon Netherton Hall, in the village of Farway, in Devon. The preliminary agreement to purchase it was made in the middle of 1919 but the sale was not closed until the following year. On January 15, 1920, Netherton Hall and land comprising 63 acres was conveyed (as they say) to Mrs. Helen Granville Barker for the sum of £6,323 17s 11d; and on May 27 of the same year a further 98 acres, known as Netherton Barton Farm, was conveyed to her for £4,159 1s 0d.[2] The property was bought with Helen's money and the title deeds remained in her name. Netherton Hall, lying in a deep, secluded valley midway between Colyton and Honiton, is an imposing and handsome grey stone mansion of the Jacobean period. It was built by Sir Edmund Prideaux in 1607 on the site of a mediaeval priory which he demolished to make way for his new house. To the Barkers in 1920 it was, it would appear, little short of a fairy castle. They approached the running of it in a way that suggests a kind of dream world. Robin Whitworth could remember his father describing the footmen who were in livery at all times; Jesse Banks, whose father was the tenant of one of the farms on the estate and whose wife was Helen's personal maid, could still tell me in 1979 the names of some of the staff and servants at 'the big house': there were fifteen of them in all – to run a house for two people to live in. The rule was that mornings, and some afternoons until tea-time, were work times and Helen and Harley retired to their separate rooms and got on with their respective pieces of writing – whatever happened to be on hand at the time. There was, no doubt, something a little unreal about it all; but they both felt that they had escaped from a series of prisons into a world of perfect freedom and a bit of fantasizing could perhaps be forgiven. The work they were doing – and neither of them was lazy – redeemed the fantasy and gave it a reality, they hoped: and the hope was not entirely a vain one.

When they moved to Netherton, Helen was working on a new novel called *Ada* (eventually to be published by Chatto & Windus in 1923). Barker, as was mentioned in Chapter 8, had begun work in New York in 1915–16 on *The Exemplary Theatre*, which he published in 1922. Along-side these two books, in 1920 at Netherton, Barker and Helen also worked together on a translation from the French of Sacha Guitry's *Deburau*: it was produced in New York by David Belasco in December 1920 and in London (where Barker himself assisted with the direction) in November, 1921. The published text (New York: Putnam, 1921) says: 'The English text by H. Granville Barker' but in the 1918 letters Barker refers several times to the fact that he and Helen intended to work on the translation together. There is nothing in the text which would suggest that this could not have been true: the translation is both accurate and speakable; the script is theatrically sound enough; the charm of the original has been in large measure captured in the lightly ironic, irregular verse form used. The texture is different from that of either Barker's dialogue in his other plays or Helen's verse in her various collections, but it is not inconsistent with either and might well have been the result of a happy collaboration. The play itself is slight, but charming. The eponymous character is that Deburau who in the third and fourth decades of the nineteenth century created in Paris the figure of the broken-hearted, eternally love-sick Pierrot in his loose white suit and floppy hat (and who, in the nineteen-forties, became the central figure of the famous French film, *Les Enfants du Paradis*). Guitry invented the device of making Deburau's off-stage life parallel the legendary life of the character he creates: Deburau falls deeply in love with a woman who, for a moment, reciprocates his feelings but then leaves him for someone else: and Guitry gives his play an added twist and an added poignancy by making the woman Marie Duplessis – the original of Dumas' Marguerite Gautier in *La Dame aux Camélias* – and having her introduce to Deburau, at the end of Act II, the young man who has supplanted him in her affections:

YOUNG MAN:	Oh, do introduce me. I've always admired him so.
MARIE:	Allow me.
DEBURAU:	Oh, please! Well, if you say I shall . . .
MARIE:	Jean Gaspard Deburau . . . Monsieur Armand Duval.

The play, which first appeared in 1918 – less than two years after the writing of *Farewell to the Theatre* – may well have had a special attraction for Barker and a special significance in that it is about the end of an actor's career. There is a passage in Act IV of Barker's version of the play which reads as follows:

> *Deburau pauses in his part and then slowly draws near the footlights. He makes an appealing gesture to the audience and silence falls.*

VOICES IN THE
AUDIENCE: He's going to speak!
            Listen!
            Fancy his speaking!
            What luck!
            First time he's done it!
            I always thought he was dumb!
            He has got pluck, I'll say that.

> *Deburau does attempt to speak, but he cannot utter a single word. So he tells his audience by a few simple gestures that he is ill, that he can't go on, that he has played for the last time. He asks their forgiveness; he says goodbye. By this time there is dead silence in the house. Deburau's tears are falling. He makes his last gesture, slowly, sadly, kissing his hand. Suddenly the curtain falls. Without another word the audience rises, without another word they move away leaving the theatre empty.*

Perhaps Granville Barker, as he read the play in French in 1918, was remembering that one of the first parts he himself played in his season at the Court Theatre in 1904 was Pierrot, in the play which he and Laurence Housman had written – a Pierrot who is without question a direct descendent of the Pierrot whom Deburau created seventy years earlier.

Barker and Helen, between 1920 and 1932, worked on thirteen other translations together, all from the Spanish. Helen – ironically enough – had learned Spanish from her second husband and from visits to Spain which she had made with him. Archer Milton Huntington had founded, in New York, the Hispanic Society of America, had made many journeys to Spain on the Society's behalf and had translated poems and stories from the Spanish. With Barker, Helen began to translate Spanish plays, he providing the theatrical element and the colloquial turn of phrase, she providing the literal translation. In 1923 they published together a collection of four plays by Sierra, in 1927 a volume of four plays by the Quintero brothers, in 1931 one further Sierra play (*Take*

Two From One) and in 1932 a collection called *Four Comedies* by the Quintero brothers. These, together, represent – to rate it at its most modest – a very considerable degree of industry. And it was, in fact, a good deal more than that: the translations introduced us to a kind of play quite different from the English plays of the time – or, for that matter, of any other time. Gentle, almost inconsequential, subtle in outlines and in character-drawing, these Spanish plays bring into the English theatre a note and a posture completely new. The time at Netherton Hall was not ill-spent.

Purdom, following Shaw's lead, says (*op. cit.*, p. 228): '. . . and he hated the Devon house, its servants, and its isolation', but the weight of evidence is against this view. There are several letters, from Barker to various people, which speak of his pleasure in his surroundings at Netherton. One typical one is a letter[3] which he wrote to Frank Sidgwick, the publisher, on June 1, 1920, which begins:

> My dear Sidgwick,
>   So glad to hear from you! Here I am and to be found more or less always. Whenever you're within reach you'd be most welcome – Devonshire hills restore one's faith in England: yes, every bit as well as the Cotswolds (more than enough be-sung); these wait their singer. Perhaps my wife may qualify; she's more English than I – at a 400 years' jump, so to speak. Anyhow, here we are – have forsworn London for work and quiet. There *is* a telephone, but no one uses it!

There are many evidences of his liking for and good relations with the people of Farway and Netherton and Colyton. He served as a member of the Board of Governors of Colyton Grammar School from 1929 to 1932 and the Minutes of their meetings show him to have been very active and vigorous. He and Helen had a small building on the Netherton estate converted for the use of the village club and showed some interest in the running of the club. Mrs. Rose Banks, who was the club's secretary for many years, showed me with some pride a letter from Barker to the Club, dated June 18, 1925, and beginning, 'My dear Neighbours': it deals with the Club's balance sheet for the previous season and says, among other things: 'You'll notice that we sold the Wireless, by arrangement, for £30. This seemed a good thing to do for new patterns are coming in and prices may be coming down. Therefore we may be able to do better by a fresh purchase.' Barker had also detailed off his secretary, Mr. Lister-Kaye, to undertake some of the administrative donkey-work involved in the running of the Club. Mr. and Mrs. William Summers, local farmers, and Mrs. H. Dimond, who has lived in Farway and neighbouring Northleigh all her life, could all remember seeing Barker (and, though less frequently, Helen) at all kinds of local events, where they gave every appearance of enjoyment. Barker was a founder-member of the Devon Archaeological Exploration Society, which was inaugurated in 1929. And Jesse Banks, brother-in-law of Rose Banks, said to me, about Barker: 'He cried when he finally had to leave Netherton, y'know.' Banks also told me that, twelve years or so after leaving, on his return to England from America after the Second World War, Barker – who was staying at the Fortfield Hotel in Sidmouth – hired a taxi for the day and went back to Farway, visiting all the local people he had known. These and other details I had from people who live in the area and who had been there in the days when the Barkers lived at 'the big house' (a delicious story about a gardener and a carpenter who would while away the time on a rainy days by meeting in one of the disused stables and giving lively impersonations of conversations between Barker and Lister-Kaye: the latter was especially easy to impersonate because he had, in Jesse Bank's words, 'a fairish stutter'; they were at this, full cry, on one day when Barker suddenly walked in, but was hugely amused rather than angry). In short, there grew up in the region around Netherton Hall a second Barker Legend, quite different from the London one. Helen sold Netherton Hall and part of the estate in 1934, the outlying land being sold two years later. Local rumour attributed this to the 1929–30 stock exchange crash in the United States in which, rumour said, Helen lost a great deal of money, but this appears doubtful. The Barkers had, in fact, entirely ceased to live at Netherton two years before: the focal centre of their life had shifted gradually to Paris, where they spent more and more time. In 1932 they took a long lease on two flats at 18, Place des Etats-Unis and settled there permanently, using the upper flat for living in and the lower one as a study-library.

Helen, while they had been living in Devon, had published four more novels and the collection of short stories called *Wives and Celebrities*. Though forgotten now, they were well-received and sympathetically reviewed at that time. *The Manchester Guardian*, commenting on *Living Mirrors*, which was published in 1928, said: 'There is much in Mrs. Granville-Barker's method which recalls Henry James . . . The qualities of the book lie in its delicate sureness . . .' and Naomi Royd-Smith, in *Time and Tide* in 1931, also compares Helen with Henry James and not wholly to her disadvantage: she describes *Come, Julia*, published that year, as 'a story of distinction by a novelist who, more intent upon inner than outer drama, justifies her choice by humour, sympathy, and a precise observation of human character.'

Barker's one venture into prose fiction during these years was the short story, *Out of these Convertites; or, Richard goes to Prison*,[4] which has already been mentioned in Chapter 6. It has never been published, though it is, I think, the most accomplished of his short stories. It is lightly ironic in tone, sure in its touch. Its plot, significantly enough, concerns a man whose wife suddenly and quite unexpectedly inherits a large fortune. Both Richard and Felicia are determined that the sudden access of wealth shall not alter the pattern of their lives, but they find that this pious resolution is more easily pronounced than practised. 'There is no domestic disturbance like a sudden increase in income;' the story says: 'even a sudden loss has no such effect. It is less embarrassing, in fact, as far as clothes and doorways and suchlike are concerned, to grow thin than to grow fat.' Richard is an engineer who has abandoned the practical side of his profession for the study of its theoretical under-pinnings. (The implied autobiographical parallels in the first half of the story are fascinating and, at a guess, their presence was probably the reason for the story's never being published: Barker did not want, even by implication, to hurt Helen's feelings. It should not be assumed, however, that the story is therefore *about* himself and Helen: the second half of it – which is much the more important part – carries no such autobiographical echoes. Barker simply took as a starting-point a domestic situation rather like his own.) When Felicia inherits the money she suggests – after one or two abortive attempts to invent quiet and undisturbing ways of disposing of it – that Richard should leave the engineering firm by whom he has been employed for many years and set up a laboratory of his own for purely scientific and theoretical studies of engineering problems – the mathematics of the matter, stress factors in various materials, and the like. The idea is attractive to Richard but he agrees to it only on one condition: he must receive from Felicia's money only a monthly salary of the same order as that paid to him by the engineering firm. She tries to persuade him to take outright half the entire inheritance, but this he resolutely refuses to do. Having, so to speak, regularized Richard's position, Felicia then goes on to tackle her own. She still has more money than she knows what to do with and it is still continuing to breed. She looks around for worthy causes or objectives upon which to bestow it and eventually hits upon the suffragette movement (the story is set in Edwardian England). Richard, although he disapproves not so much of women in politics but of political activity *per se*, takes the line that Felicia should be allowed to exercise her own choice over her own destiny and so gives her his approval and support readily when she asks him what he thinks about her idea. He again supports her later on, moreover, when she announces that she and a number of other women have decided, as a demonstration against their disenfranchisement, to refuse to pay their income tax: 'That seems to me', Richard says, 'to be, from your point of view, a perfectly reasonable thing to do.' In vain does his lawyer point out to him that if Felicia refuses to pay, the Government will then prosecute their claim against *him*, her husband. Richard is unconcerned and continues to go about his normal business. In due course, after his lawyer has exhausted all the devious delaying devices that he can exercise upon the local taxation authorities (though none of this with Richard's consent and most of it without his knowledge), Richard is threatened with arrest for non-payment of taxes.

The rest of the story, done in a deliciously, lightly ironic, comic vein, is really a moral argument between Richard and Felicia. She maintains that they have jointly done their civic duty by now and that, to keep him out of prison, there is no disgrace in her giving in and paying the tax which is due. He, on the other hand, now regards it as a matter of absolute principle: the Government is, he says, being unreasonable in seeking to enforce a foolish and unjust law and he intends to maintain his position of principle whatever the cost or consequence. Part of their first conversation on this theme goes as follows:

'You surely must see now,' she said, 'that I have just *got* to break my pledge. And give up the suffrage work.' She added this last after half a second's difficult pause.

'If you do,' said Richard, 'I swear that – in a manner of speaking – I'll never speak to you again. You needn't interpret that –' and he turned to me 'as any sympathy with suffrage. I'd take away the vote from most men if I could. I'd have them qualify for it in logic and mathematics. Then, perhaps we should be living under reasonable laws. Meanwhile what I am standing up for is a woman's right –'

The phrase with his emphasis upon it had a comically contradictory sound. He caught it himself and not to shirk the implication went back over his sentence.

'– what I am standing up for, whether I like it or not, is the woman's right to make a fool of herself if she chooses.'

'Oh, Richard,' said the poor Felicia, 'Don't say you're going to prison for that?'

'Well,' said Richard, 'resolve it to its elements and that's all political freedom consists of, for individuals or collectively. And if we were statistically wise, no doubt therefore we shouldn't want it. Where's my political freedom taking me now? To prison. Why? Because all the use I've made of it is to let a lot of idiots pass laws that I know nothing about. So now I can't complain if one of them traps me. The value of the suffrage is exactly indicated by the ridiculous antics women go through to get it. I shall go to prison because, having experienced it, I have every reason to despise political freedom and I shall go quietly and like a gentleman.'

So he goes to prison; and in response to his going, Felicia – convinced that her husband has at last seen the light and been converted to the cause of the suffragettes – abandons her passive rôle in that movement for an active one. She takes to making inflammatory speeches at meetings and throwing bricks through windows. So she finishes up in jail as well, which is too much even for Richard's dogged heroism. He immediately accepts a friend's offer to pay his taxes for him and rushes off to comfort his wife. The lawyer friend defends her when her case comes to court and, by a comic distortion of the facts and a speech of extravagant rhetoric, he manages to get the charges against her dismissed. Over dinner that night the three of them, Richard, Felicia and the lawyer (who is the narrator of the story) sum up the matter and bring the story to a close, thus:

'To be physically shut in a cell [says Richard] and to have your body hurt, is sometimes the best assurance that your mind has been set free and that your spirit is strong.'

'That's what the women find,' said Felicia. 'And, Richard, just because you're out again, you won't be less keen on our getting the vote, will you?'

'Oh, the vote!' said Richard, contemptuously, 'I would give you the vote whether you wanted it or not. And I would especially give it to those who did *not* want it. If they won't come out of prison, break the doors down. I approve of your fighting for it. I approve of their fighting against it. Not that the vote's worth having or not having, but the fighting is the thing. I approve of all fighting. Why, in the dear Lord's name the world isn't yet out of the age of fisticuffs, I don't know! Let's get it out by all means. Though – naked fists you know; there's something almost friendly in them. When my knuckles met the Sergeant's eye it was in some sense an embrace. Better to hit a man than hate him.'

'You're not sorry you did it?' asked Felicia.

Richard knocked off his cigar ash with a tender finger.

'Are you sorry you threw the brick?'

'I am sorry I broke the window,' said Felicia. 'No woman likes to see damage done. She has had too many generations of mending. But I'm not sorry I threw the brick.'

'I consider you a very dangerous and disingenuous couple,' I said.

'I'm very glad to be back at work,' said Richard.

Felicia looked at the fire.

'You know,' she said, 'I never knew until the money came and one made those extra efforts to keep alive, until we found how deadening it was, one didn't know how little lively one had ever been. Oh, but I'm tired and my back does hurt! And I can't sling a sentence together straight. Stupid efforts, crude efforts, I know, just to keep alive! I really think I'll go to bed.'

'Well' said Richard, 'as long as one *does* keep alive . . .

The story was certainly written during the years at Netherton, though the manuscript is not dated. A likely date would appear to be 1922–23. This I infer from the fact that on page 32 of the story, to illustrate the fact that the law does not always operate reasonably, Barker tells a little tale of former times:

'What are you in the stocks for?'

'Getting drunk.'

'Nonsense – they can't put you in the stocks for getting drunk.'

'Damn it, but they *have*!'

And he tells exactly the same story, though in slightly different words, in an article called 'The Heritage of the Actor' which was published in the *Quarterly Review* in July, 1923. The text of the article was at first intended as a preface to *The Secret Life*, the play that he finished in 1922 and published in 1923, but the preface grew to twenty pages in length and so was published separately, being adjudged too long to go into the book with the published text of the play. In 'The Heritage of the Actor' the stocks story figures thus:

There was once, in the 17th century, a gentleman who, coming out of church on a Sunday morning, found a week-day companion sitting in the stocks.

'What have they put you there for?' he asked.

'Getting drunk.'

'Nonsense', said the church-goer, who was a legally-minded man; 'they can't put you in the stocks for being drunk.'

'Zooks!' said the unfortunate reveller. 'But they *have*!'

It is useless to argue that actors can add nothing to and take nothing from the material the playwright gives them. The answer is that they do.

This story would seem to associate *Out of these Convertities*, at least so far as chronology is concerned, with *The Secret Life*, which – along with *The Exemplary Theatre* – was Barker's main preoccupation in the first two years at Netherton. It has no thematic connection with the play,

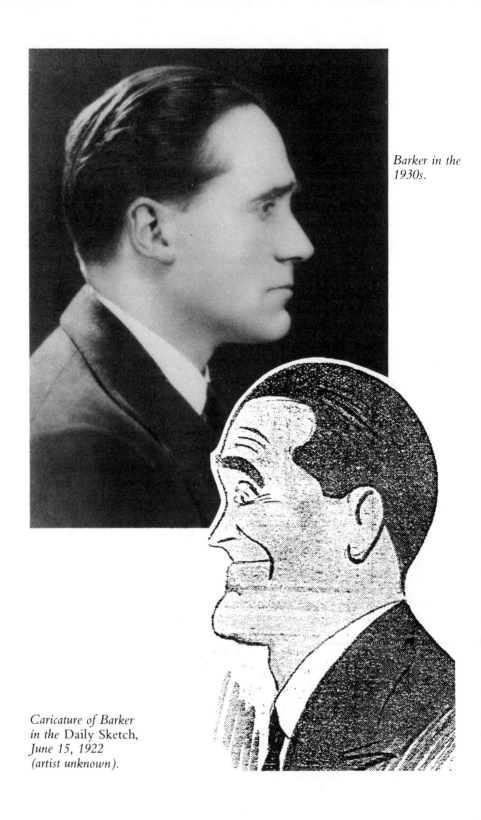

Barker in the 1930s.

Caricature of Barker in the Daily Sketch, *June 15, 1922 (artist unknown).*

however, What is interesting to observe is the way that Barker could apparently handle with ease, at more or less the same time, three works so different in tone and texture. *The Exemplary Theatre* is clear, straightforward, earnest and disquisitive; *Out of these Convertites* is tongue-in-cheek, comic narrative of a suave and sophisticated kind; *The Secret Life* is poetically sensitive, broodingly melancholy, indirect in method, technically experimental, reflecting its author's profoundest responses to life, experience and the world. The mental discipline involved in managing leaps of the imagination of this sort must have been enormous. Since *The Secret Life*, which is obviously much the most important of the three, seems in many ways to draw together all the threads of Barker's art as a dramatist, it should, perhaps, be examined separately and seen in the context of his plays purely, rather than alongside these other very different kinds of writing (excellent though these are in their own fields). *The Secret Life*, therefore, along with the one other remaining play of his career – *His Majesty*, which was started immediately *The Secret Life* was finished – will be made the subject of Chapter 10.

Meanwhile, Barker turned his attention to the writing of theatre history and criticism, alongside the continuing work on *His Majesty* and on the *Prefaces to Shakespeare*. Re-reading now the group of articles which he turned out at that time, one is struck all over again by their quality – and by the variety of their qualities. They are witty, urbane, compulsively readable, crammed with intelligence (in both senses). They are authoritative, seriously but succinctly discursive, yet elegantly stylish. Most of all, they are tied absolutely – whether he is discussing plays or players or authors – to the theatre; the theatre is the very life-blood of them and he writes, with modesty but with complete assurance, as a man of the theatre. Once again one is puzzled and re-puzzled by the Barker Legend's accusation that he *deserted* the theatre. And the suggestion that he became dull and stuffy, a 'mere professor' (Lewis Casson's sneer), writing in the language of 'mere scholarship' (C.B. Purdom's echoing sneer) – setting aside from the argument for the moment the fact that not all professors are 'mere' and good scholarship is never dull except to the completely uninformed – seems utterly incredible in the face of the liveliness, the grasp and the sheer theatricality (in the word's best sense) of most of these pieces. Since they are of such variety, it is impossible to suggest the virtues of all of them by quoting from or discussing one or two only. On the other hand, there is not space here to represent them all fully – yet they should be mentioned, for together they amount to a far from negligible contribution to the pattern of his life's work; and since a mere list of titles seems a bleak and churlish way of dealing with them, perhaps it would not be inappropriate to draw attention to some of the more striking and felicitous passages in several of the essays and articles which he wrote during these years at Netherton.

There are, for example, towards the end of the *Quarterly Review* article called 'The Heritage of the Actor' (of which mention has already been made) two brief paragraphs contrasting twentieth-century dramaturgical methods with those of earlier times which brilliantly delineate Barker's sense of the modern theatre (and incidentally comment most cogently upon his own plays):

> The dramatist's chief gain from the theatre of the new illusion and the conventions which belong to it, has been – at the price of some limitation of his power to project things in the doing – a great extension of resource in picturing things as they are. There was more need, as well as more scope, for physical action upon the older stage, even as there was for the spell-binding sway of verse. But by the new illusion the attention of an audience can be focussed upon the smallest details without either words or action being used to mark them; light, darkness and silence can be made eloquent in themselves.
> . . .
> One is tempted to imagine a play – to be written in desperate defiance of Aristotle – from which doing would be eliminated altogether, in which nothing but being would be left. The task set the actors would be to interest their audience in what the characters *were*, quite apart from anything they might *do*: to set up, that is to say, the relation by which all important human intimacies exist. If the art of the theatre could achieve this it would stand alone in a great achievement.

The thing is infinitely debatable; it is possible to argue that what Barker is doing here is trying to transform the theatre into another form of art altogether, a form so tenuous that it could not live in the rough air of public performance. Yet he is aware of this difficulty and of the basic nature of the stuff of which theatre is made (for this is, after all, an article on *acting*). He seeks to marry the craft of the actor with what he sees as a new art of the dramatist and his piece concludes in these terms:

> A play's content may be what you will, matter for nothing but laughter: its dialogue may take any form whatever, from poetical imagery to the cracking of jokes. But it will be a good play or a poor one, a living thing or dead, in so far as we are brought to accept its inhabitants as fellow-creatures or left indifferent to them.
> . . .
> But the art of theatre is not a reasonable art. A play's dialogue is an incanta-

tion, and the actors must bewitch us with it. They must seem, now to be the commonest sort of folk, now superhuman, and the form of their talk must fit them. But, for all appearance, it must ever be of a trebly-distilled strength. It must have this power of poetry in it. It must be alive with more than the mere meaning of words.

. . .

But still, too often, the worthiest plays will leave us cold, respectful, when we should be deeply moved, or paying them instead of laughter a tolerant smile. What is wrong? This, for one thing, I suggest. The dramatist of the new dispensation has yet, as a rule, to learn both what to ask of his actors and how best to help them to answer the demand.

This matter of the relationship between the actor's contribution to the final work of art and the playwright's contribution, is touched on again six years later in an essay called 'Tennyson, Swinburne, Meredith and the Theatre':

The trouble is that Swinburne seldom, if ever, sets his characters free. He conceives them, brings them to a sort of birth; but he still speaks through them, they are megaphones at his mouth. With freedom they would do as all human beings do, contest, come to cross-purposes, give way, refuse to say the things they should say, stand altogether dumb, and be a dreadful nuisance to their author, doubtless. How to round them in again and face them towards their destiny? In that lies the art of the playwright. They can be brought within conventions as formal as Racine's; but they must at some time have been free. In the theatre this freedom, as the actor inherits it, is a part of the natural order of things, is indeed its fount. The closet-dramatist can with difficulty imagine or allow for it.

The essay from which this is taken was written for a collection of papers called *The Eighteen-Seventies*, published in 1929 by the Royal Society of Literature[5], of which Barker was for that year elected president. These papers began, in fact, as lectures to the Society by various of its prominent members (Pinero lectured on 'The Theatre of the "Seventies" ', the Marquess of Crewe lectured on 'Lord Houghton and his Circle' and among the other lecturers were Hugh Walpole, Walter de la Mare, John Drinkwater and Vita Sackville-West) and Barker himself edited the volume when the papers were published, inaugurating in the process a new venture: other volumes concentrating on other decades followed in future years.

To one of these, *The Eighteen-Eighties*, edited by Walter de la Mare and published in 1930, Barker contributed an essay called 'The Coming of Ibsen'. It is, in style and tone, one of his best pieces of writing. With a lightly graceful hand and constant touches of humour, he describes the state of the English theatre immediately before the incursion of Ibsen. But the wit and humour do not make either for shallowness or for vagueness: his eye is keen and he can express incisively what it sees. Here, for instance, is his summing-up of Henry Arthur Jones, the playwright who became fashionable but who had grown up in a little market town in Bedfordshire:

> 'Henry Arthur', as he came familiarly to be, was an able craftsman. He wrote plainly and well. He had a vigorous if not very distinguished mind, which ran to humour rather than wit, which set, with the safeguards of a quite British decency and honesty and with a softening of manly sentiment, a frankly sensual value upon things. Too self-confident and self-respecting to be an intellectual snob, he was, as Archer had quickly divined, a realist in grain. But, for all his acquired knowingness, Dukes and Prime Ministers (the Victorian brand) and their womenkind of the right hand or the left, remain romantic figures to him still, and he makes woolly work of them. Whereas the butchers and bakers and candlestick makers of Market Parbury are convincing even in caricature. The vividest impressions and the truest, which we redraw into pictures, are those bitten into the consciousness of our sensitive years. Now that Henry Arthur Jones's work is done, one would give the lot of it for the single play he might have written, had circumstances with him and the theatre of his day been a little different – some mellower, more charitably humorous enshrining of the little world which was native to him. For such things live.

Then he moves on to deal with Ibsen's own plays and the impression they made when first performed in England. Their significance and their greatness he can, by 1930, comfortably take for granted, leaving himself free, rather, to observe and comment upon the responses – often comic – of the English theatre and the English public. Here is one such comment:

> But, indeed, the theatre of the 'eighties was not asking for actuality. Jones and Herman, besides collaborating in melodrama for Mr. Wilson Barrett, had produced a certain play in three acts called *Breaking a Butterfly*. It did not pretend to be original; it was drawn – via the German, one supposes – from *A Doll's House*. Its vicarious authors probably only thought of the job as an honest piece of hack-work, and the result was no better nor worse than half a hundred other plays of the time. What is interesting is to see the changes they were inspired to make. The scene is laid in some English country town. Nora becomes Flora, and to her husband, rather terribly, Flossie. He is Humphrey Goddard and we find him gifted with a mother (quite unnecessarily) and a sister (wanted for the piano playing *vice* Mrs. Linden, who disappears). The morbid Dr. Rank is replaced by a Charles-his-friend, called, as if to wipe out

every trace of his original, Ben Birdseye! He is not in love with Nora-Flora, of course; that would never do. But Dunkley, alias Krogstad, had loved her as a girl, when Humphrey Goddard stole her young heart from him; so love has turned to hate and revenge is sweet. Observe the certainty with which our operators in the English market fasten on the flawed streak in Ibsen's play and cheapen it still further. The tarantella episode, of course, will be the making of the whole affair (such was many people's judgment then, and now we rather find it marring) and this is left intact. But the third act sees the parent play deliberately stood upon its head, and every ounce of Ibsen emptied out of it. Burlesque could do no more. Torvald-Humphrey behaves like the pasteboard hero of Nora's doll's-house dream; he *does* strike his chest and say 'I am the guilty one'. And Nora-Flora cries that she is a poor weak foolish girl, '. . . no wife for a man like you. You are a thousand times too good for me', and never wakes up and walks out of her doll's house at all.

Barker also has some good, harmless fun with an early, pre-Archer, translation of *A Doll's House* into English. This translation, with the name of the translator mercifully suppressed, was published by Weber's Academy at Copenhagen in 1880. Barker quotes several passages from it, of which my own especial favourites are these:

HELMER: . . . Has my thoughtless bird again dissipated money?

NORA: But Thorvald, we must enjoy ourselves a little. It is the first Christmas we need not to spare.

HELMER: Know that we cannot dissipate.

NORA: Yes, Thorvald; we may now dissipate a little, may we not? . . .

HELMER: Nora! (*goes up to her and catches her in jest by her ear*) Is thoughtlessness again there? Suppose that I borrowed £50 today, and you dissipated this sum during the Christmas week, and a tile fell down on my head New Year's eve, and I were killed –

NORA: O fy! don't speak so badly.

HELMER: Yes, suppose that such happened, what then?

NORA: If such bad were to happen, it might be indifferent to me whether I had debt or no . . .

HELMER: What do we call the birds that always dissipate money?

NORA: Gamblers, I know it, indeed.

HELMER: . . . The gambler is sweet, but it uses up excessively much money. It is incredible how expensive it is to a man to keep a gambler . . .

and:

HELMER: Nora – may I never more become but a stranger to you?

NORA: (*takes her portmanteau*): Alas, Thorvald, then the most wonderful must happen –

HELMER:	Tell me the most wonderful.
NORA:	That both you and I changed ourselves in such a manner that – O, Thorvald, I no longer believe in anything wonderful.
HELMER:	But I will believe in it. Tell it me! Change ourselves in such a manner that –?
NORA:	That cohabitation between you and me might become a matrimony. Good-bye.

After this final quotation, Barker says: 'I am not indisposed to offer a prize at the Royal Academy of Dramatic Art to the student who could manage to speak the last line without making her audience laugh.'

The same year (1930) finds him working on something more substantial as well: he was invited by Trinity College, Cambridge to give the Clark Lectures for that year and these were afterwards published in a volume called *On Dramatic Method* (London: Sidgwick & Jackson, 1931). This, incidentally, was also the year of the publication of the second volume of *Prefaces to Shakespeare*, bringing the total number of Shakespeare plays which he had commented upon to eight. The Clark Lectures again instantly impress one with the fact that they are the voice of a practical man of the theatre. Even the purely literary aspects of the subject, without being in the least diluted or made shallow, bear this same imprint. The titles of his five lectures were as follows:

> The Natural Law of the Theatre
> The Making of Blank Verse Drama
> Shakespeare's Progress
> Wycherley and Dryden
> A Word About Form

From the lectures themselves, several points stand out as being of special interest. The first, perhaps, is to note – for the benefit of those who thought that Barker hankered after too scholarly an approach – that his first lecture begins by saying: 'The prophets of Aristotle have much to answer for. English drama at least, you may retort, has been little enough troubled by them. Still too much!' He dismisses the idea of arbitrary rules and sets out to explore the basic nature of theatre as an artistic medium, creating its own rules from the inside, so to speak. 'All arts are mysteries', he says, 'the way into their service is by initiation, not learning, and the adept hugs his secret.' And on another page of the same lecture: 'How, on the other hand, does one "naturally" set out to be a dramatist? By the way of imitation, and of trial and error. Pens and paper are needed, and a large waste-paper basket. If one is young, and unless one is a heaven-sent genius, the craft of the business will be more interesting at first than the art of it. One will have admired models, but will soon be picking these to pieces to see if they could be put together better. One will write and destroy and write and destroy. But above all one will want to be in intimate touch with the theatre, behind the curtain or before it; and this intimacy will need to be developed till the pleasures of illusion are replaced by a more critical pleasure in the processes of the scene, till one finds oneself sitting there anticipating what dramatist and actors should do – and with this one is, and knows it, in one's element, as the expressive phrase goes.'

He comes back to the same sort of point at the very end of the last lecture – and at many other places in between. As a summary of these five lectures and of his views, and as a further refutation – if any still be needed – of the Barker Legend's notion that he had forgotten the theatre and was, moreover, glad he had, the final sentences of the fifth lecture are worth quoting:

> This much is clear. We have a drama, old and new, of some quality. The best of the old sprang from a close collaboration between dramatists and actors. Those conditions are not to be repeated, and the new drama has another scope. But in the gist of them the life of the theatre abides. The dramatist must work in a medium made familiar to him by the actor's art, the actor must contribute more than his moment's success. The riddle, if it be one, is worth solving.

His belief in the craft of the theatre and in the possibilities of its art is still absolute. His trust in the actor as the essential central pillar of the edifice is still paramount and he comes back to it again and again. I know of no purely 'academic' critic or commentator, no matter how devoted to the thesis that a play should be studied in the context of the theatre, who so emphatically insists upon the supremacy of the actor or so underlines the necessity for taking into account the actor's contribution to the completed creation; and certainly one would need to search very hard indeed to find one who was able to make such points with the ease and skill that seemed to come quite naturally to Granville Barker at his best – and, during the late 'twenties and early 'thirties, he *is* at his best.

The fourth of these Clark Lectures, incidentally, gives his views on Restoration drama – trenchant and debatable, but lively and well argued: of Congreve's *The Mourning Bride*, for example, he says:

> Mr. Congreve was in poor health when he wrote *The Mourning Bride*. One sees him at Tunbridge Wells, sitting, after his morning glass and his cup of

chocolate, wrapped in his flowered dressing-gown, and delicately penning these desperate sentiments. The company at Lincoln's Inn Fields is plaguing him for the play. He knows just what they want and what their public wants – and here it is. He seems to have brought the wheel full circle. For this is indeed lofty, this is Ercles vein. It is the drama which Bottom the Weaver loved and which Shakespeare laughed at, not unkindly, and purged of dross, to make great drama from it. But the wheel has not come full circle. There was crude honest strength in the old plays. In this there is no virtue at all. It has lost its innocence, and what has it gained? Nothing can come of such fraud. Nothing did.

At the end he states his position quite candidly. 'If much in this chapter', he says 'savours more of a speech for the prosecution than a judgment, well, I think it time another one was made.'

In the same year as the Clark Lectures, Barker published a revised version of the book on a National Theatre scheme which he and Archer had written together in 1904 (see pp. 119–120). He brought it thoroughly up to date, taking into account the changes in plays and audiences and finances which had occurred in the intervening twenty-five years. In effect, he produced an entirely new work on the subject. Its title is simply *A National Theatre* (Sidgwick & Jackson).

Two years later, in 1932, he gave another lecture to the Royal Society of Literature and it, again, afterwards became an essay in a published collection, this time called *The Eighteen-Sixties* (of which John Drinkwater was the editor). Barker's contribution was called 'Exit Planché – Enter Gilbert'[6] and it told, in considerable detail and with a lot of amusing quotations, the story of the old burlesques, from Planché through Talfourd, Brough, H.J. Bryon and Reece to Gilbert; and thus to a discussion of Gilbert's gradually-developing skill and the infinite improvement he effected in light entertainment of this nature. But Barker does succeed in showing how the Savoy Operas, with all their wit and grace and sophisticated foolery, were the legitimate descendents of those rather childlike entertainments which Planché devised for Madame Vestris. In passing he has some nice comments upon Gilbert's relations with the Lord Chamberlain and the censorship of plays:

> It is not so well remembered that five years later Gilbert helped to rewrite an old pantomime of Byron's for a charity performance, played Harlequin in it himself, that the characters were made up as well-known politicians, and that in this instance the Lord Chamberlain, apparently, was never given a say in the matter at all. *Trial by Jury* seems to have passed without trouble. But there must surely have been to-ings and fro-ings at St. James's when *H.M.S.*

Pinafore was presented for licence. Would the public think that Sir Joseph Porter, K.C.B., First Lord of the Admiralty, who confesses that:

I grew so rich that I was sent
By a pocket borough into Parliament;
I always voted at my party's call
And I never thought of thinking for myself at all.
I thought so little, they rewarded me
By making me the Ruler of the Queen's Navee.

was intended for Mr. W.H. Smith, the actual incumbent of that post? Would Mr. W.H. Smith think so? In *Patience* the caricatures of Whistler and Wilde extended even to make-up and costume. This was allowable enough; they were people of no particular importance. But what happened – whatever did happen? – when the MS. for *Iolanthe* arrived? Was not the mere Commons, but the Second Estate of the Realm to be thus mocked? Were audiences to be encouraged to laugh at:

And while the House of Peers withholds
Its legislative hand,
   And noble statesmen do not itch
To interfere with matters which
They do not understand
As bright will shine Great Britain's rays
As in King George's glorious days.

– with Mr. Gladstone actually in office, what was more! The Lord Chamberlain may have learnt besides that, to make the whole affair still more absurd, the peers were to wear their coronets and robes, and the Lord Chancellor his. Was nothing said? Was Mr. D'Oyly Carte not 'sent for'? Was the Prince of Wales not acquainted with the threatened outrage? Was the Queen not told? The Reader certainly did not take the responsibility on himself, nor the Comptroller, nor in this case probably even the Lord Chamberlain. The Office does not keep records of its internal proceedings, I fancy. It is as well. The chronicle of the freedoms it first denies and then allows, seen broadening down from precedent to precedent, would not be an admirable one. It is inconceivable that on this occasion a very great deal was not twitteringly said. In no other dramatist would such hardihood have been tolerated. But Gilbert was now Gilbert, entrenched in popularity, and nothing was done.

By the time this was published, the Netherton days were over and the Barkers had decided to take up permanent residence in Paris, a city of which they were both fond and one in which they had latterly been spending more and more time. They were there for several weeks at the end of 1930, staying at the Hotel Beau Site in the Rue de Presbourg, and again in May 1931. On March 27, 1932, Barker wrote from Paris to Gilbert Murray, saying: '. . . But we're settled here permanently now (Netherton empty and to be sold: we were there so little and could not keep it on and "up" any longer) . . .' Earlier that year they had moved into the apartment in the Place des Etats-Unis. They stayed there for a little over eight years, during which time Barker produced several books and articles. The very fine *Preface* to *Hamlet*, already referred to in Chapter 7, was one of these. Another was *The Study of Drama* (Cambridge University Press, 1934), which began its life as a lecture at Cambridge in the summer of 1934; and a third was *On Poetry in Drama* (Sidgwick & Jackson, 1937) which was the Romanes Lecture for that year. These last two show, I think, some falling-off in vitality. They are very competent and quite comprehensive treatments of their subjects, but they lack any element of surprise and they lack also some of the verve and enthusiasm of his earlier writing.

Alongside this continuous output of plays, critical articles, books and lectures, from 1920 to 1940, Barker still occasionally returned to his former craft of director. The production of Maeterlinck's *The Betrothal*, in 1921, has already been mentioned, as has also the London production of *Deburau*, in the same year. Before either of these he directed a production of *The Romantic Young Lady* which opened at the Royalty Theatre in September, 1920. *The Romantic Young Lady*, by G. Martinez Sierra, was the first joint venture in translation upon which Helen and Barker embarked: they completed it during 1919, within a year of their marriage, partly while they were living at the Fortfield Hotel in Sidmouth (the purchase of Netherton Hall not having been completed at that stage) and partly during a visit to America. It was produced (in the modern sense of the word) by Dennis Eadie, who also played the lead, but it was directed by Barker. Eadie, who had worked with Barker often in the past (he was, for instance, the very striking Falder in the first production of Galsworthy's *Justice* in 1910), was a leading actor who, by 1920, was just beginning to undertake management ventures as well. Barker had persuaded him to produce the Sierra play, with Barker himself directing. This is clear from an interesting series of letters[7] from Barker to Eadie, the first of which is dated December 17, 1919 and the last, October 15, 1920. *Who's Who in the Theatre*, in its entry for Barker, says he 'was responsible with his wife for the production of 'The Romantic Young Lady', for the translation of which play, from the Spanish, they were also jointly responsible' and one of the letters to Eadie mentions that Helen had been at all or most of the rehearsals. However, there is absolutely no sign that she took any active part in the production process. I take her presence at rehearsals to be no more than a general indication of their early resolve to share their work with each other – a resolve which, in this particular instance at least, soon broke down: there is no record of Helen's ever attending rehearsals with Barker again and by the middle 'twenties the 'Lunch, Harley!' story was beginning to circulate.[8] In a letter to a friend in 1925, however, Helen does speak approvingly and excitedly of the revival of *The Madras House*, which Barker was directing. The following year he directed the first English production of *The Kingdom of God*, another of the Sierra plays which he and Helen had translated. It had been published, in a volume with three others, in 1923 and Sidgwick & Jackson re-issued it in a separate edition in 1927, to coincide with the production, which opened at the Strand Theatre on October 26. Barker was again involved in production in 1928, when he gave some directorial assistance and advice to the director and cast of a twin bill of plays by the Quintero brothers. These, again, were Spanish translations which he and Helen had done: the two plays were *Fortunato* and *The Lady from Alfaqueque*. The director was Anmer Hall and the cast included Margaret Webster and John Gielgud. In 1934, Harcourt Williams, who was then the director of the Old Vic, did a revival of *The Voysey Inheritance* at the sister theatre, Sadler's Wells, which was just being re-opened after extensive renovation. He invited Barker to take over the direction of the play and Barker agreed. Williams himself was playing the part of Edward Voysey. And two years later Michael MacOwan persuaded Barker, once again, to direct one of his own plays: the first production of *Waste*, which was presented at the Westminster Theatre on December 1, 1936. Stephen Murray, that distinguished and splendidly austere actor, whose unfortunate experience with Barker I mentioned in Chapter 1, was playing the young secretary, Walter Kent (interestingly, forty-one years later he played Cantilupe in the television production of the play) and was kind enough, when I asked him about it, to write me a description of the experience:

> When we knew he was coming over to direct the play we waited breathlessly for his arrival. His prestige then was, of course, enormous. He arrived in his dark overcoat, bowler hat and gloves, and with rolled umbrella. He was staying at the Ritz with his wife. He did take the bowler hat off but directed most of the time in overcoat and gloves. At one o'clock sharp each day his wife called for him in the car, and he would clap on the hat, grab the umbrella and bolt like a frightened rabbit. We had what was then quite a long time for rehearsals – five weeks. For the first week we sat round and read the play. Or

Barker (centre) on stage at the Old Vic, directing a scene in the 1940 production of King Lear. *John Geilgud and Lewis Casson may be seen on the extreme right.*

Jessica Tandy, who played Cordelia in the 1940 King Lear *— a drawing by Roger Furse.*

rather tried to read it. We would get two or three pages into an act and he would bellow 'No, no, no, no!' and then begin to read it himself. He would read right through to the end of the act – all the characters – in what seemed to me a rather dull monotone. He must have read the first act to us three or four times.

Margaret Webster, in her *The Same Only Different*, also confesses that, in connection with the 1928 production of *Fortunato*, she found Barker not as inspiring a director as his reputation had led her to hope for. Cathleen Nesbitt, on the other hand, speaking of both the 1912 *The Winter's Tale* and the 1925 *The Madras House*, found him marvellously sensitive and helpful and John Gielgud repeated to me personally what he has many times said in public – that he found Barker a great director and that, even as late as 1940, when he assisted Lewis Casson with the production of *King Lear* at the Old Vic (with Gielgud playing Lear), Barker's directorial hand had lost nothing of its cunning. It may be, of course, that something of Barker's sense of impatience with the theatre in general was beginning to show itself inadvertently at some rehearsals on particular occasions. His letters, certainly, as well as his more public writings of those years, are full of frustration and disappointment about the state of the theatre, both organisationally and artistically. On the other hand, his letters to individual actors, though firm and forthright in expression of opinion, are invariably gentle, kindly and very courteous. It was the artistic process itself which brought out his impatience – which, to return to our original theme, is not the characteristic sign of a man who has 'deserted'.

A summary, perhaps, would not be entirely out of order: in the twenty-one years between the wars, Granville Barker's work included –

Writing 2 full-length plays

Writing 7 books of criticism

Directing 8 productions

Translating 13 plays from the Spanish and 3 from the French[9]

Writing a dozen or so major articles on theatre history or criticism

Various jobs of editing, lecturing, exhorting and so on.

In April 1940, the moment he had finished with the *King Lear* rehearsals in London, he hurried back to Paris. Helen had, during the three weeks he had been away, written to him almost daily to tell him of the growing anxiety in the French capital. He had been back home less than a month when the German army crossed the border into France. Barker and Helen, making what hasty arrangements they could for the safeguarding of their flat in Paris, fled just in time to Lisbon. From Lisbon he wrote to various friends in England asking, rather sadly, whether he could be of any use to the national war effort if he returned. They all said no, there was no particular job that they could think of for him. He felt helpless and useless. He was by then sixty-three and years outside the conscription age limit, of course. But he was still possessed, as he always had been, by a rather naïve and boyish patriotism and he wanted to be part of the struggle, which seemed to him a just and necessary one. Even after he got to New York – which is where he and Helen went in August 1940, England having, as he felt, rejected him – he wrote in a letter to Sir John Gielgud: 'I am, for the time being, an Honorary Professor at Yale. I'm told this is of use, and other jobs of the sort and other work is in prospect, as much, I expect, as I can tackle. But I'd be happier digging trenches on the Norfolk coast, although I'd dig them badly.' This letter was written in October 1940 and from then until 1945, when he and Helen returned to England and thence to France, his real work in North America was to consist of lecturing and writing, but in the early stages of his stay in New York he held an official government position. This was chiefly because, when he and Helen reached Lisbon from Paris, some official excuse was needed for their journey to, and entry into, the United States. Strings were discreetly pulled and Barker's friend, Sir Godfrey Haggard, British Consul-General in New York (and father of Stephen Haggard, the actor) provided the necessary device by manipulating Barker's appointment as the head of the Speakers' Section of the British Library of Information in New York. Sir Godfrey's telegram to Barker in Lisbon said: 'Could you come New York official employment or Canada similar object. Important.' The visa issued to Barker, authorizing his entry to the United States, described him as a 'Government Official'. The British Library of Information was a long-established (it had been there since 1920), well respected institution of fairly modest proportions. In 1940 the British Government was just beginning to view it as a possible instrument of propaganda and by 1941 the Government had directed that it be amalgamated with the British Press Service to form a much larger organizational unit called British Information Services.[10] Barker's appointment to the British Library of Information never really amounted to more than the aforesaid official device for getting him into the United States. For a few months he moved into the organization's imposing offices at 30, Rockefeller Plaza but, in the 1941 reorganization, opportunity was taken to 'suspend' his part of the work, prior to getting rid of him altogether. He was obviously totally unsuited to such a position; he was far too complicated and idealistic a person to serve the smooth needs of propaganda and far too idiosyncratic to dance to somebody else's tune. Journalists were his natural enemies and he quite lacked the capacity to be a man for all seasons. Mr. Aubrey Morgan, an energetic British business man in New York who became the head of the new British Information Service, when I enquired of him as to the details of the matter, was so kind as to write me a detailed memorandum on the subject: it reads as follows:

REPLY TO INQUIRY BY PROFESSOR SALMON

ABOUT

HARVEY GRANVILLE BARKER AND HIS SERVICES WITH THE B.I.S.

I believe Harvey Granville Barker was appointed head of the speakers' section by Professor Charles Kingsley Webster when he was head of the British Library of Information. The Minister of Information charged me with the task of amalgamating the British Library of Information and the British Press Service which had been formed separate from the British Library of Information at the request of Lord Lothian, the then Ambassador. In my reorganization I found a number of the visiting speakers were dissatisfied in the manner in which they were handled by Granville Barker. I suspect he rather viewed them as temperamental actors and actresses which he knew so much about in his great career in the theatre. Finally he crossed swords with a Trades Unionist' visiting the United States of America as a British speaker who complained very strongly in London about Granville Barker and referred to him as a broken down playwright. If my memory proves correct, I eased him out as gently as I could. His number two was a Miss Barbara Hayes whose uncle, Sir Norman Angell, was a very well known lecturer in the U.S.A. who travelled a great deal as a most successful speaker, and she had acted as his secretary cum manager and therefore had a wide experience. I appointed her to replace Granville Barker as head of the speakers' section. During the reign of Granville Barker, we had a number of members of Parliament who came as speakers to the U.S.A. and some journalists. In those days the Ministry of Information was gradually emerging from its original chaos under the guidance of Brendan Bracken as the Minister and Cyril Radcliffe who were particularly anxious to avoid what they felt was unnecessary criticism through any misjudgments on the part of the British Information Services in New York. If my memory is correct, the change of the head of the speakers' section was prompted very largely from London. It was always a difficult section to manage because the nature of the speakers is to expect considerable attention and the production of large audiences. Unfortunately, Granville Barker succeeded in neither. I should say in these matters the chief criticism one could make about him was that he lacked judgment. I very much fear that he left the organization feeling disgruntled at what he felt was a lack of appreciation of the great talents he could bring to bear in this task which he looked upon as his contribution to the war effort.

I don't remember any more about him after his departure from the British Information Service. I deeply regretted having to take the steps I did take because obviously he was an extremely interesting man who alas, was unwilling to take direction; I suppose possibly because he had given so much to others himself.

(signed) A.N. MORGAN

There are, still extant, some of Barker's letters from New York, during that four and a half years; letters to Gilbert Murray, to C.D. Medley (his long-time solicitor and friend in London), to Pendleton Beckley (the American lawyer in Paris who was trying his best to keep the apartment in the Place des Etats-Unis from falling into the hands of the Gestapo), to various U.S. Government departments and agencies concerning his official status and his tenuous right to remain in the country. We also have some of Helen's written *to* Barker on those occasions when he was away from New York giving various lectures. Like all wartime letters they are now curiously moving because of their mixture of the portentous and the trivial: comments on the recent snowstorm in the next paragraph after the expression of anxiety about the safety of friends in the air-raids on England; a mention of the death of Paderewski, alongside a description of the intense July heat in Oneonta, New York State; Barker's constant sense of frustration at having no real work to do and his anxiety about the whereabouts of Abramsky, his Swiss-born secretary whom they had left behind in Paris; anxieties and fears for the outcome of the war expressed alongside concern for Pompey, their poodle, who was ill and had to go to a veterinary hospital. The picture which one pieces together is a sad one, as much in regard to Helen as to Barker himself.

In spite of her statement on her visa application that she was then sixty-one, she was, in fact, just turned seventy-three when they arrived in New York in September, 1940. She was no longer writing and was feeling, even more acutely than Barker, that life was over and that she was useless. She was frantically active, going to symphony concerts and piano recitals and art galleries and lectures: 'I gave lunch to Mrs. A.B. Morton. Then we went to see the Grecos again', she says in a 1941 letter: 'She is very intelligent about pictures – and other things. Then I went to

Mrs. Crane's 'class' and heard the fervent – but not very well-educated – Holiday hold forth on James Joyce . . .' But all these manoeuvres were merely diversionary tactics designed, hoping-against-hope, to distract and divert the enemy; but at the heart of the battle the enemy was steadily gaining ground and Helen was – probably for the first time in her life – aware of this. There is a tacit admission of this in the opening paragraph of the letter which I have just quoted:

> Dearest,
>   Forgive me – and don't be cross – if I don't send my book.[11] I've just read it over and I do feel the thing most to be desired for it – by us *both* – is oblivion. I do truly now desire it. I did have a poetic impulse – and perhaps some poetic feeling: nothing more. Now it only pains me to have that book given to strangers and have a kindly, polite, personal note from them. Please understand. This is all I want now – I mean the gentleness of being left alone. Don't write me a scolding letter.

But she had touched on the subject once before, over a year ago. Writing to Barker from Paris on April 8, 1940 (while he was in London directing the Old Vic *King Lear*), she had said:

> I spent this morning – after taking Kaï for a walk – doing up things for refugees of various nations (I seem to have as many shoes as a centipede would need if he needed shoes at all), ending up with a non-descript heap of things to be sold to the old-clothes man – in this case, a woman! H. le Breton came to lunch and gave first-aid to my knitting, but it was almost beyond her powers. Then we went to the Salon – not much better than, hardly as good as, the 'Independent'. After I came home, I had a go at my writing-desk, that big chest in my bedroom too – a dreadful job and most depressing. *Mountains* of typed M.S. – graves of my work, and unmarked graves at that! It's hard to have been a fool all one's life . . .[12]

Self-pity? Doubtless. But self-pity is in itself piteous and thrice-married Helen Huntington, with ambitions beyond her talents, is by the 1940s a piteous figure. Increasingly, she had begun to realize her age and the gap – never now to be bridged – between intention and achievement. In another of her letters from Paris to London in 1940, she had said:

> As usual, you see, this is all about myself – but you told me, 'once in the golden days', that you would never get tired of hearing me talk about myself. I've certainly put you to the test!

The egocentricism and the feverish round of cultural-social activities and the growing private sense of emptiness all went with her from Paris to

New York and intensified there. And something else, something unknown and inexplicable, seems to have developed there between her and her husband. The tone of her letters to him suddenly changes somewhere between 1942 and 1945. Up to 1942, the letters always begin 'Darling' or 'Dearest' ('Dearest Harley, dear', says one) and end variously with 'All love from Helen', 'Goodnight. My love to you' – followed by their joint monogram, or the like. We have no letters from 1943 or 1944, but the four written in 1945 begin either 'Dear Harley' or with no salutation at all and end 'Aff*ly*, Helen', 'Goodnight and no dreams! H', 'A very good-night to you, H' and, again, 'Aff*ly*, Helen'. The contents of these four letters are friendly enough, but in a rather distant and impersonal way, speaking exclusively and determinedly about the people she has been meeting and the places she has been visiting. One should not make too much of this, of course: it is an old lady of seventy-seven we are talking about. But the sudden change *is* noticeable, nevertheless.

The Barkers lived in New York from September, 1940 to May, 1945. During this time Barker lectured once at Yale and on two different occasions at Harvard; he gave a series of lectures (the Alexander Lectures) at the University of Toronto and a series (the Spencer Trask Lectures) at Princeton University. Out of the material of the Toronto lectures came the fifth and last series of the *Prefaces to Shakespeare*, the 'series' consisting, in fact, as has already been mentioned in Chapter 7, of one play only, namely *Coriolanus* – an interesting play for a man like Barker to finish on: a play about a man instinctively patrician, who rejects and repudiates his community, turning his back on it with the words 'I banish you! There is a world elsewhere!' The Princeton lectures also appeared in published form, under the title *The Use of Drama* (London: Sidgwick & Jackson, 1946). It is, it must be said, a rather unsatisfactory book; loosely knit, rather diffuse and even rambling, it attempts a review of theatre in relation first to the other arts, secondly to education and thirdly to society in general. The views Barker expresses are largely conventional ones (even for his own time) and the arguments he adduces – when he adduces any at all – are rather superficial.

There is perhaps some special excuse and a good reason for the falling-off which one sees in the Princeton lectures, quite apart from the general strain of those years on everyone: the lectures had to be postponed from their originally-proposed date because of an illness of Barker's and then had to be given almost immediately upon his being discharged from hospital. For many years he had been suffering from eczema which seems to have got progressively worse. The disease is, of course, neither dangerous nor contagious but Barker, apparently, found it very debilitating. He also seems to have responded to it psychologically as well, in an extremely negative way: 'the shameful thing', he calls it in a letter to C.D. Medley – almost as if he had contracted leprosy or syphilis. In October, 1944 the eczema led to what Barker describes as 'a tiresome carbuncular condition which would have meant operations'. To avoid surgical treatment, his physician put him in Roosevelt Hospital for a course of the brand-new drug, penicillin, and this caused the postponement of the Princeton lectures.

The postponed lectures in turn caused the postponement of the Barker's return to Europe. By mid-1944, when it became obvious that Germany could not possibly win the war and was rapidly losing her capacity even to be a nuisance, let alone a real danger, to the civilian populations of England and France, Barker's letters to Medley speak increasingly of plans for their return. Eventually a fairly firm plan was made for them to be back in London by November of 1944. The intervention of the illness put this off until May, 1945.

They stayed in London, at the Ritz, for a few weeks only and then went, as they had done at the end of another war in 1918, to the Fortfield Hotel in Sidmouth, Devon, where they stayed for the summer of 1945. Late in September they paid a short visit to Paris to begin the process of putting the apartment back to rights. It had been occupied by a series of tenants during the war – an American, two different Hungarians at different times and a Frenchman – frantic arrangements made, sometimes at a few hours' notice, by Pendleton Beckley in order to provide excuses for keeping the Germans out of it. Miraculously, it had sustained very little damage, and Barker's library was still intact, even though its contents had, at one point, been officially catalogued and listed by order of the German authorities (for what exact purpose is not clear). I often wonder what it must have been like to be in Barker's position in September, 1945 – to walk into that room at the end of that war, with all one's memories of what the war had done to Paris and to London, and to see one's own books again, with one's own bookplate inside the front cover, standing in their accustomed places on the shelves where one had left them six years before. Considering their relative fragility, physically speaking, what sturdy survivors books are – thank God!

It was agreed that the temporary tenants of the apartment, Mr. and Mrs. Lecsei, should be allowed to remain in possession until March 31, 1946. The Barkers returned to the Ritz and spent the winter there. It was

April, 1946 before they finally returned to their Parisian home, after an absence of almost six years. They had been back only four months when Harley Granville Barker died of arterio-sclerosis.

C.B. Purdom, in his biography (p. 275 and p. 277) has many more details about those last four months in Paris than I have been able to verify, but since he quotes no authority and no documentation to support them, they need to be regarded with some reservation, I think. He says that Barker was very unhappy, that he declared to 'a friend' that he felt his life to be useless, and that he 'was suffering from delusions' (it is not explained what the nature of the delusions was). He also says that Barker had broken two ribs in a fall and had, shortly thereafter, suffered a heart attack. Though I can find no medical records remaining to support Purdom's statement, a fall, broken ribs and a heart attack sound like fairly straight-forward, definite, practical matters which would be easy to identify and difficult to controvert. I think that Purdom's statements about these items are, therefore, probably true. I am much more suspicious, I must confess, about the delusions and the 'useless life', as I am about the story (p. 277) of his 'lying crying in his little sitting-room, while Helen upstairs heard nothing'. If he lay there crying *alone*, how did anyone ever come to hear of it? (Surely he did not relate the story himself, afterwards.) If he were *not* alone, it seems almost incredible that he would lie there crying at all, but if he actually did, why is the name and identity of so vital a witness suppressed? In short, the story is just that little bit too good to be true. It is our old friend, The Barker Legend, getting in the last word. Purdom, immediately after the story of Barker's lying crying in his sitting-room, says: 'He was alone, because he never discovered himself.' His over-simplified account of Barker needed some such ringing phrase as this to round it off and to seal it firmly within the ambit of the Legend. But neither the premiss nor the conclusion really rings true, nor will either really bear close scrutiny.

Granville Barker was within three months of his sixty-ninth birthday when he died. Helen Huntington died three and a half years later, at the age of $82\frac{1}{2}$. Lillah McCarthy, or Lady Frederick Keeble as she became when her second husband was knighted in 1922, outlived that husband by eight years, dying in April, 1960 at the age of 85.

Except for its final six years, Barker's life was, by any standards, a remarkably productive one, not only in terms of quantity but reckoned also by the quality and variety of its achievement. Something further will be said in Chapter 11 about that quality and variety, but meanwhile I have left for Chapter 10 a detailed consideration of the two last plays he wrote, twenty years before he died, which in some ways represent both the sum and the summit of his life as an artist. Both of them are, in my view, major works.

Secret Lives

*I*n the third sentence of the first of the Clark Lectures in 1930, Granville Barker says: 'For I am a practising playwright . . .' But in a letter to Nicholas Hannen on August 13, 1936 he says, talking of the difficulty of casting a proposed production of *His Majesty*: 'But I put to him [the director] for the third time the practical difficulty: *can* he provide a King and a Queen? He says he has a good company. But do *you* suppose for a moment that he can? And even if you (and some Queen) were available, *could* he make it worth your while to go and rehearse for 3 weeks and play a fortnight? The thing doesn't seem practical. But then – why write plays? So, as you have noticed, I don't any more.' In the six years between 1930 and 1936, Barker's thinking about himself and about play-writing had changed. And the reason he gives, in the letter to Hannen, is the one he gives in various other places and contexts – he begins to despair of a theatre which seems incapable of providing him with the right kind of audience or the right kind of actors or the right kind of organization for new plays of a really challenging kind. During those six years he had – so far as we know – attempted no new play. His mind seems at last made up and the theatre, if it wanted revenge for his desertion, now has it – to its own loss.

But up to 1930 at least, he thought of himself as a practising playwright and the years from 1919 to 1928, at Netherton Hall, had produced – as well as much good critical writing and occasional returns to the job of director in the theatre – the composition of the two plays which, if not the best of his career (and they may even have been that as well, if only

someone would give us the chance to see them on the stage), were in
many ways the two plays most typically *his* and the two which sum up all
that has gone before. To one of these I have already referred many times,
making it a kind of leitmotif for this book; and I do, in fact, think that all
Barker's art and all his craft came together in this play, begun in 1919 and
finished in 1922. *The Secret Life* and *His Majesty*, whether designedly or
not (and I personally incline to the view that there *was* a conscious
intention at work), are a diptych. In style they are interestingly different,
demonstrating between them the two main styles of all Barker's work
(extensions and refinements, in fact, of the differing styles represented at
the beginning – or almost the beginning – by *The Marrying of Ann Leete*
and *The Voysey Inheritance*); but in essence and spirit they are closely akin
– though not identical. *The Secret Life* brings together the two main
senses which run through all Barker's plays and which, together, constitute his vision of things – the necessity of living alone and in secret; and
the mysteriousness of the force of sex on the patterns of civilized living.
His Majesty sets aside the second of these almost entirely, in order the
better to examine the first, which it does from a point of view different
from that of *The Secret Life*. But ultimately each of these two is enriched
by being seen in the light of the other: they are companion pieces.

Alongside the reiterated theme of rejection and retreat runs, in *The
Secret Life*, the parallel theme of sexual love as a mirror of the
unattainable-desirable; and with it the whole issue of what a civilized
relationship between man and woman ought to be. Again, as in *Waste*,
there is a central character who is unmarried and whose house is kept for
him by his sister (talking about his sister Eleanor, Strowde actually refers
at one point to his 'marriage'). Whatever else Granville Barker thought
about marriage – and it is by no means clear what he did think – he
certainly did not view it as a comfortable, sensible arrangement for living
and sleeping together. His letters to Helen in the early part of 1918,
though passionate, never directly mention sex or physical love-making.
They read like the letters of a much younger man writing to a woman
whom he has placed on an impossibly high and distant pedestal. In this
connection, there is another piece of inconclusive but not insignificant
evidence which did not come to light until thirty years later. When Helen
died, in 1950, among her possessions was found a copy of Sir Arthur
Quiller-Couch's *The Oxford Book of English Verse*. Helen's name was
written, in her own handwriting, on the fly-leaf of the book and someone – Helen or Harley, one wonders? – had lightly marked, with a
vertical pencil line in the left-hand margin, the last lines of Coventry

Patmore's 'The Married Lover'. These lines read as follows:

> Because although in act and word
> As lowly as a wife can be
> Her manners, when they call me lord
> Remind me 'tis a courtesy;
> Not with her least consent of will,
> Which would my proud affection hurt,
> But by the noble style that still
> Imputes an unattain'd desert;
> Because her gay and lofty brows,
> When all is won which hope can ask,
> Reflect a light of hopeless snows,
> That bright in virgin ether bask;
> Because, though free of the outer court
> I am, this Temple keeps its shrine
> Sacred to Heaven; because, in short
> She's not and never can be mine.[1]

The woman's side of this same dilemma is stated by Joan Westbury in the third scene of the first act of *The Secret Life*:

JOAN:	Was it God tempted us then?
STROWDE:	God's the great tempter. But . . even as you now understand what you then were . . . you did love me?
JOAN:	Yes.
STROWDE:	And you've never doubted that either?
JOAN:	Never.
STROWDE:	Though the love for Mark survived. And you had your boys.
JOAN:	(*as making final confession*): I couldn't have lived my love for you, Evan . . . it would have killed me.

And a moment later she says, 'I think some power in me would always have kept me from you . . some innermost power.'

This Joan has a curious kinship with an earlier Barker character, namely Jessica in *The Madras House*. They are in many ways very different and their destinies in their respective plays are very different. But they hold one thing in common and it is the most important – though not the most immediate – thing about each of them: it is that they are impossibly divine women; exquisite, finely-tempered, beautiful and beautifully bred. Barker describes Joan, in a stage direction, as 'A woman that, in her youth, must have been very flower-like; the fragility, and a sense of fragrance about her, remains.' To Jessica, making her first entrance in Act II of *The Madras House*, he gives, it will be recalled, one of the longest and most significant of all his descriptions of a character, the sum of it all being her exquisite loveliness and her fastidiousness. He pictures Jessica as a very beautiful woman and, like all poetically sensitive men, he is both fascinated and frightened by a flawlessly beautiful woman and his instinct is to treat her as being something different from ordinary mortals and to rationalize the confusion of his feelings by worshipping her. When he wrote *The Madras House*, towards the end of 1909, he had for two years been married to Lillah McCarthy who, as well as being wilful, headstrong, a bit silly and a very fine actress, was also extremely beautiful. She never played Jessica Madras (in the original production in 1910 Jessica was played by Fay Davis and in the 1925 revival by Cathleen Nesbitt) but there are two photographs of Lillah from about that time which seem to epitomize all that Barker had in mind when he created Jessica. One picture shows Lillah as Jennifer Dubedat in *The Doctor's Dilemma* in 1907; the other is a studio portrait, infinitely composed – in both senses of the word. Apart from a slight thickening of the fingers and forearm (features which show in some of her other photographs) she looks the perfect patrician and the perfect image of Barker's Jessica. If one sits and looks at that studio portrait of Lillah while someone else, without a hint of irony in the voice, reads the description of Jessica in the stage-direction from *The Madras House*, the visual and aural images coincide with startling exactitude and clarity. Barker adored and was half-afraid of beautiful women. And Barker's ideal woman was an aristocrat (which, in a certain sense – an American sense – his second wife was).

And which, in *The Secret Life*, Joan Westbury is. So she becomes for Strowde, who is partly Barker, the divine adored one, the typification of that secret life which contains the only things of real worth, the only things that are real at all. His love for her is important to him – and to the play – not only in itself but also, and perhaps more so, because it is a symbol both of the hidden source of spiritual values and of the eternally-desired but unattainable goal. For Strowde, Joan is not merely an aristocrat in the sense of a person who is socially patrician; she belongs to the aristocracy of the spirit and is a sign of the need to resist, somewhere in the soul, the daily compromise. The opening scene of the play compels this upon us even before we know Joan's story. She sits alone on the stage, lit only by moonlight; just off-stage, as yet heard but not seen, three men who are old friends remind themselves and each other of the days when they used to meet as undergraduates and sing their way together through the whole score of *Tristan und Isolde*. We hear them,

*Lillah McCarthy as
Jennifer Dubedat in
the first production
of* The Doctor's
Dilemma *(1906).*

*Studio portrait
of Lillah McCarthy
(date unknown)*

while we gaze at the still figure of Joan, singing in snatches the end of the opera:

> In dem wogenden Schwall,
> In dem tönenden Schall,
> in des Welt-Atems –
> wehendem All –
> ertrinken,
> versinken –
> unbewusst –
> höchste Lust![2]

They are Isolde's final words. After them, Wagner's stage direction says:

> Isolde sinkt, wie verklärt, in Brangänes Armen sanft auf Tristans Leiche.
> (Isolde sinks gently, as if transfigured, in Brangaene's arms, on to Tristan's body).

Nietzsche recognized in this opera an expression of his 'love of earth' – the underlying, aimless, irrational force with which all sensitive life seeks to ally itself; the 'sea of passion' into which Isolde longs to cast herself, will-less and oblivion-seeking. The lovers' pledge, which Tristan and Isolde swear, needs to be understood clearly: it was not that they would die merely so as to be re-united in death but that they would die so that the great anonymous, unpersonified and impersonal Life Force would take them for its own. Their individual identities would be lost in it and the world's unreality would dissolve in a new sense of reality beyond death. So the two central themes of Barker's play are brought together and subsumed in the legend of Tristan and Isolde which, by being introduced into the opening scene, adumbrates them for us at the very beginning and continues to brood over the play throughout its entire length (it is worth recalling that the name of Joan's husband, for whom she deserted Strowde, is Mark). Faced with the same dilemma as was Isolde, Joan makes the opposite decision, not because of fear of social pressures but because of a scepticism within herself: 'I couldn't have lived my love for you, Evan . . . it would have killed me.'

Barker, in the play, is not talking about *his* secret life: this is not merely a piece of disguised autobiography, in spite of the obvious echoes. He is reflecting upon the secret life behind all real and sentient life and upon the necessity of this for (to use an old-fashioned expression) the soul's salvation. Nevertheless, the echoes from his own more-or-less immediate situation are remarkable. Here in an English country house, run –

apparently – on deliberately and, indeed, self-consciously archaic-aristocratic lines, he writes of people who withdraw from the market-place world. And, judging by his letters to her, his marriage to Helen Huntington – no matter how incongruous the idea now sounds – seems, at least in its first impact, to have come to Barker as an expression of the imperious inward desire to sacrifice everything in one grand gesture of renunciation to the power of that clamorous inner will which demanded some outward token of homage to the greater-than-ordinary reality which it represented. One of his letters to her, just before their marriage, said:

Monday 6.45 a.m.

My darling, this time I will write to you – in proper defiance of all lawyers and their delays – this is the day my dear one – how it has been waited for – and all it means – yet it began 'outsidely', like any other day. Even 'insidely' – oh yes deep inside one it *is* different. But I started to say – how hard to fix when things are done – the real kernel of their doing. This – in that sense is only a negative well only a registering of the actual thing done – yes, that is it – a milestone. From tomorrow (please God I say that, for all my defiance of lawyers!) it will be different, though the few yards this side and a few the other *look* the same. But we shall take a new breath as it were. In ourselves where all things happen and only there we have been 'gathering up' as it were – for a change, for a new stretch of road – nearly *our* road now every step of it. Helen darling, words meaning so little now beside even little things I do – But that is wonderful and welcome – easier to *do* with all one is than to say with only one's brain – or rather with one's brain always the final process in saying and such a ragged brain as it gets to be sometimes. I shall always love to frame thoughts for you darling, to have you as you do complete the thought as I do yours – add the true meaning. But the joy now to be *doing* and *being*. Now one can even *play* with thoughts a bit and put them in their place – a second place often – while the main accent of living is in the doing – sometimes, oh most often, of such simple things – And the being. Oh darling Helen I do pray that I shall never disappoint you. But I love you and thank God for you my dear – oh, with *more* than heart and soul and body and mind – with some quite unconscious self that *is* love for you. That *is* and it is only in external things and sometimes quite external that I must consciously try to do and be always the best I can. Be patient with me darling over those things where there is need. But you are – so dear and patient – so understanding – so *alert* to understand – My dear – My Helen – oh my darling, I love you.

This letter shows very clearly the way in which Barker, even in matters directly affecting his own immediate actions, instinctively thought of the 'real' life as being something which is secret and 'insidely' and something which has only tenuous connections with the life of overt action. He links the inner life, moreover, very firmly to the great emotional upheaval through which he was going at the time; and if the language in which he expresses this connection is neither very original, nor very striking (sounding, indeed, embarrassingly mawkish and adolescent on occasion), it nonetheless conveys both the depth and the urgency of his sense of the need for withdrawal from the world. Perhaps there is some significance, too, in the fact that, though she kept his letters, he apparently at some point destroyed hers. This need not necessarily mean that he did not value them. It may simply mean that, having read them and received their message, he was anxious that no one else should do the same.

Strowde, the central character of *The Secret Life* is, both as a dramatist's achievement and as a magnificent opportunity for an actor, outstanding in the play and sticks in the mind afterwards. He is a splendid example of what Ashley Dukes meant when he wrote, in 1924, about Barker: 'He writes for his peers in the house of cultivation, which is the true fourth estate in our national life, and by them he is understood with a mental effort that is always considerable but never goes unrewarded.'[3] The character of Strowde was much admired (and significantly) by T.E. Lawrence, who was a friend of Barker's (he was a fairly frequent visitor at Netherton Hall) and to whom Barker gave a copy of *The Secret Life* (and who retaliated by lending Barker a copy of the then-unpublished *Seven Pillars of Wisdom*, running to some 340,000 words, and asking for Barker's comments on it!) Lawrence, in a letter dated February 7, 1924, says: 'Strowde is the person who interested me most. Your women passed me by (in revenge perhaps, for I usually pass them, in the flesh); your Serocolds are too usual to be more than ornamental, and I resent a young man's taking rubbish seriously. But why did you make Strowde so weak? There is a luxury in keeping outside, but it is a poor man who will lie asleep in that; and you don't express the fear he must have had of being *pulled* back . . . the conviction that he'd have to sell the part of himself that he valued for the privilege of giving rein to the part of himself which others valued, but which he despised or actually disliked.' Obviously Lawrence saw in Strowde a lot of things with which his own alienated nature chimed[4] and that should make us to some extent wary of his judgment (he was, in any case, no dramatic critic), but the important thing for our present purpose is to note that his comments are further evidence of the force and vitality which reside in the writing of Strowde. And, indeed, in the whole of *The Secret Life*. 'It is a very great thing, that play of yours', Lawrence says elsewhere in the same letter: 'I hate plays, because I'm no theatre-goer, and the unpractised form is knobby and uncouth to my wits: but the characters come through the writing with a shout.' Further on in the same letter he says 'Your dialogue is an amazement to me; some ass said Henry James; but *he* was a porpoise, not a fencing master.' And in an earlier letter (December 2, 1923) he had said to Barker: 'I'm reading the play. It's hard, very hard, reading, and interests me enormously. I like close-woven writing, and I'm going to like this, I think.'

The Greeks said drama was action: I say that, in our sense of the word and to make sense of it in the light of all that it must now compass, drama is action taken to the point of no-action; it is action developed to the point of stasis, held in an equilibrium which is at once precarious and yet, in relation to the centre of that segment of human experience reflected in the particular work, eternally maintained. Drama is the portrayal of the progress of the soul towards that point where, within the bounds of the particular sense of life which is in that particular work being explored, there is understanding but no further progress, because the journey is complete.

In *The Secret Life*, the central dramatic conflict is between doing and being, between the ultimate unreality of the former and the ultimate reality of the latter. The central dramatic tension in the play is not between Strowde and Oliver or Strowde and Joan or Strowde and Serocold (though those conflicts and confrontations are there, in the service of the central conflict) or between any two characters or group of characters: the central dramatic tension is between the perception of human reality which leads to activity and that which leads to acceptance, resignation. This conflict, I would contend, is adumbrated at the beginning of the play, dominates the play's progress and is brought to a proper resolution at the end in the balance between Oliver's belief that Strowde will go to America even though he knows Joan is dead and Susan's belief that he will come back but come back changed.

Provided that one does not demand a completely schematic treatment of symbol and metaphor but is prepared to find the play's meaning diffused through all its parts, then the shape and pattern of this central sense of the play is quite clear. It reaches us through the structure of the plot and arrangement of incidents, through the *nuances* of dialogue and through the idiosyncrasies of character. It receives a full, immediate and ironic statement at the start of the play in the invoking, by way of *Tristan und Isolde*, of their youthful ideals by a group of middle-aged men who are now politicians, business men and civil servants. The two sides of the equation are here clearly stated and the actual subject-matter and substance of the Wagner opera are drawn into the play. This aspect of the conflict is deepened and sharpened very soon by the emergence of the story of Evan's love for Joan and hers for him. Being merges in loving and loving in death, the perfect un-activity. The value of all *doing* is denied: and behind Evan and Joan is the image of Tristan/Isolde which has been firmly planted in our minds, with its attendant images of Day vanquished by Night and perfection reached only in death, which is the supreme sublimation of all mortal passion.

What makes the play so authentic (and so powerful) is the realization one has that this division between Doing and Being, richly ambivalent and interestingly complex as the play makes it, is yet a true dichotomy, basic to all sensitive human experience, quite incapable of 'solution', a poised stasis of equal forces which reflects a division that goes down to the very centre of living and being – and this, I take it, is what 'dramatic' really means. We do not watch in order to see the division healed or the characters extricated from the dilemma; we watch to see them *try* to escape it, to see them try to reconcile the irreconcilables – and to see them come to the realization that the profundity of reality subsists in the equibalanced tension of forces, not in a reconciling of them. No god can compromise and remain a god. Nor can God resign. He Is.

Barker himself, in a brilliant aperçu (and authors are not always clear-sighted about the profounder implications of their own work), wrote to Archer:

> 'The war does for Evan's political idealism, too. I couldn't enlarge on this for fear of making it too topical. In *contrast* to this is set (beside the practical unemotional life with Eleanor) the entirely unideal Lady Peckham and the consequences of his unspiritual liaison with her. She loses her son – in an entirely opposite sense to that in which Joan loses hers – for she can no longer be of use to him, can give him nothing more that he wants. But neither can Evan take him; he was begotten only of the flesh and not of the spirit. Though – as Lady P. says – 'If you can't take what's your own I don't know what's to do you good.' That is the play's main "opposition".'

I think he is right. The confrontation of flesh and spirit is only another version of the confrontation of Doing and Being. He makes Kittredge say to Joan, in Act 3 Scene 2, 'The generation of the spirit is not as the generation of the flesh . . . for its virtue is diffused like light, generously, unpriced. Doing and suffering and the work of thought must take its toll of us. And all that life corrupts death can destroy. Then we may cease to know. But, freed from self's claim upon it, scattered, dissolved, trans-formed, that inmost thing we were so impotently may but begin, new breathed, the better to be.'

The other side of the argument has been given expression earlier in the play by Serocold: 'We philistine politicians are a poor lot . . . but we do get things done.' But Kittredge, in another conversation, has already answered that for us: 'Doing defeats itself. In disgust of mere doing men turn to destroy.'

The twin themes of withdrawal from the world and of sexual love as the epitome of unattainable perfection, which we noted at the beginning of this consideration of *The Secret Life*, may now be seen to operate not as isolated intellectual concepts or mere autobiographical echoes but as integral parts of an essentially dramatic design: they are there to serve, to illustrate and to illuminate the central conflict, the essence of the play, of Doing *versus* Being. How intimately this whole group of images is connected not only with Wagner and Nietzsche but with the whole of the later Romantic movement is both interesting and significant. Both Margery M. Morgan[5] and Colin Wilson[6] (and George Sampson,[7] too, by implication) attribute the sombreness and the nihilistic qualities of *The Secret Life* to the influence of the 1914–18 War. I think they are misled by the play itself. In it, Barker certainly makes use of the War as the great symbol of disintegration and his characters (especially, of course, Oliver, who has lost an arm and his idealism and many friends in it) regard the War as the actual root-cause of their despair. But there is more than a suggestion that though he thought of it as a symbol, Barker himself did not regard the War as a cause, let alone *the* cause, of the sensitive man's desire to retreat from life. That, he implies, was there all along: the War simply served to emphasize the imperative necessity of such a retreat if anything of worth or beauty or permanent value was to survive. In fact, as Frank Kermode points out in *Romantic Image* (London: Routledge & Kegan Paul, 1957), the notion of the *necessity* for a sensitive life to be lived apart and separate is one of the two basic assumptions that underlie a great deal of late nineteenth and early twentieth century literature and criticism, the other (and cognate) assumption being that the Image is the very substance of a work of art (and this idea, too, is not irrelevant either to Barker's view of things or Strowde's) 'To be cut off from life and action, in one way or another,' Kermode says, 'is necessary as a prepara-tion for the "vision". Some difference in the artist[8] gives him access to this – an enormous privilege, involving *joy* (which acquires an almost technical sense as a necessary concomitant of the full exercise of the mind in the act of imagination). But the power of joy being possible only to a profound "organic sensibility", a man who experiences it will also suffer exceptionally. He must be lonely, haunted, victimized, devoted to suffering rather than action . . .' Though Barker's characters are not artists, the essential idea is the same. Those of them who stand at the centre of the play are clearly intended to be taken as people of a special sensibility', all of whom embrace loneliness and suffering voluntarily and regard such loneliness and suffering as essential parts of the struggle to understand the human dilemma. They are, in other words, part of the regular Romantic tradition which was there long before the Great War (the War itself being, in a way, the ghastly, grisly obverse of the same mode of experience).

Villiers de l'Isle-Adam's play *Axël* is worth noting in this context, so astonishingly close are some of the comparisons of actual utterance. Its convoluted and inflated style, its extravagantly Gothic atmosphere and its fairy-tale plot make it a work vastly different from *The Secret Life*. But that difference serves only to make the similarities all the more remarkable. Its central character, Axël, Count of Auersperg, having just killed his wordly and trivial-minded cousin in a duel, says:

> Passer-by, you have passed away. Here you are sinking down into the Unthinkable. During your days of narrow self-sufficiency you were nothing but a dross of animal instincts refractory to all divine selection! Nothing ever *called* you from the Beyond! And you have fulfilled yourself. You fall to the depth of Death like a stone into a void – without attraction and without goal.[9]

This play was begun in either 1869 or 1870, only four or five years after the first performance of *Tristan und Isolde* and only a year or so after its author had met Wagner; and Villiers worked on it for nearly twenty years. The play is too over-blown for modern taste, almost ludicrously luxuriant in its symbols and imagery, some of which would strike a modern audience – if one could possibly imagine its ever coming to performance in modern times – as naïve and even a little trite. Nevertheless, its hero and heroine (she is more impressive than he is), Axël and Sara, are together the very prototype of the triumphal retreat into death and the play's influence has been very considerable and very widely disseminated. The early plays of Jean Anouilh show it, for instance; plays like *L'Hermine* (1931) and *La Sauvage* (1934). W.B. Yeats saw *Axël* in 1894 in Paris and was greatly impressed by it: 'Now, that I have read it all again in Mr. Finberg's translation and recalled that first impression', he wrote in his Preface to the English edition published in 1925, 'I can see how those symbols became a part of me, and for years to come dominated my imagination.' Barker, with his particular interest in Maeterlinck and the French Symbolists, must almost certainly have known the play and it does not seem to me too fanciful to suppose that, directly or indirectly, consciously or unconsciously, it may well have exerted an influence on *The Secret Life*, even though it was not published in English until eighteen months after Barker's play. (Barker, in any case, read French well.)

Contemporary comment, at the time of the publication of *The Secret Life*, tended to concentrate upon its 'difficulty' and 'obscurity'. W.A. Darlington, in the *Daily Telegraph*[10] said: 'I understand it well enough to realize that I had been introduced to a group of brilliantly drawn characters – characters who were worth the careful craftsmanship and the depth of imagination that had gone to their fashioning; but I felt, as Mr. William Archer confessed that he always felt when reading *The Marrying of Ann Leete*, that the reasons for the sayings and doings of the characters was utterly enigmatic.' He goes on to say that a second reading made the play's meaning clearer to him and confirmed the impression made rather vaguely by the first reading – 'that here we have a piece of work right above and beyond the scope of most of our leading playwrights, but a piece of work so devoid of the fundamental stage virtue of clarity that I can hardly imagine that it could be successfully produced in the theatre except before an audience of people who, like me, have read the text through carefully twice before the curtain rose.' St. John Ervine, in *The Observer* of September 30, 1923, took the same line: '*The Secret Life* is almost as long as *Hamlet*. It is much harder to understand. I will confess that when I read it for the first time, I had not the slightest idea of what it was about. It has passages of great charm, and the dialogue has a lean strength that is very attractive; but the play, as a whole, is obscure. . . . If it is hard to understand in the book, where one can turn back and re-read, how much more hard will it be to understand in performance, where the mind must be reached immediately or not at all?' However, St. John Ervine had an axe to grind: he was one of those who felt that Barker had deserted his *real* work and he makes the point very forcefully in his *Observer* review that Barker ought to be out in the theatre, directing plays and saving it, body and soul, instead of wasting his time in idle luxury writing unactable closet drama. (For his pains in this regard he drew from Barker an icy, acid letter,[11] marked PRIVATE, telling him, in effect, to mind his own damn' business; and adding: 'As to the S.L. I am mischievously tempted to tell you to read it *twice* more and to read it as you would read – if you could – an orchestral symphony.')

In that same letter, Barker also suggests – rather echoing the argument of his article in the *Quarterly Review* of July 1923 (see Chapter 9, p. 274) – that 'even such plays as *The Secret Life*, which for all their shortcomings may serve, if only by example, to set actors new problems and to widen the theatre's appeal. It needs widening.' And this seems to me a just defence. In terms of an easy and pleasant evening in the theatre, *The Secret Life* suffered in comparison with such contemporaries as A.A. Milne's *Dover Road* or *Mr. Pim Passes By* (neither of them bad plays, in their way). It acquired early the reputation for being 'difficult' and 'unactable' – the latter point drawing a mysterious sustenance from Barker's alleged 'desertion', as if there were a sort of underlying logic in believing that a man who deserted the theatre would naturally write unactable plays out of a sort of revenge. The reputation as to its unactability grew and stuck and in due time the play accreted unto itself the additional disadvantage of being 'out-of-date', 'old-fashioned', and so on. Consequently it has never really been seriously considered from the theatrical point of view, the natural conservatism of theatre audiences combining with the natural timidity of theatre managers and producers to ensure that, such plays having been successfully locked in the closet, they be permanently left there. Yet there is everything about the text of *The Secret Life* to suggest that it would live triumphantly in the theatre, given the right handling. Not that it could be made into a lightly pleasant piece, or a softly optimistic one. Beneath its urbane and civilized exterior the play is austere, severe, uncompromising as granite. It has something of Maeterlinck's 'drama of stasis' in it (and Barker much admired Maeterlinck) but nothing of the submissiveness of the Belgian playwright's gentle melancholy. It is finely and richly wrought and is – despite neglect and calumny – theatrically sound as a bell. It exists vividly in and for the medium for which it was created. But it makes no concessions to popular conceptions. Its soul is its own: cold, hard, difficult to reach; forbidding, even. Its reward is in the feeling it has of absolute authenticity. In a word, it is true.

Barker finished *The Secret Life* in 1922 and almost immediately began the composition of *His Majesty*. On the face of it, there seems to be no connection between the two: they could, on the face of it, hardly be more different from each other. *His Majesty* has a plotful of action (that is to say, surface occurrences) of an almost Ruritanian kind – complete with ruined chateaux, lost causes, brave women in distress and fancy uniforms. It is a perfectly serious play, nevertheless; and a sombre one. And it takes up, yet again, the theme which haunts *The Secret Life* – the risk of the disintegration of the ego behind the public façade. But with two differences: first, there is this time no hammering at 'the door of this sex question' – that aspect of the matter is scarcely touched upon; and secondly, it has at its end a much more robust, sturdy note of wary optimism – a kind of toughness of vision – than *The Secret Life* could manage.

His Majesty is the play in which Barker most nearly succeeded in translating his dominant theme of the protecting of the essential self, the secret life, into a complete and all-embracing metaphor which could operate, fable-like, at the level of plot and story while also containing within itself a series of subsidiary, contributory images which support and illuminate the main, central theme. This fable or tale or legend, which acquires myth-like proportions and properties, is the story of an abdication. The contributory images which throng the play are of military retreats and withdrawals, secret and half-secret diplomatic negotiations in which the right hand is not permitted to know what the left hand doeth, individual lives which face the constant choice of overt declaration or clandestine belief. The fable of the play has as its central figure King Henry XIII of Carpathia, who has been compelled by 'the war' (of 1914–18 is the inference we draw, but the further in time that we move away from that particular piece of lunacy the less it matters which war the play is talking about) to flee from his throne and his country, leaving the latter to be governed by the leaders of some kind of plebian revolution. When the play begins King Henry and his queen, Rosamund, are living in exile in Switzerland; and Carpathia, desperately divided, is on the brink of civil war. The King is hesitating as to where his duty lies. To renounce royalty and government and begin to build, at last and for the first time, a real, personal life? Or to return to Carpathia, re-establish himself on the throne – by force if need be – and thus prevent disintegration and civil strife? But would it, in fact, prevent it? Or would there not rather be the risk of its being aggravated and prolonged by his presence? While he is still hesitating, a young royalist nobleman raises an army and threatens to march on Carpathia in support of King Henry's return whether King Henry authorizes and blesses the venture or not. This would certainly cause civil war, or even war on a wider scale. The King feels that his hand has been forced; he decides to return in order to do what he can to control Count Stephen Czernyak, the young nobleman, and to prevent bloodshed. But he makes it clear to everyone that he has no intention of staying permanently or of returning to the throne of Carpathia. Once back in his own country and established at a secret headquarters in the house of Count Czernyak's mother, who was once the Queen's principal lady-in-waiting and now gladly resumes that position, King Henry begins complicated negotiations with Madrassy, the head of the revolutionary government, trying to ensure that the threatening noises which Czernyak is making do not provoke the government into violent action which would itself set off the civil war. Again he is frustrated by events: Czernyak, tired of waiting for decisions and in spite of his promise to wait the King's command, secretly begins the march on the capital with his royalist army. Even in these circumstances the King manages to stay in control of the situation. He discovers that Madrassy and the government army are very reluctant to fight and he then succeeds in persuading Czernyak not to attack first. An armistice is arranged and signed. The King, having accomplished what he came to do, prepares to leave the country once more and for the last time. He then discovers that the government will allow him to depart only on one condition, failing which they will hold him prisoner. The condition is that he sign a deed of abdication. He himself sees that this is inevitable and has few regrets – though some. Queen Rosamund, however, who has throughout approached the matter with a much less sophisticated and complex response than has King Henry, is heartbroken at what she regards as an absolute defeat. 'I could have done my duty here', she says: 'You're either a queen or you're not. I'm no use as anything else.' But he has to sign, nevertheless; and she has no choice but to accompany him when he finally leaves to go into exile.

A plain enough tale, plainly told. The language has neither the luxuriance nor the highly-charged allusiveness of *The Secret Life*. Barker relies entirely upon the accuracy, subtlety and profundity of his character-drawing to communicate the inner essence of the play. And his confidence is not misplaced: the interaction of the various figures in the play, the delicacy and sureness of their relationships, the total credibility of both their foibles and their beliefs, have resonances far beyond the importance of the tale itself. Nor is it true that the play is a 'play of ideas', though it contains many ideas. Its main gesture is not socio-political: it is metaphysical. It is a play about the journey of the soul. And the legend authentically works at that level as well as at the more obvious levels. The sense the work has of successfully existing simultaneously on several planes is very pronounced and is strongly reminiscent of Chekhov.

There is about the character-drawing, too, something distinctly

Chekhovian, especially in the cases of some of the minor characters, which are lovingly detailed, used for limited purposes and for one or two scenes only and then dispensed with; and yet are ruggedly three-dimensional and vividly alive while they *are* present. They are like Chekhov figures, too, in the sense they bear of being the unwitting and inadvertent victims of clumsy and stupid circumstances. There is, for example, a lovely portrait of a small-town mayor who comes to try to bargain about the conditions upon which the troops – of either side – would occupy his town. He is a humble man trying to do, in difficult circumstances, the job he was appointed to do, trying in the process to be both efficient and compassionate and finding it a difficult combination. He is a small-town man who has never been able to afford the luxury of an imagination, a simple man with a simple man's commonsense, down-to-earth view of things but with something of a natural turn for the philosophic.

King Henry is the most attractive of Barker's men of action. Not as polemically brilliant as Trebell, nor as doggedly virtuous as Edward Voysey, he is more resilient than either of them and more mature. He is urbane, wise and witty and never expects too much. He comes to see that public life *inevitably*, of its very nature, means chicanery and the essential loss of innocence; yet through the double-dealing of the armistice proceedings and the abdication he manages to preserve both an honour and a humanity. One of the most engaging things about him as a character – and one of the most important about him as symbol and metaphor – is his awareness of the integrity and importance of other people's lives. They may be utterly different from him and his life; they may, for that matter, be opposed to him and his objectives; but he nevertheless seems to find them continually interesting and valuable. As a personal trait this is extremely winning and agreeable and it creates a warmth and a light at the centre of the play: but, more significantly, this generous temper in the King does much to advance the sense one has – in this play far more than in any other of Barker's – of a vast, outspreading panorama of other secret lives surrounding the 'main' one (that is to say, the one we happen to have chosen for the centre of our particular picture). This gives to *His Majesty* an expansiveness not present in its predecessors: the world which Strowde rejects is represented, in the play at least, chiefly by figures whose life-gestures are the opposite of Strowde's and the same clear dichotomy is there in *The Wicked Man* and *The Voysey Inheritance* and *The Marrying of Ann Leete*; but the world which King Henry rejects, though it does include men like Bruckner, also includes Madrassy (whose point of view is not unlike the King's) and all those village Hampdens who make brief appearances in the play (Bakay, the Mayor, Jakab, and others) but who seem to bring with them a great cloud of witnesses – the little lives of all the world: and who dares to say that they should all be rejected as worthless? And yet, *somehow* their importunity must be put aside if the secret life is to be preserved inviolate. But the same is true also of and for them: they also have, or may have, a secret life to save. The image which the play throws up is a much more complex, sophisticated one, as a result, than Barker has ever managed before, much more iridescent: it is not only that the canvas seems wider than ever before and composed of more colours – muted, shifting, changing – but also that the picture gives the impression of stretching beyond the canvas itself to include a great segment of the living, ambivalent world. The world must be rejected and kept at arm's length so that the individual life may survive in the secret silences; and yet, not *all* the world must be rejected and not always or all ways. It is in this enormously complex and ambivalent vision of things that the radical originality of *His Majesty* resides. And it is, of course, this complexity and ambivalence which reminds one so strongly, in this play, of Chekhov. It used to be popular in the 'thirties to compare Ronald Mackenzie's two plays, *Musical Chairs* and *The Maitlands*, with Chekhov; and in the 'fifties the same comparison seemed apt for some of the plays of N.C. Hunter, more particularly *A Day by the Sea* and *The Waters of the Moon*. Indeed, there is some justice still in those comparisons; but nothing of Hunter's or Mackenzie's is half so truly Chekhovian as is Granville Barker's *His Majesty*. It is, moreover, a sign of the play's structural strength that it can give such authenticity and importance to a host of minor characters without fragmenting the over-all effect or blurring or decreasing the very necessary stature of the central figure. The reverse, in fact: King Henry's life is curiously locked into an eternally living pattern with the lives of these little, casually-come-across people whom we see only once and whom he will never see again: and the ultimate life of the play depends upon this integration.

One must look at *His Majesty* as a companion-piece to *The Secret Life*. One is all action, the other all introspection, but their central dichotomies are the same. *His Majesty* lacks the fierce intensity of *The Secret Life* but has a surer, deeper and wider sense of an entire world brought to the play's canvas. *The Secret Life* is, structurally, a series of brilliant 'main scenes'; set pieces, one might almost say; *His Majesty* is a continuous weaving of an intricate pattern in which the texture is more even throughout. In spite of the chances offered by its Ruritanian plot, there is a good deal less bravura in *His Majesty* than in *The Secret Life*. Both plays – John Russell Taylor[12] and a number of other critics notwithstanding – are profoundly theatrical pieces and would, if their intrinsic difficulties were firmly tackled, play extremely well. Neither has, in fact, ever been played. I am as certain as one can reasonably be that the neglect of them is accidental. They were neglected in their own time by accident, the accident of Barker's reputation of having withdrawn scornfully from the theatre. (What theatre is going to produce the plays of a man who has slighted the profession and has, the Legend says, turned his back on it?) And the habit of rejection has stuck ever since. Now, over fifty years later, when not many plays from the nineteen-twenties are produced anyway, it does not occur to anybody to consider for production two plays which are known to have been branded, even in their own immediate time, as 'closet dramas'. But brandings can sometimes be wrong and I think this one is.

A drawing of Barker made in 1912 by W. Strang and signed by Barker himself.

Man and Artist

*E*dward M. Moore, in his Introduction to *More Prefaces to Shakespeare* (which was edited by him in 1974), says of Barker that he will be remembered 'chiefly as an actor, playwright, director, and critic, but his major importance clearly lies in the latter two'. Bernard Shaw, on the other hand, in his obituary article in the Winter 1946 issue of *Drama* says:

> . . . his original contributions to our dramatic literature are treasures to be preserved, not compromising documents to be destroyed.
>
> In what has been written lately, too much has been said of him as a producer, too little as an actor, and much too little as an author.

And this was by no means the first time that Shaw had expressed such a view. Writing in *Strand Magazine* in February 1906, when Barker was only 27, Shaw said: 'Mr. Granville Barker's play, *The Voysey Inheritance*, which shows a mastery that threatens to put us all on the shelf, is a single situation in five acts, maintaining itself for three hours at the pitch an ordinary "constructed" play attains for about five minutes at the end of the last act but one.'

The argument is, perhaps, a rather futile one: was his most important and significant work that of critic, or playwright, or director, or actor? None of them solely, I think. His greatness (and it *was* such) was in his imaginative perception of the relation of theatre, at its best, to life and the arts, in his recognition – both instinctive and intellectual – of what its best was, and in his astonishing capacity for turning the force of that imaginative perception into so many different, though related, channels. It showed equally in his directing and in his acting and in his writing, both critical and creative. He was a complete *homme de théâtre*, equally at home in all the theatre's aspects and branches. Equally: for to him they were all, at their highest levels, part of the same thing and part of each other. He *felt* the rightness of great theatre and he communicated that feeling to others in all his approaches to the art, from whatever angle. He had a better intuitive understanding of both theatre and drama (and note his own beautiful exactitude in distinguishing the use of these two words) than any other English-speaking theatre artist of the twentieth century. He took the theatre immensely seriously, but was neither solemn nor pompous about it. Quite apart from artistic sensibilities and perceptions, however, he was also a craftsman of the highest order and had a truly amazing capacity for learning new crafts: his craftsmanship as a play-wright is as great as his craftsmanship as a director; his directorial skill, though immense, was not greater than his skill as an actor had been, according to contemporary accounts; his critical craftsmanship, acquired later, developed swiftly and became masterly. With major achievements to his credit in four or five different fields, it is his comprehensiveness and the ultimate unity of his vision that makes Granville Barker unique.

He created, virtually single-handed, the position of 'director' and his attitudes to the careful treating of the play, to the integrity of the text, to the obligation to follow the author's intention and to the choosing of challenging, serious and vital plays in the first place, all deeply affected the views and gave support and encouragement to the work of such pioneer directors as B. Iden Payne, W. Bridges-Adams, Barry Jackson, Lewis Casson and Norman Marshall. The example which Barker set at the Royal Court, the Little and the Kingsway had a direct bearing and influence upon the development of serious-minded theatres in the big provincial cities – the Birmingham 'Rep.', Miss Horniman's company at the Manchester Gaiety, the Playhouse at Liverpool, all of which began their work during the ten years immediately following Barker's season at the Court. And, less directly but no less certainly, he had a very considerable influence, by way both of precept and example, on the growth of the 'Little Theatre' movement after the First World War. This movement brought to the amateur theatre of Britain the same serious interest in significant plays and in theatre as a cultural force that the provincial 'reps.' were bringing to the professional theatre. Organizations such as the Maddermarket Theatre at Norwich, the Crescent Theatre at Birmingham, the Unnamed Society of Manchester, the Civic Theatre at Bradford and the People's Theatre at Newcastle-upon-Tyne

Fu Desmond

July 1937

I liked your valediction to Barrie: yes,
thank you. The best I've seen by far
—except the T.L.S. I do think that
beats you by a head or so, by its 'jury-like'
point. But you none of you take much account
of his activity —which gives me most pleasure.
But who does care for that in Whitehall now?
I suppose "art pour art's sake" puts us off it. A
pity! 'Art pour art's sake' was morbid activity.
There is, after all, a hand which is fruitful.
which makes the subject more fruitful. And
Barrie was that hand. Study the best of his
work, and how full of life it is!

Barker's handwriting in 1937.

achieved standards of performance not too far short of the best of professional production and brought to the notice of the more adventurous theatregoer scores of fine plays, both native and foreign, that never would have reached the boards otherwise. Barker, as the first chairman of the newly-founded British Drama League (which began its work in 1919) lent the lustre of his reputation and the valuable advice deriving from his experience to the new movement and exercised considerable influence in consequence. In support of the idea of a country-wide network of theatres organized on a semi-amateur, semi-professional basis, Barker wrote a short article for *The Times* in 1919 (published on February 20 of that year). In it, he said:

> Amid much reconstruction, plans for the future of the drama are emerging, and are concerned, not with the theatre of the West-end of London – where the problem is purely financial – but with enterprise which may transcend the professional theatre altogether.
>
> . . .
>
> We have been apt to think of the drama, in its lower reaches as mere tomfoolery, in its higher as a Cinderella-sister to literature. But a recognition that the art of acting is, in externals, the art of public manners and in essentials the art of self-expression, would relate it far more closely to social life. This recognition is innate in the upspringing of these companies of players.

He developed this idea further in 1927 when, as one of the principal witnesses to be interviewed by a Board of Education committee on Drama in Adult Education, he said:

> But the striking thing about the present revival of interest in drama – as apart from interest in the professional theatre – is the liking of plays for their own sake and therefore, more often than not, the liking of good plays. I suspect that the amateur clubs of my youth still go on, and perform out-of-date West-End successes, in which feeble imitations are given of the popular favourites who first played in them. But the strength of the movement lies in a variety of organisations of very recent origin, quite unrelated to these in their purpose or the taste they show. I do not think they pay very much regard to the fashions in professional drama either. I believe – though it may be because I wish to believe – that here is a genuine artistic up-growth and an endeavour not merely after self-expression, but after the far more complex co-operative expression that drama provides. Here in fact is a genuine and creative interest in a highly organic art.[1]

Himself a professional to his very fingertips, he nevertheless recognized the value of good amateur work. He tended to take the word 'amateur' in its basic, literal sense of 'done for the love of the thing' and, in this sense,

*Two views of
Netherton Hall.*

he was the perfect typification of the amateur approach himself. A great deal of nonsense has been talked about (and by!) those engaged in the pursuit of amateur theatre, but there can be no denying that the Little Theatre movement which began on a mainly amateur basis during the second and third decades of the present century has been one of the significant forces in the moulding of – and raising the standard of – public taste in the matter of plays and the theatre; and Barker's part in promoting this movement, though less spectacular than some of his other contributions to British theatre, is far from negligible. Similarly influential has been his life-long advocacy of the 'true repertory' system and the allied idea of a National Theatre. Though many forces united to bring the National Theatre of Great Britain at last into being and to encourage the growth of the Royal Shakespeare Company as a parallel organization of equal (some might even say greater) importance, Barker's personal experiments in the repertory method, combined with the massive and quite irrefutable logic of his frequently-expressed arguments in its favour, were certainly not among the least of these. Still in the sphere of practical theatre, I would designate Granville Barker the founder of a whole school of Shakespearean production, more influential – as was suggested in Chapter 7 – than either Poel or Craig. His work in the field of Shakespeare criticism influenced general methods of approach more than it changed interpretative views of particular plays. Certainly he was responsible for shifting the emphasis of purely scholarly-academic criticism towards a greater consideration of the play as a theatre piece; equally, I think, he moved the more thoughtful of practical theatre directors towards an acceptance of the true products of enlightened scholarship.

In the matter of his stature as a dramatist there has been more debate and division of opinion. Allardyce Nicoll, writing in 1973[2], describes Barker as 'the pet of a creative literary coterie' and says about his plays:

As a dramatist, then, his reputation must depend on just three plays. The first of these, *The Marrying of Ann Leete* (1902), with its complex story which ends with the heroine, a well-brought-up, relatively rich girl, suddenly calling out to the family's gardener with an inquiry as to whether he will marry her, completely baffled those who saw it at the Royalty in 1902, and it must prove as baffling to readers today. In a vague kind of way we can see what the author was aiming at but it is impossible to think that this is an important drama. Thus, in the end, we come down to two works, *The Voysey Inheritance,* presenting its pathetic picture of an honest Edward Voysey who, inheriting his father's business, finds that it has been built up on trickery and deceit, and *The Madras House*, with its kindred picture of an idealistic young man thwarted by the force of society. These unquestionably are both works which we cannot ignore, yet even here we find ourselves confronted by doubts, since neither has had a distinguished playhouse career. . . .

Nicoll goes on to remark, about *The Secret Life* and *His Majesty*, that 'they appear to have been composed with little or no thought of possible theatrical presentation', which is not only insensitive criticism but bad history. Barker's letters to Archer, to Nicholas Hannen and to St. John Ervine give the specific lie to this statement and more general comments from him elsewhere in his writings support that denial. Nicoll's view, on the other hand, is fairly widespread, though there are signs here and there now of a revival of interest in Barker's plays and of a greater appreciation of their real qualities.

This dismissing of Barker-as-dramatist is in sharp contrast with a great deal of the critical comment of his own day, much of which – especially when attempting to sum up several of his plays – rated him very highly indeed. P.P. Howe, in an article called 'The Plays of Granville Barker' in the *Fortnightly Review* for September, 1913[3], has, among other things, this to say:

> In a play by Mr. Granville Barker the things that emerge serve to suggest much more beneath, and in this much more, apprehended but perhaps not fully comprehended, the play's real unity lies.
>
> This building of a play cell by living cell, as it were, goes a good way to achieve a living organism; and it is the fact that Mr. Barker's plays have extraordinary life. What are the scenes in them which remain most clearly in the memory? Certainly those of the Voysey family summoned to the dining-room to hear the truth about the old man they have just put, with every circumstance of honour, into the grave; of the meeting of prospective ministers to decide what is to be done about Trebell; of the third-act gathering beneath the rotunda of the Madras House, whither the American financier has come to negotiate a purchase and whence he does not depart until he has enjoyed as stimulating a conversation as he can remember. Each of these scenes shows clearly what one means by the achievement of group-emotion. They show the art of Mr. Barker at its best. Each person in them, while a true person studied with the intimate humorous care we have noted, lives, not for his own sake, but for the sake of the scene. This is the triumph of dramatic characterisation.

'In its deliberate courting of the difficult', says Howe, 'Mr. Barker's is a definitely experimental drama; we may say that he is the first definite experimentalist in the modern English theatre.' He contrasts Barker's methods with those of other dramatists:

Similarly, the true answer to Constantine's 'You are a poet, Mr. State,' is Mr. State's answer, 'I never wrote one in my life, sir;' but it is not the answer another dramatist would have thought of. This, then, is the first of this dramatist's discoveries, that we really speak like that, rather than like a newspaper, as Sir Arthur Pinero would have us think that we speak. We may say of Mr. Barker, slightly varying what was said of another, 'He has an ear.'

Barker is rated in Howe's article as *the* leading modern playwright, at a time when Shaw was producing one or two plays a year and was already represented by *Man and Superman, Major Barbara, The Doctor's Dilemma, John Bull's Other Island* and *Candida*, among a growing number of other plays. Archibald Henderson, Shaw's first biographer, in his *European Dramatists* (New York: Appleton, 1913) deals with only seven playwrights – Ibsen, Maeterlinck, Shaw, Wilde, Strindberg, Schnitzler and Barker – and treats Barker as at least Shaw's equal, as well as being of the same general stature as the other six. Ashley Dukes, in *Modern Dramatists* (London: Frank Palmer, 1911), writes short essays on each of nineteen European dramatists: only three are British and one of those three is Granville Barker (the other two being Shaw and Galsworthy). A.E. Morgan, in *Tendencies of Modern English Drama* (London: Constable, 1924) has a whole chapter on Barker and begins his summing up at the end of the chapter with the words: 'Mr. Barker's contribution to English drama is certainly important . . .' And three years before Professor Morgan's book was published, Ludwig Lewisohn, reviewing (in the New York magazine *The Nation* of November 16, 1921) the first American production of *The Madras House* had this to say:

> It has remained for the Neighbourhood Playhouse to give the first American production of *The Madras House*. That production makes several things clear at once: the play 'plays'; its technical innovations, to which I shall return presently, are as fresh and suggestive as when the play was composed; its intellectual problem has not only survived its decade and the next but has gained point, force, pertinence. An infinite number of plays have been written on the relations of the sexes. But none except *The Madras House* has called attention to the pervasive and voluntary sexuality of the whole of Western civilization. Such is the intellectual content of *The Madras House*. But I am acquainted with few modern plays in which that content is more skilfully or unobtrusively handled or is more firmly and delicately woven into the concrete texture of those human lives which make the play.
> . . .

Re-reading the plays in chronological order, one is struck all over again by the astonishing rapidity with which Barker's sureness of touch developed. The plays at their best (and, for that matter, in many moments when they are *not* at their best) display a theatrical aptitude and energy of a very high order; and the radically experimental, innovative quality of the dialogue noted by Ludwig Lewisohn and P.P. Howe (among others), is everywhere apparent. But, as well, craft and technical accomplishment apart, there runs through all of them a unifying vision – sombre, melancholy, intense; idealistic, élitist, haunted by absolutes and the longing for absolutes; pivoted on the phenomenon of sex; driven towards a secret world which alone – for him – can provide the soul's salvation, a refuge from the existential anarchy and chaos. There is an eerie sense in which Barker's artistic progress actually *needed* the First World War in order to make complete its pattern of gloomy prescience, hinted at in *The Voysey Inheritance*, developed in *Waste, The Madras House* and *The Wicked Man* and completed by the War itself and the two plays which came out of it – *The Secret Life* and *His Majesty*. Barker stands in roughly the same relationship to that War as Samuel Beckett and John Whiting do to the Second World War – and a different relationship, be it noted, from that of Shaw, or the German Expressionists, or nostalgic factualists like R.C. Sherriff. His vision was essentially poetic and a-political and he developed a technique which, at its best, perfectly expressed that vision.

   J.B. Priestley, in *The Edwardians* (London: Heinemann, 1970) describes Barker as 'one of the most original and intelligent English dramatists of this century' and 'the most important figure in the Edwardian Theatre'. Margaret Webster, on the other hand, in her *The Same Only Different* (London: Gollancz, 1969 – p. 238) makes a curious, myopic, rather condescending speculation as to the *reason* for Barker's ever becoming a playwright in the first place: not for her any frippery about poetic vision or inner compulsion:

> When Vedrenne ran out of money at the Court Theatre it seemed as if Granville Barker's experiments had been indefinitely blocked. His career as a producer was frustrated, and this had forced him to turn to playwrighting. He was learning to be a dramatist of power. But he had one overriding ambition, and he never lost sight of it as long as he himself remained active on the stage: to found a British National Theatre, playing repertory. In 1910 an American manager, Charles Frohman, gave him the backing he needed. He leased the Duke of York's Theatre and prepared to try again.

She seems to me to have got it carefully wrong in almost every particular, including the spelling of 'play-writing'. But the most curious comment of all upon Barker as a dramatist comes from the man who so much admired Barker the actor and director: C.B. Purdom. In a paragraph[4] which, though short, is crammed with self-contradictions, odd juxtapos- itions, and platitudes so bland as to be breathtaking, he seems almost to be parodying himself and the very craft of criticism:

> The last two plays show that Barker's is a subjective drama – the drama within the soul – which indeed is the only true drama. Subjective drama is the drama of reality as was the Greek classic drama and the drama of Shakespeare. Barker was not fully master of it because his own drama was unresolved, while the nature of drama as an art is that the problems it presents, always personal, are always resolved – in tragedy through death, in comedy by comic reversal. Barker was obsessed by what he called factualness. In his struggle with facts, attempting to bring them into order, he lost himself for want of a guiding principle.

This, so far as I can make out, means absolutely nothing at all. It certainly has nothing at all to do with the plays of Granville Barker. It is not, in fact, the function of 'drama as an art' to 'present problems' nor is it true, in the sense in which he uses the word, that problems are 'always resolved'. True, there *is* a sense of resolution at the end of a good play, but is it a complex and sophisticated response, akin to the aesthetic satisfac- tion of hearing the dominant move finally to the tonic at the end of a symphony, and not in the least akin to the satisfactory solving of per- sonal problems; the drama (by very definition) moves not to a solution but to a final system of poised dichotomies, brought at the end into an exquisite pattern of equilibrium, sustained stasis. Why Purdom should remark that 'subjective drama is the drama of reality', I do not know: *all* good drama is the drama of reality, or at least of some facet of it. I see no evidence that 'Barker was obsessed' by what Purdom calls 'factualness' and I know of no letter, book or article in which Barker uses the word 'factualness'. The word is Purdom's own. It is certainly untrue that he lost himself in his attempts to bring facts 'into order': it was one of the things in which his technical accomplishment was most assured. The assembling of the facts of the political manoeuvres in *Waste* and of the sheer detail of Church disestablishment in that play are absolutely mas- terly, as is the organization of the many disparate items of subject-matter (including how to run a drapery business) in *The Madras House*. His grasp of legal niceties in *The Voysey Inheritance* and of revolutionary stratagems in *His Majesty*, are equally impressive. I suspect that the key to this whole extraordinary paragraph is in its last phrase – 'he lost himself for want of a guiding principle': Purdom desperately needs to believe this in order to make the main thesis of his book work, the thesis which claims that Barker ought never really to have been writing plays at all but should, instead, have been directing them. So Purdom talks himself into believing what his theory needs him to believe, and then goes searching for evidence of the truth of his belief – and finds it in odd places.

On the evidence of the work itself, it seems to me that Granville Barker was as great a playwright as he was a director – perhaps even greater. And that he was a great director is beyond question. Nor can one reasonably doubt the uniqueness and the importance of his *Prefaces to Shakespeare*. The five volumes of them are, together, a major contribution not only to Shakespeare criticism but to theatre studies generally. The truth is that he performed with equal felicity and facility in all three fields, as well as being, apparently, a fine actor. His prose writing, Shakespeare criticism apart, is less important, though fresh and lively and not unentertaining. The idea which he himself perhaps harboured – that he was meant to be 'a writer' – was (supposing he really *did* believe it) misplaced, if he meant by it that *all* his writing and only his writing mattered. There is some evidence, especially in the letters to Helen, that such was his belief. Helen herself carried this notion of him even further. She once said to a French immigration official: 'Il n'est pas un auteur: il est un homme de lettres'[5]. But he wasn't. He was, as I have already said, essentially, in everthing he did, to the very end, *un homme de théâtre*, even if, in the final stages, he became a little dispirited and the gesture flagged a little.

Even when he was at the height of his powers he was given, as was remarked in an earlier chapter, to sudden changes from optimism to despair; and though in later life he concealed this more and controlled it better, it was, judging by his letters, a characteristic of his temperament throughout his life. There was a strong streak of melancholy in his nature and, though it was not always dominant, it was never very far from the surface. One incident and one relationship stand out as exceptions to this statement. The relationship was his friendship with Gilbert Murray, especially in its early stages. The incident was a holiday which they took together in 1905. They went to Greece and Asia Minor and the letters[6] they exchanged while planning the journey, and those of happy reminiscence after they returned, are still both delightful and amusing to read. They quite obviously enjoyed each other's company enormously: the letters, from both of them, bubble over with gaiety and high spirits. Barker, in particular, seems to have been irrepressibly happy about the whole occasion: one of his letters to Murray after they got back consists almost entirely of comic verse of various kinds – limericks, rhyming couplets, quatrains, all concerned with the things they had seen and the places they had visited – and making fun of Murray's hay fever and his vegetarianism. Perhaps the beginning of the letter is worth quoting:

My dear Murray,

My old friend Baksheesh Pasha – he was Baksheesh Bey in those days – used to remark to me that a sign of high civilization both in men and states was the non-payment of debts. Ah, many is the argument we have had round the camp-fire in the summer of '78 with Hornbeam Bey snoring in the shadow of the tent, Ah, well, I shall see neither of them again. But the point of this little anecdote is, my dear Murray, that I find myself in your debt to the extent of to wit i.e. viz. q.v. (sic) passim:

1 Hairless Author
1 Hairless shaving brush
2 bottles of Pope Roach (these will be kept, for if Shaw worries me much more I must cross to Ireland and beard him in his Derry).
1 Constantinople bag – or 17 francs (Take my advice and the 17 francs)

a demi-portion of sundry monies expended by you upon creature comforts and discomforts in the latter part of our Rush across Europe (see the Star for Aug. 3). Kindly furnish an abstract of these same and oblige.

Yours faithfully,

BARKER AND BOUNCER
per H.G.B.

I next must call your attention to the fact that
There was a young man of Geneva
Who suffered a deal from hayfever
He sneezed and he snoze
Till be bust all his clothes
So his wife says. But you can't believe her.

I should also add that
The Haigite[7] is an awful brute
It feeds on milk and nuts and fruit
It never smokes, it seldom steals
It never drinks between its meals.
I wouldn't be a nasty Haig-it
No, not for all the wealth I may git
By writing verses like this 'ere
Gimme a steak and a bottle of beer.

Rather wanklin[8]. You were quite right: I don't quite know the meaning of what I've been saying. And then there's the drive wanted behind the whole thing, which comes but by prayer and fasting. I don't know how to pray and I can't fast for it gives me pains. Shaw writes me that Adolphus Cusins 'Quotes screeds of the Bacchae' (I knew it'd be the Bacchae – Blow the Bacchae!)

What are you doing – the Electra? When am I going to see that? Have you any further ideas about the music? Who is to break the matter to Miss Farr? Someone must steal her psalteries first for we shall want them. Of course, I'll ask her to come and play and chant someone else's music. She won't even answer that. Oh Lor!

Years afterwards, in 1921, Barker, in a letter to William Archer, recalled that holiday with evident pleasure and said, 'My voyage to the Mediterranean with him is red-lettered' – and that was sixteen years later. It is probably safe to say that Barker was more thoroughly at ease with Murray, especially during the ten years between 1904 and 1914, than he ever again was with anyone, for the rest of his life.

His loyalty to old friends was very touching. Jessica Tandy, who played Cordelia in the 1940 *King Lear*, told me that Barker, when he arrived in London to take over the direction of rehearsals, quietly made arrangements for a very old actor (unfortunately she could not remember his name and I have failed to identify him from the programme of the production) to play one of the walk-on parts: the actor was someone who had worked with Barker in the Court Theatre days, thirty-five years before, and was now in need of work. Barker saw that, for a little while at any rate, he got it. And J. Dover Wilson, in an essay called 'Memoirs of Harley Granville Barker and Two of his Friends'[9], tells of Barker's long-standing attachment for J.M. Barrie. Barrie and Barker had been close friends immediately preceding and during the 1914–18 War: Barrie, in fact, was one of the first people to whom Barker introduced Helen when she came to London in 1918. Dover Wilson tells how the friendship was renewed in 1936:

And when Barrie's *The Boy David* . . . was first launched in Edinburgh, nothing would do but Harley must come over from Paris to see the premiere. When he told me this I, of course, engaged him for a talk to my Honors class. Barrie never saw the performances at all, since he lay in bed all the time groaning with lumbago at the Caledonian Hotel. There Harley, the morning after his arrival in Edinburgh, went to see him; and there I came to fetch him with a car . . . And the rain poured down. At last I said: 'Harley, you must get out, I'm afraid, and help push this bloody machine over the crest.' He was as usual beautifully dressed; but he was a hero. The job was done in a trice, and we were only a few minutes late for the lecture . . . He had a very deep affection for Barrie who, I suspect, must have befriended him as a young man. At any rate, after Barrie's death in 1937, he came once again all the way from

Paris to deliver the funeral oration in the Old Quad. Whether that tribute is extant, I don't know. I could wish it were, as it was a friendship's garland that would have pleased Barrie himself as it delighted all who heard it.

Dover Wilson himself was also an old friend remembered in loyalty. During the Second World War Barker became very anxious about the safety of friends in England and wrote several times to ask if various people were all right. Dover Wilson wrote back to New York to reassure Barker and, in passing, remarked: 'It's true our clothes are wearing out, and I've lost two watches since the war began (one trodden into the mud by the Home Guard), so I now have to borrow a watch from one of my students in case I should lecture too long to them . . .' Barker replied by return, saying: 'I wouldn't have your students listen to your pernicious nonsense about Shakespeare one second longer than necessary; I am therefore sending you by the next surface mail – not my second-best bedstead but my second-best watch.' In his essay, Dover Wilson goes on to say that it was a good watch, with only one defect: 'The only thing wrong about it is it doesn't like golf, gets out of order if I inadvertently wear it when I am playing. I don't think Harley played games, so it had never been properly trained.'

There were other contradictions in Barker's personality as well as his violent fluctuations from hope to despair and from gaiety to melancholy. Much has been made, by some commentators, for instance, of his love of luxury and of what his friends would deem his aristocratic spirit and his enemies would call his snobbishness; but this inclination towards the élite co-existed in him with a genuine reformer's zeal and a very real idealism. 'If we don't keep an aristocracy of some sort alive we're damned', he wrote to Cuthbert Headlam in 1928 – but he was talking of responsibilities rather than privileges. He thought – and there are dozens of incidents in his plays which bear this out – that humanity should be led by its best and bravest spirits: but he also thought that the social structure should be such that real quality should be able to come to the top no matter what or where its origin. His life-long interest in education was evidence of this belief and there were, throughout his life, many occasions upon which this interest issued into practical action. His membership of and work for the Fabian Society before the First World War, his work with the British Drama League, his service on various government committees in the 'twenties and 'thirties, his accepting the appointment of Director of the British Institute at the Sorbonne in 1937. In his 1922 book, *The Exemplary Theatre*, he devotes one whole chapter to a detailed description of a special kind of institution which would combine the functions of school and theatre. He sees the school not in any sense as a vocational training school for actors but as a kind of institute of humane liberal studies with the theatre as an exemplar: students would be admitted at the age of fifteen and would be forbidden to act 'until the last possible moment'. He sees the theatre section of the organization as being of the highest quality professional standards and as having two playhouses under one roof, both working continuously. What he effectively does, in fact, in this chapter of his book, is to construct a paradigm showing theatre's ideal place, as he sees it, in society and demonstrating incidentally the nature of the ties which existed, for him and in his own approach, between the theatre and education. His interest in education was not a casual one, was not something separate from, or a later substitute for, his passion for the theatre: they were closely related. The theatre was, ideally, both a badge of and a vehicle for that aristocracy of spirit in which he passionately believed; and education was the path – which everyone by birthright should be allowed to tread if he so chose – towards the aristocratic state.

There was a further ambivalence in Barker that might here be remarked and it is one which shows itself also in some of the central characters of his plays – he was clearly both fascinated and repelled, simultaneously, by fame and public life: he was fiercely ambitious and capable of prodigies of effort and endeavour, yet was also strongly attracted by ease and indolence and a quiet retreat. Yet again, his feelings on patriotism also illustrate the same kind of dichotomy. In June of 1914, when the signs were beginning to be plain for everyone to read, Barker wrote to Murray:

> Dear G.M.,
>   Thank you, Sir; that is about what I thought. Shades of Ruskin! But I am not happy, Sir. I see a Tory government juggling with tariffs . . . a quarrel with Germany over some blessed market in Kamschatka or the like and then a row . . . in which you or I or both of us will be shot . . . in the back? And I won't fight, Murray; and I don't want to be shot. I want to live at peace with Hauptmann and Wilamowitz.

And on September 12 of the same year, after the war had actually begun, he mentions this same idea again in another letter to Murray. He is returning some kind of petition or protest which Murray had asked him to sign, and about it he says: 'I sign it and would sign it with my blood if anything were to be gained by shedding it, even that much of it. And I can only hope some neutral person has heard of me. My principal

admirers are alien enemies . . .' Yet alongside this tough, rebellious
sense of the stupidity of it all there was in Barker also a simple, not to say
naïve, reverence and affection for England that even W.E. Henley himself would have a hard time matching. This comes out very clearly in the
1918 letters to Helen, in many of which Barker talks about the almost
mystical sense he has of 'being English'. As Dover Wilson says about the
Second World War, in the essay already mentioned: '. . . but he was
intensely patriotic and grew very miserable while the Battle of Britain
was going on . . .'

No wonder he was a dramatist! Life bisected itself before his eyes;
every issue and every experience came to him in the form of a carefully-
poised dichotomy and life lived in him as a series of eternal confrontations: he saw everything double, and divided. Life – right down to its
very roots – was, his spontaneous sense and vision of it told him, an
inevitable, irreducible conflict, a division in nature, with the two halves
of his own nature on either side of the chasm.

*   *   *

There is, in his Introduction to the first volume of *Prefaces to Shakespeare*, a passage which accidentally reflects his ambivalent and
dichotomous self while actually talking about something quite different.
His subject of discussion is the nature of the Elizabethan stage and its
succumbing, in its last years, to the over-burdening decorativeness of the
Masque. He says:

> No great drama depends upon pageantry. All great drama tends to concen-
> trate upon character; and, even so, not upon picturing men as they show
> themselves to the world like figures on a stage – though that is how it must
> ostensibly show them – but on the hidden man.

There is a deal of relevance and significance in that phrase 'as they show
themselves to the world like figures on a stage'. The metaphor sprang
automatically to his mind and in looking at both the stage and the world
the sense in which one of them *is* the other, and yet is not, was always
something of which he was acutely aware. And the multiple ironies
which the comparison produces, both on the stage and in the world,
were never lost on him.

Perhaps, as a matter of pure critical theory, he laid too much stress
upon character and character-portrayal on the stage (an actor's mistake,
this), over-emphasizing it at the expense, sometimes, of the deeper-lying

archetypal patterns in the play and the celebratory and mythopoeic functions of the theatre. This was possibly the one weakness in his approach to Shakespeare – though, from what one can gather from contemporary report about his *productions* of Shakespeare, they showed the weakness less in practice than some of his commentary does in theory.

Not that, even in his theorizing, was Barker guilty of a downright literalism in his approach to any of the arts. When his Romanes lecture, 'On Poetry in Drama', was published in 1937, he sent a complimentary copy of it to Desmond MacCarthy, with an inscription which read:

> For Desmond
> > from H.G.B.
> > > July 1937
>
> I liked your valediction to Barrie: yes, thank you. The best I've seen by far – except the T.L.S. I do think that beats you by a head or so, by its 'fairy-tale' point. But you none of you take much account of his artistry, which gives me such pleasure. But who *does* care for that in literature now? I suppose 'art for art's sake' was *inverted* artistry. There is, after all, a kind which is fruitful, which makes the *subject* more fruitful. And Barrie's was that kind. Study the best of his work. And how full of life it is!

By 'artistry' he means more, I think, than mere craftsmanship (which is all we usually dare praise Barrie for, these days). Barker implies by the term a sense of formal control in the dramatist *and* a sense of aesthetic delight in the playgoer, an element in both the fabric and the gesture of the play more pervasive and more important than either character-drawing or plot. His instinct for theatre as pure art and pure design, transcending all discursive, descriptive and didactic purposes, was sound and sure, in spite of his intellectual preoccupation with 'character' and characters.

Let us finally recall that about the theatre, which he helped to rejuvenate and to revolutionize in two or three important ways, he always felt intensely serious, whether hopeful or despairing (and he oscillated between the two) of its future. He saw it as a major civilizing force and an important, integral element in society. Max Beerbohm, with whom Barker was very friendly for many years (the Beerbohms were frequent visitors at Netherton Hall in the 'twenties and 'thirties when the Barkers were there), made gentle and friendly mockery of Barker's seriousness in two of his light-hearted little verses. They are worth quoting, if only to remind ourselves that the lonely, serious-minded artist had a social milieu to which he belonged as well. Here are the verses:

1.

To H.G.B.

The Theatre's in a parlous state,
    I readily admit;
It almost is exanimate –
    But then, when wasn't it?
It always *was, will* always be;
    God has decreed it so.
Can'st thou rescind His grim decree?
    O, my dear Harley, No!

In Shakespeare's and in Marlowe's day,*
    In Congreve's, in Racine's,
The wretched Theatre murmured 'I'm
    One of the Might-Have-Beens!'
'O May-Be-Yet!' the critics cried,
    '*We'll* teach you how to grow!'
And were their fond hopes gratified?
    O, my dear Harley, No!

The Theatre is Exemplary,
    Now as in other ages,
Of all a Theatre shouldn't be –
    Of all that most enrages
Right-thinking men like you and me
    And plunges us in woe . . .
Mightn't perhaps the L.C.C. –
    O, my dear Harley, No!

Shall cubits come by taking thought
    And Drama gain her soul
By learning what she doubtless ought
    From dear old Mr. Poel?
Shall syllabi and seminars
    And blackboards all in a row
Somehow uplift us to the stars?
    O, my dear Harley, No!

*I meant to write in my MS
    'Time' – and wrote 'day', it seems.
This error fills me with distress
    And haunts me in my dreams.
A lover I'm of chime of rhyme,
    And to *vers libre* a foe . . .
Shall such a man rhyme 'day' with 'I'm'?
    O, my dear Harley, No!

2.

TRIOLETS
COMPOSED ON A DAY WHEN I THOUGHT
(FROM WHAT HE HAD SAID ON A PREVIOUS DAY)
THAT HARLEY WOULDN'T TURN UP FOR LUNCHEON

Harley's doing Cymbeline;
    Helen takes a car.
Behind yon castellated screen
Harley's doing Cymbeline.
Beetle-browed, athletic, lean,
    Aloof, alone, afar,
Harley's doing Cymbeline . . .
    Helen takes a car.

Helen eats and drinks with us;
    Harley plies his quill.
Gracious, fair, diaphanous
Helen eats and drinks with us . . .
Utterly oblivious
    Of Stratford's clever Will,
Helen eats and drinks with us;
    Harley plies his quill.

Helen's way is right;
    Harley's way is wrong.
As 'twere a swallow's flight,
Helen's way is right, –
To flit, to swoop, to alight
    And gladden us with song!
Helen's way is right.
    Harley's way is wrong.

(*Supplementary triolet, composed at luncheon.*)

Oh, bother and damn!
    These verses won't do!
How unlucky I am!
Oh, bother and damn!
Harley, that sham,
    Has alighted here too!
Oh, bother and damn!
    These verses won't do!

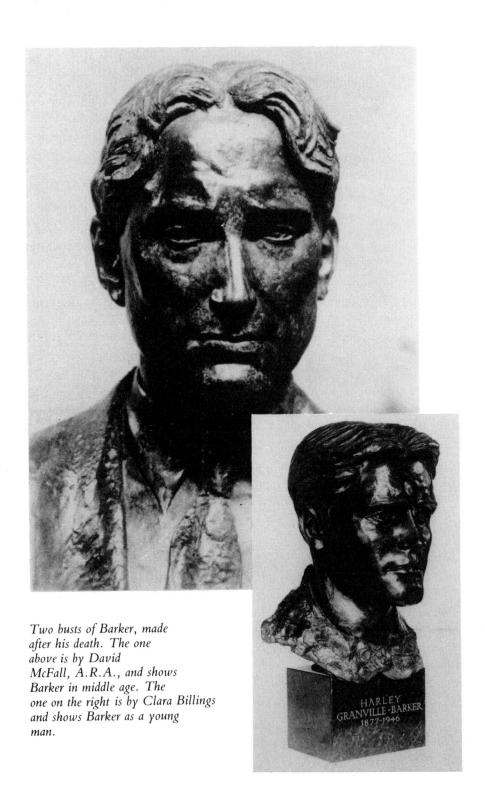

Two busts of Barker, made
after his death. The one
above is by David
McFall, A.R.A., and shows
Barker in middle age. The
one on the right is by Clara Billings
and shows Barker as a young
man.

P.S. Feb. 27.

Still, here they are,
    With my love to you both.
From perfect they're far, –
Still, here they are.
They're away below par,
    And to *write* them I'm loth.
Still, here they are,
    With my love to you both.

Perhaps, in his final years, he allowed the social milieu to become too predominant in his life. Perhaps there was a slackening of the artistry, some loss of freshness. Even if so, the record remains astonishing. Actor, director, playwright, critic: his achievements in any one of the last three would have served most men for a decent and distinguished career; and even what he accomplished in the field of acting, before starting on his three-fold main career, was not negligible. He was, in the English-speaking theatre, the most complete theatre artist of the century.

Notes

Chapter 1: The Early Years

1. London: Collins, 1972; p. 82.
2. 'Please God' and 'Thank God'. This rather undergraduate style of humour is typical not so much of Barker as of his whole circle and its era.
3. *The Exemplary Theatre* (London: Chatto and Windus, 1922).
4. *Drama*; Winter 1946 (published by the British Drama League – now called the British Theatre Association). Shaw's article had been offered to several other journals but rejected as possibly libellous.
5. See *Bernard Shaw: Collected Letters* ed. Dan H. Laurence (London: Max Reinhardt, 1972) vol. 2, p. 912.·
6. See J.P. Smith: *The Unrepentant Pilgrim* (London: Gollancz, 1965), p. 32.
7. The signature of this letter has exercised me somewhat. In my first two drafts of this book I rendered it as 'Little Boy' but felt uneasy about it. Before committing myself to this rendering in the final draft, I went back again to my photo-copy of the original (the letter is owned by the Humanities Research Center, Texas). The hand-writing is a little unclear: the final letter could easily be either 'y' or 'g'; the middle letter is indisputably an 'o'; the capital initial, which at first glance looked like a 'B' seems to me now much more likely to be a 'D' – and it also seems more likely that the family joke would be to call a young barker 'Little Dog' than to sentimentalize over a young man of eighteen by calling him 'Little Boy'. One hopes so, anyway. The three plays which Barker mentions in the letter are: *Two Roses*, by James Albery, which was written in 1870 and was one of Irving's early successes; *Money*, by Bulwer Lytton, written in 1840; 'Masks', though Barker does not put it in quotation marks as he does the other titles, is a reference to *Masks and Faces* (1852), a dramatization by Tom Taylor and Charles Reade of the latter's novel, *Peg Woffington*.
8. The quality which Shaw mocks in *Overruled* when he makes Mr. Juno say to Mrs. Lunn: 'I daresay my temperament seems tame to your boiling southern blood . . .'; to which the lady replies: 'My what!'

9.   Not, as might at first be supposed, a prayer to the Virgin, but an address to his dead wife, Tessa's erring mother.

10.   *Saturday Review*, March 13, 1895: 'Mr. Pinero's New Play'.

Chapter 2: Developing Strength

1.   'George Fleming' was the pseudonym of Julia Constance Fletcher, remembered now (if at all) as the translator, in 1900, of Rostand's *Les Romanesques*, which became in English *The Fantasticks*, a pleasant little play in light, rhyming verse. It was first produced by Mrs. Patrick Campbell.

2.   Neither version is published. The typescript of the original version is now in the Manuscript Department of the British Library (Shelfmark: Add. 53686A). The typescript of the revised version is in a private collection in England. The original version was produced for a single afternoon performance at Terry's Theatre on June 29, 1899 and proved so successful that it was transferred to the evening bill at the Comedy Theatre from July 9 to July 20.

3.   Sidgwick & Jackson (London), 1961: p. 45.

4.   Written from Paris on January 1, 1937. The letter is now in the possession of the Humanities Research Center, University of Texas.

5.   Which is what he has accused her of doing. In Act II he said to her: 'Stand sponsor to the one decided action of your life. You daren't – you're a coward – you're drifting.' And, a little further on: 'Drifting boats can't be steered. You'll drift. Back to the very point from which you started today! That'll be your progress.'

6.   Her husband is in the library, discussing with Dicky and his father the terms upon which he will 'take her back'.

7.   It was in the latter half of the nineteenth century that the West Midlands area round Wolverhampton, Walsall and Wednesbury was given the name of the Black Country because of the dreariness of its industrial landscape. 'Cardoxeter' is, of course, an imaginary town and the play nowhere mentions South Staffordshire, but the fact that Cardoxeter is represented as being close to Birmingham would seem to indicate that Barker and Thomas had the heavy industry of the West Midlands in mind.

8.   This is interesting. In the very last speech in the play, John and Griselda – and, by implication, Barker and the play itself – calmly accept, without demur or debate, the fact which so sticks in Strindberg's craw in *The Father* (written some ten years earlier, in 1887, and almost certainly known to Barker and Thomas) and sets off the whole explosive argument of that play.

9.   Perhaps we should remind ourselves, since we are not here reading the whole play and consequently are coming across things out of their proper context, that Vivien is a sincere Catholic with genuine religious convictions of which Yeo is well aware since he was formerly her priest and, presumably, heard her confession. There is, therefore, a deliberate pun on his part on the word 'prey'.

10.   The letter is in the Archer archive of the Manuscripts Department, British Library (Shelfmark: ADD 45290).

11.   Margery M. Morgan and Frederick May, in an interesting article called 'The Early Plays of Harley Granville Barker' (in *Modern Language Review*, vol. li, 1956: pp. 324–38) give a complete list of the plays written by Berte

Thomas. The titles also appear, partly under the name 'Berte Thomas' and partly under 'Herbert Thomas' in Allardyce Nicoll's *A History of Late Nineteenth Century Drama* (Cambridge, 1946) and his *English Drama, 1900–1930* (Cambridge, 1973).

12.   In an article called 'Granville Barker's Sexual Comedy', in *Modern Drama*, March 1980 (vol. XXIII, no. 1).

13.   Assuming, that is, that the verse in *Prunella* (1904) is mostly the work of his collaborator, Laurence Housman, which the correspondence between them would seem to suggest. (There are several letters from Housman to Barker, now owned by the Library of the University of Iowa, which support this contention.)

14.   This letter and the following one which is quoted are both in the Archer archive, Manuscript Department, British Library (Shelfmark: ADD 45290).

Chapter 3: The Emerging Public Life

1.   London: Heinemann; 1954, p. 149.

2.   The magazine of the British Drama League (now called the British Theatre Association).

3.   See *The Shaw-Barker Letters*, edited by C.B. Purdom (London: Phoenix House, 1956, p. 6–7).

4.   See *My Life and Some Letters*, by Mrs. Patrick Campbell (London: Hutchinson, 1922) p. 147.

5.   Written April 9, 1900. (Manuscript Dept. of the British Library – Shelfmark: ADD 45290).

6.   Margery Morgan and Frederick May in an excellent bibliography which was published by C.B. Purdom as an appendix to his *Harley Granville Barker*, tentatively conjecture 1902 as the date of the writing of 'A Miracle', but for the reasons stated in this chapter I think 1900 more likely. The only known performance of the play was on March 23, 1907, when it was given at Terry's Theatre, by the Literary Theatre Society, as an afterpiece to the *Persians* of Aeschylus. Max Beerbohm gives a short description of the play in his notice in the *Saturday Review* for March 30, 1907, which is reprinted on p. 291 of *Last Theatres* (New York: Taplinger 1970).

7.   This letter is now in the possession of Robert Eddison.

8.   In a letter to William Archer, May 19, 1923.

9.   Now in the possession of the Humanities Research Center, University of Texas.

10.   Letter now in the possession of Sir John Gielgud.

11.   Letter written in June, 1918; it is now owned by the University of Texas.

12.   *Edwardian Plays* is a paperback, published in 1962 by Hill & Wang, New York (a Mermaid Dramabook).

13.   Purdom, in quoting the passage, says 'written by William Archer seven years later in *The Old Drama and the New*', but he is in error. The play was first produced in 1905, so 'seven years later' would have been 1912. In point of fact, Archer's book, which was based on two courses of lectures which he gave in 1921 and 1922, was published in 1923, *eighteen* years after the first production of *The Voysey Inheritance*.

14.   The article, published in the July, 1914 number of *The Bookman* (Vol. XLVI, No. 274; pp. 153–162), was by Dixon Scott (1881–1915), one of the

magazine's regular contributors: his other articles for *The Bookman* at about that time included ones on Shaw (September and October, 1913), Whitman (May, 1914) and Barrie (1915). The article on Barker, under the title 'Mr. Granville Barker and an Alibi', was included (in slightly revised form) in a posthumously-published collection of Dixon Scott's pieces, called *Men of Letters* (London: Hodder & Stoughton, 1923).

15. *i.e.* the setting of the first three acts of *The Marrying of Ann Leete*.
16. The essay is contained in *Edwardians and Late Victorians: English Institute Essays, 1959* (Columbia University Press, 1960) p. 198.

Chapter 4: Director of Repertory

1. Published 1976 by Blackwell, Oxford.
2. The letter is now in the Gilbert Murray archive at the Bodleian Library.
3. Letter in the British Library, Department of Manuscripts (ADD 45,290).
4. Letter now in the possession of the Humanities Research Center, University of Texas.
5. In a painstaking article called 'Harley Granville Barker as Director', in *Theatre Research*, Vol. XII, No. 2, 1972 (pp. 126–138).
6. She became Dame May Whitty in 1917.
7. This is not strictly true. He certainly *preferred* to rehearse on the set of the play (what director does not?) and tried to do so whenever possible, but there are several letters from him both to Shaw and Murray which talk of rehearsals held elsewhere than on the stage – including the foyer of the Kingsway Theatre, where a revival of *The Doctor's Dilemma* was rehearsed. (Letter of November 21, 1913, from Barker to Shaw: British Library, Department of Manuscripts – Shelfmark ADD 50534).
8. Page 239.
9. Letter in the Archer archive, Department of Manuscripts, British Library (ADD 45290).
10. Letter in the Murray archive, Bodleian Library.
11. London: Sidgwick & Jackson, 1922 (there is also a reprint, published by Benjamin Blom, New York, in 1969).
12. Not in *Two Gentlemen of Verona* or in *The Rivals*, but in Shaw's *The Philanderer*.
13. *Old Vic Saga* (London: Winchester Publications, 1949).
14. There is an amusing 'open letter' by Shaw to Louis Calvert, the actor who first played Undershaft in *Major Barbara*, in which Shaw says: '. . . or how Barker always drops his voice when he ought to raise it . . .' The letter was published by Shaw, under the title 'Letters to His Leading Man', in *Vanity Fair*, February, 1916: it is quoted by E.J. West in *Shaw on Theatre* (New York: Hill & Wang, 1959).
15. London: Methuen, 1950.
16. His article was called 'Granville Barker & The Savoy' and appeared in the Spring number of the magazine (Vol. 52, pp. 28–31).
17. From the late nineteenth century until about the time of the First World War the process which we now call 'directing' a play was known as 'stage-managing' the play; in the period between the two wars it was (in England, at any rate) called 'producing' the play; since World War II it has been called 'directing'.
18. *Old Vic Saga*, p. 164.

19. In *Drama*, New Series No. 3 (Winter, 1946), pp. 7–14.
20. Written in May or June of 1907.
21. See *Bernard Shaw: Collected Letters*, ed. Dan H. Laurence (London: Reinhardt, 1972; vol. 2, p. 715).
22. Barker's letter of Nov. 27 1909 is owned by the Bodleian Library; Murray's letter of March 11, 1910 and Barker's reply of March 12 are both owned by Robert Eddison.
23. British Public.

Chapter 5: Major Plays

1. Now in the Bodleian Library.
2. The name is spelt Cantilupe in the second version, perhaps to avoid quite so strong a suggestion of melons (Barker had been several times to America in the meantime and the word 'cantaloup', for a certain kind of melon, is much more common in the United States than it is in England). There is a connection: the Italian village of *Cantalupo*, where that kind of melon was first cultivated, was formerly the country seat of the Pope. Barker wants to make the point that Lord Charles, though a member of the Church of England, is 'High Church' and is, therefore, like *Cantalupo*, close to Rome.
3. H.M. Harwood (1874–1959), son of an M.P., author of a long list of trivial comedies (even the titles are embarrassing now: *How to be Healthy though Married, So Far and No Father*, etc., etc.) He was, however, a quite distinguished theatre manager and was, among other things, lessee of the Ambassador's Theatre for many years. In 1921 he presented the first British production of Barker's version of Sacha Guitry's *Deburau* and in 1925 a revival of *The Madras House*. He had tentative plans to present the first public production of *Waste* in 1926 but these did not materialize.
4. He was mis-remembering again! Though there is no place in the play where two consecutive sentences are the same in both versions, here and there an effective turn of phrase in the earlier version *is* brought forward into the later.
5. This was by no means Barker's only tussle with the Censor, though it was the only one involving a play of his own. During the first dozen or so years of the century he fought a running battle with the Lord Chamberlain, sometimes on behalf of particular plays and sometimes on grounds of general principle. Along with Murray, Shaw, Archer, Barrie, Galsworthy, Pinero, Laurence Housman and a host of others, Barker several times petitioned and agitated against both the injustice and the imbecility of theatrical censorship and in 1909 appeared as a witness before the Joint Select Committee on Censorship, which had been set up in response to the pressure which the various agitations had been able to bring to bear.
6. The letters from Barker to Hannen which are quoted in this chapter are now in the possession of Athene Seyler, Hannen's widow, by whose kind permission they are quoted.
7. Margery Morgan, in *A Drama of Political Man*, chapter 7, has an excellent analysis of this imagery. There are a few occasions, I think, upon which she sees more significance and more allusions than are really there (as, for instance, her discovery of a pun on 'agapé' – the love-feast – in Barker's choice of the agapanthus for the plant whose reluctance to flower is

remarked in the Huxtable conservatory) but in the main her responsiveness to the multiple echoes of the text is at once penetrating and sensible.
8.   Quoted by Purdom (*op. cit.*) p. 230.
9.   This is not in *A Drama of Political Man* but in the Introduction to a new
edition of *The Madras House*, published by Methuen in 1977.
10. See *The Jacobean Drama* (London: Methuen, 1935).

Chapter 6: Minor Plays and Two Stories

1.   I do not name Chekhov here simply because I do not believe him ever to
have been a realistic or naturalistic dramatist, but something much greater.
2.   I can find no reference to *A Vote by Ballot* in any of the extant Barker
correspondence.

Chapter 7: Barker and Shakespeare

1.   In Canada the story is told that when he was taken, on his first visit, to see
Niagara Falls he stood for a long while in silence, watching the water, and
then said: 'Is that all?' Presumably if *he* had been staging it there would
have been some sort of exciting sequel to all that falling water!
2.   Heinemann very enterprisingly published 'acting editions' of all three of
Barker's Savoy Shakespeare productions. In each case the printed text
coincided with the text as spoken from the stage (that is to say, the full
Shakespearean text with only very minor cuts). These editions were in
paper covers and were sold for sixpence.
3.   At the opening of the Preface to the 1912 acting edition of *Twelfth Night*,
Barker confesses that he likes *As You Like It*, along with two other plays,
'as little as any plays he ever wrote'. The other two are *Much Ado About
Nothing* and *Henry V*. He finds all three, he says, 'so stodgily good, even a
little (dare one say it?) vulgar, the work of a successful man who is caring
most for success.'
4.   Letter dated February 11, 1914 and now in the Archer Archive, Manuscript Department, British Library (Shelfmark: ADD 45, 290).
5.   *The Shakespeare Revolution*, p. 121.
6.   *ibid*, p. 120.
7.   *ibid*, Chapter 6.
8.   *ibid*, pp. 120–121.
9.   See especially Wilson Knight's review, in the *Times Literary Supplement*,
July 26, 1974 (pp. 794–795) of Edward Moore's edition of *Prefaces to
Shakespeare*, volume VI. Knight quotes Purdom: 'That Barker got further
from the stage and more deeply settled in his study as time passed the
Prefaces to Shakespeare as a whole make evident' and then adds his own
opinion that: 'The *Prefaces* were, however, necessarily in large part
academic studies and were presumably conceived as such'. Barker, of
course, had claimed the opposite.
10. *Op. cit.*, p. 112.
11. I notice that W. Bridges-Adams, in his 1953 radio talk called 'The Lost
Leader', says: 'His *Othello* study is almost as moving as the play.'
12. See *Prefaces to Shakespeare*, vol. 2, p. 27 (Princeton University Press, 1947).
13. The Cambridge edition, edited by Alice Walker and John Dover Wilson,

in 1957 (the Introduction is Wilson's work); and the 'New Arden' Edition, edited by M.R. Ridley in 1958.

14.   *Prefaces to Shakespeare*, vol. 2, pp. 8–9.
15.   In her Introduction to *Shakespeare Criticism, 1919–1935* (Oxford: The World's Classics, 1936).
16.   In his Introduction to the Cambridge edition of the play.
17.   *Prefaces to Shakespeare*, vol. 2, p. 78.
18.   Later published, under the title *From Henry V to Hamlet*, in *Aspects of Shakespeare, Being British Academy Lectures (1923–1931)*, ed. J.W. Mackail (Oxford: The Clarendon Press, 1933).

Chapter 8: Barker and Women

1.   The letter was written from the Algonquin Hotel, New York, on January 3, 1916. It is now in the possession of the Humanities Research Center, University of Texas.
2.   It is in the Library of the University of London.
3.   Barker and Lillah were married in 1906 at the same Register Office at which Bernard Shaw and Charlotte Payne-Townsend were married in 1898.
4.   A further strain may well have been caused by Lillah herself. The following story, taken from p. 95 of Constance Babington Smith's *John Masefield: A Life* (O.U.P., 1978), illustrates the point: 'Masefield's professional association with the Granville Barkers led to a close friendship (he sometimes stayed with them in Kent and they helped him a great deal with his next play, *The Tragedy of Pompey the Great*). Lillah McCarthy was one of the first of the beautiful and talented women who, throughout his life, inspired him and at whose feet he worshipped. Yet his devoted dependence on Constance, and their mutual trust, remained unshaken, and she – loving, maternal, dominating – watched him and guided him at every step. 'I don't *think*, if I were you,' she wrote to him apropos of Lillah, 'I should go on dining with Mrs. Barker any more. I fancy she rather loves having bevies of men round her when she is alone, and I don't think it is a very dignified position for the men . . .'
5.   There has been some dispute, even some mystery, about her place and date of birth. Purdom confesses (*op. cit.*, p. 278) that he had been unable to ascertain her age, though he does (p. 188) give the place of her birth (slightly mis-spelled). I confirmed the place by reading some Huntington family letters in the George Arents Research Library at Syracuse University, Syracuse, N.Y. The date I was able to obtain from a marriage certificate in Orange, New Jersey, where in December 1889, at the age of twenty-two, Helen had married Thomas Dall Criss.
6.   For much of this information I am indebted to the Huntington Library, the Library at Syracuse University (see above) and to a fascinating book, privately published in Hartford, Connecticut in 1915, called the *Huntington Genealogical Memoir*. It is published by the Huntington Family Association and it traces every known descendant of Simon Huntington, who left Norwich, England, in 1633 to emigrate to New England but died of smallpox on the voyage: his widow, Margaret, and four children, survived however and arrived in Roxbury, Mass. later that year.
7.   Purdom says (*op. cit.*, p. 188) that C.P. Huntington never married, but this is untrue.

8. Letter now in the possession of the Department of Manuscripts, British Library (Shelfmark: ADD 56660).
9. There are copies of them in the collection of the Theatre Museum, Victoria and Albert Museum, London. *The Fire that Burned in the Corner* is in typescript, with a few very minor hand-written corrections; 'The Bricks of the Temple' (an earlier title for *The God of Good Bricks*) is in manuscript and is probably a first draft – it has multiple emendations, some of them quite extensive.

Chapter 9: The Lost Leader?

1. In *G.B.S., A Postscript* (N.Y.: Harper & Brothers, 1950 – p. 113).
2. For the beautiful exactitude of these dates and figures I am indebted to the courtesy and co-operative kindness of Mr. Michael B. Harris of Messrs. Stone & Co., Solicitors, Exeter, to whom my best thanks are due.
3. The original is now in the possession of the Theatre Museum, Victoria and Albert Museum, London.
4. There is a typescript of this story in the Theatre Museum, Victoria and Albert Museum, London.
5. Barker's essay was also published in the May, 1929 issue of *Fortnightly Review* under the title 'Three Victorians and the Theatre'.
6. It was also published, in two parts, in *The London Mercury* of March and April, 1932.
7. These letters are now owned by Sir John Gielgud.
8. The story has become legendary: several actors have told me, in relation to several different productions, that whenever Barker directed rehearsals during these years, Helen would arrive at the theatre promptly at 1 p.m. every day to fetch him to lunch. Some versions of the story say that she leaned over the dress circle rail and called down to him; others say that she scorned to come into the theatre at all but sent the chauffeur.
9. Two of these have not been mentioned in the text of this Chapter (or elsewhere in this book): they are *Doctor Knock* and *Six Gentlemen in a Row*, both by Jules Romains.
10. There is an interesting chapter on 'B.I.S.' in Sir Robert Marett's book, *Through the Back Door* (London: Pergamon Press, 1968).
11. Her most recently published book was *Poems* (London: Sidgwick & Jackson, 1939), and it is probably this to which she refers. The books immediately before that were *The Locked Book* (an anthology which she had put together) in 1936 and *Traitor Angel* (a novel) in 1935. There was one further publication by her after 1941: this was *Nineteen Poems* (London: Sidgwick & Jackson, 1944).
12. The letters of Helen Huntington which are quoted in this chapter are now in the collection of the Humanities Research Center University of Texas.

Chapter 10: Secret Lives

1. The book thus marked, is now in the possession of Mrs. Alfreda Rushmore, of New York. Mrs. Rushmore is the daughter of Constant Huntington, Helen's cousin.
2. In the heaving swell,
    In the resounding echoes,

> In the universal stream
>   of the world-breath –
>   to drown –
>   to founder –
>   unconscious –
>   utmost rapture!

(trans. John Kehoe)

3.   *The Youngest Drama* (London: Ernest Benn, 1924) p. 26.
4.   The connection between Lawrence and Barker is interestingly explored in Colin Wilson's *The Outsider* (London: Gollancz, 1964).
5.   In *A Drama of Political Man.*
6.   In *The Outsider* (see Note 4, above).
7.   In *The Concise Cambridge History of English Literature,* 1st Edition (C.U.P., 1941); the editor of the 2nd Edition (1965), R.C. Churchill, though he glancingly mentions Barker, does not refer to *The Secret Life* at all.
8.   Difference from ordinary men, that is.
9.   Translated by Marilyn Gaddis Rose (Dublin: The Dolmen Press, 1970).
10.   His review of *The Secret Life* is reprinted in his *Literature in the Theatre* (London: Chapman & Hall, 1925).
11.   Letter dated October 2, 1923, now in the collection of the Humanities Research Center, University of Texas.
12.   See *The Rise and Fall of the Well-Made Play* (London: Methuen, 1967) pp. 114–115.

Chapter 11: Man and Artist

1.   See *The Drama in Adult Education: A Report by the Adult Education Committee of the Board of Education, being Paper No. 6 of the Committee* (London: H.M.S.O., 1927).
2.   In *English Drama, 1900–1930* (Cambridge University Press, 1973); pp. 392–396.
3.   The article was reprinted in Howe's book, *Dramatic Portraits* (New York: Mitchell Kennerley, 1913): in the *Fortnightly Review* it appears on pp. 476–487.
4.   On p. 204 of *Harley Granville Barker.*
5.   I had the story from Mr. J.C. Medley, the son of C.D. Medley, Barker's solicitor.
6.   Some of these letters are now in the Gilbert Murray archive at the Bodleian Library; some of them are owned by Robert Eddison, the actor.
7.   A reference, I think, to Arthur Ellam Haigh (1855–1905), classical scholar, editor of classical texts and author of *The Attic Theatre* (1889), etc. Murray is comically pictured in Barker's verse as a follower of Haigh.
8.   'Wanklin' is a Scots and North-of-England dialect word, a favourite of Barker's: I have come across it half-a-dozen times in his letters: it means 'feeble' or 'unsteady', 'insecure, delicate in health'.
9.   The essay is in *Elizabethan and Jacobean Studies* (Oxford University Press, 1959): the book was edited by Herbert Davis and Helen Gardner and presented to Frank Percy Wilson in honour of his seventieth birthday.

Bibliography

Works by Granville Barker

Plays

A Comedy of Fools (in collaboration with Berte Thomas) Unpublished, 1895.
The Family of the Oldroyds (in collaboration with Berte Thomas) Unpublished, 1895–96.
The Weather-Hen (in collaboration with Berte Thomas) Unpublished, 1897.
Our Visitor to 'Work-a-Day' (in collaboration with Berte Thomas) Unpublished 1898–99.
The Marrying of Ann Leete (London: Sidgwick & Jackson, 1909).
A Miracle (unpublished; 1900).
Agnes Colander (unpublished; 1900–01).
Prunella, or Love in a Dutch Garden (in collaboration with Laurence Housman) (London: A.H. Bullen, 1906).
The Voysey Inheritance (London: Sidgwick & Jackson, 1909).
Waste (London; Sidgwick & Jackson, 1909).
The Madras House (London; Sidgwick & Jackson, 1911).
Rococo (London; Sidgwick & Jackson, 1917).
Vote By Ballot (London; Sidgwick & Jackson, 1917).
The Wicked Man (unfinished; unpublished; 1914).
Farewell to the Theatre (London; Sidgwick & Jackson, 1917).
Harlequinade (in collaboration with Dion Calthrop) (London; Sidgwick & Jackson, 1918).
The Secret Life (London: Sidgwick & Jackson, 1923).
His Majesty (London: Sidgwick & Jackson, 1928).

Foreign Plays in Translation

Anatol, by Arthur Schnitzler (London: Sidgwick & Jackson, 1911).
Deburau, by Sacha Guitry (London: Heinemann, 1921).
Doctor Knock, by Jules Romains (London: Ernest Benn, 1925).
Six Gentlemen in a Row, by Jules Romains (London: Sidgwick & Jackson, 1927).

Commentary and Criticism (Books)

A National Theatre: Scheme and Estimates (London: Duckworth, 1907) (in collaboration with William Archer).
Introduction to acting edition of *Twelfth Night* (London: Heinemann, 1912).
Introduction to acting edition of *The Winter's Tale* (London: Heinemann, 1912).
Introduction to acting edition of *A Midsummer Night's Dream* (London: Heinemann, 1914).
The Exemplary Theatre (London: Chatto & Windus, 1922).
Prefaces to seven vols. of *The Players' Shakespeare* (London: Benn, 1923–27).
Prefaces to Shakespeare: First Series (London: Sidgwick & Jackson, 1927).
A National Theatre (London: Sidgwick & Jackson, 1930).
Prefaces to Shakespeare: Second Series (London: Sidgwick & Jackson, 1930).
On Dramatic Method (London: Sidgwick & Jackson, 1931).
The Study of Drama (Cambridge: University Press, 1934).
Prefaces to Shakespeare: Third Series (London: Sidgwick & Jackson, 1937).
On Poetry in Drama (London: Sidgwick & Jackson, 1937).
The Use of Drama (Princeton: University Press, 1945).
Prefaces to Shakespeare: Fourth Series (London: Sidgwick & Jackson, 1945).
Prefaces to Shakespeare: Fifth Series (London: Sidgwick & Jackson, 1947).

Commentary and Criticism (Articles)

'The Heritage of the Actor' (in *Quarterly Review*, CCXL, No. 476, July, 1923).
'From *Henry V* to *Hamlet*' (in *Proceedings of the British Academy*, XI, 1924–35).
'Three Victorians and the Theatre' (in *Fortnightly Review*, CXXV, May, 1929).
'The Coming of Ibsen' (in *Theatre Arts Monthly*, XIV, October and November, 1930).
'Exit Planché, Enter Gilbert' (in *London Mercury*, XXV, March and April, 1932).

Short Stories

Georgiana (in *English Review*, February and March, 1909).
The Bigamist (unpublished: 1910–1914).
Souls on Fifth (Boston: Little, Brown, 1917).
The Fire that Burned in the Corner (unpublished: 1919).
Out of these Convertites; or, Richard Goes To Prison (unpublished, 1923?).
The God of Good Bricks (in *The Century Magazine*, May 1924).

Spanish Plays Translated by Helen and Harley Granville Barker

A. Plays by Gregorio Martinez Sierra

The Kingdom of God
The Two Shepherds
Wife to a Famous Man
The Romantic Young Lady

in *The Plays of Sierra*,
Vol. 2 (London: Chatto
& Windus, 1923)

Take Two from One (London: Sidgwick & Jackson, 1931).

B. Plays by Serafin and Joaquin Alvarez Quintero

The Women Have Their Way
A Hundred Years Old
Fortunato
The Lady From Alfaqueque

in *Four Plays*
(London: Sidgwick &
Jackson, 1927)

Love Passes By
Don Abel Wrote a Tragedy
Peace and Quiet
Dona Clarines

in *Four Comedies*
(London: Sidgwick &
Jackson, 1932)

Index

(NOTE: The Preface, the Chronology and the Bibliography are not included in the following Index: the Notes – pp. 336–44 – are included.)